Competition in
Telecommunications

Munich Lectures in Economics
Edited by Hans-Werner Sinn

The Making of Economic Policy: A Transaction Cost Politics Perspective, by Avinash Dixit (1996)

The Economic Consequences of Rolling Back the Welfare State, by A. B. Atkinson (1999)

Competition in Telecommunications, by Jean-Jacques Laffont and Jean Tirole (2000)

In cooperation with the council of the Center for Economic Studies of the University of Munich

Martin Beckmann, David F. Bradford, Gebhard Flaig, Otto Gandenberger, Franz Gehrels, Martin Hellwig, Bernd Huber, Mervyn King, John Komlos, Richard Musgrave, Ray Rees, Bernd Rudolph, Agnar Sandmo, Karlhans Sauernheimer, Klaus Schmidt, Hans Schneeweiss, Robert Solow, Joseph E. Stiglitz, Wolfgang Wiegard, Charles Wyplosz

Competition in Telecommunications

Jean-Jacques Laffont
Jean Tirole

The MIT Press
Cambridge, Massachusetts
London, England

First MIT Press paperback edition, 2001

© 2000 Massachusetts Institute of Technology

This book was set in Palatino by Windfall Software using ZzTEX and was printed and bound in the United States of America.

Library of Congress Cataloging-in-Publication Data

Laffont, Jean-Jacques.
    Competition in telecommunications / Jean-Jacques Laffont, Jean Tirole.
      p. cm. — (Munich lectures in economics)
    Includes bibliographical references and index.
    ISBN 0-262-12223-5 (hc : alk. paper), 0-262-62150-9 (pb)
    1. Telecommunication. 2. Competition. I. Tirole, Jean. II. Title. III. Series.
HE7631.L34   1999
384'.041—dc21   99–41518
                                                           CIP

10   9   8   7   6   5   4

Contents

Series Foreword

Every year the CES council awards a prize to an internationally renowned and innovative economist for outstanding contributions to economic research. The scholar is honored with the title "Distinguished CES Fellow" and is invited to give the "Munich Lectures in Economics."

The lectures are held at the Center for Economic Studies of the University of Munich. They introduce areas of recent or potential interest to a wide audience in a nontechnical way and combine theoretical depth with policy relevance.

Hans-Werner Sinn
Professor of Economics and Public Finance
Director of CES
University of Munich

Laudation for Jean Tirole

In deciding to honor Jean Tirole the CES has further dispelled the notion that economics is a dismal science. Jean Tirole is one of those individuals who clearly enjoys "doing economics" and transmits this pleasure to his readers and audiences. His research agenda is complex and far from my own area of competence, but the occasional reading of some of his papers has convinced me over the years that he is one of the most productive, original, and ultimately socially useful economists of his generation.

Jean initially trained in engineering. Graduating top of the class from Ecole Polytechnique, a prestigious school established by Napoleon to train top artillery sharp shooters, he became a specialist in road and bridge construction at the Ecole des Ponts et Chaussées. This is the archetypal course of honor for the brightest mathematically minded French students. Most of them go on effectively administering the network of roads or railways. Few escape, and among those can be found many of France's economists with international reputations (Maurice Allais used to teach in the sister institution, Ecole des Mines, which nominally trains engineers to dig and exploit iron mines that no longer exist.) Jean went from math in engineering schools to applied math at the University of Paris and finally to economics at MIT where he received his Ph.D. in 1981 under the supervision of Eric Maskin. Since then he has moved between France and the United States, taking up positions at the Ecole des Ponts et Chaussées and MIT, with visiting positions at Harvard, Ecole des Hautes Etudes en Sciences Sociales, Stanford, and the University of Lausanne. He has now settled in Toulouse and is affiliated with CERAS (Ecole des Ponts et Chaussées) and MIT.

Over the past fifteen years, Jean has produced a steady flow of work, publishing six or seven papers each year in the top reviews, plus six books. One of his books, *The Theory of Industrial Organization*, has been

translated into many languages, including Mandarin Chinese. To graduate students all over the world, and their teachers, it is known as "the
Tirole," and is required reading from the first to the last page.

How can one person be so productive? The first answer is that more
than one person is involved. Indeed, Jean has formed high-power part-
nerships with Mathias Dewatripont, Drew Fudenberg, Bengt Holmström, Jean-Jacques Laffont, and Eric Maskin, to name the most regular
ones. The second answer, however, is that he is remarkably effective.
Good ideas come in quickly and are executed speedily to guarantee a
rapid progress from idea to end-product.

Along with his co-authors, Jean has changed the field of industrial
organization. It used to be a mixture of conventional wisdom and empirical work, with little theory. Jean has contributed rigorously to build
a rich body of theory. Industrial organization has now become a field
that attracts a large contingent of thesis writers, a sure sign that major
improvements are taking place. As I understand it, the new field was
born when two theories—game theory and information theory—began
to be applied to the analysis of strategic behavior in firms and markets.
Utilizing game theory, firms can be formally analyzed as strategic units.
Information theory contributes another feature that may seem obvious
today: each firm has more knowledge about itself than about its competitors. Putting these two theories together provides an analysis of the
marketplace that allows each firm to discover what the others are up to
and react by changing its prices and its products in an infinity of ways,
including design, variety, advertisement, and so forth.

Having accomplished this, Jean has gone on applying his toolbox
to other issues, transforming more fields along the way. For example,
he has explored sociology through organization theory by studying
how bureaucracies and hierarchies structure themselves. He further
extended his foray into sociology by asking whether the experience of
private firms can be used to better design public organizations. He even
went on wondering about the social and economic functions of lawyers
(as a profession, of course).

Pursuing this line of questioning in another direction quickly leads
to the perennial debate of competition versus efficiency. This has led
Jean to revisit the issue of regulation: how to make it more efficient, and
how to use information instead of applying a heavy hand. *Competition
in Telecommunications* is a perfect example of the line of thought that
Jean and his colleagues now follow. This is not pure armchair theory
anymore. Many of the new ideas that have emerged from this research

have found their way into regulation reform all over the world. From antitrust to incentive regulation and access policies, new legislation bears the imprint of new ideas developed over the last decades by Jean.

Finally, for someone who wonders about the transmission of information, it is a natural step to look into the functioning of financial markets. This has led Jean to produce some papers influential in as far a field as macroeconomics. He has clarified the logic of speculative behavior. In particular, he has offered a rigorous analysis of speculative bubbles: Under what conditions may such irrational phenomena arise in markets dominated by rational traders? And then he has produced works that are currently influencing those in charge of regulating banks and financial markets.

It seems a safe bet that regulation of the telecommunications industry will one day reflect some of the ideas presented in the following text, and that we will all be better-off for that.

Professor Charles Wyplosz

Preface

Purpose and Audience

This book fills a gap. The telecommunications industry has been changing rapidly for years, but academic research is still lagging behind. Telecommunications theory and policy lie at the intersection of regulation and competition, yet their study has often been treated informally, and important policy decisions have been and are being made on ad hoc reasoning in the absence of clear guidance from economic theory. We regret this state of affairs; in our experience, policy choices could often be improved through abiding by some simple principles derived from theory. *Competition in Telecommunications* provides a conceptual apparatus for thinking through the key issues facing the new competitive environment. It studies the rich field of telecom theory and policy using economists' state-of-the-art theoretical knowledge of industrial organization.

We devote this enterprise to two tasks. The first is to synthesize and draw the policy implications of a framework developed during the 1990s to promote environments conducive to a harmonious development of competition. The second, equally important task is to enrich this approach in several relevant directions, as well as to identify some of the remaining challenges for the economics profession.

The book is written for a wide audience: practitioners (telecommunications executives and consultants, regulators, and antitrust officials), academics, and students (advanced undergraduates and graduate students). To accommodate the wide variety of approaches, we present the material in a nontechnical manner in the text and provide separate boxes for the theoretically inclined economist. Thus the entire book can be comprehended by readers averse to mathematics.

Overview

The book is organized as follows. Chapter 1 provides the unfamiliar reader with some background knowledge concerning the technology and regulatory debate in the telecommunications industry.

The book then covers the four central topics of the recent deregulatory movement. Chapter 2 discusses the introduction of incentive regulation. It recalls the main considerations behind the design of performance-based regulation: the incentive–rent extraction trade-off, the provision of quality, the issue of regulatory commitment, and the structuring of efficient retail pricing. It explains the rationale for the introduction of price caps and discusses their drawbacks at length.

The second main topic of the book is one-way access, that is, access given by a local network to the providers of complementary segments, such as long-distance or information services. Chapter 3 provides an intuitive description of the implications of economic reasoning for the setting of access charges. Chapter 4 contains an in-depth discussion of four possible access policies and their variants: embedded costs, forward-looking costs, ECPR, and global price caps. The emphasis is on regulatory policy viewed in the light of the theoretical principles developed in chapter 3.

With the advent of local competition, as well as the coexistence of mobile and fixed-link networks, the issue of two-way interconnection arises, and it is tackled in chapter 5. When multiple networks coexist (as opposed to the previous situation of a single network to which providers of complementary services need access), the networks must set access prices that they charge to each other for mutual termination of calls. Chapter 5 (based on joint work with Patrick Rey) analyzes this form of cooperation among competing networks.

The fourth central topic of interest in the current reform movement is universal service. Universal service was previously provided through cross-subsidies among services supplied by the incumbent monopoly. The introduction of new modes of regulation and, even more, the advent of competition have made it impossible to keep providing universal service in this way. Chapter 6 first goes back to the foundations of universal service. It then studies in detail the two leading contenders for the "competitively neutral" provision of universal service: the use of engineering models to compute subsidies and the design of universal service auctions.

Last, chapter 7 discusses the Internet and regulatory institutions.

Some General Lessons

Key insights that emerge from our treatment include the following:

1. *Desirability of some price discrimination:* Marginal-cost pricing for all services is not viable in telecom industries (at least in certain important segments involving large joint and common costs), so the relevant benchmark requires some markups. Allowing at least some price discrimination can therefore reduce the pricing distortion. Price discrimination may also be the prerequisite for the viability of certain investments.

2. *Implications for access pricing:* Because wholesale prices (access charges) guide retail prices, it is not surprising that the desirability of price discrimination at the retail level translates into a need for price discrimination for wholesale prices. Using illustrations drawn in particular from recent policy debates, we show that undifferentiated access prices may substantially distort competition and reduce welfare.

3. *Problems with asymmetric regulation:* Relatedly, a different regulatory treatment of an infrastructure owner's access services and its retail services (access and network elements typically being regulated more tightly than retail services) creates a built-in incentive to discriminate against competitors in access, whereas more symmetric regulation would induce the firm to treat them more like customers/subcontractors.

4. *Pitfalls with price cap regulation:* Beware expecting too much from price caps. But don't neglect the benefits created by flexible pricing.

5. *The special nature of competition in an industry requiring two-way access:* With the advent of competition in local access (local loop unbundling; alternative access supports such as wireless, cable, or power lines), as well as the rapid growth of the commercial Internet, networks need to provide termination transmission to each other. The design of "two-way" access policies conditions competition at the retail level. We identify efficient interconnection arrangements and explain why some standard intuition does not carry through. For example, an agreement on

the mutual interconnection price may not raise final prices because of firms' incentives to expand market shares so as to minimize their termination outpayments.

6. *Efficient provision (as opposed to financing) of universal service:* We identify some intricacies of establishing competitively neutral yet economically efficient subsidies for providers: competition *for* the market versus *in* the market, optimal area size.

Acknowledgments

An early version of this book was used as the basis for a lecture series given November 26–28, 1996, at the University of Munich by the second author. The latter was honored and happy to have the opportunity to deliver the Munich lectures. He is grateful to the Center for Economic Studies at the University of Munich, to its director, Hans-Werner Sinn, and to his colleagues for inviting him and for their warm hospitality during his stay in Munich.

We are grateful to Suzanne Schennach for able research assistance and, for helpful comments, to Jerry Hausman, Michael Riordan, and Marius Schwartz on chapters 3 and 4, to Patrick Rey on chapter 5, and to Gary Biglaiser and Evan Kwerel on chapter 6. We are extremely grateful to William Baumol for a very careful reading of the entire draft. We also thank Paul de Bijl, Hans-Werner Sinn, David Sevy, Etienne Turpin, Ingo Vogelsang, and reviewers of an earlier draft for helpful insights. We are very grateful to our colleagues at the Institut d'Economie Industrielle for many stimulating discussions related to the material covered in this book. We also thank Patrick Rey for letting us borrow unrestrainedly from the joint research conducted with him in the writing of chapter 5.

We are grateful to the sponsors of the Institut d'Economie Industrielle, and in particular on this occasion to France Telecom, for their continued support for research, without which this book would not have been possible.

Finally, warm thanks to Pierrette Vaissade for dealing so professionally with this manuscript. She performed a remarkable job. Many thanks, too, to Nancy Lombardi for an excellent editing of the final draft, and to Terry Vaughn and the MIT Press team for their continuous support.

Competition in Telecommunications

1   Setting the Stage

1.1   Introduction

Broadly speaking, this book analyzes regulatory reform and the emergence of competition in network industries. Incentive regulation and competition are being introduced worldwide in telecommunications, electricity, gas, postal services, and railroads, among others. Yet we have elected to limit the scope of most of our analysis to the telecommunications industry. This choice was motivated by two considerations. First, networks in these industries differ in their technological attributes, such as the routing of services, the location of bottlenecks, the speed of technological change, and the storability of output, as well as in their demand characteristics, such as the existence of network externalities or the cost of service breakdown. While the principles enunciated in this book have some universality, careful adjustments are required in order to apply the analysis performed for one industry to another industry. Second, the telecommunications industry has been at the forefront of incentive regulation reform, and competition there has developed faster than in other industries. The experience gained in the telecommunications industry will be useful for other industries.

While not necessarily representative of the network industries, the telecommunications sector is fascinating in many respects. First, technology is progressing rapidly. "In the old days" (a few years ago) the cozy monopolists who ran the industry offered a small variety of "POTS" (plain old telephone services) such as local, long-distance, and international calls. The advent of high-capacity and intelligent networks has multiplied the number of offerings, or "PANS" (pretty amazing new services, such as calling cards, toll-free or paying numbers to call businesses, name or number identification, voice messaging,

routing of calls, facsimile, data transfers, home banking, video on demand, videoconferencing, and Internet services).

Second, the industry structure too is evolving rapidly. Networks
proliferate, and they need to be interconnected: public switched telephone networks, cable companies, competitive access providers, mobile operators, local area networks linking computers, Internet service
providers.

With digital technology, telecommunications, cable TV, broadcasting,
and computers have become a single industry, which will be a critical
element of our economies' backbone. New entrants, such as software
companies, information service providers, and media, as well as infrastructure owners (electricity, gas, water, and railroad companies) who
can lay telecommunications cables along their networks, are preparing
themselves to tap the new markets.

With the impending opening of competition, industrial restructuring
is progressing at a fast pace. Through mergers and alliances, telecommunications operators are preparing themselves to offer the full range
of services. "One-stop shopping" will enable business and residential
users to purchase all services from a single supplier. Forty- to sixty-
billion-dollar mergers have become commonplace in the United States.

On the economic front, to which we will naturally devote our attention, two fundamental reforms have been or are being implemented.
First, incumbent operators are being privatized and are provided with
better incentives to minimize cost, as well as more flexibility to rebalance rates in conformity with business and economic principles. Second, markets have been largely deregulated in Anglo-Saxon countries
and were legally liberalized in continental Europe on January 1, 1998.
Similar reforms are taking place in other network industries such as
electricity, gas, railroads, and postal services.

The economics of incentives and organization, political economy, and
the new theory of industrial organization all can help us understand
regulatory reforms in these industries and their impact on economic efficiency. Economists have been at the forefront of the incentives reform.
They are currently playing an important role in designing the competitive environment, although, as we will argue, their deregulatory fervor
is often guided more by a gut feeling that competition is efficient than
by a clear conceptual framework embodying the specificities of these
industries. The telecommunications or electricity market is not the same
as the wheat or restaurant market, and competition there does not come
about as easily.

For decades, telecommunications services have been provided by a secure monopolist, a public enterprise in most of the world and a private regulated corporation (AT&T) in the United States. The absence of competition was motivated by the existence of large fixed costs in several parts of the network, whose duplication was neither privately profitable nor socially desirable; the telecommunications industry was deemed to be a "natural monopoly."

At least two economic factors contributed to the reform movement.[1] First, motivating the two fundamental reforms was the growing awareness of the inefficiency of the incumbent monopolists. On the one hand, the monopolist would typically face poor incentives to reduce its costs, which formed the basis for the setting of future prices: Should the monopolist spend wastefully, its prices would be adjusted accordingly (although with a lag) to make up for the revenue shortfall. One does not need to have studied much incentive theory to understand that the "cost plus" nature of the so-called rate-of-return regulation would not deliver brilliant cost and price performance.

On the other hand, the price structure, and not only its level, was also severely distorted. Individual prices were determined through a fairly arbitrary cost allocation accounting procedure that had little connection with sound business practice. Cross-subsidies among services were substantial, with business, mobile, and long-distance services subsidizing residential, local, and rural ones. Innovative pricing such as time-of-day pricing or the design of menus of tariffs tailored to the needs of heterogeneous customers were not widespread.

While some politicians and regulators were satisfied with the status quo that enabled them to tinker with the pricing structure, economic efficiency was sacrificed. As is often the case, the inefficiencies generated by high and poorly structured prices were large but invisible. Some concerns were raised, though, when some possibly inefficient entrants that were allowed to come in took advantage of archaic regulatory rules and benefited from the regulatory price umbrella to skim the cream (business users) in central business districts and specific long-distance services.

---

1. As usual, political economy considerations played a substantial role, from the lobbying by large business user organizations (such as the International Telecommunications Users Group and the Telecommunications Managers Association in the United Kingdom) to the desire to break the power of trade unions or the overall ideological shift in the attitude toward markets.

The second development, technological change, created a force toward deregulation. Some traditional segments as well as some new ones, such as information services, could be served equally well, and sometimes better, by new players than by the incumbent telephone operator. For example, progress in microwave technology, a technology that exhibits only moderate returns to scale, paved the road for the opening of the American long-distance market to competition and ultimately to the 1984 AT&T breakup into a long-distance operator (still called AT&T) and seven regional Bell operating companies, or RBOCs. (Ironically, the microwave technology was by and large leapfrogged in the 1980s, and the big three long-distance carriers, AT&T, MCI, and Sprint, all installed a full-size long-distance network with fiber optics, a high-fixed-cost, low-marginal-cost technology.)

1.1.1   Incentive Reforms

Starting in the mid-1980s, many network industry incumbents became subject to price caps.[2] In a nutshell, price caps define an average price level (adjusted each year to account for inflation and expected technological progress) not to be exceeded by the firm. The firm is otherwise free to adjust its individual prices (often up to some constraints on the speed of price rebalancing). Besides reducing political interference in the setting of individual prices, this price flexibility enables incumbent operators to become more business oriented. Although they cannot affect the average price they charge, they, like ordinary firms, can adjust their individual prices to reflect costs, elasticities of demand, complementarities and substitutabilities between segments, and competitive pressure. Economists say that the structure of prices is thereby Ramsey oriented and thus more consistent with economic efficiency. Moreover, the firm's past cost performance in principle is not meant to be reflected in the revision of the price cap. That is, the price cap scheme aims at suppressing the link from cost inefficiencies to price increases, and at thereby providing the firm with powerful incentives for cost reduction.

---

2. In the United States rate-of-return regulation for the long-distance provider AT&T was replaced by a price cap, or rather three price caps on three service baskets (residential and small business services, toll-free 800 services, business services). The February 1996 Telecommunications Act mandates the use of incentive regulation. Only 20% of the revenue stream of the regional Bell operating companies and GTE (a large non-Bell, primarily local operator) was regulated under a price cap scheme; this proportion had become 70% by mid-1996.

Theoretical analysis predicted, and practice confirmed, that, while useful, there was only so much that could be expected from the price cap revolution:

1. When regulators have imperfect information about the operator's costs, there is an unavoidable trade-off between the provision of incentives and variations in profitability. This trade-off is easy to apprehend: In order for a firm to be fully accountable for its performance, the firm must receive $1 whenever it reduces its cost by $1. But this sensitivity of reward to cost also implies that the firm is highly exposed to exogenous shocks in profitability and thus will often receive large rents or incur large losses.

This point raises the issue of the credibility of the price cap. Large rents are politically hard to sustain. A case in point is the 1995 breach of the price cap contracts with the U.K. regional electricity companies, when Professor Steve Littleschild, a designer of price cap regulation in the 1980s who had become the U.K. electricity regulator, had to yield to intense political pressure and reduce the caps substantially ahead of the planned review because the companies were making large profits. Conversely, large losses force regulators to raise prices to keep operators alive.

2. Relatedly, price caps and more generally "high-powered incentive schemes" (schemes that provide operators with powerful incentives to reduce cost) give regulators substantial discretion over the firm's profitability. This raises two opposite concerns. In the first scenario, called regulatory capture, the regulator is too soft on the firm and voluntarily inflates its rent. In the second scenario, called regulatory taking, the regulator is too harsh on the firm and does not adequately compensate the firm for its investments and efficiency improvements. The use of price caps reinforces the need for regulatory independence vis-à-vis the regulated firm and other interest groups.

3. High incentives to reduce cost create a concern for quality. Because the firm bears a higher fraction of its expenditures, it is more prone to skimp on services, and so the regulatory reform should be accompanied by increased attention to quality issues. Regulators in the United Kingdom learned their lesson in the matter when they were forced to design new quality measures in response to a degradation of BT service quality a few years after the introduction of a price cap. Similarly customers of U.S. West complained of increased delays after it laid off many workers in response to a switch to incentive regulation.

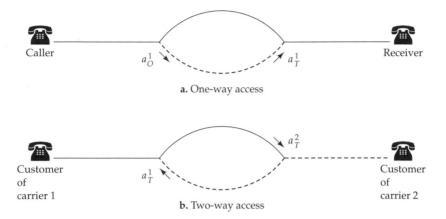

Figure 1.1
a^i_O, access charge received by carrier i for originating a call; a^i_T, access charge received by carrier i for terminating a call; solid line, carrier 1; dotted line, carrier 2

1.1.2   Liberalization

Let us now discuss the opening to competition. It is now widely accepted that entrants should be able to compete on most telecommunications segments. But there still exist bottlenecks to which the providers of competitive services must have access in order to compete with the incumbent. For example, a long-distance entrant or information service provider needs access to the incumbent's local network. The issue is then one of "one-way access," in which one company needs access to the other, but the reverse does not hold. In figure 1.1a, carrier 1 provides local loop services for both the caller and the receiver. The caller uses carrier 2, a company specialized in long-distance services, for long-distance calls. Carrier 2 therefore buys both originating and termination access from carrier 1 in order to be able to offer the long-distance service.

The setting of access charges is a highly difficult exercise:

1. The stakes are high, and negotiations are highly contentious. Often half of the entrants' costs are access charges and thus are controlled by their competitors. Conversely, access charges represent a substantial source of income for the incumbent (today about 30 percent for the regional Bell operating companies in the United States). Intense lobbying

by interest groups and political intervention do not simplify the regulator's task.

2. The setting of access charges regulates the rate of return on the incumbent's investment in infrastructure. There is in general a trade-off between promoting competition to increase social welfare once the infrastructure is in place and encouraging the incumbent to invest and maintain the infrastructure. That is, regulators must encourage entry without expropriating incumbents.

3. The access pricing rule must impose reasonable informational requirements on the regulator in terms of computing the access charges and monitoring compliance. This simplicity helps to reduce the regulatory costs and limit the influence of politics in the determination of access charges.

The currently dominant paradigm for setting access charges for elements of telephone networks (such as local networks, transmission facilities, and switches) is marginal cost, or more precisely *forward-looking long-run incremental cost*. To compute these costs, the regulator will perform a cost optimization based on an engineering model, compute an economic depreciation (physical depreciation plus technological progress), and forecast the likely future usage of the elements. This paradigm has not been used much to date, but it was favored by Congress in the 1996 U.S. Telecommunications Act (although recent Federal Communications Commission writings argue for more flexibility in the pricing of access), was adopted in 1995 by the Office of Telecommunications in the United Kingdom for 1997 on, and dominates the thinking in continental Europe.

This dominant paradigm raises several concerns:

1. It does not obey basic economic principles. While marginal cost pricing is the proper benchmark in a competitive industry, the very concept of a bottleneck and the need for regulation stem from the existence of a large fixed cost or more generally large returns to scale. Networks involving large fixed costs would never be built if their owners were allowed to charge only marginal cost. This consideration must, for instance, be born in mind at a time when experts and politicians envision the building of a very costly information superhighway.

2. Relatedly, marginal cost pricing of access prevents incumbents from making money on the access business and gives them incentives to

extend their untapped market power on that segment to the competitive segments, by denying access to their rivals by nonprice methods. This possibility calls for close regulatory monitoring and interference with the operators' business judgment.

3. The computation of marginal costs leaves regulators in charge of setting individual prices and is discretionary. The last two points raise the concern that, beyond the liberalization and free-market rhetoric, one may be creating an environment that will lead to heavy-handed regulation. Regulation should be more in line with economic principles as well as light-handed.

Besides these one-way-access pricing issues, a new set of "two-way" interconnection issues will develop if the deregulation of telecommunications succeeds in creating local competition. The two-way interconnection situation is illustrated in figure 1.1b, in which customers calling each other belong to two different local networks. Each carrier must then buy termination access from the other network. The 1996 Telecommunications Act aims at promoting local competition in order to break the local monopoly position of the incumbent local exchange companies (LECs). It envisions three types of local entry:

• Facilities-based entry by mobile operators or by fixed-link operators (cable companies, competitive access providers, and long-distance companies such as AT&T).

• Resale entry, through the resale of the LECs' services by entrants. (The consumers would notice that their service is actually provided by the incumbent only when they see the incumbent's repairman.)

• Mixed entry, whereby entrants lease some facilities (e.g., transmission) and provide others (e.g., switches). This is entry through "unbundled network elements."

Regardless of the exact mode of entry, the various networks will need to interconnect to have access to their mutual bottlenecks, namely, the final access to the consumer. (If I want to call you, my network will have to pay termination charges to yours.) Many experts argue that regulation should end once local competition has developed and that regulation should be replaced by standard competition policy (as is the case, say, in New Zealand, where regulatory agencies have been abolished). This (perhaps correct) view is unfortunately not supported by any economic analysis. A tempting analogy with other industries may suggest that competition will yield a socially desirable outcome. This analogy, however, ignores the fact that interconnection requires an agreement among competitors. This feature, which also arises in various guises in the connection of fixed-link and mobile operators, in credit cards and automatic teller machine (ATM) markets, and in cross-licensing arrangements, raises two concerns. The first is that strong players may refuse to enter interconnection agreements with smaller ones. The second is that the strong players may be able to use the interconnection agreements among themselves as an instrument of tacit collusion in the retail markets. The economics of two-way interconnection, like those of one-way interconnection and of incentive regulation, will be a central focus of this book.

1.2   A Brief Guided Tour through the Telecommunications Industry

This section does not provide an exhaustive description of the telecommunications technology[3] and industry structure. (Indeed, both are changing rapidly, and any attempt at a careful description is bound to become quickly obsolete!) Rather, we list a few key characteristics of the industry that are necessary, first, to understand the regulatory evolution and, second, to motivate the economic analysis undertaken in this book.

Telephone networks are made up of two main elements: switches and transmission. *Switches* allow the routing of voice, video, and data signals throughout the network. *Transmission* can be decomposed into wireline (twisted pair of copper wires, coaxial cable, fiber optic) and wireless (via satellite, cellular radio, microwave, personal communications services, or PCS). Relative to wireline transmission, wireless transmission offers end users the benefit of mobility; however, wireless equipment, especially if it is to offer advanced services, is expensive, and wireless transmission faces interference and especially bandwidth (capacity) problems.

Traditional wireline transmission technology since the 1920s has been the twisted pair of copper wires, which still link the customer premises to a remote terminal or a central office (first switch). Copper wire pairs are well suited to carry voice, but they have rather limited capacity,

---

3. A good reference (although too exhaustive for an economist) for the description of telecommunications networks is Tanenbaum (1996).

although recent progress in data compression techniques (ADSL: asymmetric digital subscriber line systems, more generally xDSL)[4] has substantially increased that capacity and allows telephone companies to offer video programming as well as telephony and thus to compete with cable operators.

The transmission technology of the future is fiber-optic cables (glass). Fiber-optic cables have a large capacity (an excess capacity given the current usage pattern in local networks) and thus incur a very low marginal cost. Fiber-optic cables are already in place for long-distance transmission. They have made an appearance at the local level—for example, with the building of MANs (metropolitan area networks, which are fiber-optic loops installed by the competitive access providers—the CAPs—or by the incumbent local operators), or of high-capacity connections between a local operator's switches (central offices).

The recent technological evolution has been a sharp *decrease in the cost* of transmission and switches. The second recent key development has been the substantial increase *in the intelligence of the network*. Until recently, the signaling—that is, the transmission and reception of control information associated with a phone message—was conveyed within the same channel as the voice message; now, with "out-of-band signaling," it is conveyed through a separate channel. This development, as well as the adoption of new signaling protocols (signaling system 7, or SS7), has permitted a richer set of offerings and more efficient utilization of the networks. (For example, SS7 allows networks to seek unobstructed paths in order to increase call completion and to economize on network resources.)

Plain old telephone services are now complemented by a wide and rapidly changing array of new services: calling card, 800 numbers (toll-free calling to a business), 900 numbers (which allow vendors to charge a premium for their information services and to use the telephone company as a billing and collecting agent), automatic call back, name or number identification, selective call rejection or acceptance, voice mes-

---

4. Variants of ADSL (HDSL, VDSL, . . .) provide different speeds of transmission (bits per second). They can also offer the same data transmission rate in both directions. In contrast, ADSL offers much higher speeds for information going from the network to the user (downstream bit rate, e.g., that associated with downloading web pages) than for information from the user of the network (upstream bit rate). The efficiency of these techniques depends on the length of the local loop, which must remain short for them to be effective. For example, it is estimated that the downstream bit rate decreases from 8 Mbit per second to 2 Mbit per second when the distance increases from 1 km to 5 km.

saging, selective routing of calls (for instance, a pizza chain can direct a call to the caller's nearest franchise), facsimile, database access, video on demand, home banking, videoconferencing, Internet offerings, and so forth. Many of these new services require more intelligent networks and larger transmission capacities than were available until recently.

To this proliferation of services corresponds a multiplication of networks.[5] The basic network is the *public switched telephone network,* to which we will come back later. Historically, entry first took place in the *long-distance segment.* MCI[6] and Sprint, which entered the U.S. long-distance market in the 1970s, have, like the incumbent AT&T, since covered the country with fiber-optic cables and are individually able to serve the entire current long-distance demand. The U.S. long-distance segment includes many other actors as well. In particular the big three sell wholesale to (nonfacilities-based) resellers who sell at retail; the activity of these resellers is motivated in part by the profitability of arbitrage between the large discounts observed in the wholesale market and the substantial markups in the retail market. Resellers have also created value by offering highly personalized service in some market niches such as small businesses. Competition in long-distance markets has developed in some other countries as well. For example, Mercury, Clear, and Optus have challenged the incumbents, BT, Telecom, and Telstra, in the United Kingdom, New Zealand, and Australia, respectively. The Japanese giant, NTT, faces some competition from three long-distance providers (telephone markets were liberalized in Japan in 1985). Competition in long distance is likely to develop rapidly in continental Europe now that markets are fully liberalized with the implementation of the interconnection and licensing directives of the European Commission in 1998.

There have been various forms of entry at the local level as well. *Competitive access providers* (CAPs) provide special access, that is, unswitched (point-to-point) links, from central business districts and large urban users to specific long-distance companies. They also provide special access between the long-distance companies' points of presence,[7] and private lines between an end user's multiple locations. Their entry

---

5. See, e.g., Hausman (1995).

6. In 1998, MCI merged with another large telecommunications operator, Worldcom.

7. The points of presence (POPs) are the locations at which the long-distance companies receive local traffic corresponding to long-distance calls or interconnect for local termination of calls.

is partly encouraged by specific aspects of the regulatory environment. In particular, in the United States, CAPs in the 1980s benefited from the price umbrella provided by the high regulated access prices charged by the local telephone companies (the local exchange carriers—the LECs) for connections to long-distance operators; indeed almost half of the CAPs' revenue stems from connecting large customers in central business districts to the long-distance carriers' points of presence.[8]

Another group of entrants at the local level are *cable operators* (CATV). Unlike CAPs, they already had a network in place, but cable TV networks have a one-way tree-and-branch structure that is ill-adapted to the two-way telecommunications services. Cable TV networks have nevertheless started to compete in telephony, especially in the United Kingdom where they have added a copper twisted pair to their coaxial cable and now compete forcefully with BT for telephone services through stand-alone telephone offers as well as bundled telephone-cable offers. Two other networks complete the description of the local scene: *wireless services* (including personal communication services), which include both mobile wireless services and fixed wireless services, which do not allow the subscribers to roam from their premises; and *local area networks* (LANs), which are rings connecting computers with outside networks through routers designed for high-speed data applications.

Let us return to the public switched network, and in particular to the local loop, which is still widely perceived as a bottleneck and figures prominently in the regulatory reform that we will later describe. While the description of the local configuration of the public switched network must constantly be adjusted to reflect technological change, the key point that we will emphasize is that *some elements of the local network, such as the link close to customer premises, are essentially a fixed cost, and that because they are crucial parts of the network, lawmakers and regulators have been preoccupied with the access of all telecommunications actors to these elements.*

The traditional representation of the local loop is given in figure 1.2. Starting from the end users, the individual connections from the interface at the customer premises form the distribution plant. The cost of the distribution plant is by and large non–traffic sensitive (NTS); that is, at current usage levels it does not vary much with the customer's

---

8. According to the FCC Preliminary 1993 Common Carrier Statistics, CAPs in 1993 had market share 3.10% in special access and 0.20% in switched access. So they have remained small compared to the LECs. In 1995, the regional Bell operating companies still received over 99% of the calls terminating in their territories.

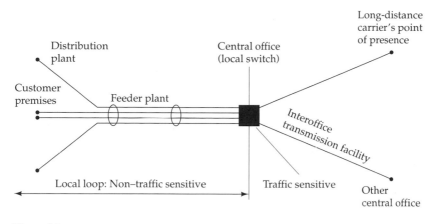

Figure 1.2
The old-fashioned local loop

telecommunications usage (volume). The feeder plant then gathers the lines of the distribution plant and thus consists of concentrated bundles of cables that terminate at the central office (switches). While the feeder plant exhibits "economies of shared plant," it too is rather traffic insensitive. Altogether, the cost of the transmission from the customer to the switch (the local loop) is non–traffic sensitive. It really involves a (large) fixed cost and no marginal cost. Or, putting it differently, the marginal cost relates to the decision of connecting the customer (or creating a new line for a customer) rather than the traffic this customer generates.

Then comes the first switch. Part of the cost of the central office is non–traffic sensitive (existence of office, design of software, . . .); part (the interface) depends on the number of connecting lines; and the third part (the switches themselves) varies with volume, that is, is traffic sensitive. Last, further (usually digital) transmission facilities take the call from the central office to a long-distance carrier or to another switch in the local area (the switch also connects customers linked to the same switch). There is in general a trade-off between the number of central offices and the cost of the distribution and feeder plants.[9]

---

9. The British terminology differs from the American one. In Britain, the local network is decomposed into *access* and *conveyance*. Conveyance starts at the first switch and is traffic sensitive. Access is the part from the customer premises to the first switch and is non–traffic sensitive. The Office of Telecommunications' (Oftel's) December 1995 consultative document "Pricing of Telecommunications Services from 1997" estimates that 61% of BT's local network costs correspond to access and 30% to conveyance, the remaining 9% being considered costs common to access and conveyance.

This description of local networks has been modified a bit because of advances in fiber-optic technology (such as digital loop carrier, DLC, and asynchronous transfer mode switching, ATM). Those modifications have in particular modified the nature of the feeder plant: see Marcus and Spavins (1993) for details.[10]

Three other features of the telecommunications industry should be noted before we review recent regulatory efforts. First, there is a *large number of actual or potential players.* Besides the traditional operators (fixed-link and mobile), other network operators such as cable companies, railroad infrastructure owners, and electricity, gas, and water utilities can be efficient providers of transmission facilities if the public switched-telephone network is to be duplicated. Large software companies, information service providers, and media also may play an important role in the restructuring of the industry. Deregulation prospects and the new demands of customers have led to a number of strategic mergers and alliances: between regional operators (the recent $44 billion and $43 billion mergers of Bell Atlantic and NYNEX and of Pacific Telesis and SBC communications),[11] between long-distance and cellular operators (AT&T and McCaw), between regional operators and cable operators (BOC's alliances with or acquisition of out-of-region cable TV operators), between long-distance companies and CAPs (the $23 billion merger between Worldcom, the fourth-largest long-distance carrier in the United States, and MFS, which has fiber-optic networks in 50 American cities and is the largest Internet access provider), and between operators and railroad and electricity companies (for example, in France and Germany). A number of global networks designed to provide a worldwide service are in the process of being formed (the Sprint–France Telecom–Deutsche Telekom alliance, or AT&T's alliance with BT).

---

10. See also Hatfield Associates (1994, chap. 3) for the description of a "generic distribution technology mode" for fixed-location telephone service, meant to apply not only to the LEC's network, but also to cellular radio/PCS, cable telephony, and CAP fiber ring. Starting from the customer, one can distinguish (1) the customer connection (including the customer interface unit)—the distribution plant in the case of a LEC, (2) a remote terminal (serving area interface for a LEC), (3) backhaul facilities (feeder plant for a LEC), (4) network interface unit, (5) switch, (6) interoffice facilities (LEC circuits), and (7) signaling.

11. At this writing, two further mergers of the remaining large U.S. local exchange carriers were pending: the $62 billion merger of SBC and Ameritech and the $47 billion merger of Bell Atlantic and GTE. AT&T has also been involved in mega mergers with cable companies. Its merger with TCI was approved by the FCC in early 1999 and, at this writing, its takeover of MediaOne is pending.

Second, as in several other network industries, *universal service obligations* have always been an important instrument of income redistribution among individuals and among geographical areas. In a nutshell, business and urban customers subsidize residential and rural customers, and long-distance, value-added, and wireless services subsidize fixed-link local services. Until recently these cross-subsidies were built into the rate structure of the monopoly operator. The advent of competition forces incumbents to rebalance their tariffs as competitors enter the profitable markets and leave the subsidized markets to them. This rebalancing in turn obliges regulators to find alternative ways, which we will later discuss, of ensuring universal service in a "competitively neutral" way.

Third, we ought to mention the existence of a debate in several network industries about whether (fixed) line rental charges can by themselves fully pay for the deficit engendered by the fixed costs of the network and for the cost of universal service obligations. The importance of this debate stems from the fact that markups over marginal costs on services other than subscription would no longer be needed to ensure the operator's budget balance if high line rental charges were economically and politically feasible.

Whether one can indeed eradicate the deficit by using high, distortion-free line rental charges is, in our view, an empirical question whose answer is likely to be time and industry-dependent. Three factors may make deficits hard to eradicate solely through the subscriber line charge in the telecommunications industry. First, the elasticity of demand for subscription may not be negligible. Although few customers forgo telephone service altogether because of small increases at the current line rental charges, they may forgo the use of multiple lines at home (for business or family purposes or for Internet access) or in secondary dwellings.[12] And, more and more, they may start bypassing the network through mobile phones or to arbitrage tariffs by grouping lines (shared tenant services). A proper computation of the elasticity of demand must also take into account the loss in revenue from phone users who would have called the disconnected customer. Second, and relatedly, there may be constraints in the pricing of the connection charges. For instance, bringing optic fiber or an electricity cable into a remote village may have some features of a public good, so that efficient pricing

---

12. This part of demand is quite elastic. For example, BellSouth recently increased its residential additional lines by 21% year-over-year through an aggressive marketing effort.

is unlikely to cover the corresponding fixed cost. Third, there may exist political constraints. As an illustration, consider the argument that some of the customers who would disconnect because of a high line rental charge are people who badly need access to a phone (to be able to call a doctor or relatives); the proper reaction to this argument is that one can offer either resource-based "social tariffs" or self-selecting "menus" of telephone contracts including some with very low rental line charges and very high marginal prices for calls beyond some low volume (as is sometimes done). Politicians may be reluctant to adopt such policies, however, or else the necessary information to implement them may not be available.

1.3   Regulatory Reforms

The telecommunications industry has always been and still is a heavily regulated industry. There are two complementary paradigms for regulation. The political economy approach to regulation emphasizes the impact on policy of interest groups (industry participants, suppliers, customers, etc.). The public interest approach looks at market failures to motivate government intervention and usually assumes that governments are benevolent. These two approaches will be featured prominently in chapter 2 where we describe the normative and positive paradigms for monopoly regulation. There, we will discuss how incentive regulation must trade off cost efficiency and the limitation of operator's rent, and how service pricing should be structured in order to attain economic efficiency. The advent of competition reduces the attention paid to the incentives—rent-extraction trade-off and raises a set of new issues, such as the entry of efficient competitors, the coordination of investments in facilities and new technologies between operators, the duplication of networks, and so forth.

A number of features must be borne in mind with respect to the telecommunications industry:

1. Networks are multiplied, and, because of network externalities, must be interconnected.

2. The telecommunications industry is one with large fixed costs. Some of its segments are, technologically, natural monopolies. And, to the extent that they are produced by one or a small number of operators, these segments become bottlenecks to which other operators must have ac-

cess in order to be able to compete. Interconnection policies must be designed so as to allow efficient entrants to come in and to keep out inefficient ones. They must provide entrants with the right price signals for their "make-or-buy decision," that is, with respect to the decision of building their own facilities versus leasing them from bottleneck owners. Interconnection policies must also provide reasonable compensation to bottleneck owners so that they have incentives to build and maintain the bottlenecks and not to exclude their rivals from access to them. Last, interconnection prices must induce an efficient use of the network.

3. The location of the bottlenecks changes with the evolution of technology. When AT&T was in the process of being broken up (the divestiture took place in 1984), experts envisioned a competitive long-distance market supplied by a low-returns-to-scale microwave technology. This technology, however, was leapfrogged with the introduction of fiber optics, a technology with high fixed cost and a small marginal cost; so, experts soon emphasized that long distance had become a natural monopoly, implying that the buildup of three full-scale fiber-optic networks by AT&T, MCI, and Sprint was technologically wasteful. Another illustration of the fact that technological change makes predictions of bottleneck location somewhat hazardous is the introduction of private virtual networks. In 1987, Peter Huber, a well-known expert and then consultant to the Department of Justice, predicted that the local exchange network was changing from a hierarchical structure to a geodesic structure in which, in particular, switching would be moved out toward the end user (Huber 1987). An example of this evolution was the development of private branch exchange (PBX) switching facilities that, together with leased lines, allowed large users (businesses, government, universities) to operate their own private network (the PBXs located at the user's premises switching intracompany calls). The development of intelligent networks, however, has allowed operators to offer a replacement to this inefficient duplication of switching facilities by offering areawide Centrex services and virtual private networks. In a nutshell, large users can have their own private network supported by the public switched telephone system. Intracompany calls are now switched, like other calls, by the network's central offices. This development (and others related to signaling, etc.) have raised the issue of competitors' access to the network's intelligence.

1.3.1   The U.S. Telecommunications Act of 1996

The Telecommunications Act of 1996, which supersedes the 1934 Communications Act, is a major step in the evolution of the telecommunications industry in the United States. Before discussing its main features
it is useful to recall earlier developments.[13]

Until the 1960s the U.S. telephone industry was mostly run by a mas-
sive, vertically integrated and regulated monopolist, AT&T (the Bell
system). Among other things, AT&T offered long-distance services and
owned Western Electric (its equipment manufacturer), the Bell Labora-
tories (R&D arm), and the local Bell operating companies (BOCs), now
called regional Bell operating companies, the RBOCs. Except for the existence of some independent local phone companies, which were also
protected by a legal monopoly status and provided about 20 percent of
local service, AT&T provided almost all telephone services.

Entry was considered almost impossible until a 1956 court decision[14]
that allowed the marketing of non-AT&T-built customer-premises
equipment (in this instance, a device called Hush-A-Phone that could
be snapped onto the telephone handset to provide speaking privacy)
and a related 1968 Federal Communications Commission (FCC) decision that allowed an independently produced and marketed connecting arrangement (in this case, the Carterfone, which connected mobile
radiotelephone systems to the telephone network). The introduction of
long-distance competition, an important step in the liberalization of the
U.S. telecommunications industry, began with the 1963 filing by MCI
for the right to offer microwave communications between St. Louis and
Chicago. The FCC's 1969 approval of this application as well as MCI's
offering of switched long-distance services in the mid-1970s generated
heated debates on interconnection with the local operating facilities
of the Bell system involving the operators, the FCC, and the courts,
and opened the way for the development of competition in the long-
distance market.

In 1974 the Department of Justice (DOJ) filed an antitrust suit alleg-
ing monopolization by AT&T of the long-distance, local, and equipment markets and sought divestiture. AT&T was perceived to use

---

13. See, e.g., Brock (1986) and Temin (1987) for very detailed accounts of the evolution
leading to the breakup of AT&T.
14. *Hush-A-Phone Corp. v. United States*, 238 F.2d 266(D.C. Cir.). The court overturned the
FCC decision.

its bottleneck—the local phone networks—in order to favor its long-distance operations to the detriment of other interexchange carriers such as MCI. The Department of Justice argued that the FCC would always find it difficult to prevent AT&T from charging excessive prices and providing inferior quality for its rivals' access to the local networks. In the equipment market, the BOCs were said to favor their affiliated supplier, Western Electric, even when Western Electric's equipment was more expensive or of lower quality than that of its rivals. There were widespread accusations of cross-subsidies, according to which Western Electric's inflated prices were subsidized by regulated local phone rate increases, as well as cases in which the BOCs and Bell Labs communicated information about technical requirements to Western Electric ahead of its equipment manufacturing rivals in order to give the former a head start.

A consent decree (the so-called Modification of Final Judgment, or MFJ, announced in 1982) resulting from negotiations between the administration[15] and AT&T led to the 1984 breakup. AT&T kept its long-distance operations, its manufacturing subsidiary (Western Electric),[16] and its R&D facilities (Bell Labs). AT&T was not subject to lines of business restrictions and thus was allowed to enter other markets as well. In contrast, the seven divested BOCs or Baby Bells (NYNEX, Bell Atlantic, Bell South, Southwestern Bell Corporation, Pacific Telesis, U.S. West, and Ameritech) were restricted to local telephone service.[17] The BOCs, together with GTE (a non-Bell local operator of a size similar to that of the BOCs) and a number of smaller companies, are called LECs (local exchange companies), or, now that entry into local exchange is contemplated, ILECs (incumbent local exchange companies). The parts of the country served by the Bell system were divided into 192 LATAs (local access and transport areas), each LATA being served by a LEC. InterLATA services were considered long-distance services and were therefore not meant to be offered by the BOCs, but rather by the IXCs (interexchange carriers) such as AT&T, MCI, or Sprint.

A central focus of the twelve-year debate that preceded the Telecommunications Act of 1996 was the line-of-business restrictions imposed

---

15. The administration was initially against the breakup, except DOJ (in particular, Bill Baxter).

16. Western Electric, now called Lucent Technologies, was voluntarily divested by AT&T in 1995. See Rey and Tirole (1996) for a theoretical discussion of this divestiture.

17. The BOCs were allowed to market, but not manufacture, customer-premises equipment and to produce and market "Yellow Pages" directories.

on the RBOCs. A clause in the consent decree stated that a line-of-business restriction could be removed if an RBOC could show that "there is no substantial possibility that it could use its monopoly power to impede competition in the market it seeks to enter." In other words, the RBOCs had to demonstrate that they could not or had no incentive to use their strong market power in the local phone segment in order to gain market power in a complementary segment. (The issue of whether local phone rates could be raised by a cross-subsidy from the local phone segment to the complementary segment—an issue that we will take up in section 4.3—was later declared irrelevant by a circuit court.)

There were reviews of the RBOCs' line-of-business restrictions in 1987 and 1993. In 1987 the Department of Justice, in a change of position and on the basis of the Huber report, recommended the complete removal of the manufacturing, nontelecommunications, and information restrictions (as well as some modification of the long-distance restriction). The district judge who had jurisdiction lifted the nontelecommunications restriction but left basically intact the three "core restrictions" (long-distance, equipment, and information services). The RBOCs were allowed to offer information services in 1993.

In 1994 the RBOCs sought vacation of the Modified Final Judgment so that they could be let into long-distance services and equipment manufacturing. They sponsored a collection of 47 supporting affidavits written by 56 leading economists, accountants, and telecommunications policy experts.[18] In 1995, Congress, which had a choice between letting the Department of Justice and the district judge review the line-of-business restrictions and enacting a law, decided to lift the long-distance and equipment restrictions. After a threat of veto by President Bill Clinton, an agreement was found with the administration, which resulted in the February 1996 Telecommunications Act.[19]

In August 1996, the FCC released a "Report and Order" to implement the local competition provisions of the Telecommunications Act (unbundling requirements and interconnection pricing; dialing parity;

18. These affidavits are summarized in *Motion of Bell Atlantic Corporation, Bell South Corporation, NYNEX Corporation, and Southwestern Bell Corporation to vacate the Decree*, July 1994.
19. See Schwartz (1996) for a useful account of the debate leading to the Telecommunications Act, and Wiley, Rein, & Fielding (1996) for a good summary of the FCC Order.

nondiscriminatory access to telephone numbers, operator services, directory assistance, and directory listings; network disclosure; and numbering administration).[20]

The thrust of the Telecommunications Act is to allow the creation of companies that can offer a large array of complementary services. These "one-stop shops" will offer long-distance, local, PCS, multimedia, and Internet services. In a nutshell, the act aims at fostering local market competition and will enable the RBOCs to enter the long-distance market once there is "sufficient competition" in the local call markets. Its key focus is thus the creation of competition by the so-called CLECs (competitive local exchange carriers) to eliminate the incumbent local exchange carriers' (ILECs') ability to use their bottleneck monopoly to impede competition in complementary segments.

We describe in detail some of the key provisions of the Telecommunications Act and of the FCC's report and order for three reasons: First, these have received much prominence in the political debate; second, a large number of the leading experts in industrial organization and telecommunications policy have devoted substantial amounts of time to their conception; and, third, chapters 3–6 will offer an economic analysis of a number of their provisions, and so they constitute a useful introduction to the theoretical analysis.

1.3.1.1 Entry into Local-Call Markets
The Telecommunications Act envisions three patterns of entry in the local market: facilities-based, resale, and unbundling.

---

20. FCC's *Report and Order (FCC96–325) Regarding Implementation of the Local Competition Provisions in the Telecommunications Act of 1996. CC Docket no. 96–98.*

Key parts of the FCC interconnection rules were suspended on October 15, 1996, by a panel of judges in St. Louis (a ruling upheld by Supreme Court Justice Clarence Thomas on October 31, 1996), putting on hold the application of the rules. The St. Louis court froze two parts of the FCC rules, one concerning the interconnection charges to be paid to the RBOCs and the other governing the services that the RBOCs would have to make available to new competitors. The RBOCs and GTE (another large LEC) had argued that the FCC rules took power away from state regulators. The St. Louis court ruled that the FCC exceeded its authority by prescribing methodologies that states must use in setting prices; after the court's stay, some states reclaimed jurisdiction on pricing. Nevertheless, a number of states have chosen to use the FCC methodology or similar methodologies to compute interconnection charges.

On December 31, 1997, Federal Judge Kendall in Texas ruled against a key feature of the 1996 Telecommunications Act, ruling that the RBOCs should not have to prove that their local market is competitive before they can get into long distance. This decision was immediately challenged by the federal government and the long-distance companies.

Facilities-Based Entry   The first possibility, which we already evoked, is for the entrant to build its own local loop, switches, and so on. While Congress expresses no formal preference among the three patterns of entry, it seemed to favor the development of new local networks even though such a development entails a nonnegligible duplication of the cost of such networks. Leaving aside possible interest-group-pressure explanations, the economic motivations for Congress to prefer buildup of facilities over the other two patterns may be that (a) even carefully monitored access requirements may not be fully satisfactory, and (b) the monitoring of compliance with such requirements will, as we will later argue, most likely involve heavy-handed regulation, and therefore may well conflict with Congress's long-term vision of an industry in which competition policy might substitute for regulatory supervision. As reported by the *Congressional Quarterly* (1995, p. 6):

The House and Senate have passed competing bills to promote competition and deregulation in telecommunications, both of which drew broad, bipartisan support. The two proposals (HR 1555—H Rept 104–204 Part I; S 652—S Rept 104–23) have the same goal: to allow all telecommunications companies to compete head to head in one another's markets, with as little government regulation as possible.

Facilities-based competition involves several social costs. First, where an incumbent's network already exists, the infrastructure is duplicated. In particular, wiring every home twice might well be prohibitively expensive. Second, and even if no infrastructure is initially in place, competition implies losses in economies of density and scope. Third, competition, to be effective, requires number portability, so that consumers not be too penalized when they switch operators. Number portability involves software upgradings to ensure that the phone number is still recognized when the consumer switches to a new network.

Because the buildup of a proprietary network is a costly option, the long-distance companies in particular are more likely at this time to experiment with the unbundling and resale options for entry into local markets rather than to engage in facilities-based entry. And if they do choose the facilities-based option, they are likely to enter into agreements with existing facilities' owners such as competitive access providers (CAPs) for the central business districts, cable operators (after upgrading of their coaxial cable to carry telephony) for the residential areas, and wireless service providers.

Resale   Second, an entrant can buy the ILECs' local services at a discount under the price charged by the ILECs to their customers and resell these services to its own customers. Resale is generally considered to be an easy way of creating "entry," although it is unclear whether the entrant is really offering a new product or even the same product at a lower cost, since the differentiation is limited to the marketing component. U.S. regulators view resale as strategically important to the development of competition, with entrants using resale on a temporary basis before they install their own facilities.[21] Resale is not limited to basic telephone services. With a number of exceptions,[22] the a priori scope for resale items is determined by the carrier's retail list.

The *pricing* methodology is basically that of the *efficient component pricing rule* (ECPR), which we will later analyze in detail. The entrant compensates the ILEC for its opportunity cost, that is, for the difference between its retail price for the service and the cost that the ILEC economizes when the service is resold by the entrant. This "avoided cost" or "avoidable cost" corresponds to the direct cost of serving the customer. The FCC established a list of costs that are presumed avoidable, with the burden of overcoming the presumption belonging to the ILEC: product management, sales, advertising, customer services, call completion services, number services, together with a proportional share of some joint costs (corporate operations, . . .). For states that are unable to conduct an avoided cost study, the FCC order sets a default discount

---

21. There have already been some recent attempts by ILECs to enter resale agreements with long-distance carriers. For example, Ameritech has allowed AT&T to enter the IntraLATA market in Illinois on a resale basis, and AT&T has now a 15% market share. (AT&T also entered, but has been less successful in California, where, unlike Illinois, it does not enjoy dialing parity—that is, its customers have to dial more numbers than the local phone company's customers.)

There are also some bundled local resale agreements between ILECs and CAPs. Ameritech has a five-year local resale agreement with a 17% discount relative to retail price and a ten-year agreement with U.S. Network at a 20–25% discount. These agreements include volume requirements. Ameritech has also reached unbundled local loop resale agreements with MFS and CBG at discounts of about 30%.

22. Vertical switching features (call forwarding, etc.) are not classified as retail services, because they are features and functions of the network element's "switch," which is otherwise available for leasing on an unbundled basis (to be discussed later). Special (unswitched) access also is not considered a retail service.

It should also be noted that volume discounts must be available for resale at a wholesale price. However, an ILEC's promotional offering of up to 90 days need not be made available at wholesale, that is, need not be discounted.

in the range of 17–25 percent of the retail price (the exact number being set by the state).

Unbundling   Entry through unbundling is a priori a hybrid of facilities-based and resale entries, although, as we will see, the pricing methodologies differ substantially for unbundling and resale. Under unbundling, an entrant can lease elements of the local network à la carte. For instance, the entrant can lease the ILEC's wires and provide its own switches. The ILEC remains responsible for maintaining, repairing, and replacing the unbundled elements.

The *level* of unbundling is widely perceived to be an important interconnection decision. Entrants are concerned that incumbents may force them through excessive bundling to purchase services they do not need. In contrast, incumbents are worried that detailed unbundling could increase the transaction and interface compatibility costs and also could provide more opportunities for the entrants to arbitrage within necessarily imperfect pricing structures. (The entrants' incentive to lease undervalued facilities and to supply overvalued ones themselves is likely to increase with the degree of disaggregation.) The elements to be unbundled are (1) local loops (transmission between the interface at the customer premises and the central office), (2) switching[23] (including basic capabilities as well as vertical features such as caller ID, Centrex, etc.—the embedded features and functions within the switch cannot be removed from it), (3) interoffice transmission facilities, (4) databases and signaling systems (access to the SS7 network, access to the toll-free calling database, access to the number portability dababase, access to service management systems so entrants can create, modify, or update information in call-related databases, etc.), and (5) operator services and directory assistance.

The *prices* of unbundled elements will be *cost based*.[24] They must be based on *total element long-run incremental cost* (TELRIC) plus a "reasonable share of forward-looking joint and common costs." (The incumbent bears the burden of proof if it wants to include a share of joint

---

23. Except packet switching.
24. The FCC order argues that ECPR (which, recall, is used for resale) is an improper method to set prices for interconnection and network elements because the methodology is not cost based and provides no mechanism for forcing retail prices to competitive levels.

Note that it is not obvious what ECPR would mean, since many of the pieces offered as unbundled elements are not sold retail and thus, individually, do not have a clear opportunity cost.

and common costs.) The TELRIC methodology basically attempts to obtain a measure of the marginal cost of the element on the basis of an engineering model of the network. The forward-looking long-run incremental cost is the direct unit cost attributable to the use of the element under the "most efficient technology deployed" using the incumbent's current network. Such per-unit costs are obtained by dividing total costs by a projection of the element's total usage (by the incumbent and the entrants). So, the marginal cost defined by TELRIC does not refer to the embedded or accounting costs associated with past decisions, but rather results from an optimization based on an engineering model and a forecast of the future use made of the element (see sections 4.2 and 4.4 for a discussion of embedded and forward-looking costs). Some geographic deaveraging (perhaps a decomposition into three or more geographic zones) will be allowed to account for cost differences,[25] but "usage-based" pricing, in which different classes of customers pay different rates, is prohibited. Last, an entrant can lease all ILEC facilities on an unbundled basis; that is, an entrant is not required to install any facilities in order to lease others (this case is called virtual resale or virtual unbundling or rebundling).

As in the case of resale, the FCC order sets default prices for unbundled elements to be applied by states that are unable to conduct cost (in this case, TELRIC) studies. For instance, it sets a state-specific default monthly price for the unbundled local loops in the $10–25 range. Entrants must then add, if they do not build their own facilities, 0.2–0.4 cent per minute for switching, plus 0.15 cent per minute for tandem switching if relevant, plus possibly additional costs for local transmission between the ILEC's central offices, plus a per-query or per-message charge for directory assistance or operator services, and so forth.

1.3.1.2   Interconnection Agreements
Even a pure facilities-based entrant must interconnect with the incumbent so that each provides termination (the so-called "transport and termination") of the other's off-net calls. That is, when an entrant's customer calls an incumbent's customer, the call must terminate on

---

25. One of the factors determining costs is density. In the absence of geographic deaveraging, carriers serving rural areas, for instance, would be penalized. For example, GTE, which is an ILEC in Virginia that serves areas with an average 48 lines per square mile, is concerned that it would have the same standards applied to it as to Bell Atlantic, another Virginia ILEC serving areas with an average 180 lines per square mile.

the incumbent's network, and conversely. The Telecommunications Act states that mutual interconnection charges should be negotiated between the operators. But the outcome of such negotiations depends heavily on the interconnection charges that the state public utility commissions (or, on appeal, the courts or the FCC) would set in case of negotiation breakdown.

The important features of the Telecommunications Act and the FCC order with regard to interconnection[26] are as follows:

• *Cost-based pricing*: As in the case of unbundled elements, the incumbents' charge must be based on a forward-looking cost study. Indeed, the same TELRIC standards are meant to apply to both unbundled elements and interconnection. (Interconnection can be seen as a simple element consisting of transmission and routing of a terminating call.)

As in the case of resale and unbundling, the FCC order sets a default range to be applied by the states in the absence of cost study. This range is 0.2–0.4 cent per minute for end office termination.[27]

• *Symmetrical access charges*: The ILECs must enter into reciprocal[28] compensation arrangements with other telecommunications carriers, including commercial mobile radio services (cellular, broadband PCS, . . .).[29] The symmetry of access charges is motivated by the FCC by the elimination of the incumbent's bargaining strength and by the incentives given to entrants to minimize their own costs of termination given that their termination charges are exogenously determined by the ILEC's forward-looking incremental costs. States may also if they want opt for a bill-and-keep arrangement (an arrangement in which the car-

---

26. We focus on the pricing of interconnection. There are also important provisions relative to the technically feasible points of interconnection. (The ILEC must provide interconnection at the line side and trunk side of a local switch, the trunk interconnection points for a tandem switch, the central office cross-connect points, the out-of-band signaling transfer points, and the points of access to unbundled elements.) ILECs may be required to modify their facilities—for example, in case of lack of space—to allow interconnection. In case of new services requested by entrants, the latter must compensate the ILEC for conditioning their networks to the new services.

27. Plus possibly 0.15 cent per minute for termination involving a tandem switch.

28. Current interconnection arrangements are not necessarily reciprocal. For instance, the ILECs charge for calls originating with mobile operators, but do not pay when their calls terminate on mobile networks. (Indeed some ILECs currently charge mobile operators for ILEC-originated traffic.)

The European Commission and the French Regulator (ART) are less keen than U.S. regulators on imposing symmetry.

29. Except paging operators (who terminate but do not originate calls).

riers do not compensate each other) if neither carrier has rebutted the presumption of symmetrical rates and if the volumes of traffic between the two networks are approximately equal and expected to remain so.

• *Nondiscrimination*: The ILECs must offer the same interconnection conditions (enforced through an automatic most-favored-nation status) to all telecommunications carriers. So, for instance, the ILECs cannot charge different rates to mobile operators, CAPs, or cable companies.

In contrast, entrants may not be forced to provide other operators the same rates that they charge in their reciprocal arrangement with ILECs.

1.3.1.3   Checklist for RBOC Entry into Long-Distance Services

The Telecommunications Act says that RBOCs will be allowed to enter the long-distance market if they face significant facilities-based competition.[30] (This fact, of course, may not encourage the big three long-distance operators—AT&T, MCI, and Sprint—to invest in facilities-based local networks, although each might actually end up committing such investments thinking that the others would do so anyway.) An RBOC must satisfy two conditions before it may be allowed to provide long-distance services: (a) it must enter into at least one access and interconnection agreement with a competing facilities-based carrier or at least offer such agreements under terms approved by the state, and (b) it must comply with a "competitive checklist." Furthermore the FCC must determine, after consultation with the Department of Justice, whether RBOC entry is in the public's best interest.

The competitive checklist includes the requirements relative to resale, unbundling, and interconnection listed earlier as well as some others such as access by rivals to poles, ducts, conduits, and rights of way, and interim number portability through remote call forwarding until the FCC requires full number portability.[31]

---

30. Non-RBOC ILECs, such as GTE, are not subject to the line-of-business restriction imposed by the consent decree because they were not affiliated with AT&T. For example, GTE has been free to offer long-distance services since 1992. The non-RBOC ILECs have so far been successful entrants in long-distance services. (For example, Southern New England Telephone has converted 25% of its local customers to its long-distance services.)
31. Local number portability allows users to retain their telephone numbers when switching telecom carrier. The absence of local number portability is an important obstacle to the introduction of local competition. Introducing full number portability, however, requires costly software modifications by the incumbent. In the meantime, interim number portability is ensured by forwarding calls and making a much more extensive use of transmission and routing through the existing network.

Once allowed into long distance,[32] the RBOCs are expected to act
as resellers. Unlike the existing resellers, they will benefit from well-
established brand names. But, like existing resellers, they will take
advantage of the large discrepancies between retail prices and marginal
costs on the long-distance market (which, recall, is a very-large-fixed-
cost, very-low-marginal-cost market). The marginal cost of long-
distance transport (not including the taxes levied on long-distance
services—see below) is estimated around 1 cent per minute while the
retail rate (net of access) is about 10 cents a minute.[33] Indeed, RBOCs
have already entered into resale agreements with long-distance carriers even though they are not yet allowed into long distance. Bell South
has announced a large three-year contract with AT&T. Bell Atlantic
and NYNEX have signed up with Sprint. The transactions occur at an
80–90 percent discount relative to retail (for instance, the Sprint deals
involve rates of about 1.5 cents a minute).

1.3.1.4   Universal Service
As will be discussed in more detail in chapter 6, the United States has
two main universal service programs for telecommunications. One provides subsidies on basic services to low-income consumers. The other
aims at making telecommunications services "affordable" in high-cost
areas (rural or insular areas). These programs are currently financed
through "taxes" on long-distance services.

The 1996 act prohibits the previous practice of subsidizing universal service programs from revenues from interconnection and unbundled network elements. Universal service, furthermore, will be funded
through a "competitively neutral mechanism." Two main such mechanisms, which are reminiscent of those used in other industries for
the provision of universal service (education, health, water, railroads,
. . .), contend for the provision of universal service in high-cost areas. One consists in using engineering models to determine a per-line
subsidy to which all eligible operators would be entitled. That is, each
household or business would receive a voucher that could then be al-

---

32. The RBOCs will then have to provide in-region interLATA services through a separate subsidiary for a minimum of three years; this policy is viewed as a safeguard against
cost misallocation and foreclosure. They also should not share proprietary information
concerning a carrier with its affiliate.
33. International services exhibit a similar pattern: The marginal cost is around 10 cents
a minute and the average retail rate 90 cents a minute.

located to the carrier of the user's choice. The other contending mechanism is the design of auctions for universal service, in which carriers would announce the subsidy that they would demand for providing supported services at a prespecified price within a given area. Chapter 6 will analyze in detail the costs and benefits of both mechanisms.

1.3.2 Other Reforms: United Kingdom, New Zealand, Europe

Other countries have chosen different reform paths. To illustrate this diversity, we briefly review the experience with deregulation in two other Anglo-Saxon countries, the United Kingdom and New Zealand, and the projects for the European market.

1.3.2.1 *United Kingdom*

Until it was privatized in 1984, the incumbent operator, British Telecom (BT), was a public enterprise and had a virtual monopoly on all services.[34] Unlike AT&T, BT was not broken up. In particular, it kept its local telephone operations and in 1998 was still widely dominant in this segment. (BT still had 94% of local lines in 1995.)[35]

A second nationwide network operator, Mercury,[36] was licensed in 1982 and began competing seriously with BT in 1986. The government's policy was to create and protect a duopoly for a period of time over which Mercury could build its network and gain market share. Mercury built direct links to large businesses (e.g., in the city of London) and competed with BT for residential users' long-distance and international services through access to BT's local network. The duopoly policy period expired in 1991, when several new operators were licensed.

The 1984 Telecommunications Act in the United Kingdom created an independent regulator, the Office of Telecommunications, or Oftel, headed by a director general of telecommunications (in contrast, the Federal Communications Commission in the United States has five commissioners). Parties can further refer issues concerning anticompetitive behavior to the Monopolies and Mergers Commission (MMC).

---

34. For good surveys of the U.K. reforms, see, e.g., Armstrong (1997a, 1997b, 1997c) and Armstrong, Cowan, and Vickers (1994, chap. 7).

35. An exception to this absence of line-of-business restrictions is the later (1991) prohibition preventing BT (and its long-distance rival Mercury) from offering television services on its telecommunications network until at least 2001.

36. Mercury is a subsidiary of Cable & Wireless, formerly an international telecommunications carrier specialized in former U.K. colonies and privatized in 1981.

Long-Distance and International Services   As we have mentioned, Mercury was licensed as a common carrier in 1982, and it had installed a full-scale switched long-distance network by 1986. At the end of the duopoly period (1991) it had acquired about 10 percent of the market.[37] For most customers, Mercury relies on its competitor, BT, for originating and terminating calls. Its penetration in the local market, as we will see, is quite limited.

Much controversy has surrounded the setting of access charges (or rather "interconnect charges," as they are called in the United Kingdom) since the inception of long-distance competition. Methods for computing such charges on the basis of BT's "opportunity costs" were designed by Oftel in the early 1990s. A simplified version of these methods will be described in section 4.6. Let us simply mention here that access charges were meant to reflect the loss in revenue incurred by BT when losing a customer to Mercury. Thus access charges were governed by demand considerations because they reflected BT's markups on competitive long-distance and international services, and not only by the cost of giving access to Mercury. This aspect of access charge determination generated substantial controversy, which we will later analyze in the light of economic theory.

Another controversial aspect of the access charge setting was its implementation. The director general of telecommunications often and discretionarily waived access charges to be paid to BT by Mercury. This form of entry assistance raised two concerns. First, it reinforced the general policy initiated by the imposition of a duopoly period of picking BT's competitor. Many observers have argued that Mercury may not have been the best choice (as illustrated by its low market share and low profits despite substantial entry assistance) and that market forces would have done a better job at selecting worthy competitors to BT. Second, the linkage of waivers to Mercury's market share (the idea that the partial or complete waivers would stop once Mercury reaches a given market share) reduced Mercury's incentives to build market share, as was recognized, for example, by Oftel in December 1994.[38]

In December 1995, Oftel proposed a new regime for the determination of access charges.[39] Simplifying somewhat, the new policy makes

---

37. In 1996, Mercury had 10.7% of domestic call minutes and 15.6% of international call minutes, against 79.1% and 57.9% for BT, respectively (Oftel, *Market Information Update,* July 1997).
38. Oftel, "A Framework for Effective Competition," December 1994.
39. Oftel, "Pricing of Telecommunications Services from 1997."

a distinction between terminating access and originating access. Oftel wants termination access charges to be based on long-run incremental costs plus some contribution to common costs. Termination charges are also meant to be reciprocal, at least for similar networks. That is, BT's rivals that have local operations should charge the same termination charge as BT.

In contrast, Oftel accepts the principle of flexibility for origination access charges. The latter are subject to a price cap on a single basket, with some downward and upward constraints on individual access charges (a floor at incremental cost, and a ceiling, perhaps equal to stand-alone cost).

To this *network* or *wholesale* cap is added a *retail* cap for BT's retail services. (There are still some constraints on the speed of rebalancing of rates, in particular for monthly subscribers fees, that are not allowed to increase too fast. There are also separate caps for some services such as leased lines, while some others such as telex, public phone booths, or ISDN services are deregulated.)

Mobile Telephony   As in most countries, competition in mobile telephony has developed faster than that in other telecommunications services. The United Kingdom now has four mobile network operators. Two analog licenses were granted in 1984 to Cellnet and Vodafone. The latter, as well as Mercury and Orange, received GSM licenses in 1991. We refer to Armstrong (1997b) for a discussion of some of the economic issues in the U.K. mobile market.

Local Competition   Like U.S. regulators, Oftel is trying to encourage facilities-based entry in the local market. In 1991 cable TV companies were allowed to offer telephony, and were protected against the competition of BT and Mercury through a prohibition faced by both from offering television services on existing phone lines (BT offers video on demand, however). Cable companies do not supply long-distance and international services themselves, but enter wholesale agreements with BT's competitors on those segments and thus can offer to their consumers a wide range of services including local, long-distance, international, television/cable, rapid access to Internet, and value-added services. More recently (1996), Ionica entered the local market through a fixed wireless service. For businesses, competitive access providers such as MFS and COLT have installed fiber-optic networks in central business districts (such as the city of London) and created an opportunity to bypass BT's local network.

In December 1996, BT still had a 90.6 percent market share in terms of subscribers (86.1% for local call minutes), Mercury 1 percent (2.4%), cable companies 7.5 percent (9.8%), and other companies 0.9 percent (1.7%).[40]

Two other points are worth noting. First, Oftel does not want to promote local competition through unbundling and resale;[41] in contrast, we saw that, even though in principle U.S. regulators would prefer facilities-based entry, some of the action in the American policy of promoting local competition is through policies that do not duplicate or only partly duplicate the local bottleneck (and indeed it is expected that some of the local entry in the United States will take place through unbundling and resale). Second, Oftel is providing active entry assistance in local markets;[42] besides the prohibition that prevents BT and Mercury from providing television services over their telecommunications network, which benefits cable companies, BT and Mercury are not allowed to offer fixed wireless technology except in sparsely populated areas, a prohibition that favors Ionica. Third, BT is required to set geographically uniform tariffs for connections, quarterly rentals, and call charges; this rule encourages cream skimming in profitable (mostly urban) markets. Last, BT is not forced to offer equal access to long-distance and international markets, a fact which reduces the competition in markets faced by cable companies and other entrants in the local markets. These distortions of competition, it is hoped, will create multiple companies in the local markets and thus facilitate or even eliminate regulation in those markets in the long run.

Universal Service   Universal service obligations are a smaller issue in the United Kingdom than in other countries such as the United States or France; for one thing, there are fewer sparsely populated areas. BT is required to offer affordable prices for vocal telephony and to enable users to receive calls and call emergency services even after unpaid bills. Of-

---

40. Business and residential users together (Oftel, *Market Information Update*, July 1997).
41. BT must interconnect with "certified facilities-based carriers." BT is not forced to lease its local loops, according to the 1996 Oftel document "Policy on Indirect Access, Equal Access and Direct Connection to the Access Network." Furthermore, resellers pay the same retail rate as end-use customers to BT.
42. See Armstrong (1997a) for more detail.

tel in 1996[43] stated that BT should continue to offer a special subsidized tariff for very low usage and to charge geographically uniform prices for network connection, line rental, and calls.

1.3.2.2 New Zealand

The deregulation in New Zealand offers an interesting contrast with those in the United States and the United Kingdom, since the regulatory authority has been abolished. Competition was opened in 1989, and the incumbent operator, Telecom, was privatized in the following year.[44] Telecom, owned by a consortium led by two U.S. RBOCs (Ameritech and Bell Atlantic), faced two main competitors: Clear in long-distance services and BellSouth New Zealand in the mobile market (BellSouth runs a GSM network, while Telecom still has an analog technology). In 1995, Clear's market share in value was 21 percent for domestic long distance and 24 percent for international calls; BellSouth New Zealand had 10 percent of the subscribers and 22–24 percent of the value in the mobile market.

Effective competition is meant to be secured through the application of the 1986 Commerce Act, and mainly through its Section 36, "Use of Dominant Position in a Market,"[45] and its Section 27, "Contracts, Arrangements, or Understandings Substantially Lessening Competition."[46] Furthermore, unlike, say, the Department of Justice in the United States, the government cannot sue on behalf of the consumers (unless the government itself is affected by an anticompetitive practice).

---

43. See also its December 1995 *Consultative Document on Universal Telecommunications Services.*

44. The state kept a "Kiwi share," which is used to run the universal service program. This program caps residential line rentals for users who were served in 1990 (grandfathering), but it does not protect new subscribers.

45. Whose paragraph 1 stipulates, "No person who has a dominant position in a market shall use that position for the purpose of

a. Restricting the entry of any person into that or any other market; or

b. Preventing or deterring any person from engaging in competitive conduct in that or in any other market; or

c. Eliminating any person from that or any other market."

46. Whose paragraphs 1 and 2 stipulate, "(1) No person shall enter into a contract or arrangement, or arrive at an understanding, containing a provision that has the purpose, or has or is likely to have the effect, of substantially lessening competition in a market."

"(2) No person shall give effect to a provision of a contract, arrangement, or understanding that has the purpose, or has or is likely to have the effect, of substantially lessening competition in the markets."

There is widespread agreement in New Zealand that reregulation is unwarranted.[47]

Interconnection agreements have been a central and thorny issue.
The setting of access charges is left to negotiations, with possible resort to courts under the competition policy law. Clear and Telecom
were involved in a famous dispute in the early 1990s. Clear entered
the long-distance market in 1991 and negotiated originating and terminating access with Telecom. Soon after, Clear drew plans to offer
local service to business users and demanded a new type of interconnection, which Telecom refused. In August 1991, Clear took the case to
court. Telecom, advised by William Baumol and Robert Willig, embraced the efficient component pricing rule (ECPR, see section 4.6)
for the determination of access charges. After a series of contradic-
tory court rulings, New Zealand's Supreme Court, the Privy Council
(in London), ruled in October 1994 that ECPR does not conflict with
Section 36 of the 1986 Commerce Act. There have also been multiple
disputes between BellSouth New Zealand and Telecom, concerning
the absence of wholesale discounts (access charges were set by Telecom at retail prices for terminating calls and above retail for originating calls) and various technological choices by Telecom (interconnection standards, slow upgrading of network intelligence, control
of numbering plan, . . .) that were deemed to handicap the wireless
entrant.

The New Zealand experience is a fascinating, perhaps extreme, one.
It demonstrates the difficulty of ensuring competition in the absence
of regulation. It also highlights the reluctance of courts to get involved
in technical, yet crucial, issues concerning the determination of access
charges.

1.3.2.3   Europe
The deregulation in Europe is characterized by its hierarchical structure
with general rules defined by the European Commission and, according to the subsidiarity principle, implementation of these rules with
some degree of freedom by the national regulatory agencies (NRAs).

---

47. For example, the joint discussion paper of the Ministry of Commerce and the Treasury
(August 1995) argues that regulators, while potentially sophisticated, are much more
likely to be captured than courts. It recognizes, however, that courts tend to be slow and
ill-informed, and recommends considering compulsory arbitration as an intermediate
arrangement.

Full deregulation in telecommunications services and infrastructures with transition periods for some member states has been in place since January 1, 1998. An interconnection directive of June 30, 1997, is particularly relevant here. The general principle is free negotiation on a commercial basis of interconnection agreements within European law and under the supervision of the NRA. Interconnection pricing must be transparent, nondiscriminatory, and cost oriented. Nondiscrimination implies in particular that interconnection tariffs for termination offered by powerful operators (i.e., having more than 20% of the market) cannot discriminate between calls originated from fixed-linked networks and calls from mobile networks. They should be based in the future on forward-looking long-run incremental costs but can include a share of common costs. Meanwhile, the NRAs may use benchmarking with access prices abroad and best practice; ECPR is clearly rejected as a principle for pricing interconnection. Collocation and sharing of infrastructures is encouraged but can be only imposed after a complete public inquiry.

The European Commission defines the minimal level of universal service obligations (USOs). Member states can extend the domain of USOs but cannot use taxes on the industry to finance these extensions.[48]

The pace of deregulation and privatization varies across member states.[49] Future issues include the possible creation of a European Regulatory Agency and the respective roles of regulation and competition policy.

---

48. Under Article 90(1) of the European Community Treaty, member states can grant special rights and obligations to operators. Article 90(2) specifies that such provision of services of general economic interest must comply with competition rules, as long as competition does not prevent the operators from performing the tasks assigned to them.
49. See CEPR (1998).

2   Incentive Regulation

As we discussed in chapter 1, the currrent reforms serve a dual purpose. They aim at improving the incumbent operators' incentives and at encouraging competition in their lines of business. While this book is concerned with the introduction of competition, the understanding of several important aspects of the liberalization process requires a good command of the incentive reform. That is, the regulatory schemes offered to the incumbent operators affect the development of competition and the design of access policies. Chapter 2, therefore, is devoted to a brief study of the key theoretical and practical aspects of incentive regulation.

The incentive reform exhibits roughly two main features. The two features are often lumped together under the heading of performance-based ratemaking (PBR), mainly because they were introduced simultaneously in a number of industries and countries; but they are conceptually separate, and we will accordingly review them sequentially. First, the current reforms try to increase productive efficiency by making incumbent operators accountable for a higher fraction of their costs. We will call this approach performance-based or incentive regulation. In practice, the reforms have altered the sharing of efficiency gains between the consumers and the firms. The new sharing rules, together with the improved incentives for cost reduction, have thereby affected the *average* level of prices. Second, the reforms have given operators more freedom to set their rates in accordance with standard business practices. This flexibility on the *relative* price structure has led, as we will explain, to more Ramsey-oriented prices.

This chapter is organized as follows. Section 2.1 describes the key theoretical considerations behind performance-based regulation: the basic trade-off between incentives and rent extraction, the extent of disaggregation of incentive schemes, and the factors limiting the power of these schemes. Section 2.2 reviews the rationale for Ramsey pricing to final users, its possible implementation through price caps, and some limits to Ramsey pricing. It also applies Ramsey pricing to the case of a structurally separated infrastructure owner supplying wholesale services to downstream industries. Section 2.3 discusses the practical aspects of regulatory reforms with respect to incentives and price flexibility. Readers familiar with incentive regulation and Ramsey pricing can move directly to chapter 3.

2.1   Economic Principles: Performance-Based Regulation

2.1.1   The Rationale for Performance-Based Regulation

One of the motivations for the design of new regulatory schemes is the perception of a poor cost performance of regulated firms. Depending on the situation, this poor performance may take several forms: insufficient internal control, labor hoarding, incompetent management, undue perks, lack of innovation, imprudent investments, and so forth. The suboptimal performance is generally attributed to a lack of incentives. Deregulated firms have traditionally operated under a regime in which cost increases were automatically passed through to consumers in the form of higher charges for the operators' services. Recent reforms have been trying to make firms accountable for a substantial fraction of their costs.

2.1.1.1   *A Procurement Example*
To get a good grasp at the incentive issues, let us abstract from pricing considerations in a first step. Suppose that a government wants to procure some (fixed amount of) public good. Only one firm has the know-how or capacity to supply this public good. Unfortunately, the government has imperfect information about the cost that will be incurred by the firm. Its expected cost depends on both exogenous and endogenous variables.

Exogenous variables refer to the technological requirements that the firm will be facing in producing the public good and to the firm's opportunity cost—that is, the profit forgone by the firm when producing the public good instead of undertaking an alternative project for another principal. To the extent that the firm is better informed about these exogenous factors when contracting with the government, as is likely to be the case, the government faces an *adverse selection* problem. Roughly speaking, the government does not know whether a low payment will suffice to convince the firm to undertake the project or whether it will have to "pay the high price." Needless to say, the firm will not be eager to reveal that its production cost is low even if this is the case, since it is in its interest to persuade the government that only a high price will do.

Endogenous variables refer to those postcontractual decisions taken by the firm that, together with the exogenous variables (and some ex post uncertainty), determine the firm's final production cost and that cannot be contracted upon because they are not verifiable by a court of law. These discretionary choices by the firm create the scope for poor performance that we alluded to earlier. That is, the government faces *moral hazard* on the firm's side. Only if the firm is made accountable for a large fraction of its realized cost will it not abuse this discretion.

2.1.1.2   The Basic Trade-Off between Incentives and Rent Extraction

Suppose that the government wants to buy the public good but would like to pay as little as possible. Its instrument is the payment to the firm, which can be made contingent on the firm's ex post realized cost (provided, of course, that the firm is willing to provide the public good under the conditions offered by the government). That is, the government offers a *cost reimbursement rule* specifying the payment that will be made to the firm for each realization of the cost.

A key concept is that of the *power of the incentive scheme*. A *high-powered incentive scheme* is one in which the firm bears a high fraction of its cost at the margin. That is, when the firm raises its cost by $1, its net payment (that is, the payment it receives over and beyond the reimbursement by the government of the realized cost) is reduced by an amount close to $1, or, equivalently, its gross payment (that is, the payment it receives if, by accounting convention, it pays the cost itself) hardly moves with the realized cost at the margin. In a procurement context, a fixed-price contract, in which the contractor receives a fixed gross payment, is the prototypical high-powered incentive scheme, since the firm is made fully accountable for its cost savings. In contrast, a *low-powered incentive scheme* is one in which a $1 increase in the firm's realized cost translates into about a $1 payment by the government, and so hardly affects the firm's profit. In particular, in a cost-plus contract, the firm's cost is reimbursed, and so the firm is not made accountable for its cost savings or overruns.

If the government were fully informed about the firm's cost, that is, if there were no adverse selection, the government's design of a contract for the firm would be a simple matter: by offering a fixed-price contract, the government would give perfect incentives to the firm. The latter would fully internalize its cost savings and therefore would exert the socially optimal level of effort to reduce costs. Besides, the government would not have to worry about paying too high a price. Being well-informed about the firm's technology, it could perfectly choose the fixed price so as to leave the firm with no rent; that is, it could select the lowest price that is consistent with the firm's being willing to agree to produce the public good. We conclude that, in the absence of adverse selection, the government would offer a high-powered incentive scheme.[1]

In the presence of incomplete information about the firm's technology or opportunity cost, though, the government faces a trade-off between giving good incentives to the firm and capturing its potential rent. Recall that proper incentives for effort are created by a fixed-price contract (or more generally by a high-powered incentive scheme). But a contract that yields $1 to the firm each time the firm endogenously reduces its cost by $1 also gives it $1 whenever its cost is lower by $1 for exogenous reasons; that is, a firm is residual claimant also for cost factors that are outside its control. This fact generates substantial rents. In contrast, a cost-plus contract (or, more generally, a low-powered incentive scheme), while providing poor incentives to keep cost down, is efficient at capturing the firm's potential rent. Indeed, the firm does not benefit when it is lucky and its cost is exogenously reduced by $1, since the cost is fully borne by the government.

To illustrate this adverse selection problem and the impact of the power of the incentive scheme, suppose that there is no moral hazard problem—that is, that the firm's cost is exogenously determined. This cost can be either 5 or 10. If the government is constrained to offering a fixed-price contract, and if the public good is socially sufficiently valuable so that the government must supply it, then the government has no choice but offering 10 to the firm. While this offer ensures that

---

1. The reader may object that the firm enjoys a monopoly position and may therefore be able to extract rents even if the government has full information. Assuming that the firm has substantial bargaining power, however, does not modify the conclusion that the contract is a fixed-price contract. It affects only transfers via fixed fees. More generally, the insights obtained in this chapter carry over even when the government is unable to make a "take-it-or-leave-it offer" to the firm.

the firm is willing to produce the public good, it also leaves a rent equal to 5 if the firm has a low cost. In contrast, a cost-plus contract pays only what is needed to let the firm break even. To be certain, the realized cost is then, say, 8 or 13 (depending on the firm's intrinsic efficiency),[2] but the payment matches the cost.

We thus conclude that *there is a basic trade-off between incentives, which call for a high-powered incentive scheme, and rent extraction, which requires, in the presence of adverse selection, low-powered incentives.*

This simple implication of the theory is too often forgotten. High-powered incentive schemes (price caps in a regulatory contract) have repeatedly been hailed as a breakthrough in the economics of regulation. While they indeed deliver a good cost performance, they are also likely to leave substantial profits to the firms' owners. There is no magic cure. Those who support or just accept the use of high-powered incentive schemes should be ready to refrain from forcing contract renegotiation when they observe large profits.[3] Experience (the 1995 early review of the U.K. regional electricity companies is a case in point) shows that this point is not always understood.

2.1.1.3 One Size Does Not Fit All

A second insight, "One size does not fit all,"[4] can be gleaned from our procurement example. The same contract in general does not fit all types of supplier. The point is more subtle than the incentives–rent-extraction trade-off, but it is equally important. In the presence of asymmetric information between the firm and the government, the key issue for the latter is how to screen the firm's type through its contractual choice.

Recall that the difficulty encountered in extracting the firm's rent resides in the firm's ability to pretend to face a high cost when it actually has a low cost. The government can, however, reduce the gain enjoyed by a low-cost firm by making this strategy unappealing. To build a simple example, suppose that the firm's intrinsic cost can be "high" or "low" (that is, the exogenous cost parameter can take one of two values). And suppose that the government offers a *menu* of two contracts,

---

2. We assume here that the most egregious forms of cost overruns can be prevented through audits, so that a low effort translates into an excess cost of 3.

3. This point was made clear by theory as early as 1986. See Laffont and Tirole (1986).

4. We borrow this phrase from Sappington and Weisman (1996). Their book draws a very useful link between the theoretical precepts and recent regulatory reforms.

a fixed-price and a cost-plus contract, from which the firm selects one (or none). The fixed-price contract is designed so as to let the firm just break even (that is, enjoy no rent) when it has a low cost. Yet the firm when it has a low cost is not tempted to choose the cost-plus contract, since its cost efficiency yields no gain under a contract that reimburses all costs anyway. And it is easy to see that the firm strictly prefers the cost-plus contract when its cost is high because it would lose money under the fixed contract, which, as we have seen, is designed so as to let the more efficient type just break even.

This menu of a fixed-price contract for a low-cost type and of a cost-plus contract for a high-cost type allows the government to ensure participation by the high-cost type while not giving rents away to the low-cost type. This "perfect screening" is of course purchased at a high expense: The high-cost type faces no incentive whatsoever to control cost. But it illustrates nicely the scope for screening. The general insight, developed in box 2.1, is that *it is optimal to design a menu of contracts in which the firm self-selects: a high-powered incentive scheme when it is efficient and lower-powered incentive scheme when it is less efficient.*

Regulators have traditionally refrained from offering menus of regulatory contracts. They are starting to do so, however. For instance, some U.S. state regulators have offered regulated firms a choice between remaining under a cost-of-service regime, staying with a scheme somewhat akin to a cost-plus contract, or switching to a price cap, a higher-powered incentive sheme. The federal regulator, the FCC, has similarly designed a menu of incentive schemes for the local exchange companies relative to the provision of local access for the long-distance companies.

There are also probably more menus than meet the eye. When regulators do not formally offer a menu of contracts, they may consider several options when bargaining with the firm. In other words, menus may exist but not be observable by industry outsiders.

The possibility of formal or informal menus of contracts actually complicates econometric analyses of the impact of the power of incentive schemes on cost efficiency.[5] As we have seen, firms that are confident that they can keep their cost low are likely to select or lobby for high-powered schemes. So, while high-powered schemes are conducive to efficiency, they also attract a priori efficient firms. In other

5. See, e.g., Feinstein and Wolak (1991), Wolak (1994), Wunsch (1994), Thomas (1995), Gagnepain (1996), and Gomez-Lobo (1997).

Text continues on p. 51.

Box 2.1
Choosing the Power of Incentive Schemes

Let us sketch the procurement version of the Laffont and Tirole (1986) model. That model was designed in particular so as to allow us to identify the determinants of the power of optimal incentive schemes. Consider, as in the text, an indivisible project with social value S. There is a single, risk-neutral firm with the know-how to realize this project. Its cost function is

$$C = \beta - e \qquad (1)$$

where β (the exogenous factor in the cost function) is an efficiency parameter and $e \geq 0$ (the endogenous factor) is the firm's postcontractual effort to keep the cost down.

The government ex post audits the firm's cost C, but observes neither β nor e. Let us adopt the convenient accounting convention that the government reimburses the cost and also pays a net transfer t to the firm. (Equivalently, the government pays a gross transfer $t + C$, and the firm bears its cost.) The firm's private cost or disutility of effort is $\psi(e)$ with $\psi' > 0$, $\psi'' > 0$, $\psi''' \geq 0$ (a technical assumption that guarantees the second order condition), $\psi(0) = 0$, and $\psi'(0) = 0$. The firm's utility is then

$$U = t - \psi(e) \qquad (2)$$

We further normalize the firm's utility when it does not contract with the government (that is, its reservation utility) at 0, and so the firm's particpation constraint is

$$U \geq 0 \qquad (3)$$

With this convention, the firm's utility is equal to its rent; that is, it is equal to the difference between the utility and the reservation utility.

To highlight the role of informational asymmetries, we assume here that the government is benevolent and maximizes a utilitarian social welfare function. There is, however, a shadow cost of public funds associated with the distortionary nature of taxation. That is, a \$1 transfer to the firm imposes a cost of \$$(1 + \lambda)$ on the taxpayers, with $\lambda > 0$ (econometric studies often estimate $\lambda \simeq 0.3$ in developed countries). Provided the project is implemented, the social welfare function is therefore

$$\begin{aligned} W &= S - (1 + \lambda)(t + C) + U \\ &= S - (1 + \lambda)[C + \psi(e)] - \lambda U \end{aligned} \qquad (4)$$

In words, social welfare is equal to the gross surplus S engendered by the project, minus the total monetary and nonmonetary cost of the project, $C + \psi(e)$, evaluated at one plus the shadow cost of public funds, minus the shadow cost of public funds times the firm's rent. The key feature of this social welfare function is that leaving a rent to the firm is socially costly.

The socially optimal allocation is therefore characterized by the absence of rent:

$$U = 0 \qquad \text{or, equivalently,} \qquad t = \psi(e)$$

and by the equality of the marginal cost of effort and marginal cost savings:

$$\min_{e} [\beta - e + \psi(e)] \qquad \text{or} \qquad \psi'(e^*) = 1$$

Box 2.1 (continued)

For simplicity, we will assume that the government designs a contract that the firm then accepts or refuses.

The Full-Information Benchmark

Suppose, first, that the government has perfect information about the firm's technology, as summarized by the parameter β. The government can then easily obtain the optimum defined previously by offering a *fixed-price contract:*

$$t(C) = \alpha - C$$

The firm, which is residual claimant for its cost savings, then chooses the socially optimal level of effort e^*, since it minimizes $C + \psi(e)$. To suppress the rent, the government then chooses the fixed price α at the minimum level that induces the firm to agree to implement the project, which is equal to the total (monetary and nonmonetary) cost of the project:

$$\alpha = (\beta - e^*) + \psi(e^*)$$

Asymmetric Information

Obviously, the government is unable to select the proper fixed price when it is not perfectly informed about the firm's technology. To depict this situation, let us assume that, while the firm knows the parameter β when contracting with the government, the government only has a Bayesian prior, with cumulative distribution $F(\beta)$ and density $f(\beta)$ on some interval $[\underline{\beta}, \bar{\beta}]$. For technical reasons, we will assume that the hazard rate of the distribution, f/F, is weakly decreasing. (This assumption, which is satisfied for most common distributions, is used to guarantee that the second-order conditions are satisfied.) For a given incentive scheme $t(C)$, the final allocation $\{e(\beta), C(\beta) = \beta - e(\beta), U(\beta) = t[C(\beta)] - \psi[\beta - C(\beta)]\}$ is now contingent on β.

Assuming that the project is sufficiently valuable that the government always wants to realize it, the government now maximizes the expectation of social welfare, $E[W(\beta)]$, where $E[\cdot]$ denotes an expectation with respect to the parameter β. It now faces two types of constraints: the participation constraint

$$U(\beta) \geq 0 \qquad \text{for all } \beta \tag{5}$$

and an "incentive compatibility condition." Facing an incentive scheme $t(C)$, the firm chooses e, or equivalently $C = \beta - e$, so as to solve

$$U(\beta) = \max_C \left\{ t(C) - \psi(\beta - C) \right\} \tag{6}$$

The envelope theorem then implies that

$$\frac{dU}{d\beta} = -\psi'[e(\beta)] \tag{7}$$

Equation (7), which is a rewriting of equation (6), shows that, as expected, the

Box 2.1 (continued)

firm's rent increases with its efficiency. This result implies that equation (5) boils down for the worst type $\bar{\beta}$ to

$$U(\bar{\beta}) \geq 0 \tag{5'}$$

And, because rents are costly, equation (5') will be binding at the social optimum.

More interestingly, equation (7) embodies the basic trade-off between incentives and rent extraction. More powerful incentives for type β, that is, a higher $e(\beta)$, raise the slope of the rent curve, thereby raising the rent of all types with parameter lower than β, as depicted in figure 2.1.

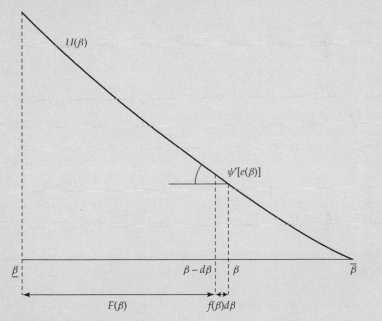

Figure 2.1

The government then solves

$$\max_{\{e(\cdot), U(\cdot)\}} E[W(\beta)] = \int_{\underline{\beta}}^{\bar{\beta}} \left(S - (1+\lambda)\{C(\beta) + \psi[e(\beta)]\} - \lambda U(\beta)\right) f(\beta)d\beta$$

subject to the participation constraint (5') and the incentive compatibility constraint (7). We leave to the reader to show that the first-order condition for effort is, for all β,

$$\psi'[e(\beta)] = 1 - \frac{\lambda}{1+\lambda}\frac{F(\beta)}{f(\beta)}\psi''[e(\beta)] \tag{8}$$

yielding a decreasing function $e(\beta)$, with $e(\underline{\beta}) = e^*$.

An intuitive derivation of equation (8) goes as follows: Suppose that a change in the cost reimbursement rule $t(C)$ is contemplated that induces types in

Box 2.1 (continued)

$[\beta - d\beta, \beta]$ to raise their effort $e(\beta)$ by a unit amount. The total cost for these types, in number $f(\beta)d\beta$, is reduced by $1 - \psi'[e(\beta)]$, to be weighted at one plus the shadow cost of public funds. But the rent of type $\beta - d\beta$ is increased by $\psi''[e(\beta)]d\beta$ [from equation (7)], and, ceteris paribus, so is the rent of all types in $[\underline{\beta}, \beta - d\beta]$, in number $F(\beta)$. At the optimum these incentive and rent increase effects must exactly offset, and so

$$(1 + \lambda)\{1 - \psi'[e(\beta)]\}f(\beta)d\beta = \lambda F(\beta)\psi''[e(\beta)]d\beta$$

which yields equation (8). We will ignore the study of the second-order conditions for simplicity.

Implementation

The preceding treatment is abstract, and we must explain how the government can implement the optimal allocation if we are to draw useful implications for the desired power of incentive schemes. In practice, regulators offer a cost reimbursement rule (CRR) $t(C)$. We must therefore recover the underlying CRR from the optimal allocation. Note that

$$C(\beta) = \beta - e(\beta)$$

and, from equations (2), (5'), and (7),

$$t(\beta) = \psi[e(\beta)] + U(\beta) = \psi[e(\beta)] + \int_{\beta}^{\bar{\beta}} \psi'[e(x)]dx$$

Substituting β in these two equations yields the desired CRR $t(C)$. Straightforward computations show that the CRR is decreasing and convex

$$t' < 0 \qquad \text{and} \qquad t'' > 0$$

That it should be decreasing is intuitive. We will shortly come back to the reason why it is convex.

A key property of convex functions is that they are the envelope of their tangents, see figure 2.2. Concretely, this means that, rather than offering the CRR $t(C)$, the government can indifferently offer the menu of linear incentive schemes defined by the tangents to the CRR.

$$t = \alpha(b) - bC$$

where α is an increasing function of the slope b of the incentive scheme selected by the firm. Facing technology β, the firm selects a linear incentive scheme with slope

$$b(\beta) = \psi'[e(\beta)] \tag{9}$$

where $e(\beta)$ is given by equation (8).

The firm, when it is more efficient (β decreases), is willing to bear a higher fraction b of its cost. Indeed, the most efficient type, $\underline{\beta}$, selects a fixed-price contract ($b = 1$) from equations (8) and (9). But quite generally, the efficient contract involves some cost sharing between the firm and the government [$b < 1$, also from equations (8) and (9)]. As discussed in the text, this cost sharing

Box 2.1 (continued)

is costly because it reduces the firm's incentive to control cost, but it limits the rent of the efficient types.

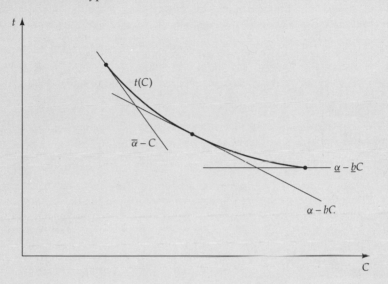

Figure 2.2

The intuition for the convexity of the CRR is provided by this menu of linear incentive schemes: More efficient types want to bear a higher fraction of their cost, which they know to be low; that is, self-selection implies that the slope of the incentive scheme is high when the cost is low. Note, incidentally, that intrinsic cost differences (differences in β) are compounded by the fact that more efficient types also exert more effort to reduce their cost.

Besides its practical appeal, the menu of linear contracts also has the advantage that it is robust to the introduction of ex post cost uncertainty. Suppose that

$$C = \beta - e + \varepsilon$$

where ε is a random variable with zero mean and is independent of β. On the one hand, the presence of the noise ε does not impact the firm's choice among the linear contacts, and so social welfare is unaffected by the noise. On the other hand, the noise does not create any value and might conceivably reduce welfare by garbling the information available to the government. Thus linear contracts are still optimal in the presence of noise.

Potential Criticisms and Applications of the Bayesian Approach

There are two possible readings of the theory that we have developed. One emphasizes its *quantitative* implications for the power of incentive schemes. Critics of the Bayesian approach point out that the quantitative implications of the

Box 2.1 (continued)

model rely on some assessment of the distribution of the unknown variable(s) [here of $F(\beta)$]. One may then want to calibrate this distribution using data from related situations and/or reasonable guesses on the magnitude of the informational asymmetries. This approach has been advocated by Schmalensee (1989) and Gasmi, Ivaldi, and Laffont (1994). Calibration of the range of asymmetric information can be derived from independent experts' range of uncertainty about costs. Gasmi, Laffont, and Sharkey (1997) use engineering models of the local loop to calibrate the extent of potential asymmetric information. Alternatively, when various contracts coexist and costs are observable, econometric methods can be used to recover the distributions of the unknown variables (see Laffont [1997] for a survey of the literature on the econometrics of auctions).

In the absence of dependable data, one may have to rely on the regulator's subjective distribution. Critics of the Bayesian approach will here object on the basis that the distribution is then indeed subjective and therefore subject to potential manipulation. This critique should actually be viewed in a constructive way. The manipulation alluded to may well stem from regulatory capture by some interest group (e.g., the firm). As we will later point out, the implications of the theory must be amended in the presence of potential collusion between the regulator and specific interest groups.

An alternative reading of the theory focuses on *qualitative* implications. Rather than trying to compute the slopes of optimal incentive schemes, one studies how various factors impact those slopes. This qualitative approach suggests that schemes should be low powered in some circumstances and high powered in others. We will draw such implications later in the section.

Competition for the Market

We have assumed that there is a monopoly supplier. Suppose, in contrast, that m firms, with cost functions

$$C^i = \beta^i - e^i \qquad i = 1, \ldots, m$$

can compete for the market. The efficiency parameters β^i are the only factors differentiating the firms ex ante and are independently drawn from the same distribution $F(\cdot)$ with density $f(\cdot)$. These parameters are private information to the firms. The government organizes an auction to select a single supplier among the m firms. It can be shown (Laffont and Tirole, 1987a; McAfee and McMillan, 1987; and Riordan and Sappington, 1987, obtain closely related results in different contexts) that in the optimal auction,

1. The most efficient supplier, namely the one with the lowest β^i, is selected.
2. The winner is given a linear incentive scheme, with the same slope as if it had been a monopoly supplier. The fixed fee in contrast is reduced relative to the monopoly case.

That the slope of the CRR given to the winner depends only on its cost function, but not on the information that the firm won the auction, can be grasped as follows. Suppose, without loss of generality, that the most efficient

Box 2.1 (continued)

firm is firm 1, the second most efficient is firm 2, and so forth. Firm 1's win indicates that β^1 belongs to the interval $[\underline{\beta}, \beta^2]$. In contrast, in the absence of competition for the market, "winning" generates no information, and so the government only knows that β^1 belongs to $[\underline{\beta}, \bar{\beta}]$. Thus the impact of the auction is to reduce the asymmetry of information between the winner and the government. Now, recall from equations (8) and (9) that the slope of the incentive scheme is entirely determined by the hazard rate of the distribution. But the hazard rate is invariant under an upward truncation of the distribution:

$$\frac{\left[f(\beta)/F(\beta^2) \right]}{\left[F(\beta)/F(\beta^2) \right]} = \frac{f(\beta)}{F(\beta)}$$

and so $b(\beta^1)$ is the same whether there is or is not competition for the market.

While the power of the winner's incentive scheme is independent of the existence of competition for a given β^1, the winner's efficiency may depend on the number of competing firms. For example, with independent draws from the same distribution, the first-order statistic of the winner's type improves (in the sense of first-order stochastic dominance) with the number of firms,[6] and so the winner's incentive scheme is more high powered when there is more intense competition for the market.

Benchmarking

Let us return to the case of a monopoly supplier for the production of a given public good, but assume that there are two regions, $i = 1, 2$, each with its own public good provision and single supplier. Supplier i's cost function is

$$C^i = \beta - e^i$$

Note that we assume that the two suppliers use the same technology (have the same β). Let the government in region i (it would not make any difference if the government were the same for both regions) offer a fixed-price contract to its monopoly supplier

$$t^i(C^i) = \alpha - (C^i - C^j)$$

with $\alpha = \psi(e^*)$. That is, the supplier's reward is determined by its relative, rather than its absolute, performance. The supplier then is residual claimant for its cost savings and selects the socially optimal effort $e^i = e^*$. Provided government $j \neq i$ also offers a fixed price contract to supplier j (which it optimally does), then the performances are the same, and the choice of the fixed fee ensures that supplier i enjoys no rent. Thus, benchmarking here allows the government to mimic the full-information outcome even if it does not know the firm's technology.

---

6. The cumulative distribution of the winner's type is $1 - [1 - F(\beta^1)]^m$.

Box 2.1 (continued)

Multiple Product Lines, Managerial Cross-Subsidies, and Regulation on a Global Basis

In Laffont and Tirole (1990a), we derived sufficient conditions under which observing the subcosts of a multiproduct regulated firm is useless and regulating the firm on the basis of its total cost (implying a uniform power across activities) is optimal. Here is a simple example.

Suppose the firm undertakes n projects, $k = 1, \ldots, n$, each yielding social surplus S. The firm's subcost on project k,

$$C_k = \beta_k - e_k$$

depends on a project-specific technological parameter β_k known only to the firm, and the firm's effort e_k to reduce subcost C_k. The firm chooses both a total effort $e = \Sigma_k e_k$, which involves disutility $\psi(e)$, and its allocation among projects; that is, the firm allocates headquarter attention, personnel, nonverifiable investment, and so forth to the various projects. Let

$$C \equiv \Sigma_k C_k$$

denote total cost, and

$$\beta \equiv \Sigma_k \beta_k$$

As earlier, λ, t, and U denote the shadow cost of public funds, the net transfer to the firm, and the firm's rent, respectively. Welfare is (the expectation of) $W = nS - (1 + \lambda)(t + C) - U$.

Intuitively, the derivative of the net transfer $t(C_1, \ldots, C_n)$ with respect to subcost C_k must be the same for all k. Otherwise, the firm would reallocate its effort away from projects with low $|\partial t/\partial C_k|$ to those with high $|\partial t/\partial C_k|$. In other words, the transfer function can depend only on total cost C, and there is no point auditing the subcosts.

Slightly more formally, note that the firm's rent is equal to

$$\max_{\{C_1,\ldots,C_n\}} \left\{ t(C_1, \ldots, C_n) - \psi(\beta - \Sigma_k C_k) \right\}$$

From this it follows that the rent depends only on β, that $dU/d\beta = -\psi'(\beta - C)$ depends only on total cost C, and that for a given C, the firm allocates effort (or equivalently subcosts) in such a way that

$$\frac{\partial t}{\partial C_1} = \cdots = \frac{\partial t}{\partial C_n}$$

That is, incentives are necessarily uniform. The rest of the analysis is then the same as in a single-project case for the distribution on β (obtained from the convolution of the distributions on the β_k's).

words, there is a biased selection in the sample of firms subject to high-powered schemes.

Last, let us notice that there is nothing unusual about menus of contracts. Indeed, the telephone companies themselves routinely offer their customers optional tariffs, some with a low fixed fee and a high usage price and others with a higher fixed fee and lower usage price. While the former are geared to low users, the latter are targeted to heavy users. Telephone companies design menus for their customers for the same reason regulators should design menus for regulated firms: to better screen them. The low-fixed-fee, high-usage-price option (the counterpart of the cost-plus contract) is somewhat unappealing to heavy users who care most about the variable charge. While this option involves a price for the marginal minute far above the firm's marginal cost and is therefore inefficient, it forces heavy users to choose the option that is designed for them and thereby limits the heavy users' net surplus (the counterpart of the firm's rent in the regulatory context).

2.1.1.4   Why Are Rents Costly?
Our analysis is based on the assumption that the government "wants to pay as little as possible" for the supply of the public good. There are three possible, and conceptually very similar, foundations for this assumption. The first is that the government puts a lower weight on the firm than on the other agents in the economy. Then $1 received by the firm is counted at less than $1 in the social welfare function, and thus has a net social cost. Second, the government may put the same weight on the firm as on the rest of the economy, but transfers to the firm must be financed through distortionary taxation on labor, savings, and so on. The existence of a shadow cost of public funds implies again that unwarranted transfers to the firm create a social loss (this assumption is adopted in box 2.1). Third, and more relevant for the rest of the book, when the firm is subject to budget balance, the firm's rent is financed through markups on the firm's services. These markups distort the consumers' consumptions and are therefore undesirable. Which of these three reasons motivates the social cost of rents has no impact on the insights obtained in this section.

2.1.1.5   Competition for the Market and Benchmarking Allow Higher-Powered Incentive Schemes
We saw that low-powered incentive schemes are motivated by the asymmetry of information between the firm and the government and

by the concomitant concern to keep the firm's rent at a reasonable level. Factors that reduce the asymmetry of information naturally alleviate this concern and lead to the adoption of higher-powered schemes. Competition and benchmarking are two such factors.

Competition in an auction for the monopoly position reduces the asymmetry of information by forcing firms not to overinflate their cost announcements because they are then likely to lose the market. Box 2.1 shows that competition for the market pushes the winner's incentive scheme toward a fixed-price contract.

Benchmarking (or "yardstick competition" or "relative performance evaluation") consists in comparing the performance of the firm with that of other firms facing a related (technically: correlated) situation. For example, other firms might produce the same public good in different geographical areas. To the extent that the technologies used to produce in different areas are similar, one can compare the performances of these other firms to gather relevant information about the firm one is regulating. In particular, the government becomes suspicious if its contractor announces and produces at a very high cost while the supplier in a neighboring area produces at a low cost. The comparison of performances of producers facing similar technological conditions thus reduces the asymmetry of information and enables the use of higher-powered incentive schemes.

Despite high hopes, explicit contractual benchmarking is rare in regulation because of alleged heterogeneities. In the electricity sector, it underlies the "Marco Estable" regulating the power companies in Spain; but the need for adjusting costs to each firm's specificities weakened the mechanism. It is used within Electricité de France, which has numerous identical nuclear power plants.

Benchmarking often plays a more informal role through improvement of regulators' and the public's information derived from observing similar situations elsewhere. Benchmarking leads to higher-powered incentive schemes by decreasing the need to rely on the regulator's beliefs about the firm's efficiency. A case in point was the use of British information on the cost of universal service obligations in telecommunications by the French regulator to assess the cost of universal service obligations in France.

2.1.1.6   How Many Performance Measures?

Regulated firms rarely produce a single service. Rather, they are "multiproduct firms." A question often encountered by regulators is whether different services should be subject to differentiated cost-sharing rules.

That is, should the power of incentive schemes vary across product lines? For example, deregulated segments (competitive telecommunications activities, equipment manufacturing, . . .), which involve no cost sharing, are usually subject to higher-powered incentives than regulated ones, which exhibit varying degrees of cost sharing between the regulated firm and the consumers. Another common situation with differentiated incentive powers arises when different activities are regulated by different authorities—for example, state and federal—which do not fully coordinate their regulations.

A differentiation of the powers of incentive schemes across product lines creates the concern that the firm may engage in cross-subsidies. Suppose that a firm keeps 75 cents per dollar of cost reduction on activity 1 and only 25 cents per dollar of cost reduction on activity 2. Then saving $1 on activity 1 and increasing the cost of activity 2 by $1 yields a net benefit of 50 cents for the firm.

This cost transfer may occur in two ways. The first, and the one the regulatory debate has focused on, involves *accounting cross subsidies*. The firm benefits from allocating costs that are incurred in the provision of activity 1 to activity 2. This may involve reporting that personnel or other variable inputs that were used in activity 1 were dedicated to activity 2, or (and harder to detect) the firm may allocate a large share of jointly incurred costs to activity 2. In an attempt to prevent accounting cross-subsidies, regulators routinely impose "accounting separation" between activities, together with rigid (and arbitrary) rules for allocating the joint costs that are incurred in the simultaneous provision of these activities.

Careful accounting procedures, however, cannot prevent the second type of transfers, associated with managerial decisions. *Managerial cross-subsidies* refer to real (as opposed to accounting) allocations betwen the activities. For example, the firm may allocate its inexperienced or underperforming personnel to the activity with the highest cost sharing (that is, with the lower-powered incentive, activity 2) and the trained and best-performing employees to activity 1. And, when investment decisions involve assets that are jointly used by the two activities, the firm benefits from biasing its technological choices toward technologies that involve low variable costs for activity 1 and high variable costs for activity 2. As a last illustration, the company's CEO and top management often devote a substantial share of their energy to deregulated segments.

No accountant can control such managerial cross-subsidies, since doing so would substitute one's business judgement for the firm's, a practice that would run against the standard mission of accountancy. Clearly, managerial cross-subsidies severely constrain the differentiation of powers of incentive scheme across activities undertaken under a unified management. Box 2.1 shows that they may even force regulators to regulate the firm *on a global basis*, with all activities subject to the same, uniform power.

We will use these insights in chapter 4, where we discuss the impact of cross-subsidies on the choice of an access pricing rule.

2.1.2   Three Factors Limiting the Power of Incentives

We have already observed that asymmetric information allows regulated firms to extract large rents under high-powered incentive schemes. This possibility in turn motivates the use of cost- or earnings-sharing schemes. This section investigates three factors that make sharing by consumers or by the government particularly desirable.

2.1.2.1   *Quality Concerns*
A well-known drawback of high-powered schemes is that they make it very costly to firms to supply quality. The provision of quality raises cost and is therefore borne entirely by the firm if the latter is residual claimant for its cost performance. The firm may, therefore, decide to skimp on quality if quality is not minutely specified in the regulatory contract. In contrast, low-powered schemes, by failing to make the firm accountable for its cost performance, make it very cheap to supply quality.[7]

This point is well known. Indeed, the U.S. Department of Defense has often invoked it to motivate the use of cost-plus contracts in contexts in which quality is a sensitive issue and its specifications are hard to pin down exactly in the initial procurement contract with the defense contractor (Scherer, 1964). Similarly, the argument has been made several times that the introduction of incentive regulation for power companies conflicts with the safe operation of nuclear power plants. As a last illustration, quality started deteriorating shortly after British Telecom's 1984 privatization and design of more powerful incentives in the form of a price cap, and quality standards and verification mechanisms had to be set up as a consequence (Vickers and Yarrow, 1988).

---

7. For formalizations of this "multitask issue," see, e.g., Holmström and Milgrom (1991) in the context of internal organization and Laffont and Tirole (1991a) in the context of procurement.

There is a natural complementarity between powerful incentive schemes and a close monitoring of quality standards. If the regulator is unable to specify the standards or to monitor compliance with these standards, then there may be no other choice than the adoption of low-powered incentives.

2.1.2.2   Regulatory Commitment

Regulatory contracts are generally much shorter than the relationship between the regulatory authority and the regulated firm. They do not exceed five years for price cap regulation and are usually shorter under other forms of regulation.

Let us for the moment assume that the official length of the contract is respected, so that the regulatory review will occur at the expiration of the current regulatory contract. And consider a high-powered incentive scheme covering the length of the regulatory contract. It is clear that even though the firm is formally residual claimant for its cost savings, an effort to reduce cost by $1 is not rewarded $1 overall. A lower cost will convince the regulatory authority of a higher efficiency and will make it more demanding in the regulatory contract designed for the firm at the next regulatory review. So while a $1 cost reduction yields $1 to the firm in the short run, it also entails a long-term penalty in the form of higher performance requirements at the next review. This is the well-known *ratchet effect*.[8] The ratchet effect imposes a bound on the incentives that can be provided even by formally high-powered incentives.

In practice, the actual length of the regulatory contract may be shorter than its formal length. That is, the contract may be renegotiated before the next regulatory review. On the one hand, the regulator, usually under political pressure, may be tempted to force the firm to renegotiate before the end of the contract when the latter makes substantial profits. Such renegotiation exacerbates the ratchet effect and makes the firm even more cautious about taking full advantage of (formally) high-powered incentives to reduce cost. On the other hand, the firm may force the regulator to renegotiate midway and offer more favorable terms if the initial contract proves unprofitable and makes credible the threat of bankruptcy or at least that of forgoing investments that the regulator deems necessary. The firm is then said to face a "soft budget constraint," since it is rescued by the regulator despite a commitment

---

8. See Freixas, Guesnerie, and Tirole (1985) and Laffont and Tirole (1987b, 1988b).

not to intervene before the next regulatory review. A high-powered incentive scheme raises the likelihood of the occurrence of either situation (very high or very low profits) and therefore of contract renegotiation. Because *in both cases* contract renegotiation ex post rewards the firm's inefficiency (punishes its cost-reducing effort), early regulatory reviews further decrease the *real* power of *formally* high-powered incentive schemes.

2.1.2.3   Regulatory Capture

The debate on incentive regulation focuses on the agency problem between the regulator and the regulated firm. There is in practice a second agency problem, namely, that between the general public and the regulator. And, as we will see, the two agency problems may interact in an interesting way.

Understanding the second agency problem requires asking why there is a regulator in the first place. Quite clearly, the regulator is an *informational intermediary*. The members of the collectivity face a collective action problem. They individually have no incentive to make the very heavy investment required for a good understanding of both the technology and the economics of telecommunications. This free-riding problem is somewhat alleviated by the election of political representatives, who themselves are informational intermediaries. But the free-riding problem subsists, in an attenuated but still substantial way, at the congressional level. It is resolved only (and still imperfectly) by the creation of specialized congressional committees and bureaucratic agencies.

In a nutshell, congressional committees and regulatory agencies are "informational intermediaries," "delegated monitors," or "supervisors." Their role is to fill some of the informational gap between the collectivity and the industry. But this informational expertise is precisely what provides the delegated monitors with discretionary power and what creates the second agency problem. This second agency problem can be divided into two parts. First, the informational intermediaries may not have sufficient incentives to collect the information about the technology and the economics of the industry, in the same way the regulated firms may not have enough incentives to control their cost. Second, when endowed with a given amount of information, the informational intermediaries may not make use of this information in the direction that would benefit the collectivity. That is, they may abuse their discretion.

Here, we are interested in this potential for abuse, and in particular in the possibility that the informational intermediaries are captured by interest groups. Political scientists (Montesquieu, the American Federalists, Marx, Bernstein, . . .) and economists (the Chicago school with Stigler, Posner, Becker, and Peltzman, and the Virginia school with Buchanan and Tullock) have long recognized the threat posed by interest-group politics for the efficiency of economic regulation.

For an economist interested in regulatory design and reform, the interesting question, though, is not the existence of a threat of capture, but rather what is to be done about it. To approach this question, we must, as we discussed, first explain why regulators have discretion and so may collude with interest groups. Their role as informational intermediaries seems crucial in this respect:[9] *It is precisely because their principal (the full Congress or the collectivity as a whole, depending on the interpretation) is uncertain as to the ranking of alternative policies that informational intermediaries can get away with policies that favor specific interest groups to the detriment of the collectivity.* Furthermore, a delegated monitoring approach not only explains why there is scope for regulatory capture, but also suggests policies that will reduce the likelihood of capture, as we now illustrate in the context of incentive regulation.

Recall that high-powered incentive schemes are associated with high rents, and therefore with high *stakes* for the regulated firm. High-powered incentives thus generate for the regulated firms a large benefit from capturing their regulators. Using a procurement example, and in the presence of uncertainty about the firm's cost, the regulator has a lot of discretion when designing a fixed-price contract, in that the level of the fixed price is highly subjective and affects the firm's welfare substantially. In particular, when the regulator obtains information that the firm has a low cost, a piece of information that if disclosed would permit the elimination of the firm's potential rent, the regulator may be lenient with the firm and "forget" the information he acquired. In contrast, a cost-plus contract is more mechanical, and regulatory decisions have a much lower impact on the firm's welfare.[10] A cost-plus contract

9. Our approach is explained in much more detail for example in chapters 11–16 of Laffont and Tirole (1993), which are devoted to various aspects of regulatory capture.
10. Except with respect to the regulator's measurement of the firm's cost (see Laffont and Tirole, 1992).

is therefore less sensitive than a fixed-price contract to the risk of regulatory capture by the regulated firm (at least when good accounting procedures are in place).

The reader may wonder whether the influence of the regulated firm might not be offset by that of interest groups with opposite interests. Indeed, taxpayers in a procurement context and consumers in a regulatory context are hurt when the firm enjoys a rent, since they then have to pay higher taxes and prices for the services, respectively. It can be shown, however, that, *even if they solve their collective action problem and are properly organized, taxpayers or consumers do not form an effective counterpower to the industry when they lack the information about policy rankings.*[11] But this lack of information is precisely what motivated the use of an informational intermediary in the first place. Put differently, collusion may occur among members of a "nexus of information," that is, between economic agents sharing information; it is for this reason that collusion is an important matter in situations of delegated monitoring.

The delegated-monitoring view of regulatory agencies, therefore, leads to the following implication for incentive regulation: low-powered incentive schemes, because they are less discretionary (make less use of the regulator's private information), are more robust to regulatory capture; it is therefore advisable to lower the power of incentive schemes when the threat of capture by the regulated firm is serious. Or put differently, the adoption of high-powered schemes must go hand-in-hand with the existence of political and bureaucratic institutions that alleviate the capture problem.

More generally, the delegated monitoring view identifies four types of policies with a potential to curb regulatory capture. The first two aim at reducing the gains from collusion; the last two make it more difficult for the parties to collude to reap those gains.

Reduction of Regulatory Discretion   The use of low-powered incentive schemes is an illustration of a more general principle: Substantial regulatory discretion—that is, a high sensitivity of regulatory decisions to the regulatory agency's assessment of the regulated firm's cost and demand environment—creates high stakes for the interest groups and therefore a concern about regulatory capture. The potential for regulatory capture, therefore, reduces the use that is made of the regulators'

---

11. On this topic, see Laffont and Tirole (1991b).

private information and thereby creates a more bureaucratic environment. We will later offer other examples of reduced stakes and less discretionary policies.

Making Regulators Accountable by Offering Them a Stake   Another way of fighting capture is to make regulators internalize at least partly the welfare of other groups so as to induce them not to favor a specific interest group. Let us here provide some analogy. A lead investment bank, leveraged buyout specialist, or venture capitalist brings investors to buy a new debt or equity issue; it thereby acts as a delegated monitor. It specializes in acquiring information about the issuer not held by the other investors. But, of course, it may also collude with the issuer, possibly getting some kickback on the side. To reduce the risk of collusion (as well as to encourage the collection of information), investors require the lead investment bank, leveraged buyout specialist, or venture capitalist to take a stake in the issue. The incentives of the delegated monitor and the principal (the investors) are then better aligned. Stake taking by delegated monitors is actually a widespread institution in situations in which the principal's welfare is easily measurable.

Alas, what works well in financial environments is less effective in a regulatory context. Stake taking by the regulator would mean that the regulator's salary would be made contingent on the amount of money paid by taxpayers (in a procurement context), on the level and structure of consumer prices (in a regulatory context), and possibly on the quality of service (in both contexts). It is clear that such performance measures either are hard to specify exactly ex ante, or when they can be easily described, as in the case of the taxpayers' bill, they lack a natural benchmark (in contrast, the benchmark can be the market rate of return in the financial investment analogy). So, in general, it is difficult to prevent capture by providing regulators with monetary incentives that would align their interests with those of taxpayers or consumers.

Making Collusion More Difficult   We have not yet discussed the process of capture. In general, the regulator may be willing to do a favor to an interest group if a quid pro quo is available. This quid pro quo in practice takes many forms: direct monetary transfer (as in most cases of corruption), campaign contributions for politicians, lack of complaint about the regulatory activity, future employment as a top executive or consultant (the revolving door), friendship, entertainment expenditures, and so forth. The nature of the *bribe* varies greatly with the situation and with the personality of the parties involved in the capture process.

One may try to reduce capture by making these quid pro quos more costly to the parties. But such policies have also a cost. For example, the prohibition of the revolving door may make it difficult to find qualified regulators if industry executives envision that they will not be able to return to the private sector when they quit the regulatory agency. It is only recently that economists have started developing formal models of the impact of regulatory institutions on the ease with which transfers can respond to stakes and facilitate capture.[12]

Reduction of the Asymmetry of Information between Regulators and Their Principal   To the extent that capture is related to the regulators' informational superiority over their principal (full Congress, collectivity), a reduction in this informational asymmetry reduces the scope for capture. Obviously, one should not expect too much from such policies, since delegated monitoring is the heart of the problem. But some steps can be undertaken that reduce the manipulation of information by regulators. In particular, and following the Anglo-Saxon tradition of transparency, one can force regulators to adopt a very open process: open regulatory hearings, use of consultative documents, independent appeal procedures, written and detailed explanation of decisions, and so forth. Transparency gives the regulators' principal access to other sources of opinion (interest groups such as customers and competitors), to data, and to the regulators' reasoning. It alleviates, although it does not eliminate, informational asymmetries between the delegated monitor and its principal.

2.2   Economic Principles: Pricing Services to the Consumer

2.2.1   Ramsey-Boiteux Prices and Marketing Principles

In their first courses students of economics learn that social efficiency obtains when prices are equal both to the marginal costs of production and to the willingnesses to pay for the products by the marginal consumers. Only later on do they realize that this idealized benchmark

---

12. See in particular Martimort (1997) on repeated game aspects of collusion, Laffont and Meleu (1997) on mutual supervision, and Laffont and Martimort (1999) on the separation of regulatory powers.

holds only under strong assumptions. In particular, lectures on economic regulation emphasize the impossibility for firms operating in industries with increasing returns to scale to cover their costs when pricing at marginal cost, and the need to charge markups above marginal costs to achieve budget balance; they further learn that these markups ought to follow the rules enunciated by Marcel Boiteux (1956) for public monopolies, in a contribution very closely related to that of Frank Ramsey (1927) on optimal taxation.

This section provides an informal treatment of Ramsey-Boiteux pricing and of its practical implications for utility regulation. It assumes that the utility is constrained to cover its cost, although it should be realized that exactly the same principles would hold if deficits were covered by the taxpayers, since distortions implied by taxation (implying a shadow cost of public funds) raise an analogous concern about the firm's profit. To simplify the exposition, we will assume that the firm incurs a joint and common cost, and then produces services at constant marginal costs (this assumption is not essential).

2.2.1.1 Ramsey-Boiteux Pricing

Let us first, following Ramsey and Boiteux, assume that the regulator has full information about cost and demand, and thereby ignore incentive problems; we just ask, What is the optimal price structure for a multiproduct regulated firm given that the overall price level must enable it to break even? Answering this question entails looking for prices of the various services that are preferred by the consumers among the prices that yield a nonnegative profit to the firm. The criterion, therefore, is the consumers' net surplus, that is, their gross surplus from consumptions minus the firm's revenue. With the firm's revenue covering its cost, we can rewrite the criterion as the difference between the gross surplus and cost.

Note that in the absence of a budget constraint, social welfare, as defined as the difference between consumer gross surplus and cost, would be maximized when the price of each service is equal to its marginal cost; for, as illustrated in figure 2.3, consumers' gross surplus increases by the price of the service when the consumption of this service increases by one unit, or, putting it differently, the willingness to pay for a service of the marginal consumer is equal to the service's price.

Let us now worry about budget balance and look for prices that maximize social welfare subject to the firm's profit (revenue minus cost) being nonnegative. By definition, this optimization yields the

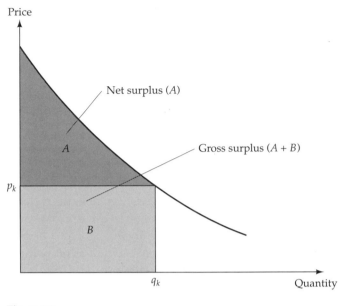

Figure 2.3
Consumer surplus

Ramsey-Boiteux social welfare level. Equivalently, the socially optimal prices can be obtained by solving the "dual program" of maximizing the firm's profit subject to social welfare being at least at its Ramsey-Boiteux level. This reformulation of the problem may seem abstract or odd, but it underlies much of the practical implications of Ramsey-Boiteux pricing. We have reinterpreted the problem as one in which a firm maximizes its profit and so behaves like an ordinary firm, except that it must provide some minimum level of welfare to the consumers.

Let us assume, in a first step, that the demands for the services are *independent*. Unconstrained profit maximization would lead the firm to equate, for each service, the marginal revenue to the marginal cost, where the marginal revenue is equal to the price minus the price divided by the elasticity of demand for the service. The need to provide the consumers with a given level of social welfare implies that a unit increase in the quantity of a service is penalized by an amount proportional to the marginal social welfare, that is, to the difference between price and marginal cost (technically, the proportional coefficient determining the penalty is the shadow price of the consumers' welfare constraint). To sum up, for each service k, and letting p_k, q_k, η_k, and c_k denote the price, quantity, elasticity (where $\eta_k = - \left[dq_k/dp_k \right] / \left[q_k/p_k \right]$), and marginal cost of service k and $\propto$ stand for "proportional to"

$$p_k \left(1 - \frac{1}{\eta_k}\right) - c_k \propto p_k - c_k \tag{1}$$

or

$$\frac{p_k - c_k}{p_k} = \theta \frac{1}{\eta_k} \tag{2}$$

where $\theta < 1$ is the same for all k. We see that like an unregulated monopolist the Ramsey-Boiteux utility charges prices that are inversely proportional to the elasticities of demands for the services [see box 2.2 for
a formal derivation of equation (2)]. Therefore, the price *structure* is the
same in the presence or absence of regulation: The ratio of the relative
markups over marginal costs of two services is equal to the ratio of the
inverse elasticities of demand. Put more crudely, the Ramsey-Boiteux
prices are the same as those of an unregulated monopolist, just a notch
down. We will therefore say that Ramsey-Boiteux prices are business
oriented.

The fact that the structure of Ramsey-Boiteux prices conforms to
standard business practice generalizes straightforwardly to the case
of *interdependent demands*. Services can be complements or substitutes.
A telecommunications operator's off-peak discount may lower the
demand for peak services if customers shift some of their peak consumption to the off-peak period. Conversely, a price reduction on an
information service will increase the demand for calls and not only that
for the service itself. Also, telecommunications services may sometimes
be complements and sometimes substitutes. Historically, the introduction of mobile services has increased the use of the fixed-link network,
but as their price plummets mobile services are substituting more and
more for fixed communications.

Standard marketing principles regarding complements and substitutes thus apply to utilities. It is optimal to lower the price of a service
[below the level that is implied by equation (2)] if doing so raises the
demand for a complementary service on which the utility charges a
markup. Conversely, the price of a service should be raised [starting
from the level given by equation (2)] if it competes with another service
sold by the utility at a price above marginal cost.

To sum up, the overall picture is that each service should contribute
toward the coverage of the firm's fixed cost in a way that minimizes
the economic distortion. It would be absurd (on efficiency grounds) to
charge high markups on those services for which consumers are not

Box 2.2
Ramsey-Boiteux Pricing

A utility produces services $k = 1, \ldots, n$ in quantities $q = (q_1, \ldots, q_n)$. The demand functions for price vector $p = (p_1, \ldots, p_n)$ are $q_k = D_k(p_1, \ldots, p_n)$. The symbol $\eta_k = -[\partial D_k/\partial p_k]/[D_k/p_k]$ denotes the own elasticity of demand of service k. In the case of independent demands, q_k is a function of p_k only and $\eta_k = -[dD_k/dp_k]/[D_k/p_k]$. The firm's revenue is $R(q) \equiv \Sigma_{k=1}^{n} p_k q_k$. Let $C(q_1, \ldots, q_n)$ denote the cost function. For example, with a joint and common cost k_0 and constant marginal costs $c_1, \ldots, c_n$,

$$C(q_1, \ldots, q_n) = k_0 + \Sigma_{k=1}^{n} c_k q_k$$

Let $S(q)$ denote gross consumer surplus, with

$$\frac{\partial S}{\partial q_k} = p_k$$

The Ramsey-Boiteux pricing problem, as we have seen, consists in maximizing social surplus subject to the budget constraint

$$\max_{q} \{S(q) - C(q)\}$$

subject to

$$R(q) - C(q) \geq 0$$

or, equivalently, in maximizing the firm's profit subject to providing the Ramsey-Boiteux level of social surplus:

$$\max_{q} \{R(q) - C(q)\}$$

subject to

$$S(q) - C(q) \geq S(q^*) - C(q^*)$$

where stars refer to the Ramsey-Boiteux levels. Letting $1/\lambda$ denote the shadow price of the constraint in the latter program, the first-order condition with respect to q_k is

$$\lambda \left(p_k - c_k + \Sigma_{j=1}^{n} \frac{\partial p_j}{\partial q_k} q_j \right) + p_k - c_k = 0$$

In particular, for independent demands,

$$\frac{p_k - c_k}{p_k} = \frac{\lambda}{1 + \lambda} \frac{1}{\eta_k}$$

When services are complements or substitutes, "elasticities" must be replaced by the so-called "superelasticities." In a nutshell, the pricing rule must be corrected to account for the impact of service k on the demand for the other services. If service k cannibalizes the demand for another service ℓ (for example k and ℓ are two long-distance services, or they stand for demands for calls at nearby hours under time-of-day pricing), then the price of good k ought to be raised above the level implied by the mere consideration of the elasticity of good k; similarly, if service k boosts the demand for service ℓ (for example, an increase in the number of subscribers raises the demand for calls), then the price of service k should be set below the level implied by the preceding rule. Since we will not use the general treatment of Ramsey prices in this book, we do not develop them in further detail here. We will provide explicit formulas in the special case of access charges; see box 3.1.

willing to pay much above marginal cost. Cost recovery should place a higher burden on those services with relatively inelastic demands. The structure of markups must thus reflect the structure of demand elasticities. Furthermore, the cross-elasticities must also be accounted for. The structure of prices, though, is no different from the one that would be selected by the marketing division of an ordinary firm.

It is important to stress the "broad tax base" aspect of Ramsey-Boiteux pricing. All costs go to a "common pool"; the resulting total cost is recovered through prices on all services. This statement implies that there may be a loose relationship between individual costs and prices; for example, a substantial part of the investment cost to provide a new service may be covered by consumers who do not benefit from this new service. There is thus no compartmentalization or earmarking of specific revenues to specific services. We will later come back to this principle and demonstrate some of its limits.

2.2.1.2 Ramsey-Boiteux Pricing and Incentive Regulation

In practice, regulators have less information about the firm's environment than is presumed by the Ramsey-Boiteux paradigm. As we discussed, informational asymmetries lead to inflated costs. Should utility prices still abide by the business principles enunciated by Ramsey and Boiteux? As we will see, the answer to this question has important implications for regulatory design.

Intuitively, deviations from the Ramsey-Boiteux precepts would be warranted only if they facilitated the regulator's extraction of the firm's rent. The primary instrument for limiting the firm's rent is the earnings-sharing rule, that is, the fraction of profit that the firm is allowed to retain. This fraction embodies the trade-off between incentives and rent extraction. Given this instrument, it is not clear that the price structure should be distorted. Indeed, the latter's main object is to allocate the "taxes" or markups on services in a way that least distorts the consumption decisions. Departures from Ramsey-Boiteux pricing raise the prices of some services and lower those of other services. One can provide sufficient conditions[13] under which such a rebalancing of rates away from the Ramsey-Boiteux structure does not help alleviate the informational asymmetry and reduce the firm's rent, and is therefore undesirable. In such circumstances, a "dichotomy" obtains: Prices are confined to their allocative role, and rent extraction is performed through the earnings-sharing scheme. This dichotomy seems a reasonable benchmark, unless

---

13. See Laffont and Tirole (1990a).

there is a good presumption that raising the price of a service and lowering that of another helps reduce the firm's rent.[14]

2.2.2   Price Caps

In principle, the choice of Ramsey-Boiteux prices can be decentralized to the firm through price caps. Suppose the firm is faced with an average price ceiling, with weights $w = (w_1, \ldots, w_n)$:

$$\Sigma_{k=1}^n w_k p_k \leq \bar{p}$$

and is otherwise free to maximize its profit. That is, the price level is constrained, but not its structure. It is easily demonstrated (see box 2.3) that if weights are equal to the future realized quantities (which we denote by $\bar{q}_k$), then optimality conditions for the firm yield Ramsey prices *in structure*. To see why this statement is true, recall what is wrong with monopoly pricing: The firm does not internalize the undesirable effects of an increase in its prices on consumer net surplus: When the firm raises the price of service k by \$1, then the consumers' net surplus is lowered by the amount they consume of service k.

A price cap amounts to a "tax" on the increase of the price of service $k, k = 1, \ldots, n$, proportional to the weight w_k put on service k. And so, if the weight turns out to be equal to the quantity of service k, then the "tax" vector faced by the monopolist is (proportional to) the vector of externalities imposed on the consumers by the monopolist's price increases. The monopolist is thereby induced to adopt an efficient (Ramsey-Boiteux) price structure. The level of earnings is determined by the cap $\bar{p}$. If the chosen cap is too low, the firm incurs a deficit; if it is set too high, the firm makes a profit.

The price cap described in this section can be called a "perfect price cap." In practice, regulators lack the information needed to institute such a perfect price cap.[15] Indeed, if they had perfect information, they

---

14. Using a calibrated engineering model for local telecommunications, Gasmi, Laffont, and Sharkey (1997) show that the dichotomy holds approximately.

15. Vogelsang and Finsinger (1979) have analyzed the dynamic properties of a regulatory scheme in which the firm can choose its prices each period subject to the constraint that the new prices would not have generated a positive profit in the previous regulatory period using last period's cost and outputs. That is, the price cap constraint at date t can be written as $\sum_{k=1}^n q_k(t-1)p_k(t) \leq C[\mathbf{q}(t-1)]$. They show that with a myopic firm and in a stationary environment, the allocation converges toward the Ramsey allocation; that is, the weights in the price cap formula converge to the optimal quantities.

Box 2.3
Price Caps and Ramsey-Boiteux Pricing

Using the notation of box 2.2, suppose that the utility maximizes its profit subject to the price cap constraint

$$\max_{q} \left\{ R(q) - C(q) \right\}$$

subject to

$$\Sigma_{k=1}^{n} w_k p_k \leq \bar{p}$$

Letting v denote the shadow price of the price-cap constraint, the first-order condition with respect to q_k is

$$p_k - c_k + \Sigma_{j=1}^{n} \frac{\partial p_j}{\partial q_k} q_j - v \Sigma_{j=1}^{n} \frac{\partial p_j}{\partial q_k} w_j = 0$$

and so if the weights w turn out to be the quantities q, and letting $\lambda = (1/v) - 1$, one obtains the Ramsey-Boiteux conditions.

would be able to set the prices directly, and price caps would be unnecessary. We will return to the role of price caps under imperfect regulatory information in section 2.3.

2.2.3   Reinterpretations and Corrections

The Ramsey-Boiteux precepts have wide applicability. In the following paragraphs we remind the reader of situations in which (simple) reinterpretations provide insights about optimal pricing.

2.2.3.1   Intertemporal Aspects
The Ramsey-Boiteux model is apparently a static, "one-period" model. Therefore, it would seem inappropriate for an analysis of long-term investment and regulation. Economists, however, have long realized that one way to think about intertemporal situations is to consider that the same service offered at different dates should be thought of and treated as different services.[16] Thus, formally, the Ramsey-Boiteux model with n services and T regulatory periods can be reinterpreted as a static one with nT services.

---

16. This reinterpretation, for example, underlies the Arrow-Debreu modeling of time in general equilibrium models; see, e.g., Debreu (1959) and Wildman (1997) for an application to access pricing in a context similar to that of chapter 3.

Let us think through the implications of this reinterpretation. First, the intertemporal version of the Ramsey-Boiteux model implies the existence of a *single, intertemporal budget constraint* rather than a sequence of per-period budget constraints. Clearly, this vision is consistent with regulatory practice of looking at per-regulatory-period profitability only if per-period profitability takes into account the firm's debt service, as debt allows the firm to smooth temporary imbalances between cost and revenue and thus to come closer to a single budget constraint. A second, closely related point is that pricing distortions should be spread out over time so as to least distort consumptions. Concretely, a substantial investment in a telecommunications network today would lead to an extreme distortion in consumption if it were defrayed fully through markups on today's consumptions (assuming such markups could cover the investment cost, which may well be impossible as they would discourage demand). Part of the "tax" required to finance the investment must be raised on future consumptions. This reinterpretation of Ramsey-Boiteux may seem abstract. But, as usual, the reader should recall the correspondence with standard business principles. The latter do spread the markups over multiple periods, and the intertemporal structure of markups should be the same in both cases.

There is a difference, though, between unregulated and regulated firms: A utility may be concerned about the regulator's future willingness to let it recover its past investment costs through markups on services. That is, the reinterpretation of the Ramsey-Boiteux model assumes that the regulator can commit to approval in the future of the intertemporal sequence of markups implied by Ramsey-Boiteux prices. The regulator, however, may be tempted to force prices down once the investments have been committed. Facing the threat of such expropriation, the firm is then forced to "front-load" the markups—that is, to charge higher markups than those prescribed by Ramsey-Boiteux ordinary business principles—immediately after the investment is made. We will return to this issue in section 4.4 where we discuss deregulatory takings in the context of access pricing.

2.2.3.2 *Nonlinear Pricing*

The basic Ramsey-Boiteux model assumes linear prices. However, it generalizes to nonlinear pricing as well. The benefits of nonlinear pricing are the same as for an unregulated firm with market power: It reduces economic distortions and raises revenue by, for example, offering low marginal prices to high-volume customers and high marginal prices to low-volume ones.[17]

Though extending the Ramsey-Boiteux model to nonlinear pricing involves no theoretical difficulty, there are some practical difficulties with the decentralization of Ramsey-Boiteux prices through the use of price caps. This decentralization remains straightforward in the case of two-part tariffs, as we indicate shortly, but becomes daunting when more and more detailed menus of sophisticated offers are proposed to the consumers, as is now the case in telecommunications.

To illustrate why the treatment of nonlinear pricing involves a mere reinterpretation of the one for linear pricing, consider a two-part tariff composed of a fixed (subscription, monthly, connection) fee together with a (per-minute) variable charge. A two-part tariff should economically be analyzed as the provision by the firm of two services: the fixed fee entitles the consumer to connect[18] to the service, and the variable charge covers the actual use of the service. These two services ("connection" and "consumption") are complements: The more consumers are connected to the service, the higher the variable consumption; similarly, a reduction in the variable charge raises the number of consumers who are willing to pay the fixed fee to connect. The two prices should therefore be coordinated. It is worth losing some revenue on connections if doing so boosts variable consumptions, and conversely.

This reinterpretation also has implications for price caps. Theoretically, a two-part tariff should be treated as two prices corresponding to two distinct (although interdependent) services. Furthermore, in a perfect price cap, the weights on the fixed fee and on the variable charge are (the forecast of) the number of consumers who will purchase the service and the variable consumption of these consumers, respectively.

Box 2.4 shows that this reasoning applies more generally to fully nonlinear prices.

2.2.3.3   Externalities

We have equated social welfare with the consumers' net surplus. That is, consumption of the various services is valued at the consumers'

---

17. See, e.g., Mitchell and Vogelsang (1991) and Laffont and Tirole (1993, chaps. 2, 3) for a treatment of nonlinear prices by regulated firms, and Wilson (1993) for a broader treatment.

18. We here avoid the use of the word "access," which is more widely used in this context than "connection," because this book discusses at length the issue of the access provided by one network to another. In common parlance, the word "access" is used in both situations.

Box 2.4
Price Cap and Nonlinear Pricing

(This box is somewhat technical and can be omitted in a first reading even by the analytically oriented reader.)

The production technology for a single good entails a fixed cost k_0 and a constant marginal cost c. There is a continuum of consumers indexed by a parameter θ. A consumer of type θ confronted with a nonlinear tariff $T(q)$ and consuming $q(\theta)$ has a net utility $U(\theta) = \theta V[q(\theta)] - T[q(\theta)]$.

The parameter θ is distributed according to the c.d.f $G(\theta)$ with density $g(\theta)$ on $[\underline{\theta}, \bar{\theta}]$ with $g(\theta)/[1 - G(\theta)]$ increasing. Let $(1 + \lambda)$ denote the shadow cost of the firm's budget constraint. Maximizing social welfare (or consumer net surplus) subject to the budget balance constraint is equivalent to maximizing

$$\int_{\underline{\theta}}^{\bar{\theta}} \{\theta V[q(\theta)] - T[q(\theta)]\}\, dG(\theta) - (1 + \lambda) \int_{\underline{\theta}}^{\bar{\theta}} \{cq(\theta) + k_0 - T[q(\theta)]\}\, dG(\theta)$$

Changing variables, $U(\theta) \equiv \theta V[q(\theta)] - T[q(\theta)]$, we obtain the program defining optimal pricing

$$\max \int_{\underline{\theta}}^{\bar{\theta}} \left((1 + \lambda)\{\theta V[q(\theta)] - cq(\theta) - k_0\} - \lambda U(\theta) \right) dG(\theta)$$

subject to

$$\dot{U}(\theta) = V[q(\theta)] \qquad \text{and} \qquad \dot{q}(\theta) \geq 0 \qquad\qquad (1)$$
$$U(\theta) \geq 0 \qquad \text{for all } \theta \qquad\qquad\qquad\qquad (2)$$

where expressions (1) are the incentive constraints and formula (2) the participation constraint. Letting $\theta(q) = p(q) = T'(q)$ denote the marginal price defined by the optimal tariff, we obtain

$$\frac{p(q) - c}{p(q)} = \frac{\lambda}{1 + \lambda} \frac{1 - G(\theta)}{\theta g(\theta)}$$

To generalize price caps to nonlinear pricing we must decompose the demand function into independent demands for marginal units of consumption. Fix a quantity q and consider the demand for the qth unit of consumption with price $p(q)$.

Demand for this unit is

$$D_q(p) \equiv 1 - G[\theta_q^*(p)]$$

where the marginal consumer $\theta_q^*(p)$ is defined by

$$\theta_q^*(p) V_q'[\theta_q^*(p)] = p$$

Consider a generalized price cap as

$$\int_0^{\bar{q}} w(q)p(q)dq \leq \pi$$

where $\bar{q}$ is the maximal quantity demanded.

The firm maximizes under this constraint

$$\int_0^{\bar{q}} [p(q) - c]\{1 - G[\theta_q^*(p)]\}dq$$

Box 2.4 (continued)

The first-order conditions are

$$1 - G[\theta_q^*(p)] - [p(q) - c] g \left[\theta_q^*(p)\right] \frac{d\theta_q^*}{dp} = \mu w(q)$$

hence

$$p(q) - c = \frac{1 - G[\theta_q^*(p)] - \mu w(q)}{g[\theta_q^*(p)] \frac{d\theta_q^*}{dp}}.$$

Noting that $\frac{d\theta_q^*}{dp} = \frac{\theta_q^*}{p}$ we have

$$\frac{p(q) - c}{p(q)} = \frac{1 - G[\theta(q)]}{\theta(q)g[\theta(q)]} \left\{1 - \frac{\mu w(q)}{1 - G[\theta(q)]}\right\}$$

If π is chosen so that $\mu = \frac{1}{1+\lambda}$ and $w(q) = 1 - G[\theta(q)]$, optimal pricing is induced. Note, again, that the weights are equal to the quantities.

With nonlinear prices, the price cap implied by the theory consists in treating increments of the same good as different goods. For example, the price cap for a nonlinear price $T(q)$ for consumption q in $[\underline{q}, \bar{q}]$ can be approximated by dividing the consumption segment into intervals $[q_0, q_1], [q_1, q_2], \ldots, [q_{n-1}, q_n]$ with $q_0 \equiv \underline{q}$ and $q_n = \bar{q}$. Let p_0 denote the price of the first q_0 units, $p_1 = \frac{T(q_1) - T(q_0)}{q_1 - q_0}$ the unit price of the $q_1 - q_0$ next units, $p_2 = \frac{T(q_2) - T(q_1)}{q_2 - q_1}$ the unit price of the following $q_2 - q_1$ next units, and so forth. The price cap can be written as

$$\sum_{k=0}^{n} w_k p_k \leq \bar{p}$$

Optimal weights are equal to the forecasts of the quantities. So if N_k consumers consume at least q_k, then

$$w_k = N_k \left(q_k - q_{k-1}\right)$$

willingnesses to pay for them. When consumption creates externalities, then Ramsey-Boiteux prices should be corrected to adjust to the externalities.[19] For example, freight services offered by a rail operator reduce road maintenance, and environmental damage is created (and not fully internalized) by the trucking industry. Similarly, local trains reduce congestion in cities. Conversely, some trains may create negative externalities for the environment.

As shown in box 2.5, a positive (negative) externality amounts to a reduction (increase) in the cost of producing the service (with the

---

19. We treat here the case of externalities from consumers to third parties. Another interesting issue is that of externalities among consumers. See in particular Mitchell and Vogelsang's treatment of Ramsey pricing under network externalities (1991, pp. 55–60).

Box 2.5
Accounting for Externalities

Using the framework of box 2.2, let us introduce externalities, so the objective function is

$$S(q) + \Sigma_k b_k q_k - C(q)$$

where b_k is the marginal benefit (or cost, if negative) of the externality created by the consumption of service k. We assume that these externalities are not subsidized (or taxed if they are negative) from the general budget, and therefore must be internalized by the industry. The (dual of the) Ramsey-Boiteux program becomes

$$\max_q \{R(q) - C(q)\}$$

subject to

$$S(q) + b \cdot q - C(q) \geq S(q^*) + b \cdot q^* - C(q^*)$$

For example, for independent demands, prices are given by

$$\frac{p_k - \left(c_k - \frac{b_k}{1+\lambda}\right)}{p_k} = \frac{\lambda}{1+\lambda} \frac{1}{\eta_k}$$

twist that the benefit [or cost] of the externality should be deflated by one plus the shadow cost of the budget constraint, because of the fact that other [private] costs are monetary [and therefore tighten the budget constraint] while externalities are not).[20] Therefore, ignoring interdependences among services, the firm should lower its prices in the case of positive externalities and raise them in the case of negative externalities.

Externalities also require a correction when decentralizing Ramsey-Boiteux prices to the firm through price caps. The counterpart of the standard instrument used to force economic agents to internalize their externalities, namely, Pigovian taxes and subsidies, here is the manipulation of weights. In reference to a perfect price cap, the weight on a service should exceed the (forecast of) the quantity of the service in the case of positive externalities and be lower than this quantity for a negative externality. This manipulation of weights provides the firm with an incentive to lower the prices on the former services and raise the prices on the latter. If, however, one is concerned about the possibility of abuse of these weight corrections, the alternative is to use the general budget

---

20. Here we are assuming that externalities affect the consumer's utility directly. If externalities affected the industry's or the government's budget, the accounting would be different.

to impose taxes and subsidies that will make the firm internalize the externalities and will allow the regulator not to correct weights.

2.2.4   Four Factors Limiting the Use of Ramsey Pricing

This section reviews some *theoretical* limitations on the use of Ramsey pricing. Section 2.3 will discuss some further, *practical* difficulties.

2.2.4.1   Redistributive Concerns

The Ramsey-Boiteux assumption that the consumption of various services is valued at the consumers' willingnesses to pay for them, and thus that consumer net surpluses are simply added up, can be objected to on redistributive grounds.[21] Recall that Ramsey-Boiteux markups are levied primarily on services with inelastic demands. These may sometimes be primarily purchased by poor consumers who have no other alternative than using the service. Or, as in the case of a monthly subscriber fee, they may be levied on all consumers. In proportion to telephone usage, though, the markup is higher for low-income consumers than for high-income ones.

We delay until chapter 6 the discussion of whether utility prices should reflect distributive concerns and whether these concerns are not better addressed by other fiscal instruments. Let us here simply mention that, whether for economic or political reasons, substantial deviations from Ramsey prices have historically been the norm. For example, in telecommunications, "reverse Ramsey pricing" with high prices for businesses and long-distance and low prices for residential customers and monthly subscriber charges has only recently given way to a more Ramsey-oriented structure (and the rate rebalancing is not yet completed).

2.2.4.2   Regulatory Capture

One of the main (and, in our opinion, overstated) concerns about Ramsey pricing is that its fine tailoring to demand creates substantial discretion and therefore is prone to regulatory capture. In particular, if interest groups A and B consuming the same service are to pay different prices, each will lobby the regulator to pay the lower price. In such circumstances, the main determinant of price discrimination between

---

21. One can obtain modified Ramsey-Boiteux formulas by weighting consumers' net surpluses differently; see, e.g., Deaton (1977) and Laffont and Tirole (1993, sec. 3.9).

the two interest groups may not be the demand elasticities (or, possibly, the difference in the cost of serving the two types of consumers), as Ramsey and Boiteux would recommend, but rather the relative political strength of the interest groups, their relationship with the regulator, or their willingness to transfer income to politicians and their parties. Adopting nondiscriminatory pricing rules has the benefit of reducing the risk of favoritism, that is, of economically unjustified price discrimination.

Our view on this matter is that this concern is real; indeed, in one paper (Laffont and Tirole, 1991b), we showed that the possibility of regulatory capture by interest groups pushes toward nondiscrimination rules. We feel, however, that the argument can be exaggerated. The abuse of price discrimination is primarily a concern in a world in which the regulators select the prices and are subject to regulatory capture. Many still view Ramsey-Boiteux pricing as a structure of prices that are handpicked by regulators, and we therefore sympathize with their concern. In practice, however, regulators rarely select Ramsey-Boiteux prices themselves; rather, price caps confer this task on the regulated firms. Although the latter may indeed collude with specific interest groups, they are less likely to do so because, first, they are politically more independent than regulators and, second, because such capture reduces their profit. For this reason, we would favor Ramsey pricing more in a world in which pricing decisions are delegated to profit-maximizing firms than in one in which they are made by regulators and politicians.[22]

2.2.4.3   Utility Opportunism and Nondiscrimination Rules
Nondiscrimination rules may sometimes protect the firm against its own "bad behavior." Suppose that an aluminium producer builds a plant planning to use electricity rather than an alternative source of energy. Once the plant is built, the power utility can demand a very high price. Indeed, ex post Ramsey pricing implies that the utility fully extracts the aluminium producer's profit (gross of the investment cost which is then sunk anyway). Anticipating this "special deal" and knowing that it will lose the investment cost, the aluminium producer

---

22. To be sure, even when pricing decisions are decentralized, the regulator may still have some impact on final prices through the setting of weights. But this impact is more indirect; furthermore, regulators do not have complete freedom in setting weights (see section 2.3).

ex ante either does not build the plant or else selects its location and technology to fit a different source of energy, even though electricity may be the most cost-effective energy input. That is, the demand for electricity is more elastic ex ante than ex post. This example represents the familiar problem of expropriation of specific investment.[23] The same problem is common in telecommunications. For example, a long-distance company or a value-added-service provider may be held up by the local loop provider after having made substantial investments.

A standard response to this problem is a long-term contract. The aluminium producer and the electricity company may agree before the plant is built on the terms at which the producer will purchase electricity. Despite the usual difficulties involved in designing good long-term contracts, this is often a decent way to resolve the hold-up problem. In a regulated context, though, some new difficulties arise. For example, the multiplication of personalized deals may make price-cap regulation very complex. Furthermore, price caps apply over some limited period (four or five years). Long-term agreements covering regulatory periods must be decomposed into agreements covering each a regulatory period, but the agreement between the regulated firm and its client is an overall deal and is therefore hard to split into pieces (in the same way that a joint and common cost is hard to allocate among the services that make use of the corresponding facility). Or, put differently, the regulated firm and the client can structure payments and terms of service in many equivalent ways that are different in accounting terms, and thus may try to arbitrage across regulatory periods.

In practice, the hold-up problem is also partly resolved through the external imposition of nondiscriminatory pricing. The aluminium company may not need to insist on a long-term contract if it knows that it will be able to buy electricity at the same price as other customers who are less dependent on electricity.

Thus, although we are generally in favor of price discrimination (for the reasons discussed so far, as well as those presented in the context of access pricing in the rest of the book), we also see some benefits from nondiscrimination and do not think that utilities should be given blanket permission for price discrimination.

---

23. See, e.g., Williamson (1975) and Klein, Crawford, and Alchian (1978).

2.2.4.4   Single-Cost-Recovery Approach versus Budget Compartmentalization

As we discussed, the Ramsey-Boiteux paradigm treats the regulated firm as a single entity. In particular, the various fixed costs incurred in different activities are lumped together, and the overall cost must be recovered through markups on all services. This principle means that each expense is financed from the broadest possible tax base.[24] This practice ensures that the marginal costs of the financing of the various services (as measured by the marginal welfare cost of distortions in consumptions) are equalized across services.

Ramsey and Boiteux's "single-cost-recovery-problem," "single-till," or "one-budget" principle implies that a service may be financed largely by consumers who do not purchase the service. This attribute puzzles many, sometimes for good reasons. We can level three criticisms at the concept of a single budget constraint:

Compartmentalization Creates a Viability Test for Lumpy Decisions   Many regulatory choices involve lumpy decisions. A power company may build a transmission link in its territory or one that connects to another power system. A railroad company may ponder over whether to open a new line, whether to close a low-traffic one, or whether to transform a mixed freight-passenger line into one that carries only freight.[25] A telecommunications company may contemplate an upgrade of its network to offer new services (e.g., ISDN or broadband).

Under full information about the cost and demand for the service whose existence is in question, matters would be relatively simple: Conditionally on the service being provided, the Ramsey-Boiteux price for the service should be charged. This price would generate both a net consumer surplus[26] from the service and a loss (or perhaps profit) equal to the difference between the extra cost of providing the service and the corresponding increase in revenue. If the net consumer surplus gener-

---

24. In the industry. Note that the tax base would be even broader if the financing could come from the general budget (for example, if the local loop costs were financed by the income tax, the gasoline tax, and all other fiscal instruments). There is already a compartmentalization in that regulated industries must pay for their own costs. Presumably, the reasons that we will discuss will shed some light on the requirement that an industry not be able to draw funds from the rest of the economy.

25. The fixed cost of maintaining the line is lower for a freight-only line because of lower safety standards.

26. For simplicity, we have assumed that this service is neither a complement to nor a substitute for the utility's other services.

ated by the service exceeds the monetary loss (weighted at the shadow cost of the budget constraint), then the service should be provided, otherwise not (see box 2.6).

Suppose, in contrast, that the demand curve is unknown. In particular, one may have some "local information" about the elasticity of demand around the price that is charged by the firm, but little information about the demand at much higher prices, and therefore about the surplus generated by the service. Thus while the provision of the service may be "locally efficient" in that its price is optimal conditionally on the service being provided, it may not be "globally efficient," as the service may not generate enough surplus to vindicate the cost.

If provision of the service is required to break even on a stand-alone basis (and thus is not allowed to be partly financed from markups on other services), and if the service indeed succeeds in generating enough revenue to cover its cost, then we are certain that the provision of the service is socially desirable, because the consumers' net surplus from the service is always positive. This observation provides some intuition for why some compartmentalization may be desirable: Compartmentalization avoids situations in which undesirable activities are undertaken or perpetuated.

Of course, compartmentalization creates a risk of a different type of error: A service may be unable to cover its cost and thus not pass the stand-alone test, and yet generate a high surplus. Compartmentalization will then imply (at least in the long run) that the valuable service is not provided. Or else, costs may be covered at high prices only, but economic efficiency would call for lower prices. Last, and relatedly, it is unclear that a *permanent* compartmentalization is optimal even if its drawbacks are smaller than those of the single-budget approach. Indeed, once one has learned that the service is socially desirable because its costs can be covered by pricing at a sufficiently high price, and assuming that cost and demand are stationary, it would seem optimal then to lower the price toward its Ramsey level.[27]

Our reasoning here is a mere reinterpretation of an old argument made by classical economists from Adam Smith (1776) to Coase (1945). These have worried about the possibility that marginal-cost pricing may allow the provision of services that are socially wasteful, and have

---

27. See Laffont and Tirole (1993, pp. 24–29). The overall issue of optimal price experimentation by a firm, be it regulated or unregulated, is complex.

Box 2.6
Stand-Alone Viability or Ramsey Pricing?

Consider a utility practicing Ramsey-Boiteux pricing for a given set of services. And let λ denote the shadow cost of the budget constraint. (See the previous boxes.) Suppose the utility contemplates introducing a new service. For expositional simplicity, let us assume that this service is small relative to the rest of the firm so that its introduction would not affect λ, and that the service does not interact, on the cost or demand side, with the services already offered by the firm. The service can be produced at constant marginal cost c and involves a fixed cost F.

Known Demand

In a first step, suppose that the demand curve, $q = D(p)$ (with elasticity of demand η), for the service is known. To decide whether to introduce the service, Ramsey and Boiteux would offer the following procedure:

1. Conditionally on being provided, the service should be priced at p^*, given by the inverse elasticity rule:

$$\frac{p^* - c}{p^*} = \frac{\lambda}{1 + \lambda} \frac{1}{\eta}$$

2. If the service then generates a stand-alone profit $[(p^* - c)D(p^*) \geq F]$, then it should indeed be introduced. If it generates a loss $[(p^* - c)D(p^*) < F]$, the cost of financing this loss must be compared with the increase in consumer net surplus. That is, the service should be introduced if and only if

$$(1 + \lambda)\left[F - (p^* - c)D(p^*)\right] \leq \int_{p^*}^{\infty} D(p)dp \tag{1}$$

Unknown Demand

With unknown demand, even if the firm succeeds in finding the Ramsey-Boiteux price p^* through local experimentation and learning of the demand curve, it may still not know whether equation (1) is satisfied as long as it does not know the value of demand at much higher prices, as illustrated in figure 2.4. In the figure, the firm's knowledge of the demand curve around p^* does not tell it whether that full demand curve is D_1 or D_2 (D_2 differs from D_1 in that consumers have a substitute at the higher price $\hat{p}$). Now, if

$$B < (1 + \lambda)(F - A) < B + C$$

it is unclear whether the service should be provided. It may then be optimal to experiment with prices around $\hat{p}$ in order to learn whether the service should be provided.

Box 2.6 (continued)

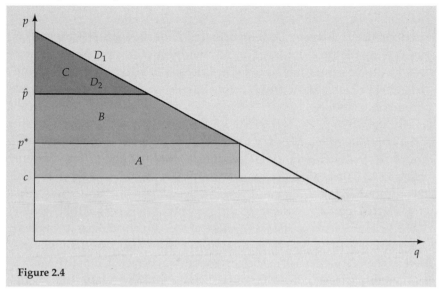

Figure 2.4

sometimes recommended average-cost pricing as a second-best solution. Our argument is simply an application of theirs to the more general concept of Ramsey-Boiteux prices.

To sum up: For lumpy decisions and in the presence of uncertainty about whether a service should be provided, a proper application of Ramsey-Boiteux prices requires consideration of the learning and experimentation process. Prices then differ from the Ramsey-Boiteux prices that would obtain were the provisions of the service a foregone conclusion. Some compartmentalization may be considered, although it may have serious drawbacks.

Matching Revenues and Expenses Encourages Cost Monitoring Another possible argument[28] against the one-budget principle is that it dilutes the impact of a deficit or inefficiency on a product line over many different categories of users. Because the cost of providing service k is borne not only by the users of service k (through the price of service k) but also by the users of all other services, the users of service k have fewer incentives to monitor the efficient provision of service they consume. More precisely, the fixed cost associated with service k is

---

28. This argument is developed and formalized in Laffont and Tirole (1990b).

covered primarily by the users of other services (in contrast with the marginal cost, which more directly affects the welfare of the users of service k under Ramsey-Boiteux pricing). Thus, in a situation in which one has moderate confidence in regulatory monitoring of costs, and in which one would like to enlist users as watchdogs, it may become desirable to match costs and revenues to provide users with enhanced incentives to monitor.

Compartmentalization May Reduce Regulatory Capture   Consider a variant of the problem enunciated under the subheading "Compartmentalization creates a viability test for lumpy decisions" and suppose that the introduction of a new service or the closure of a low-usage service is contemplated, and that the regulator may favor the users of this service. The regulators may overstate the size of the consumer surplus associated with this service so as to allow it to be supplied, and let the users of the other services pay for the corresponding deficit. Compartmentalization, in contrast, makes it more difficult for the regulator to provide undue benefits to the users. In a similar vein, even if the provision of the service is taken for granted, the regulator may favor low prices (below Ramsey level) to provide greater benefits to the users, to the detriment of users of other services. As usual, the concern just discussed is weaker if decisions are decentralized to a profit-maximizing utility.

2.2.5   Structural Separation and Pricing of Access to an Independently Owned Infrastructure

In some industries and countries a bottleneck segment with natural monopoly characteristics has been separated from the potentially competitive segments. For example, electric transmission grids in the United Kingdom, Argentina, Norway, New Zealand, and probably soon in most of the United States have been transformed into regulated monopolies that are not vertically integrated into electricity generation. Similarly, railroad infrastructure (tracks, stations) in some countries (France, Germany, and the United Kingdom, for example) is now separated from freight and passenger train operators. In telecommunications, the 1984 AT&T divestiture created operators of local infrastructure (the RBOCs) who have been prohibited from entering some competitive segments such as long-distance services. A similar situation could arise (although this is unlikely) if it were decided that the Internet backbone should become a vertically disintegrated regulated utility, or if regulators tried to encourage the development of an

ADSL local loop that would be providing services to all operators on complementary segments. Such situations exhibit "structural separation."

Under structural separation, the utility in general sells *wholesale services* to other firms who then market final services to the consumers. It should, however, be realized that the utility's infrastructure access charges orient the final prices and that Ramsey-Boiteux principles are still relevant.[29]

A simple illustration is provided by the case in which the final services are produced by competitive industries at some constant unit cost. Then, everything is *as if* the utility were vertically integrated and produced the final services itself at a unit cost equal to its own cost of providing access to the competitive downstream firms plus the latter's unit cost of producing the final services. The Ramsey-Boiteux formulas can be applied to the prices charged for access to the utilities' infra structure:[30] See box 2.7 for more details. And they can be decentralized through a price cap on access charges.

Perhaps one attribute of infrastructure utilities (as compared to utilities producing services for final consumers) is that the users of the infrastructure are often large and have market power. Whereas the power grid in California currently faces many small power producers as a result of intense horizontal disintegration at the generation level,[31] most independent transmission utilities face producers with nonnegligible market power. Similarly, railroad infrastructure companies often face one or two operators nationwide or at the regional level. And at the divestiture the regional Bell operating companies faced a handful of long-distance companies with AT&T holding a very strong position.

Downstream market power requires some corrections to Ramsey pricing. Here, we will content ourselves with a few remarks. First, the infrastructure owner may want to charge two-part tariffs to a large user. This policy helps to capture the rent, if any, of the large user and so reduces the social cost of having the other users contribute to

---

29. See, e.g., Feldstein (1971), Yang (1991), and Chang (1996).

30. In practice, firms which negotiate access to the infrastructure produce several services. The infrastructure utility can recover the relevant elasticities for Ramsey pricing only if the firms truthfully reveal their use of access, a probably unrealistic assumption; then, the infrastructure utility must reason on the basis of elasticities of average uses of access.

31. Mandated spinoffs by the large power utilities, however, have not eliminated local market power held by generators, who at certain points of time have a "strategic" position in the network and thus can exert market power despite a small market share in the state of California.

Box 2.7
Ramsey-Boiteux Access Charges for a Vertically Separated Infrastructure

As in box 2.2, we assume that there are n final services, $k = 1, \ldots, n$. To simplify the exposition, the services have independent demand curves, $q_k = D_k(p_k)$ with elasticity η_k for $k = 1, \ldots, n$. The infrastructure cost is composed of a fixed cost k_0 and a unit cost, c_k^u, incurred in providing access to firms supplying service k, $k = 1, \ldots, n$ (u stands for "upstream"). Final services are produced by competitive industries, with unit costs c_k^d (d for "downstream"). One unit of output requires using one unit of the infrastructure input.

Let

$$c_k \equiv c_k^u + c_k^d \tag{1}$$

The infrastructure utility charges access prices $\{a_k\}_{k=1,\ldots,n}$. The final services are sold by the competitive downstream industries at prices

$$p_k \equiv a_k + c_k^d \tag{2}$$

That is, the choice of access charges fully determines the final prices in that they are entirely passed through to the final consumers. The Ramsey-Boiteux final prices that would be charged by a vertically integrated industry—that is, a fictitious industry in which the infrastructure owner could absorb the downstream suppliers—would be given by

$$\frac{p_k - c_k}{p_k} = \frac{\lambda}{1 + \lambda} \frac{1}{\eta_k} \qquad \text{for all } k \tag{3}$$

where λ is the shadow price of the industry budget constraint

$$\Sigma_{k=1}^{n} \left(p_k - c_k \right) D_k(p_k) - k_0 \geq 0 \tag{4}$$

Using equations (1) and (2), equation (3) yields, for the vertically separated infrastructure,

$$\frac{a_k - c_k^u}{a_k + c_k^d} = \frac{\lambda}{1 + \lambda} \frac{1}{\eta_k} \qquad \text{for all } k \tag{5}$$

where λ is also the shadow price of the infrastructure owner's budget constraint (since the downstream industries break even):

$$\Sigma_{k=1}^{n} \left(a_k - c_k^u \right) D_k(a_k + c_k^d) - k_0 \geq 0 \tag{6}$$

Example: To illustrate these formulas, suppose that the infrastructure owner sells to two competitive downstream industries, with independent linear demand curves

$$q_k = D_k(p_k) = \alpha_k - \gamma_k p_k \qquad k = 1, 2$$

We assume that demand is higher (relative to costs) in industry 1, say, because industry 2 faces strong competition from substitute services, in that

$$\frac{\alpha_1}{\gamma_1} - c_1^d > \frac{\alpha_2}{\gamma_2} - c_2^d$$

Let us assume that the cost of giving access for the two services is the same, namely c^u. (The two services use the same infrastructure, but there is no congestion. We leave it to the reader to modify the analysis for the case in which

Box 2.7 (continued)

the services compete for scarce infrastructure capacity.) Formula (5) yields, for linear demand,

$$\frac{a_k - c^u}{p_k} = \frac{\lambda}{1 + \lambda} \frac{\alpha_k - \gamma_k p_k}{\gamma_k p_k}$$

and so

$$a_k = \left(\frac{1 + \lambda}{1 + 2\lambda}\right) c^u + \left(\frac{\lambda}{1 + 2\lambda}\right) \left(\frac{\alpha_k - \gamma_k c_k^d}{\gamma_k}\right)$$

And so

$$a_1 > a_2$$

infrastructure cost recovery. Two-part tariffs may also be a good instrument to correct the downstream market power of the large user, as shown in box 2.8. Indeed, it may be optimal to lease the infrastructure at a marginal access charge *below* the infrastructure's marginal cost and to use the fixed fee paid by the large user for cost recovery purposes. (Of course, this policy requires substantial knowledge by the infrastructure owner of the profitability of the large user.) The point is that the downstream user already imposes a markup, indeed a markup above the Ramsey markup in case of a monopoly. To bring down the total markup to the Ramsey level, the infrastructure owner must subsidize use of the infrastructure at the margin.

Box 2.8
Downstream Market Power

Suppose that service k is supplied by a downstream monopoly producer. Facing marginal access charge a_k, this producer charges monopoly price p_k given by

$$\frac{p_k - \left(a_k + c_k^d\right)}{p_k} = \frac{1}{\eta_k}$$

Letting λ denote as usual the shadow price of the infrastructure owner's budget constraint, the Ramsey price of service k is given, as usual, by

$$\frac{p_k - c_k}{p_k} = \frac{\lambda}{1 + \lambda} \frac{1}{\eta_k}$$

Thus the marginal access charge should satisfy

$$\frac{a_k - c_k^u}{p_k} = -\frac{1}{1 + \lambda} \frac{1}{\eta_k}$$

It is thus optimal for the infrastructure to offer a two-part access tariff, $A_k + a_k q_k$, to the downstream monopoly, where A_k is computed so as to extract the latter's profit {equal to, say, $[p_k - (a_k + c_k^d)]D_k(p_k)$, in the absence of downstream fixed cost}.

In the absence of long-term contracts, the presence of large users also creates some potential for expropriation, through high access charges, of the large user's investments. As we discussed in section 2.2.4, the prohibition of third-degree price discrimination, that is, of price discrimination based on the identity of the user, may then help the infrastructure owner to commit itself not to expropriate the large user. But the prohibition generates other problems: How can the infrastructure owner then discriminate between two users with the same usage of the infrastructure but with different degrees of downstream market power or facing different elasticities of demand? And is the no-price-discrimination rule always workable? For example, if a user is much larger than the others, second-degree price discrimination (that is, nonlinear pricing) may substitute for third-degree price discrimination.[32]

A second attribute of infrastructure utilities is that the downstream users of an infrastructure may compete among themselves, whereas final consumers consume the good for their own benefit and in general do not exert externalities on each other. In this respect, we note that published, nondiscriminatory tariffs may help the infrastructure owner to prevent downstream competition from eroding the "tax capacity" of the corresponding segment. In contrast, and as is well-known in the economics of foreclosure,[33] secret deals struck between the infrastructure owner and competitors on the downstream segment tend to erode profits that can be made by the upstream monopolist, and this erosion is more intense, the more competitive is the downstream industry. Nondiscriminatory tariffs, therefore, allow the infrastructure owner to recoup some of the fixed cost through markups on the segment.

2.3   Practical Aspects

2.3.1   From Rate-of-Return Regulation to Price-Cap Regulation

2.3.1.1   *Rate-of-Return Regulation and the Review Process*
For many years, the dominant method of regulation for private monopolies was so-called rate-of-return regulation. The regulated firm was allowed to charge prices that would cover its operating costs and give

---

32. Although expropriation of the large user's investment would take the form of price premiums in this case, whereas in practice second-degree price discrimination often takes the form of price discounts for large users.

33. See Rey and Tirole (1996) for an overview of the theory.

it a fair rate of return on the full value of its capital. If costs moved out of line with those prices, the firm would ask for a new set of prices. The main virtue of this "regulatory contract or compact" was to guarantee that the company would recover its costs. This absence of risk could attract capital at a low price. However, this method did not give incentives to the firm to keep its costs down.

To improve efficiency, "prudency reviews" were introduced to assess whether a new investment was necessary. If an investment was not judged "used and useful," then the regulator might not allow it to enter the rate base. Prudency reviews raise the concern of excessive micromanagement by regulators. Furthermore, by allowing regulators to substitute their own business judgement for that of the utilities' managers and boards, they potentially jeopardize the guarantee against expropriation afforded by rate of return regulation. Prudency reviews have therefore remained relatively limited.

The bureaucratic delays of the lengthy process leading to price revisions generated so-called regulatory lags, which had the beneficial side effect of creating some incentives for cost minimization. Indeed, during such lags, the firm was residual claimant of any cost decrease. To mitigate the effects of these delays on profits regulators introduced indexation clauses, for some items outside the control of firm, or pass-through clauses. For example, an electric company might be entitled to a complete pass-through to the consumer of its energy purchase expenditures in the wholesale market. A danger, then, is that the firm has little incentive to bargain for low prices of the corresponding inputs.

Another important feature of rate-of-return regulation is that individual retail prices are determined through accounting procedures and therefore do not obey commercial principles. In particular, they poorly reflect demand considerations. As discussed earlier, the review process determines a revenue requirement meant to cover operating costs plus a fair rate of return on undepreciated capital. Loosely speaking, this revenue requirement sets an average price or price *level*. It does not yield the price structure. The latter is the outcome of a cost allocation process. Costs that can unambiguously be allocated to a service are included in the price of this service; costs that are common to several services (which is the case for most equipment, be it wires or switches) are allocated according to some accounting rule to the different services. We refer to section 4.2 for illustrations of this process in the context of the setting of wholesale and retail prices, and to Baumol-Willig (1987) for a more extensive discussion of full cost allocation.

2.3.1.2   Price-Cap Regulation

Price-cap regulation was introduced in the United Kingdom under the name of "RPI − X". The firm is required to keep the weighted increase in a basket of its prices to less than the increase in a specified price index (for example, the retail price index, RPI), less x percent. The x percent factor induces a decline in real terms to account for anticipated technological progress.[34] The price control remains in place for a fixed period of four to five years during which the firm fully bears its cost.

In practice, price-cap regulation resembles rate-of-return regulation in some respects. On the one hand, the revision of price cap every four or five years uses all the information available about the firm including its present and projected operating costs, its assets, its investment plans, and its demand forecasts. This information enables the regulator to constrain the rate of return of the firm on the upside. (Sometimes rent extraction is performed more explicitly when earning-sharing schemes are appended to the price cap to redistribute excessive profits to consumers. A consequence of such profit sharing, of course, is a weakening of the incentives for cost minimization, as we discussed in section 2.1.) On the other hand, the profit downside is also partly insured through a common understanding that the regulator should allow a reasonable rate of return; indeed, regulatory statutes include an appeal mechanism to protect the company against excessively zealous regulators.

Price-cap regulation differs from rate-of-return regulation in other respects. First, the revision of the regulatory constraint is in principle less frequent, thus providing stronger incentives for cost reduction. Second, and conceptually a more drastic departure, the firm has flexibility as to the choice of its price structure. As we have seen, the firm is then able to price-discriminate in a way that minimizes the social distortion associated with cost recovery. In contrast with the regulator, the regulated firm has strong incentives to acquire the information about demand elasticities and to make use of this information; if it misjudges demand elasticities or does not act on knowledge of them, its profit will be substantially smaller.

---

34. It is also used to index the cap on the value of verifiable variables, such as the market price of inputs.

2.3.2 Some Practical Difficulties with Price Caps

Whereas a "perfect price cap" can yield the social optimum, frictions imply that its implementation is likely to be less efficient than the theoretical analysis predicts. Let us briefly recall a few difficulties encountered when regulating firms with price caps:

• *Treatment of nonlinear tariffs.* As demonstrated in box 2.4, the inclusion of nonlinear prices into a price cap poses no theoretical difficulty (since nonlinear prices are particular instances of Ramsey-Boiteux prices). Yet, the transposition of these principles to practice is still quite rough. In practice, regulators often take price averages or ignore discounts for the purpose of monitoring compliance with the price cap.

• *Treatment of new services and of upgrades, and phasing out of existing services.* Again, innovations in the spectrum of services of a regulated firm are treated in an essentially pragmatic way, such as the exclusion of new services from the price cap during the year of their introduction. Too little theoretical work has been devoted to providing reasonable guidance to regulators in the matter.

• *Lack of intertemporal price cap.* Price caps are defined over some limited period. Therefore, they deal imperfectly with the intertemporal dimension of some contracts (such as guarantees on future prices) or of investments in goodwill through low prices.

• *Ratchet effect.* As we discussed previously, there is no pure price cap. Regulatory reviews imply some form of profit sharing (which is not equivalent to contemporaneous profit sharing). Conversely, a price cap may not be credible if it leads to financial losses and jeopardizes the operator's survival.

• *Setting of weights in case of substantial demand and cost uncertainty.* Weights should equal realized quantities in a perfect price cap. Uncertainty about cost, about market demand, and about the competitors' market share may, however, make it difficult to forecast these quantities accurately. We can of course avail ourselves of mechanisms for updating weights on the basis of past outcomes.[35] Yet the properties of such mechanisms (whether they converge to the socially optimal prices) are known only for simple situations. We will come back to this point shortly.

---

35. See, e.g., chapter 2 of Laffont and Tirole (1993) and the early work of Vogelsang and Finsinger and of Sappington discussed therein.

• *Need for monitoring the provision of a service priced below marginal cost.* All price caps that involve bundles give rise to the following hazard: The operator may charge a very low price for a service and ration consumers of that service. The price cut allows the operator to raise prices on other services and still comply with the requirement defined by the price cap. Rationing consumers is profitable when the price of the service falls below marginal cost.

Even though such behavior may not be quite as profitable in the long run (rationing leads to a lower weight for the service in future regulatory reviews), it can substantially enhance profit in the short run. Two regulatory responses to this hazard are conceivable. First, the regulator can monitor rationing, perhaps using consumers as whistle-blowers. Second (as is already the case under some regulatory schemes), prices can be required to exceed marginal costs.

• *Price cap and the provision of quality.* Provided the quality of a service is observed by consumers when purchasing the service (the service is then called a search good), the demand-expansion effect of an increase in quality provides the utility (just like any unregulated firm) with an incentive to supply quality. However, there is no guarantee that the provision of quality will be appropriate. First, as has been well known since Spence's 1975 article, the choice of quality is guided by the impact of quality on the *average* consumer. Accordingly, quality may be too low or too high depending on the relationship between the value of quality for the marginal consumer and its value to the average consumer. When quality is underproduced (overproduced), one can manipulate price-cap weights so as to introduce an upward (downward) distortion in the price with respect to Ramsey pricing to improve the quality performance. Such action in turn raises (reduces) the incentive for provision of quality.

This discussion brings us to a related, and potentially more important, point. Price-cap regulation is about constraining margins. With low margins, the regulated firm has mild incentives to provide quality. It bears the full cost of the provision of quality and reaps a small fraction of its benefits to the extent that the demand expansion is multiplied by a small margin. It is for this reason that price cap regulation is often accompanied by the introduction of measurements of new indicators of quality.

• *Exclusion of competitive goods.* Most price-cap controls exclude goods that are produced by the regulated firm in competitive markets. The idea is that for such goods, the utility's price is constrained by market forces and therefore need not be regulated. For example, if the good is produced under a freely available constant-returns-to-scale technology, Ramsey pricing reduces to marginal cost pricing. Including or excluding competitive goods from the cap leads to the same pricing formulas. There are, however, two limits to this argument, which will be developed in more detail later in the book. First, it must be the case that the market is indeed competitive. If the competitiveness of the market relies on access to a crucial input supplied by the firm, then excluding the "competitive" retail good from the price basket gives the firm an incentive to deny its rivals access to the essential input and then raise the retail price in the now less competitive retail market. The second caveat is that the deregulated segment and the regulated ones exhibit different patterns of profit sharing between the firm and consumers. The firm retains its entire profit in the deregulated segment, but usually only a fraction of its profit in the regulated ones (either through explicit earnings-sharing rules, or implicitly through the revision of the price cap). Therefore, the exclusion of these goods may provide incentives for cross-subsidies—for example, by shifting the best inputs toward the production of the competitive good and leaving the inefficient inputs for the regulated part of the activity.[36]

The pure price-cap mechanism sets specific weights for a number of prices and controls their weighted average. In practice, a simpler form of regulation is often used: the revenue-control regulation. In this case, there is no need to list individual prices, and the weights are the current quantities effectively sold. However, this simpler regulation cannot generate Ramsey pricing and provides the firm with incentives to expand sales to low-price segments excessively and to contract sales to high-priced segments[37] (see box 2.9). Intuitively, a revenue-yield control refers to an average price $\bar{p}$ and requires that the average deviation weighted by actual quantities (q_k for service k) from this average be nonnegative:

$$\sum_k \left(p_k - \bar{p} \right) q_k \leq 0$$

---

36. Practical implementation of price-cap regulation also raises a large number of technical and accounting issues related to the dynamics of price controls, benchmarking, depreciation rules, cost of capital, revenue forecasting, proper discounting, and quality standards (see Green and Rodriguez-Pardina, 1997).

37. See Armstrong and Vickers (1991), Bradley and Price (1988, 1991), Law (1995), and Waterson (1992) for more on the distortions induced by an average revenue constraint.

Box 2.9
Revenue-Yield Control

Assuming independent demands and constant marginal costs for simplicity, the firm maximizes profit under a cap on the revenue per unit of sales, that is,

$$\max \sum_k p_k D_k(p_k) - \sum_k c_k D_k(p_k)$$

subject to

$$\frac{\sum_k p_k D_k(p_k)}{\sum_k D_k(p_k)} \leq \bar{p}, \qquad (\tilde{\lambda})$$

yielding the first-order conditions

$$\frac{p_k - c_k}{p_k} = (1 - \tilde{\lambda}) \frac{1}{\eta_k} + \tilde{\lambda} \frac{p_k - \bar{p}}{p_k}$$

where $\tilde{\lambda}$ is a function of $\bar{p}$. In particular suppose that one can choose $\bar{p} = \bar{p}^*$ such that $1 - \tilde{\lambda} = \frac{\lambda}{1+\lambda}$ where λ is the shadow price of the budget constraint under optimal (Ramsey-Boiteux) pricing. Then

$$\frac{p_k - c_k}{p_k} = \frac{\lambda}{1+\lambda} \frac{1}{\eta_k} + \frac{1}{1+\lambda} \frac{p_k - \bar{p}^*}{p_k}$$

The formula identifies the distortion from Ramsey pricing: the firm can ease the cap by expanding sales for low-price services ($p_k < \bar{p}^*$).

Consider for example a low-cost service $k(p_k < \bar{p})$. The firm has an incentive to lower the price of service k further, that is, to increase q_k in order to relax the price cap constraint. More generally, it has an incentive to expand the production of services whose price lies below the average price.

Revenue-yield control is used primarily when the different services sold by the firm are still relatively homogeneous (comparable). For example, it has been used in the United Kingdom in the electricity sector.

Another common type of price cap is the so-called revenue-weighted price basket (which has been applied, for example, to British Telecom). This price cap constrains the average relative increase in price, with weights set equal to the previous year's revenue shares. The increase should not increase the rate of inflation minus the expected rate of technological progress

$$\sum_k w_k \frac{p_k(t) - p_k(t-1)}{p_k(t-1)} \leq RPI - X$$

where $w_k^{\circ} = \frac{p_k(t-1)q_k(t-1)}{\sum_l p_l(t-1)q_l(t-1)}$

2.3.3   Weight Setting under Imperfect Information

Price caps dispense the regulator from setting individual prices. It is often argued, though, that this cutback in the regulatory burden is fictitious, for the regulator must still select the weights, and errors in weight setting result in errors in retail prices. A low weight on a service induces an unduly high price on that service, while a high weight forces a low price. Indeed, it is often further argued that "setting proper weights requires as much information as setting the proper prices." This argument has some grain of truth, but falls short of proving that price caps offer nothing beyond administered prices, that is, prices that are set directly by the regulator and therefore do not leave the firm with any flexibility. To be certain, setting the weights that induce the *exactly* optimal prices in general will require perfect information (at least locally) about cost and demand functions, in which case the regulator might set the individual prices in the first place. However, inducing the exact Ramsey optimum will always be an infeasible task for a regulator. In practice, one can at best shoot for Ramsey-orientated prices. With this perspective, it would be incorrect to deduce from the previous argument that price caps cannot improve on administered prices.

We should warn the reader that the theory of weight setting under imperfect information is still in its infancy. We therefore content ourselves with a few remarks, examples, and intuitions.

First, price caps allow the firm to *rebalance* its tariffs as a response to news concerning costs, demand, and competitive pressure *during* the regulatory period.[38] As we noted, price caps are usually in effect for

---

38. Armstrong and Vickers (1996) study a couple of such examples, in which information accrues after the regulatory contract. Their focus is on "price flexibility" or "price discretion" more generally, rather than on price caps. On the basis of a couple of examples, they formulate the following interesting conjecture:

"The desirability of pricing discretion depends on whether private and social interests concerning its exercise are aligned or opposed. When uncertainty is about costs they are aligned: it is good for both profits and welfare to have higher relative prices in markets where relative costs are higher. With demand uncertainty, however, private and social interests may or may not be aligned. It is socially desirable (for Ramsey reasons) to have higher prices where demand *elasticities* are lower, but it is generally profitable to have higher prices where the *scale* of demand is greater. If the elasticity and scale of demand are negatively related, discretion is therefore desirable. But if they are positively related (and there is no cost uncertainty), there might be no way to exploit the firm's private information that is both incentive compatible and socially beneficial; in that case zero discretion is best."

four to five years. It would be illusory to think that the prices set by even a well-informed regulator at the regulatory review can remain adequate for that long in a fast-changing industry such as the telecommunications industry. Flexibility is therefore needed. Consider, for instance, the following trivial example. Suppose that the demand for a service, access to the network for a certain category of customers, say, is relatively inelastic at the beginning of the regulatory period. The minimization of economic distortions (Ramsey pricing) then commands imposing a high markup on this service. But perhaps at midterm a cheap bypass technology will appear that will make it socially efficient to lower the price of access for these customers in order to compete effectively with the bypass technology and make effective use of the existing access infrastructure. Price caps let the firm react to the competitive threat.[39]

Second, the regulator lacks information about cost and demand *at the regulatory review stage.* Unlike administered prices, which reflect the regulator's "average beliefs," a price cap allows the firm to rebalance its price structure to reflect its privy information about cost and demand. Services that turn out to be cheaper (more expensive) to produce than is anticipated by the regulator can thereby be marketed at a lower (higher) price. Similarly, the firm can adjust its prices to the privy information it has about demand; for example, it can lower its price when confronting a competitive threat whose strength the regulator underestimates.

Last, let us note that even if the regulator's toolbox is limited in the way implicit in the price-cap institution (no use of cost or profit observations, and industry budget balance), a single price cap in general is not optimal. As is often the case in situations in which the regulated firm has private information, a *menu* of options is in general desirable.

Box 2.10 illustrates these points through simple examples.[40] It first demonstrates the benefits of flexibility; in two examples in which the firm has privy information about its cost or demand structure, we show that a price cap, by making use of this information, may raise welfare relative to an administered price process. We also start analyzing the impact of the asymmetry of information about this structure on the Ramsey pricing structure.

---

39. So does an administered price *ceiling*, that is, an administered price that allows for downward flexibility. However, unlike the price cap, the price ceiling does not allow the firm to recoup the revenue loss on this segment by charging higher prices on other segments.

40. We are grateful to Marius Schwartz for prompting us to write this box.

Box 2.10
Administered Prices, Price Cap, and Flexibility

Privy Information about the Demand Structure

Consider a two-product firm. Producing goods $k = 1, 2$ involves no marginal cost (for notational simplicity), and a joint cost k_0. Demands are linear:

$$q_k = \theta_k - p_k$$

While the regulated firm knows perfectly its demand functions (knows the θ_k's), the regulator only knows the average $\bar{\theta}$ of the intercepts:

$$\theta_1 + \theta_2 = 2\bar{\theta}$$

However, one service (the other service) faces a higher (lower) demand than predicted by this average. Let us assume that the distribution of θ_1 (and therefore that of $\theta_2 = 2\bar{\theta} - \theta_1$) is symmetric around $\bar{\theta}$. More precisely, $\theta_1 = \bar{\theta} + \frac{\Delta}{2}$ with probability 1/2 and $\theta_1 = \bar{\theta} - \frac{\Delta}{2}$ with probability 1/2. We will focus on the case of small uncertainty (Δ small). The regulator either sets prices directly or sets a price cap so as to maximize social welfare subject to the firm's break-even constraint.

Administered Prices

Suppose, first, that the regulator sets the prices directly. By symmetry, he sets the same price $p_1 = p_2 = p^*$ for both. The administered price p^* allows the firm to break even, or

$$2p^*(\theta - p^*) = k_0$$

The consumer net surplus (welfare) is then equal to

$$W^{ap} = \Sigma_k \frac{(\theta_k - p_k)^2}{2} = (\bar{\theta} - p^*)^2 + \frac{\Delta^2}{4}$$

Price Cap

Suppose now that the regulator offers price cap

$$\frac{p_1 + p_2}{2} \leq \bar{p}$$

Then, knowing (θ_1, θ_2), the firm sets (p_1, p_2) so as to maximize its profit,

$$\pi = p_1(\theta_1 - p_1) + p_2(\theta_2 - p_2) - k_0$$

subject to the price-cap constraint. This optimization yields

$$p_k = \bar{p} + \frac{\theta_k - \bar{\theta}}{4}$$

and

$$\pi = 2\left[\bar{p}(\bar{\theta} - \bar{p}) + \frac{3\Delta^2}{64}\right] - k_0$$

Box 2.10 (continued)

This example has been designed so that the firm's profit is known to the regulator despite asymmetric information about the demand structure. Note also that price flexibility raises the firm's profit, and so, if $\bar{p}$ is chosen so as to yield zero profit,

$$\bar{p} < p^*$$

Welfare is

$$W^{pc} = \Sigma_k \frac{(\theta_k - p_k)^2}{2} = (\bar{\theta} - \bar{p})^2 + \frac{9\Delta^2}{64}$$

Clearly, for $\Delta = 0$, $W^{pc} = W^{ap}$. A simple Taylor expansion shows that for Δ small but positive, $W^{pc} > W^{ap}$ if k_0 is large enough.

Privy Information about the Cost Structure

We can perform a symmetrical exercise for the case in which the firm has privy information about its marginal cost structure rather than about its demand structure. Let

$$q_k = 1 - p_k, \qquad k = 1, 2$$

Marginal costs are $c_1 = \bar{c} + \frac{\Delta}{2}$ and $c_2 = \bar{c} - \frac{\Delta}{2}$ with probability 1/2, and $c_1 = \bar{c} - \frac{\Delta}{2}$ and $c_2 = \bar{c} + \frac{\Delta}{2}$ with probability 1/2.

Administered Prices

It is easy to see that welfare under an administered price is independent of uncertainty:

$$W^{ap} = (1 - p^*)^2$$

where

$$2(p^* - \bar{c})(1 - p^*) = k_0$$

Price Cap

The reader will check that

$$W^{pc} = (1 - \bar{p})^2 + \frac{\Delta^2}{16}$$

where $\bar{p} = (p_1 + p_2)/2$ solves

$$2\left[(\bar{p} - \bar{c})(1 - \bar{p}) + \frac{\Delta^2}{16} \right] = k_0$$

A Taylor expansion again shows that for Δ small

$$W^{pc} > W^{ap}$$

Box 2.10 (continued)

Impact of Informational Rents on the Pricing Structure

The preceding examples were designed to isolate the impact of price flexibility. The utility had privy information about its cost or demand structure, but because of the two-point symmetric uncertainty was unable to extract any rent; while abiding by the two-type paradigm, we now introduce an asymmetry and study the impact of rent extraction on the price structure.

Again, we consider a regulated firm producing two services with cost function

$$(c + \theta)q_1 + (c - \theta)q_2 + k_0$$

where, for simplicity, the private information θ can take two values, $\underline{\theta}$ and $\bar{\theta}$, with $\Delta\theta \equiv \bar{\theta} - \underline{\theta}$ and $v = Pr(\theta = \underline{\theta})$. We assume $\underline{\theta} > 0$.

The demand functions for the two goods are separable with the same constant price elasticity η. A regulatory mechanism here is two pairs of prices $(\underline{p}_1, \underline{p}_2)$ and $(\bar{p}_1, \bar{p}_2)$ designed for types $\underline{\theta}$ and $\bar{\theta}$, respectively. Let $\underline{U}$ and $\bar{U}$ denote the associated profit levels of the two types:

$$\underline{U} = \left(\underline{p}_1 - c - \underline{\theta}\right) D(\underline{p}_1) + \left(\underline{p}_2 - c + \underline{\theta}\right) D(\underline{p}_2) - k_0$$

$$\bar{U} = (\bar{p}_1 - c - \bar{\theta}) D(\bar{p}_1) + (\bar{p}_2 - c + \bar{\theta}) D(\bar{p}_2) - k_0$$

Type $\bar{\theta}$, by mimicking type $\underline{\theta}$, obtains rent

$$\underline{U} + (\Delta\theta) \left[D(\underline{p}_2) - D(\underline{p}_1) \right]$$

Since $\theta > 0$, good 1 is more costly to produce than good 2 and we can expect $q_2 - q_1$ to be positive. As usual, the incentive constraint of type $\bar{\theta}$ and the participation constraint of type $\underline{\theta}$ are binding:

$$\bar{U} = \underline{U} + (\Delta\theta) \left[D(\underline{p}_2) - D(\underline{p}_1) \right] \tag{1}$$

$$\underline{U} = 0 \tag{2}$$

Maximizing expected welfare yields

$$\frac{\bar{p}_1 - c - \bar{\theta}}{\bar{p}_1} = \frac{\bar{p}_2 - c + \bar{\theta}}{\bar{p}_2} = \frac{\mu}{1 + \mu} \frac{1}{\eta} \tag{3}$$

$$\frac{\underline{p}_1 - c - \underline{\theta}}{\underline{p}_1} = \frac{\lambda}{1 + \lambda} \frac{1}{\eta} - \frac{1 - v}{v} \frac{\mu}{1 + \lambda} \frac{\Delta\theta}{\underline{p}_1} \tag{4}$$

$$\frac{\underline{p}_2 - c - \underline{\theta}}{\underline{p}_2} = \frac{\lambda}{1 + \lambda} \frac{1}{\eta} + \frac{1 - v}{v} \frac{\mu}{1 + \lambda} \frac{\Delta\theta}{\underline{p}_2} \tag{5}$$

where $(1 - v)\mu$ and $v\lambda$ are proportional to the multipliers of equations (1) and (2), respectively.

We obtain Ramsey pricing for type $\bar{\theta}$ (and here Lerner indices for the two goods are equal because elasticities of demand are identical) and an incentive correction with respect to Ramsey pricing for type $\underline{\theta}$. Note that *this* incentive correction brings the two prices p_1 and p_2 closer to each other. Indeed its purpose is to decrease the information rent $(\Delta\theta) \left[D(\underline{p}_2) - D(\underline{p}_1) \right]$.

Box 2.10 (continued)

If the parameter θ were drawn from a continuous distribution, the optimal price regulation would take the form of a nonlinear relationship $p_2 = P(p_1)$; the firm would select a point on this curve on the basis of its realized cost structure. If this curve is convex, it can be replaced by the family of its tangents, which can be interpreted as a menu of price caps. If the curve is not convex, a menu of price caps is not optimal, but such a menu in general can still improve on a single price cap. A single-price-cap constraint in general is not an optimal regulation, even under the no-transfer and absence-of-cost-observability constraints. What a menu enables the regulator to do is to maintain prices of firms with very asymmetric cost structures close to Ramsey pricing despite asymmetric information. This process entails giving to a firm that is relatively less efficient in the production of a good a lower weight for this good in the price-cap formula. Incentive compatibility, of course, requires that the weight on the other good should increase.

3   Essential Facility and One-Way Access: Theory

3.1   Background

The provision of a telecommunications service often requires the combining of multiple elements. A long-distance phone call may flow through the local exchange carrier's local loop, switches, and inter-office transmission facilities at the originating and terminating ends and through a long-distance company's trunk lines in between. New service offerings such as voice messaging, video on demand, call forwarding, or Internet services (ftp, gopher, e-mail, World Wide Web, etc.) rely on the use of the telecommunications infrastructure and, for many, its signaling and call-related database facilities.

The existence of complementarities is not unique to telecommunications or even to network industries. Indeed, it is pervasive in all industries. Most goods and services we purchase are bundles of various elements. A car comes with seats, radio, tires, and engine. In general, bundling adds economic value to the products. Economists are naturally preoccupied with situations in which it may not. They, as well as courts and regulators, have wondered whether competition on some segment can be preserved when another complementary segment is monopolized. Monopolization of the latter segment may stem from economies of scale or of scope, network externalities, innovation, or patent ownership. In all cases the segment will be called a bottleneck.

Examples of bottlenecks in regulated industries are the local loop for telecommunications, the power transmission grid for electricity, mail delivery for postal services, pipelines for natural gas, and tracks and stations for railroads; see figure 3.1. Examples of bottlenecks (essential facilities) to which competition law has been applied include stadiums, harbors, computer operating systems, computer reservation systems, and R&D or marketing joint ventures.

Industry	Bottleneck	Potentially Competitive Segment
Telecommunications	Local loop	Long distance
Electricity	Transmission grid	Generation
Gas	Pipelines	Extraction
Rail transportation	Tracks, stations	Passenger and freight services
Postal services	Local delivery network	Complementary segments (consolidations, presort bureaus, . . .)

Figure 3.1

In antitrust, the foreclosure or essential-facility doctrine states that the owner of an essential facility may have an incentive to monopolize complementary or downstream segments as well. This doctrine was first discussed in the United States in *Terminal Railroad Association v. U.S.* (1912), in which a set of railroads formed a joint venture owning a key bridge across the Mississippi River and the approaches and terminal in Saint Louis and excluded nonmember competitors. The Supreme Court ruled that this practice was a violation of the Sherman Act. A version of the doctrine was invoked by the European Court of Justice in the celebrated United Brands (1978) decision, in which it held that United Brands Corporation enjoyed substantial market power in the banana market in Europe and engaged in exclusionary practices in related markets (distribution, ripening). The Clear case in New Zealand provides an example of application of this antitrust doctrine to telecommunications, where the dominant operator (Telecom)'s network was viewed as an essential facility. This book focuses mostly on a regulatory environment and therefore will not further discuss the antitrust approach. We refer to Rey and Tirole (1996) for a review of the theoretical considerations and an exposition of restrictive practices, efficiency defenses, and court remedies.

It is generally agreed that an intelligent interconnection policy is the key to harmonious development of competition in the telecommunications industry. To this end, interconnection charges must reflect multiple objectives. They must induce an efficient use of networks, encourage their owners to invest while minimizing cost, generate an efficient amount of entry into infrastructure and services, and do all of this at a reasonable regulatory cost.

Regulators may strike many rocks. High interconnection charges erect barriers to entry and maintain the incumbents' monopoly position in their potentially competitive segments. They also may induce inefficient bypass or duplication of the incumbent's bottleneck segments. Conversely, low interconnection charges may generate entry by inefficient entrants. They may also induce incumbents to foreclose access to their bottleneck and discourage them from maintaining and upgrading their networks. They may, furthermore, dissuade entrants from building their own facilities.

Thus the choice of the overall *level* of access charges is delicate. So is the determination of the relative *structure*[1] of these charges. An inadequate rate structure provides the wrong signals for the incumbents' choices of investment in infrastructure and for the entrants' decisions on which segments to enter. For example, incumbents often complain about the entrants' strategies to "skim the cream."

Two factors make it difficult for regulators to set interconnection charges. First, regulators generally lack the information required for a good interconnection policy. Being understaffed, they know too little about the incumbents' and entrants' cost structures, about demand functions, and about the intensity of competition. Second, the high stakes attached to the interconnection policy in most countries generate intense lobbying by incumbents and entrants as well as political intervention. These "political economy considerations" matter more, the more discretionary the interconnection policy and the wider the divergence between policy and sound economic principles.

We first lay out the economic principles for interconnection. Second, we examine current and proposed institutions in the light of economic incentives, and warn against the (often poorly understood) dangers of "asymmetric regulations" such as those in place in the United States and the United Kingdom, which represent the dominant paradigm within the European Union. We then study alternative methods of determination of access charges.

---

1. When discussing the "structure" of access prices, we take as given the set of access services. An important issue is the definition of this set, for example, the choice of the locations of the points of interconnection (e.g., before or after the first switch).

3.2   Economic Principles

3.2.1   The Cost-Recovery Problem

For illustrative purposes we use the paradigm, depicted in figure 3.2, of long-distance competition cum local-exchange bottleneck. A telephone operator, the incumbent, controls the local bottleneck and faces competition by one or several competitors, the entrants, in the long-distance market. (While we consider a single competitive segment for simplicity, it is clear that the principles to be derived carry over to an arbitrary number of competitive segments. And, indeed, we will consider multiple competitive segments in some of our applications.) The entrants need access to the local network in order to reach end users.

From a social viewpoint, the presence of entrants in the competitive market may be desirable for several reasons. Entrants often offer a differentiated service not offered by the incumbents. They may also provide existing services at a lower cost. Last, entrants may force the incumbent to produce more efficiently.

For future reference, we will let c_0 denote the marginal cost of the local loop. That is, c_0 denotes the traffic sensitive cost of the local loop—mainly the additional cost of switching brought about by the originating or terminating long-distance traffic. This cost does not include the less traffic sensitive parts of the local network, such as the access lines connecting central offices to homes. The latter cost (as well as any universal service deficit incurred by the incumbent) is treated as a fixed cost of the incumbent. We let c_1 and c_2 denote the incumbent's and entrants' marginal costs in the long-distance segment. We make the strong assumption that entrants behave competitively, so that they stand ready to supply at marginal cost. We will later comment on entrant market power.

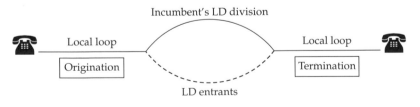

Figure 3.2
Long-distance competition

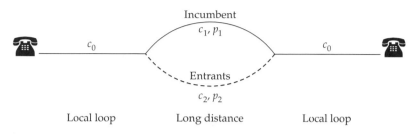

Figure 3.3
Summary of marginal cost and price structure

Let a denote the access charge to be paid (per minute, say) by the entrants to the incumbent. Access is said to be priced at marginal cost if the access charge is equal to the incumbent's total cost of carrying a call at the originating and terminating ends, that is, $a = 2c_0$. The determination of the access charge is then said to be (purely) *cost based*. In contrast, an access charge in excess of marginal cost ($a > 2c_0$) is said to involve a *markup*, and one below marginal cost ($a < 2c_0$) a *subsidy*. Last, we will let p_1 and p_2 denote the (per-minute, say) prices of long-distance services offered by the incumbent and the entrants. The incumbent may (and typically does) offer other services such as local phone service, which we can add to our description (see box 3.1), but these do not play any major role for this discussion of access. Figure 3.3 summarizes the mathematical notation.

3.2.2   Efficient Access Pricing: A Level Playing Field

The key to understanding the determination of the *efficient access charge* (see box 3.1) is to note that the incumbent (voluntarily or involuntarily) *subcontracts* the provision of a new long-distance service to entrants whenever the latter gain market share. The incumbent can then be viewed as producing two long-distance services, one internally and one outsourced. It thus faces a standard make-or-buy decision. It produces its own long-distance service at cost $2c_0 + c_1$ and, with competitive entrants, can supply the alternative long-distance service at cost $2c_0 + c_2$.

In a first-best world, a necessary condition for optimality would be that entrants internalize the bottleneck's marginal cost ($a = 2c_0$). And so the access charge would be cost based. The retail goods (long-distance offerings) would also obey marginal cost pricing. The incumbent's

Box 3.1
The Mathematics of Efficient Access Pricing

Let q_1 and q_2 denote the quantities (expressed in minutes, say) of long-distance services supplied by the incumbent and the entrants, respectively. Let q_0 denote the quantity of local calls, that is, the end users' demand for local calls. The total number of calls using the local network is thus $Q = q_0 + q_1 + q_2$.

For expositional simplicity, all activities exhibit constant returns to scale, except for the existence of a fixed cost k_0 in the local network. The symbol k_0, which will represent the access deficit broadly defined in this framework, can be thought of as having two components. The first is the setup (non–traffic sensitive) cost of the network. The second is the difference between a universal service deficit (linked with the constraints of creating easy access to phones and of national uniform pricing) and the fixed subscription charges paid by the consumers, unless a universal service fund explicitly covers this difference.

The cost functions are $C_0 = 2c_0 Q + k_0$ for the local network, $C_1 = c_1 q_1$ for the incumbent's long-distance service, and $C_2 = c_2 q_2$ for the long-distance entrants. Note that we adopt the convention that a local call involves the same use of the local network, namely, an origination and a termination, as a long-distance call. Any correction to reflect a discrepancy in the use of the local network is straightforward.

Let $S_0(p_0)$ and $S(p_1, p_2)$ denote the consumer *net* surpluses for local and long-distance services. Recall that the derivative of a net surplus with respect to a price is equal to (minus) the corresponding quantity; that is, when the price of service i is raised by \$1, the consumers must increase their expense by \$$q_i$. They also reoptimize their consumption pattern, but this action locally has only second-order effects on their welfare.

Let π denote the incumbent's profit. We noted that in the absence of entrants' market power, one can either consider that the incumbent produces at cost $2c_0$ and sells at price a an access service that is resold without markup at price $p_2 = a + c_2$, or envision an equivalent situation in which the incumbent produces the entrants' retail service itself at cost $2c_0 + c_2$ and sells it to final consumers at price p_2. And so

$$\pi(p_0, p_1, p_2) = (p_0 - 2c_0)q_0 + (p_1 - c_1 - 2c_0)q_1 + (p_2 - c_2 - 2c_0)q_2 - k_0$$

We have thus transformed the access-pricing problem into a standard Ramsey-Boiteux determination of retail prices through the maximization of social surplus subject to the constraint that the incumbent breaks even:

$$\max_{\{p_0, p_1, p_2\}} \left\{ S_0(p_0) + S(p_1, p_2) + \pi(p_0, p_1, p_2) \right\}$$

subject to

$$\pi(p_0, p_1, p_2) \geq 0$$

Let λ denote the shadow cost of the budget constraint. In the absence of fixed cost to be covered ($k_0 = 0$), the optimal prices would be the marginal costs $2c_0$, $2c_0 + c_1$, and $2c_0 + c_2$, respectively. These would maximize the objective function and allow the incumbent to break even ($\pi = 0$). The shadow cost of the budget constraint would then be equal to zero. In the presence of a fixed cost,

Box 3.1 (continued)

marginal-cost pricing is inconsistent with budget balance, and the shadow cost λ is strictly positive. Simple computations then yield

$$\frac{p_0 - 2c_0}{p_0} = \frac{\lambda}{1 + \lambda} \frac{1}{\hat{\eta}_0}$$

$$\frac{p_1 - c_1 - 2c_0}{p_1} = \frac{\lambda}{1 + \lambda} \frac{1}{\hat{\eta}_1}$$

$$\frac{p_2 - c_2 - 2c_0}{p_2} = \frac{\lambda}{1 + \lambda} \frac{1}{\hat{\eta}_2}$$

The numbers $\hat{\eta}_i$ are price "superelasticities." Superelasticities are modified elasticities of demand, which account for possible substitution and complementarity among goods. If we assume, as we did, that the demands for local calls and long-distance calls are independent, then the superelasticity of good 0 is equal to the ordinary elasticity of demand for local calls. In contrast, to the extent that the two long-distance services are *substitutes*, the superelasticities $\hat{\eta}_1$ and $\hat{\eta}_2$ are smaller than their respective ordinary elasticities. Namely, let $\eta_k \equiv -\frac{\partial q_k}{\partial p_k}\frac{p_k}{q_k}$ denote the ordinary demand elasticities and $\eta_{kl} \equiv \frac{\partial q_k}{\partial p_l}\frac{p_l}{q_k}$ denote the cross-price elasticities. We have $\hat{\eta}_0 = \eta_0$, $\hat{\eta}_1 = \eta_1 \frac{\eta_1 \eta_2 - \eta_{12}\eta_{21}}{\eta_1 \eta_2 + \eta_1 \eta_{12}} < \eta_1$, and $\hat{\eta}_2 = \eta_2 \frac{\eta_1 \eta_2 - \eta_{12}\eta_{21}}{\eta_1 \eta_2 + \eta_2 \eta_{21}} < \eta_2$ (assuming goods 1 and 2 are substitutes).

To confirm this reasoning, consider a decrease in the access price. This decrease creates more competition for the incumbent's long-distance service and therefore generates a revenue loss for the incumbent on the competitive segment, that is, a shortfall in the covering of the fixed cost. Superelasticities are just meant to reflect the global impact of a change in the price of a service on the incumbent's total profit. Note also that the precepts embodied in the Ramsey formulas are not limited to the case of substitutes. Suppose that service 2 is mobile calls, and that for legal or technical reasons the incumbent is not in the mobile market. Suppose further that mobile communications do not compete with local calls. (This assumption might be a rough approximation of the current situation, although it will become quite unrealistic when the price of mobile calls plummets.) Rather, they increase the incumbent's demand for long-distance calls. In this application services 1 and 2 are complementary. Their superelasticities are higher than their ordinary elasticities, reflecting, for example, the fact that a lower price of mobile calls raises the incumbent's revenue on long-distance calls.

The optimal access price $a = p_2 - c_2$ follows from the formula

$$a = 2c_0 + \frac{\lambda}{1 + \lambda} \frac{p_2}{\hat{\eta}_2}$$

This demonstrates that the access price contributes to covering the fixed cost. The Ramsey formulas for access charges were developed in Laffont and Tirole (1994). A useful rewriting of the Ramsey access charges is offered by Armstrong, Doyle, and Vickers (1996). They show that

$$a = 2c_0 + \delta(p_1 - 2c_0 - c_1) + \frac{\lambda}{1 + \lambda} \frac{p_2}{\eta_2}$$

Box 3.1 (continued)

where the "displacement ratio" $\delta \equiv -[(\partial q_1/\partial p_2)/(\partial q_2/\partial p_2)]$ is the change in incumbent retail sales divided by the change in its sales to rivals as the access price varies. So, the markup embodied in the access charge can be divided into two markups. One is the standard own elasticity markup; and the second markup reflects the substitution between the retail and access activities of the incumbent. This type of decomposition of the Ramsey price is emphasized in Armstrong, Doyle, and Vickers (1996), which also allows for variable input proportions.

This rewriting illuminates our discussion of usage-based pricing of access. Recall that access charges should both reflect the elasticity of demand for the entrants' services and the possibility of business stealing. Our first illustration in section 3.2.3 assumes that the new service offered by the entrants does not interfere with the incumbent's retail business; that is, the new service is pure value creation ($\delta = 0$). Our second illustration emphasizes the business-stealing effect.

deficit, equal to the non–traffic sensitive cost of the local loop and to the universal service deficit, would be covered through a lump-sum payment from the treasury.

In the absence of government subsidies, the incumbent must balance its budget by offering at least some, retail or wholesale, services at prices above marginal cost. There is thus a need for markups above cost. Recall from chapter 2 that optimal second-best prices for a regulated firm are Ramsey-Boiteux prices. These reflect marginal costs and demand elasticities so as to minimize the distortions brought about by the recovery of fixed costs. Reinterpreting demand as a residual demand given competitive offers, one immediately infers that Ramsey-Boiteux prices must also reflect competitive pressure on the firm's various segments. For instance, it is inefficient to tack a substantial markup over marginal cost on the price of a wholesale or retail service if this induces customers to purchase from a less efficient competitor or a product less adapted to their needs. Concretely, Ramsey-Boiteux prices reflect the possibility of bypass and cream skimming, which make the (residual) demand for the operator's services more elastic. Last, Ramsey-Boiteux prices take into account the complementarity or substitutability between services. For example, the price of a service should be higher when a price increase boosts demand for another service; that is, the division in charge of the former service should internalize the markup over marginal cost on the latter service. Conversely, the prices of complementary services should be set below the "myopic" levels that result from looking at the demand of individual products in isolation.

Putting together our two observations—the incumbent can be viewed as a supplier of multiple long-distance services, and optimal prices are Ramsey prices—yields optimal pricing formulas for the *retail* services, in particular the two long-distance services. The long-distance prices must in general exceed the corresponding marginal costs in order to contribute to the coverage of the deficit. The markups on these retail prices are higher, the higher the fixed costs to be covered are. The markup on a retail service should be higher, the lower the elasticity of demand for this service is and the less substitutable this and the other retail service are.

Because the price charged by long-distance entrants should involve a markup above marginal cost ($p_2 > 2c_0 + c_2$), so should the access charge they pay to the incumbent ($a = p_2 - c_2 > 2c_0$). We thus conclude that the wholesale price should, like the incumbent's retail prices, participate in the coverage of the network's fixed costs. It is inefficient to destroy the level playing field between the entrants and the incumbent by pricing access at marginal cost and thus applying no markup on the former's offering, and by concomitantly raising the markup on the incumbent's offerings. In other words, giving the incumbent responsibility for covering fixed network costs all by itself, and letting the entrants free ride on the provision of this public good distorts consumer choices toward the offerings of entrants if the incumbent's retail prices in the competitive segments are not aligned with those of the entrants. And, whether this alignment occurs or not, marginal-cost access pricing places the full burden of cost recovery on the incumbent's monopoly segments (such as the local retail services in our framework) implying large distortions in these segments.

3.2.3 Applications

We have observed that efficient access prices depend on demand as well as cost. That is, they are cost and usage based. This observation has several implications, which we illustrate through a series of examples.

3.2.3.1 Application 1: Third-Degree Price Discrimination in the Retail Segment (Elasticity-Based Access Pricing)

Let us first set aside the issue of substitution between the incumbent's wholesale and retail services associated with a cross-elasticity of demand for the retail services offered by the incumbent and the entrants. To this purpose, we assume in this application that technological or regulatory reasons prevent the incumbent from offering retail services that would compete with the entrants' services. We will thereby isolate the impact of the elasticity in the retail market on the efficient wholesale price. The impact of cross-elasticities will be studied in the next application.

The pricing of access should reflect conditions of demand in the retail market. Optimal third-degree price discrimination requires that the retail price be lower, the more elastic the demand in the retail market. Because competitive entrants charge purely cost-based retail prices and so are unable to price discriminate, this discrimination must be performed through the access charge. To do so requires that *the access charge be lower, the more elastic the demand in the final market.*

A simple illustration of this proposition goes as follows: Suppose that there are two retail markets labeled A and B. As mentioned earlier, we ignore rivalry by assuming that the incumbent offers no services in those markets (because of either line-of-business restrictions or his high marginal costs in those markets). Thus the delivery of these two independent final services is fully outsourced. Suppose that the services offered by the entrants in the two retail markets allow business users to economize on their production costs. They reduce production costs by v_A and v_B per unit, respectively, where $v_A > v_B$. That is, the retail service is more useful to end users in market A than in market B. The entrants' production cost, c_2, is otherwise the same in both markets. Let us assume that the service is socially valuable in both markets (so $v_B > 2c_0 + c_2$).

Optimal access prices are clearly usage based. Entrants in market A should be charged $a_A = v_A - c_2$, while entrants in market B (perhaps the same entrants) should pay $a_B = v_B - c_2$. This pricing policy enables the incumbent to obtain the maximal contribution toward the coverage of the network's fixed cost without creating any distortion in final consumption; thus, ceteris paribus, an entrant should pay a higher access charge, the less elastic the demand for the usage that is made of the interconnection facility.[2]

Note that a cost-based rule for pricing access ($a = 2c_0$) is inefficient because it deprives the incumbent of the opportunity to use markets A and B to reduce its deficit. Fixed costs must then be recouped by

---

2. Here, demands in markets A and B are "inelastic" up to the reservation prices, but the reservation prices differ in the two markets, so that the demand in market A should be considered less elastic than that in market B.

increasing prices and thus by raising distortions in consumption in other segments. A cost-based rule with a uniform markup, an often-recommended alternative to marginal-cost pricing of access, allows some recovery of the deficit in markets A and B in contrast with the pure cost-based rule, but again cannot discriminate between markets A and B.

Usage-based pricing of access conflicts with nondiscrimination rules that are encountered in most regulatory environments and is usually frowned upon in regulatory circles. The European Open Network Provision calls for nondiscrimination in access. In the United States, the Communications Act of 1934 barred carriers from practicing "unjust and unreasonable discrimination" in rates and conditions; section 251 of the Telecommunications Act of 1996, which supersedes the 1934 act, imposes more stringent standards by requiring that rates and conditions for interconnection be "just, reasonable, and nondiscriminatory."

Yet, usage-based pricing would seem natural to any marketing executive in the private sector. The same seat on a given flight can be priced in a range of 1 to 5 or 1 to 10 by the airline for different usages (occupational activity, date of purchase, length of stay, etc.). Or, academic journals fetch a very different price for students, researchers, and libraries. Ramsey pricing is but a transposition of standard marketing techniques to a regulated firm, and once it is understood that the wholesale services belong to the incumbent's overall product line, it should come as no surprise that efficient access pricing follows the standard marketing principles.

3.2.3.2 Application 2: Value-Creation versus Business-Stealing Impact of Entry (Cross-Elasticity–Based Access Pricing)

Let us now focus on the rivalry aspect. We noted that the incumbent's retail and wholesale services can be substitutes or complements. Its pricing of access should thus depend on whether the entrants create value (through product differentiation or cost efficiency, say) or merely steal customers away from the incumbent.

Again, an illustration may prove helpful. Suppose that prior to entry the incumbent supplies (among other products) at marginal cost c_1 a service, service 1, that economizes a known v_1 for business users. So, prior to entry, the incumbent charges price $p_1 = v_1$, and makes profit $v_1 - (2c_0 + c_1)$ per unit on the service, which can be used toward the coverage of the network's fixed cost. Suppose now that entrants can enter with a different service, service 2. This service's marginal cost is equal to that of service 1, $c_2 = c_1$, but service 2 reaches a new clientele that dislikes or is unable to consume service 1. This clientele is willing to pay v_2 per unit, where $2c_0 + c_2 < v_2 < v_1$. Its size is equal to β times the size of the incumbent's initial clientele. However, a fraction δ of the incumbent's clientele can switch to the new service offered by the entrants and values this service as much as the incumbent's service (that is, the new service also economizes v_1 for the incumbent's displaceable clientele). The complementary fraction $(1 - \delta)$ has no taste for service 2 or is unable to switch.

In order for the new service to create a new clientele, the access charge, a, must not exceed the new clientele's willingness to pay for the new service minus the entrants' marginal cost, that is $v_2 - c_2$. Conditional on creating a market for the entrants, the access charge is thus equal to $v_2 - c_2$, and the profit made on access is equal to $\beta[v_2 - (2c_0 + c_2)]$. However, the incumbent loses $[v_1 - (2c_0 + c_1)] - [v_2 - (2c_0 + c_1)] = v_1 - v_2$ on the "displaced" fraction δ of his customers who switch to the new service. (There is no point matching the entrants' price in order not to lose customers because doing so would not raise profit on potential switchers and would lower price for the nonswitchers.) If

$$\beta[v_2 - (2c_0 + c_2)] \geq \delta[v_1 - v_2]$$

that is, if the value creation exceeds the cost of business stealing, then entry does not reduce the incumbent's profit. It is then socially optimal to provide access at a price that generates entry, since consumers also enjoy extra surplus $\delta(v_1 - v_2)$.

Suppose now that

$$\delta(v_1 - v_2) > \beta[v_2 - (2c_0 + c_2)]$$

Whether it is socially optimal for the incumbent to deny access to the entrants depends on the magnitude of the cost-recovery problem. In the absence of the cost-recovery problem or if the firm's budget constraint is only mildly binding, entry should be allowed because it creates social surplus $\beta[v_2 - (2c_0 + c_2)]$ and the higher markup on the firm's other services needed to keep the budget balanced does not create much distortion. However, if the cost-recovery problem is serious and/or if the value creation is small (either because it affects a small number of new customers: β small; or because the value added per customer is small: $[v_2 - (2c_0 + c_2)]$ small), then access should be denied.

More generally, the incumbent may need to raise the access price[3] in order to avoid inefficient business stealing and balance his budget. In particular, for a given elasticity of demand for the entrants' service, the incumbent should charge a higher access charge, the higher the fraction of his own customers who switch to the new offering. Thus, ceteris paribus, the incumbent should charge higher access charges when entry is primarily motivated by the desire to divert lucrative segments from the incumbent and lower access charges when the entrants create value.

Again, such precepts correspond to standard business practice in the private sector. A division of a car manufacturer raises its prices if it competes directly with an affiliated division. More generally, marketing executives are wary about the possibility of "cannibalization" between products. Conversely, a razor manufacturing division sets a low price, perhaps below cost, for razors in order to boost the profit of the razor blade division. The fact that the telecommunications incumbent's interacting services include wholesale as well as retail service does not alter the general insight that optimal prices should reflect the complementarities or substitutabilities between products.

As for the other applications, it is worth noting that a purely cost-based rule for access ($a = 2c_0$) may incapacitate the cost-recovery process. This rule automatically generates entry under our assumption and prevents any arbitrage between value creation and business stealing.

Remark on the "Burden Test"   The condition $\beta[v_2 - (2c_0 + c_2)] < \delta(v_1 - v_2)$ is equivalent to a failure of the burden test (see Temin, 1997). The burden test, developed by William Baumol in the 1960s on behalf of AT&T,[4] is the ancestor of the efficient component pricing rule (see section 3.2.5). The repricing of an existing service or the pricing of a new

---

3. One can embellish this example by introducing two types of new customers who cannot be told apart by the entrants or the incumbent. Some value the new service at $v_2 < v_1$, as is the case here. Others value the new service at $v_3 \geq v_1$. Suppose that the proportion of those valuing the new service at v_2 relative to those valuing at v_3 is large enough that it is optimal to reach the low-valuation customers, that is, charge $p_2 = v_2$, when there is little or no business-stealing effect, that is, when $\delta \simeq 0$. An increase in business stealing, that is, in δ, may then raise the efficient access price from $v_2 - c_2$ to $v_3 - c_2$.

4. It was used by the FCC in a context markedly different from the one considered here. The issue was whether AT&T's low Telpak prices for private point-to-point communication were predatory. This difference has to be kept in mind, since the low price in our illustration is associated with a positive externality to consumers, while it was assessed

service fails the burden test if the gain from selling more of the service is outweighted by the loss of net revenue (revenue minus cost) from the firm's other services.

3.2.3.3   Application 3: Second-Degree Price Discrimination in the Retail Segment

Incumbents often offer menus of calling plans. For example,[5]. France Telecom has introduced a "low-user scheme" that offers a low monthly subscription fee (half the regular monthly fee) in exchange for a higher variable charge for calls (twice the per-minute regular charge). A slightly more complex low-user scheme had earlier been introduced in the United Kingdom.[6]. So far, so good: Economists have long insisted on the virtues of segmenting the market. For example, Willig (1978) showed that it is always possible to add additional two-part tariffs to an existing set of two-part tariffs and to generate a Pareto improvement, that is, to maintain or to increase the firm's profit, since the consumers are obviously made better off by the increased offering.

Concretely, the low-user scheme allows the incumbent to raise the nondistorting subscription fee for those consumers who value telecommunications services highly while still serving those consumers who might disconnect if they had to pay a high monthly fee—for example, owners of secondary residences, low-income consumers not covered by universal service programs, or simply consumers with limited demand for telephone services. Figure 3.4 illustrates the incumbent's offerings. For clarity, the regular scheme will be labeled the "high-user scheme," in contrast to the "low-user scheme."

Let us now introduce competition. For expository simplicity, besides connection, suppose that there is a single retail segment, long distance, and that the monthly subscription charge is paid to the incumbent, who owns the local loop bottleneck; that is, we simplify the basic para-

---

by the FCC in the Telpak case as inflicting a negative (long-term) externality on the consumers because of predation. Thus failure of the burden test is viewed as a *necessary* condition for avoiding a low access charge in our context, while it was viewed in the Telpak case as a *sufficient* condition for considering low prices as predatory.

5. Another example of menu offered by a bottleneck owner is the choice between measured service and a flat rate for local calls. Miravete (1997) provides an econometric analysis of second-degree price discrimination by a monopoly local exchange carrier, using data from a tariff experiment by South Central Bell in two cities in Kentucky in 1986.

6. Under the "light-user scheme" offered by BT in 1995, customers whose call charges placed them in the lowest 20% by usage could claim a tapered discount on line rental charges, up to a maximum rebate of 60% if no outgoing calls were made.

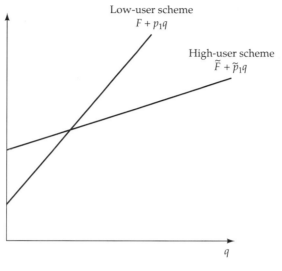

Figure 3.4
Optional calling plans

digm of section 3.1 by ignoring local calls. Thus, p_1 and $\tilde{p}_1$ are the per-minute prices charged by the incumbent for long-distance calls to the customers who elect the low-user scheme and the high-user scheme, respectively, where $\tilde{p}_1 < p_1$.

Entrants (Mercury in the United Kingdom and Cegetel in France, say) need access to the incumbent's local loop in order to compete in the long-distance market. A hotly debated issue is whether the entrants should pay a differentiated access charge (a and $\tilde{a}$, respectively) when obtaining access to the customers subscribing to the incumbent's low- and high-user schemes. Standard nondiscrimination rules as embodied in various directives and laws as well as the precept of cost-based access pricing suggest that such discrimination is unwarranted, implying that $a = \tilde{a}$. Regulators in the United Kingdom and in France, however, have taken a wholly different stance, without *formally* violating the nondiscrimination rule. Namely, they have allowed the incumbent to foreclose the entrants' access to those customers electing the low-user scheme. This regulation (which amounts to setting $a = +\infty$) has naturally infuriated the entrants, who complain that they are barred from competing for a substantial number of consumers. Though the entrants definitely have a point, the regulators and the incumbents in our opinion can lay out a very sound case in favor of discrimination. The culprit, as we will see, is the common lack of understanding of Ramsey access pricing reflected in the no-discrimination rule.

Our argument is simple. Suppose that access pricing is uniform: $a = \tilde{a}$. Consumers then choose among four two-part tariffs, namely the two (depicted in figure 3.4) offered by the incumbent and two offered by the entrants. Note, however, that, since $p_2 = \tilde{p}_2 = a + c_2$, one of the calling plans offered by the entrants dominates the other, namely, $F + p_2 q < \tilde{F} + \tilde{p}_2 q$ for all q. In words, consumers have an incentive to declare themselves "low users" rather than "high users" if they choose an entrant as their long-distance service provider; by so doing, they reduce their monthly fee and still get the same long-distance offering from the entrants.

It is now clear that uniform access pricing deprives the incumbent of its ability to offer an efficient menu of tariffs tailored to the needs of its clientele. Suppose, for instance, that the entrants' and the incumbent's long-distance services are reasonably close substitutes. First, consider setting the uniform access charge high enough, namely, in the vicinity of $p_1 - c_2$, for the incumbent to be able to compete with entrants for customers who select the low-user scheme. The entrants then cannot compete for high-user-scheme customers, as their total marginal cost, $a + c_2$, far exceeds the marginal price, $\tilde{p}_1$, charged by the incumbent for these customers. The entrants are then de facto prevented from competing for the high-end market. Now consider instead setting the uniform access charge low enough, say, in the vicinity of $\tilde{p}_1 - c_2$, so that the entrants and the incumbent can compete for the high-user-scheme customers. This policy, however, de facto eliminates the incumbent from the long-distance market, since its high-user scheme cannot compete with the overall tariff offered by the entrants. In sum the nondiscrimination rule leads to the abandonment by the incumbent of the distinction between high- and low-user schemes.

It is, therefore, important to allow discrimination in the access charge if we are to preserve optional calling plans. Entrants should pay a higher access charge when the calls originate from customers electing the low-user scheme ($a > \tilde{a}$). Box 3.2 makes this point more formally in a context in which it is socially optimal to offer a large number (technically, a continuum) of two-part tariffs to tailor offerings to the needs of a heterogenous clientele; see figure 3.5. Its main result, summarized in figure 3.6, is that *the efficient access charge paid by the entrants is a decreasing and convex function of the monthly fee paid by the customer to the incumbent.*

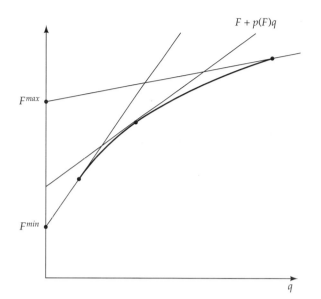

Figure 3.5
Optimal second-degree price discrimination

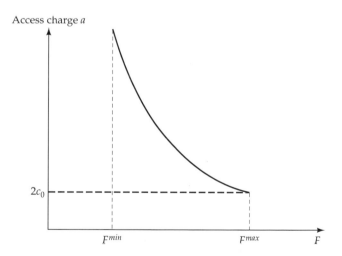

Figure 3.6
Discrimination in the access charge

Box 3.2
Optional Calling Plans and Access Pricing

(This box applies the analysis of Stole [1995] and Rochet and Stole [1997] to access pricing.)

The incumbent and the entrants offer two differentiated long-distance services. They are equally efficient in providing these services, and so their marginal costs are the same: $c_1 = c_2 = c$. As in the text we omit local calls for notational simplicity.

There is a continuum of consumers, indexed by a parameter θ, differentiated by their demand for long-distance calls. They choose either of the two long-distance services (incumbent or entrants). A consumer with type θ enjoys gross surplus $\theta V(q)$ from consuming q units of a long-distance service. When confronted with a tariff $T(q)$, this consumer chooses consumption $q(\theta)$ so as to maximize $\theta V(q) - T(q)$.

Let

$$U(\theta) \equiv \theta V[q(\theta)] - T[q(\theta)] \qquad (1)$$

The parameter θ is distributed in the population of consumers according to the cumulative distribution function $G(\theta)$, with density $g(\theta)$ on $[\underline{\theta}, \bar{\theta}]$. We make the standard assumption that the hazard rate $g(\theta)/[1 - G(\theta)]$ is increasing. (The monotone hazard rate condition is used in particular to guarantee concavity of the objective functions. See, e.g., Fudenberg and Tirole [1991, chap. 7] for more detail.)

The incumbent and the entrants are differentiated à la Hotelling. Consumers differ not only in their demand for long-distance calls, but also in their location x on a segment $[0, 1]$. The incumbent and the entrants are located at $x_1 = 0$ and $x_2 = 1$, respectively. A consumer with parameter (θ, x) then derives net surplus

$$U(\theta) - t|x - x_i|$$

from consuming from supplier $i, i = 1, 2$. We assume that consumers are located uniformly on the segment; this assumption, together with the overall symmetry of the model, implies that in a socially optimal allocation, half of the consumers, namely, those located at $x < 1/2$, should buy from the incumbent, and the other half, namely, those located at $x > 1/2$, should buy from an entrant. We further assume that $\underline{\theta} > 0$ and the "transportation cost" t is sufficiently small so that it is optimal to serve all customers; this assumption in turn implies that $U(\theta)$ should exceed the maximal "transportation cost," $t/2$, for all θ.

We first solve for the *Ramsey-Boiteux optimum* and then show how this social optimum can be implemented in a competitive environment. By symmetry, the Ramsey-Boiteux optimum is characterized by a consumption function $q(\theta)$ and a surplus function $U(\theta)$. Assuming that there is a cost-recovery problem, that is, that the budget constraint is binding, the Ramsey-Boiteux optimum is obtained by solving

$$\max_{\{q(\cdot), U(\cdot)\}} \int_{\underline{\theta}}^{\bar{\theta}} \left\{ \theta V[q(\theta)] - (2c_0 + c)q(\theta) \right\} g(\theta) d\theta$$

Box 3.2 (continued)

subject to

$$\int_{\underline{\theta}}^{\bar{\theta}} \left\{ \theta V[q(\theta)] - (2c_0 + c)q(\theta) - U(\theta) \right\} g(\theta)d\theta \geq k_0 \qquad (2)$$

$$\dot{U}(\theta) = V[q(\theta)] \qquad (3)$$

$$U(\underline{\theta}) = t/2 \qquad (4)$$

The objective function represents the expected gross surplus minus the expected variable cost; it omits two constant terms: the fixed cost k_0 of the local loop and the average transportation cost, $t/4$, per customer. Constraint (2) is obtained by eliminating transfers, using expression (1), from the budget constraint:

$$\int_{\underline{\theta}}^{\bar{\theta}} T[q(\theta)]g(\theta)d\theta \geq k_0 + \int_{\underline{\theta}}^{\bar{\theta}} (2c_0 + c)q(\theta)g(\theta)d\theta.$$

Constraint (3), obtained from expression (1) and the envelope theorem, gives the slope of the rent function. Last, constraint (4) says that all consumers subscribe to a long-distance service. We ignore the second-order conditions, which happen to be satisfied at the optimum.

The solution to this program is obtained in the standard way: One substitutes

$$U(\theta) = \frac{t}{2} + \int_{\underline{\theta}}^{\theta} V[q(\tau)]d\tau$$

into the budget constraint, and integrates by parts to obtain the following first-order condition:

$$\theta V'[q(\theta)] = (2c_0 + c) + \frac{\lambda}{1 + \lambda} \frac{1 - G(\theta)}{g(\theta)} V'[q(\theta)] \qquad (5)$$

where λ is the shadow cost of the budget constraint.

Let

$$p(q) = T'(q) = \theta V'(q) \qquad (6)$$

denote the marginal price. Then

$$\frac{p - (2c_0 + c)}{p} = \frac{\lambda}{1 + \lambda} \frac{1 - G(\theta)}{\theta g(\theta)} \qquad (7)$$

Condition (7) can be interpreted as the standard inverse elasticity rule (see Tirole [1988, pp. 154–158] for more detail). Furthermore, it is easily shown that equations (6) and (7) define (after eliminating θ) an increasing and concave schedule $T(q)$, so that the optimal allocation can be implemented through a menu of two-part tariffs

$$T_F(q) = F + p(F)q$$

where $p(F)$ decreases with F as depicted in figure 3.5 (Laffont and Tirole, 1986; Tirole, 1988, pp. 157). Note also that equation (7) implies that for $\theta = \bar{\theta}$, $p(F^{max}) = 2c_0 + c$ (price equals marginal cost), and so there is "no distortion at the top."

Let us now come to the *implementation of the Ramsey-Boiteux optimum in a context in which service 2 is provided by entrants*. Second-degree price discrimination

Box 3.2 (continued)

by providers of service 2 must be induced by discriminatory access charges. Specifically, suppose that entrants must pay per-unit access charge $a(F)$ to serve customers paying monthly subscription fee F to the incumbent. Such customers electing to be served by entrants face a two-part tariff

$$\hat{T}_F(q) = F + [a(F) + c]q$$

For $\hat{T}_F(\cdot)$ to coincide with $T_F(\cdot)$, it must be the case that

$$a(F) = p(F) - c$$

Thus the access charge decreases with F. Furthermore,

$$a(F^{max}) = 2c_0$$

The definition of $a(F)$ and the consumer's optimization over the choice of two-part tariff for a given consumption imply that

$$\frac{da}{dF} = \frac{dp}{dF} = -\frac{1}{q}$$

and so

$$\frac{d^2a}{dF^2} > 0$$

as claimed.

This access charge exceeds the marginal cost of providing access, except for the highest-demand consumers for which the access charge is equal to marginal cost ($a = 2c_0$).

3.2.3.4 Application 4: Peak-Load Access Pricing

Our last illustration of efficient access prices is a straightforward one: time-of-day pricing. The bottleneck's capacity may be fully employed part of the day (peak period) and be partly used during the rest of the day (off peak). The entrants should internalize the variations in the congestion cost (zero off peak, substantial on peak) that they impose on the incumbent's bottleneck. Thus, in theory, the access charge should be substantially higher on peak than off peak.

A uniform or slightly differentiated access charge that would purport to be some average of optimal peak and off-peak charges would have grave consequences for the exploitation of the bottleneck. The entrants would be prevented from competing off peak with an incumbent who (efficiently) offers its customers off-peak discounts. Conversely, the entrants would overutilize the bottleneck on peak, forcing the incumbent to ration the use of the bottleneck, or to curtail its own services, or else to engage in wasteful investments in peak capacity.

Box 3.3
Peak-Load Access Charges

Consider the following simple and symmetric example of competition in long distance. Demands for the long-distance services offered by the incumbent (service 1) and by the entrants (service 2) are given by

$$q_1 = \mu D(p_1, p_2)$$

and

$$q_2 = \mu D(p_2, p_1)$$

where $D(\cdot, \cdot)$ is a constant-elasticity demand function. The variable μ is equal to μ^L off peak and μ^H on peak, where $0 < \mu^L < \mu^H$. We further assume that the incumbent's and entrants' marginal costs on the local loop and the long-distance segment are c_0^L and c^L off peak and $c_0^H = K c_0^L$ and $c^H = K c^L$ on peak, where $K > 1$. The increments, $(K-1)c_0^L$ and $(K-1)c^L$, represent the marginal costs of adding capacity, that is, the difference between short- and long-run marginal costs. Note that we implicitly assume that there is no "shifting peak," in that low pricing off peak derived from the absence of capacity constraint does not make the capacity constraint binding off peak.

At the Ramsey optimum, the (symmetric) retail price charged by the incumbent and the entrants to consumers, p^τ, depends on the time of the day ($\tau = L, H$), and satisfies the inverse elasticity rule:

$$\frac{p^\tau - (2c_0^\tau + c^\tau)}{p^\tau} = \frac{\lambda}{1 + \lambda} \frac{1}{\hat{\eta}}$$

where $\hat{\eta}$ is the superelasticity (see box 3.1). And so

$$p^H = K p^L$$

Efficient access prices are given by

$$a^\tau = p^\tau - c^\tau$$

and so

$$a^H = K a^L$$

In this very special example, the time-of-day modulation of access charges mirrors the variations in marginal cost.

While the theory of peak-load access pricing is straightforward (see box 3.3 for an example), its application in practice is complex, especially if the regulator sets the structure of access prices herself. Even a perfect knowledge of the short-run and long-run marginal costs of the bottleneck does not enable a regulator to determine the incumbent's marginal cost of giving access to entrants. Peak and off-peak periods are endogenous and depend on the demand functions and the pricing structures and levels of the incumbent and the entrants. Thus, even if there were no cost-recovery problem so that efficient access charges could be set equal to the marginal costs of providing access, the setting of efficient access charges would still require a fine knowledge of demand and entry variables.

3.2.4   Access Markup or Retail Tax on Entrants?

It should be noted here that the entrants' contribution toward the fixed cost of the network could alternatively be provided through a retail tax on the entrants' offerings that would be paid back to the incumbent. The level of this tax should be set equal to the previous markup, $a - 2c_0$, on the access charge; the access charge should then be set equal to marginal cost. The two policies are equivalent here, since the entrants have a fixed demand for the local loop per minute of long-distance output.

A markup on access and a tax on entrants differ when the entrants can use alternative (bypass) technologies to get access to the end users. A markup on access then creates an incentive for the entrants to over-invest in these alternative technologies; that is, they will bypass the incumbent whenever the cost of bypass is lower than the access charge, and these situations include those in which the incumbent supplier is a superior provider of access (see figure 3.7). Suppose that a competitive access provider (CAP) can offer access at marginal cost, $\hat{c}_0$, greater than the incumbent's marginal cost but lower than the access charge: $c_0 < \hat{c}_0 < a$ (or alternatively that the CAP has the same marginal cost, $\hat{c}_0 = c_0$ as the incumbent, but incurs a small enough fixed cost when duplicating part of the incumbent's network). Then end users at the originating end, who are those who pay for phone calls, have an incentive to turn to the CAP to obtain access to the long-distance operators. This bypass, however, is socially inefficient, since the end users do not make use of the cheaper facilities offered by the incumbent at the originating end.

It is widely acknowledged that the raison d'être of entry by CAPs such as MFS and Teleport in the 1980s in the U.S. central business districts was the existence of large markups on regulated charges for access to the local exchange carriers' (LECs') networks. Businesses, government agencies, or universities could thereby obtain better rates for long-distance calls by connecting to long-distance operators through the CAPs.

Although a tax on the incumbent's rival reconciles the objectives of universal participation to the coverage of the network's cost and (in

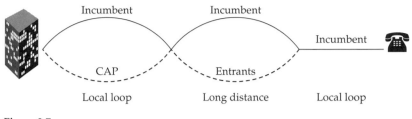

Figure 3.7
Bypass at the originating end

the presence of bypass opportunities) of cost-based pricing of access, it should be noted that this tax should depend on the usage that is made of the network. We should point out, furthermore, that such a tax is politically unlikely and that it is almost never mentioned in the regulatory debate, even though it could in principle be repackaged as a tax on the whole industry (as will be the case for the funding of universal service) in order not to make it look discriminatory. We will, therefore, proceed as if it were infeasible, keeping in mind that depriving oneself of this instrument may generate inefficiencies in the presence of bypass opportunities.

3.2.5 Relationship to the Efficient Component Pricing Rule

We may wonder whether the efficient pricing of access satisfies the *efficient component pricing rule* (ECPR). This rule, first proposed by Robert Willig (1979) and variously called the parity pricing principle or the Baumol-Willig rule (after its two main proponents), has been argued before courts and regulatory agencies in several industries throughout the world. It is a partial (incomplete) regulatory rule that links retail and wholesale prices. ECPR forces the incumbent to charge an access price that does not exceed its *opportunity cost* on the competitive segment. In our notation,

$$a \leq p_1 - c_1$$

To understand this condition, suppose that an entrant diverts one minute of long-distance phone call from the incumbent. This stealing of business costs the incumbent an amount equal to the markup on his long-distance offering, $p_1 - (2c_0 + c_1)$, plus the marginal cost of giving access, $2c_0$, to the entrant. The marginal cost of access, of course, washes out in this calculation of the incumbent's opportunity cost, since the local loops must be used regardless of the identity of the long-distance operator. The loss in revenue for the incumbent is thus equal to the difference, $p_1 - c_1$, between his retail price and his marginal cost on the competitive segment. For future reference, this cost c_1 on the competitive segment is often called in regulatory proceedings the *avoided cost*.[7]

An alternative and equivalent approach to ECPR is the so-called *imputation* procedure. Suppose that the incumbent's long-distance service is provided by a separate division (or subsidiary) and that there is proper "accounting separation," in that transfers between local and other operations of the incumbent and the long-distance division are fully transparent (we will discuss the limits of accounting separation in section 4.3). Assuming away any fixed cost of long-distance operations, and taking the incumbent's long-distance price as given, let us compute the maximum access charge that the local network division can set for its long-distance affiliate without forcing the latter to lose money. This (fictitious) access charge clearly must satisfy $p_1 - (a + c_1) \geq 0$, and so we are back to ECPR.[8]

Baumol, Willig, and others have repeatedly stressed that the proper yardstick for defining access prices is that of the perfectly contestable market and that, when supplying an intermediate good to another firm, a supplier must be permitted to price the intermediate good at a level sufficient to compensate it for the sacrifice in profit due to the supply to the other firm. The expected social benefits of charging the opportunity cost for interconnection are as follows (see, e.g., Baumol and Sidak, 1994a, 1994b):

1. The rule sends the right signal to entrants. Potential entrants can enter profitably if and only if they are more efficient than the telephone

---

7. The link between ECPR and Baumol's "burden test" (see section 3.2.3.2) goes as follows: A reduction in the price of the incumbent's wholesale service (that is, in the access charge) generates an increase in the volume of wholesale transactions, creating a surplus $a - 2c_0$ on each added unit. If we make the (strong) assumption that the increase in the volume of wholesale transactions is offset one-for-one by a decrease in the incumbent's retail transactions, which generate per-unit profit $p_1 - (2c_0 + c_1)$, then the burden test is satisfied if and only if the extra gain in the wholesale market outweighs the loss in the retail market, or

$$a - 2c_0 \geq p_1 - (2c_0 + c_1) \Leftrightarrow a \geq p_1 - c_1$$

8. There are in general some nuances distinguishing ECPR and the imputation rule. See Hausman and Tardiff (1995) for a detailed discussion of imputation.

operator. Indeed, note that they must charge at least their total (access plus long-distance) cost, $a + c_2$, but less than the incumbent's long-distance price p_1, if they are to make a profit. Under ECPR the entrants' total marginal cost is equal to the incumbent's long-distance price minus the entrants' cost advantage (or plus the entrants' cost disadvantage), $a + c_2 = p_1 - (c_1 - c_2)$, and so only a cost advantage can generate entry.

2. Entry has no effect on (is neutral regarding) operating profit for the telephone operator. This fact has several consequences. Entry on the competitive segment does not interfere with the historical cross-subsidization of the bottleneck segment by the competitive segment; this benefit has been a powerful political argument because politicians are eager to maintain the subsidies embodied in the connection of remotely located households or in the pricing of local calls. More important from an economic viewpoint, revenue neutrality also reduces the telephone operator's incentive to destroy the level playing field by skimping on (or even deliberately degrading) the quality of access. These two properties have deservedly attracted attention, and certainly have contributed much to the popularity of ECPR.

The conceptual framework advanced to defend ECPR—contestable market theory—makes strong assumptions and yet does not provide completely convincing foundations for the necessity of the ECP rule. Standard perfectly contestable market theory (Baumol, Panzar, and Willig, 1982) assumes that all firms (incumbents and entrants) face identical cost functions and the same demand function in the competitive segment. Because it also abstracts from incentive issues, it provides no reason for having more than a single firm in the competitive segment in the absence of diminishing returns in that segment. So in the standard framework of cost symmetry, there is no clear motivation for entry. Proponents of ECPR, therefore, must have in mind an extension of perfectly contestable market theory in which entrants are (at least sometimes) more efficient than the telephone operator in the competitive segment, that is, in which $c_2 < c_1$. However, ECPR implies that the entrants undercut the incumbent, $a + c_2 < p_1$, if entrants are more cost efficient, $c_2 < c_1$, and therefore that the telephone operator in equilibrium supplies only access and exits the competitive segment. The access price defines who (incumbent or entrants) will corner the potentially competitive segment. But the prediction of absence of in-market competition is too stark.

One should not nitpick on this particular aspect of the argument of ECPR proponents. Indeed, we do not view this argument as building an important case against ECPR. The unpalatable property of absence of competition can be eliminated as just shown; the framework that we have described builds on the useful insights of the proponents of ECPR to develop a reference model delivering actual competition on the competitive segment. This model introduces product differentiation as a motivation for competition[9] and allows cost and demand asymmetries between the telephone operator and the competitors.

Let us consider the following assumption:

Full Symmetry Assumption
The symmetry assumption consists of two maintained assumptions and two new assumptions:

• *Symmetric cost of providing access:* The incumbent's marginal costs of providing access to itself and to entrants are the same.

• *No entrant market power:* Entrants behave competitively given the access charge and their marginal cost on the competitive segment.

• *Demand symmetry on the competitive segment:* The demand functions faced by the incumbent and the entrants on the competitive segment are symmetrical.

• *Cost symmetry on the competitive segment:* The incumbent's and the entrants' marginal costs on the competitive segment are equal.

Some readers may wonder why "no entrant market power" is a symmetry assumption. After all the incumbent is the only supplier of service 1 on the competitive segment; but recall that the incumbent is regulated and therefore in principle cannot exploit his market power on the competitive segment.

A simple but powerful result emerges: *The efficient access charge satisfies ECPR under full symmetry.*[10] The proof is straightforward: Under symmetry, the incumbent and the entrants should charge equal prices, $p_1 = p_2$. The access charge then satisfies

---

9. This extension is also suggested by Baumol and Sidak (1994a, p. 109), who argue that, in practice, the business an entrant gains is not always business lost by the incumbent; entrants offer differentiated services and also "beat the bushes for customers who were not previous users of the product in question."

10. The absence of fixed entry cost is assumed all along. See the next section for the introduction of entry costs.

$$a = p_2 - c_2 = p_1 - c_1$$

that is, ECPR.

When there is an asymmetry along at least one of the four dimensions (access cost, market power, retail demand, and retail cost), ECPR is in general not satisfied by optimal prices. Corrections must then be included that take the access price below or above the ECPR level.

For instance, suppose that because of brand loyalty or name recognition a fraction of the incumbent's customers are captive and do not consider switching to the entrants. As a result, the demand curve faced by the incumbent is more inelastic than that faced by the entrants. The incumbent accordingly should charge a higher price than entrants on the competitive segment ($p_1 > p_2$). Hence under access and retail cost symmetry the access charge ($a = p_2 - c_2$) should be set below the incumbent's opportunity cost ($p_1 - c_1$), that is, below the ECPR level.

Suppose, next, that the incumbent and the entrants differ in their retail cost, $c_1 \neq c_2$, and that they face symmetric and linear demand curves. The low-cost operator (incumbent or entrant) must then charge the lowest price. But the price difference does not fully reflect the cost difference. Indeed, "cost absorption" is implied by linear demands. So, for instance, if the incumbent is the low-cost operator, $p_2 - p_1 < c_2 - c_1$, this fact implies that $a = p_2 - c_2 < p_1 - c_1$, and so the access charge lies below the incumbent's opportunity cost. Conversely, if entrants are more cost efficient, the access charge should exceed the incumbent's opportunity cost.

While such corrections should be included in practice, we view ECPR as a useful benchmark for the subsequent discussion.

3.2.6 Recap

We conclude this section with a summary of the main economic principles governing efficient access pricing:

• Wholesale and retail prices must together contribute to the recovery of the network's fixed costs. A cost-based pricing of access generally tilts the level playing field toward inefficient entry in the contested segments and forces the incumbent to shift the burden of recovery to consumption in monopolized retail segments.

• Efficient access charges are cost and usage based. They decrease with the elasticity of the demand for the usage that is made of the interconnection facility; they also reflect the relative magnitudes of value creation and business diversion associated with entry.

• Efficient access charges satisfy ECPR under full symmetry (access cost, retail-demand and retail-cost symmetry, and absence of entrants' market power), but in its absence the two criteria do not generally coincide.

3.3   Refining the Theory: Lack of Instruments and Multiple Goals for Interconnection Charges

This section refines the theoretical analysis of section 3.2 by allowing for entrants' market power on the retail market, bypass of the whole-sale segment, and incentive-for-cost-minimization considerations. The uninitiated reader is advised to skip this section, which is not needed to understand the subsequent ones.

In the idealized case developed in the previous section, the setting of the access charge had a single purpose; it was only meant to regulate the otherwise undistorted price of the competitors' good and thereby obtain a proper rate structure in the competitive segment, given that the prices in that segment ought to include a markup contributing to the coverage of the fixed cost. In practice, the need to cover the deficit is not the only source of distortion.

First, entrants may themselves have market power. This arises in particular when there are large fixed entry costs. Two new distortions may appear in such situations. The competitor's price (or competitors' prices) includes a markup above its perceived marginal cost (that is, its marginal cost plus the unit access charge). And, if entry costs are large, entry may not occur even when it is socially desirable.

Second, as we noted earlier, the bottleneck segment may not be a pure bottleneck. Although expensive, entry on that segment is feasible. Two widely noted paradigms, the bypass and the network duplication paradigms, have been the object of intense policy debate in the telecommunications industry. On the one hand, large business customers (perhaps through a competitive access provider) may be able to bypass the local loop and connect directly to a long-distance company in order to economize the markup on the access charge. On the other hand, the incumbent's long-distance competitors can install a second local network either by themselves or by entering an agreement with a cable, water, or electricity company. Ensuring that the right amount of bypass and of network duplication occurs provides two more targets for public policy.

Third, as we discussed in chapter 2, the incumbent may not produce efficiently when the regulators' imperfect technological information prevents them from imposing cost minimization. A new target for
public policy is then to create proper incentives for cost minimization
while not giving excessive rents to the incumbent. Should the interconnection policy contribute to the definition of proper incentives for
the incumbent? For example, it has been argued in regulatory proceedings that ECPR neglects the fact that the incumbent's marginal cost on
the bottleneck segment may be inflated, unduly penalizing the entrants
through a high access charge. Baumol's response to this criticism has
been that the access charge has no role in regulating incentives and that
other controls are needed for the purpose.

These three classes of further concerns can be analyzed as follows.
More goals require more instruments. If these further instruments are
available to the regulators, what we have said needs only to be reinterpreted. However, those instruments may not belong to the regulatory
toolbox, particularly because of the separation of powers. The access
charge then needs to contribute to the achievement of conflicting goals.
It becomes a "jack of all trades and master of none."

3.3.1   Entrants' Market Power

Let us first consider the case of large fixed entry costs.

3.3.1.1   *Profitable Entry*
Suppose that, because of a large fixed entry cost, the incumbent faces
a single entrant on the competitive segment. This competitor charges a
markup above its marginal cost $a + c_2$.

The analysis is straightforward when the competitor's profit (net of
the fixed entry cost) can be taxed and redistributed to the incumbent.
The profit tax disposes of the issue of capturing the competitor's profit
to contribute to the coverage of the fixed cost. The access price, as earlier, only guides the competitor's final price. It should be reduced so
as to exactly offset the markup imposed by the competitor. This yields
the same price structure on the competitive segment and does not affect the incumbent's budget relative to the case in which the competitor
charges its marginal cost. The new distortion is eliminated by a reduction in the access charge computed so as to yield the Ramsey price once
the competitor's markup m is added to $a + c_2$.

For example, recall from the previous section that in the symmetric case the optimal access charge obeys the ECPR. In the presence of

competitor market power, the optimal access charge is equal to the ECP level minus the competitor's unit markup m:[11]

$$a = p_1 - c_1 - m$$

We thus obtain an "ECP–m" rule.

However, the redistribution of the competitor's profit to the incumbent is likely to be unrealistic. In the absence of such taxation, the access price is assigned a second role; namely, it must substitute for the missing profit tax to limit the competitor's rent. The access price is then raised above the ECP–m level, and can even in some circumstances exceed the ECP level.[12]

3.3.1.2   Unprofitable Entry

Our analysis so far has assumed that the competitor is profitable, so that its entry is not an issue. This assumption is not realistic for very large fixed costs; the challenge then becomes to raise the entrant's profit to the break-even point rather than to capture its excess profit.[13]

We can apply the previous argument. The ECP–m rule still obtains (in the symmetric case) when a lump-sum subsidy is feasible. The lump-sum subsidy is then to be included in the computation of the access deficit as yet another unallocated cost.

But suppose now that the lump-sum transfer to the entrant is not feasible. Then the access charge must subsidize entry. One correspondingly obtains a "below ECP–m" access price:

$$a < p_1 - c_1 - m$$

This policy has been extensively used to promote entry in the telecommunications industry. Mercury has benefited in the past from generous access conditions. (Its "access deficit contribution" has often been waived, so it has benefited from access charges below marginal cost and even equal to zero.) Similarly, the access charge paid by MCI and

---

11. In general this unit markup m depends on the access charge. So this equation should be understood as determining a and m endogenously.

12. The exact nature of the correction depends on the kind of competition the firms are waging; see Masmoudi and Prothais (1994) for Cournot competition and Laffont and Tirole (1994) for price competition.

13. It may be socially beneficial to subsidize an unprofitable entrant because the latter does not internalize the full social value of its entry. However, the subsidy policy may be dangerous for various reasons associated with incomplete information (capture, irreversible errors, . . .).

Sprint has not reflected their high connection cost to the local exchange companies compared with AT&T. This "asymmetric regulation" is now often perceived as dangerous because it may induce entry by inefficient firms.

3.3.2   Bypass and Network Duplication

New policy issues arise when the incumbent's natural monopoly position in the bottleneck segment is challenged. In particular, concern has been expressed that bypass and network duplication (PBXs, cellular, competitive access providers), which in specific instances provides cost savings or complements the public switched telephone network, in general may prevent the exploitation of substantial economies of scope.

3.3.2.1   Bypass

Large long-distance customers oftentimes can establish a radio link or lay a cable in order to connect directly with the incumbent's long-distance competitors. Such bypass may be socially efficient. Yet the inclusion of a markup into the access price may give large customers an excessive incentive to bypass the local loop.

Regulatory policy must now be concerned with inducing the efficient amount of bypass. In essence, it needs one more instrument. This is where the distinction between access charge and excise tax made in section 3.2.4 becomes important. The use of an excise tax (perceived by the incumbent) to help cover the access deficit frees the access charge from its deficit recovery role. The access charge can then be used to guide large customers in their bypass decisions.

The division of labor between the access charge and the excise tax works *roughly* as indicated in the following reasonable rule of thumb:[14] To provide the large customers with the right signal, the access charge is set near the marginal cost of access. The excise tax then picks up the access deficit contribution; in the case of full symmetry in the competitive segment (see section 3.2.5), the excise tax is set approximately equal to the incumbent's opportunity cost on the competitive segment.

In practice, however, regulators usually have no mandate to levy taxes in their industry, even though they regulate the incumbent's final prices. In the absence of excise tax, the access price must now arbitrate

---

14. See Laffont and Tirole (1994) for more details. "Roughly" refers to the fact that bypass affects the total marginal cost of long-distance calls, and to the regulator's desire to extract some of the bypassers' rent.

between two conflicting goals. A low access price prevents wasteful bypass but substantially increases the incumbent's deficit. The incumbent must then set its price on the competitive segment even higher and may well be squeezed out of that segment. This move toward a de facto (rather than de jure) vertical separation not only deprives the competitive segment of one of its main actors, but also raises the question of how the cost of the local loop is to be recovered.

We thus come to the following conclusions. It seems logical to depart from custom and to let the regulator (when feasible) regulate the competitors' prices through an excise tax designed to cover the network's fixed cost. To be certain, a tax set by regulators is more information demanding than a price decision delegated to the firm. Furthermore, it is risky to extend regulatory powers in this direction. Indeed, we conjecture that the combination of limited statutory powers (the regulators are prevented from regulating the entrants) and of a mechanistic access pricing rule is intended to prevent regulatory capture by the industry by freeing entrants from regulatory control.

If one is concerned with this extension of regulatory powers, there is a particularly strong case for allowing substantial quantity discounts in the pricing of access. While quantity discounts are no panacea, they exploit well the fact that high-demand customers are those with the highest incentive to bypass.[15] The incumbent can profitably offer a menu of two-part tariffs, with the fixed fee inversely related to the per-unit charge.[16] Small customers would be charged (or rather would select) a low fixed fee with a high per-unit charge (which in practice would be collected by the long-distance operators and repaid to the incumbent). The main change relative to the present situation is that large customers would choose to pay a high fixed fee in order to face a low per-unit charge (close to marginal cost of access).

---

15. See Laffont and Tirole (1990c) and Curien, Jullien, and Rey (1998).

16. It is interesting to note in this respect that the California Public Utility Commission accepted the argument according to which quantity discounts on access prices can prevent uneconomic bypass, and estimated that the corresponding efficiency gain overshadows a potential favoritism in favor of AT&T and to the disadvantage of smaller interexchange carriers (PUC of the State of California, 1994, pp. 123–126). The California decision came in response to GTEC's "Switch Access Volume Election" (SAVE) proposal. The SAVE plan offers volume discounts on access to compete with high-speed digital private lines. (Interestingly, a higher threshold of originating minutes of use than terminating minutes of use is required to qualify for SAVE credits. Bypass is more common at the originating end than at the terminating end. This fact also provides a rationale for charging higher access prices at the terminating end than at the originating end.)

3.3.2.2   *Network Duplication*

While bypass is, say, the phenomenon in which large customers dispense with the incumbent's services to reach the competitors on the long-distance market, network duplication consists in the competitors' building a local network in order to reach customers who would not have bypassed by themselves. Network duplication substitutes advantageously for individual bypass when bypass connections exhibit returns of scope among customers. Network duplication is often quite costly, and its main justification is that it facilitates the regulatory task of providing incentives for low costs in the local loops.

Taking for granted the optimality of network duplication, the arguments laid out in the discussion of entry in the competitive segment resurface in the analysis of entry in the complementary segment. One could either encourage the building of a rival network through a subsidy, or, if subsidies are not available, charge high access prices in order to discourage the use of the incumbent's network by its competitors.[17] One should also note that, if network duplication is contemplated, the rival networks should face the same universal service obligations as the incumbent network. That is, networks should be treated symmetrically.

3.3.3   Access Charges and Incentives for Cost Minimization

The analysis has until now ignored the important issue of the incumbent's incentive to minimize cost. One may wonder, as some policy analysts and judiciary do, whether access charges should also be employed for cost-minimization purposes.

3.3.3.1   *Incentives to Minimize Bottleneck Cost*

In Laffont and Tirole (1994) we offered a comprehensive analysis of the impact of incentive considerations on pricing. We showed in particular that under some conditions pricing and incentives issues are decoupled.[18] That is, the price formulas are the same as when the regulator has perfect information about the technology and incentives are not an

---

17. Let us here note that the latter policy (high access charge as an inducement for network building) may require discrimination in access prices, for most suppliers in the competitive segments using the local loop will not build their own network and will need to face a reasonable access price.

18. This is the "dichotomy property." Technically, it holds whenever quantity levels do not affect rates at which technological improvements can be converted into rents by the firm. Incentives are then provided solely by the cost reimbursement rule.

issue. In particular, the Ramsey formulas described in section 3.2 still hold for the realization of marginal costs, whether or not these marginal costs are inflated by the incumbent's poor incentives. We feel that this decoupling is a reasonable rule of thumb in the absence of detailed information about the cost function. (Incidentally, it provides a foundation for Baumol's position that the access price is not meant to correct poor incentives for cost minimization.)

3.3.3.2   Incentives to Minimize Cost on the Competitive Segment

The previous decoupling applies equally well to the incumbent's incentives on the competitive segment as long as the behavior of the incumbent's competitors does not provide information about the incumbent's cost structure on that segment. Recall that we assumed that the competitors' marginal cost is a known c_2. More generally, their marginal cost could be unknown to the regulator as long as it does not convey information about the incumbent's cost structure. That competition per se brings no information about the incumbent's costs may be a reasonable assumption if the competitors use a different technology. In contrast, when technologies on the competitive segment are similar, one may use the competitors' performance as a benchmark to control the incumbent's efficiency. This "yardstick competition" (also called relative performance evaluation or benchmarking) is indeed one of the arguments for the creation of competition.

Are the access pricing principles altered when benchmarking is a further motivation for competition? To take a simple example, suppose that the regulators do not know the incumbent's marginal cost function on the competitive segment. They only know that, regardless of this function, entrants suffer a per-unit cost disadvantage equal to some Δ. ($\Delta > 0$ would be due to some experience advantage or unique access to a scarce resource; $\Delta < 0$ might stem from the use of a more technologically advanced input by the entrants.) Because the cost differential is known to the regulators, entry by competitive entrants perfectly reveals the incumbent's technology. So, in this highly stylized example, yardstick competition brings us back to the case of complete information.

We can thus apply the results of section 3.2.5 to state that in the symmetric linear demand case (see section 3.2.5 for a further correction in case of asymmetric demand), the access price should lie below its ECP level, $p_1 - c_1$, if $\Delta > 0$ and above it if $\Delta < 0$. Although a more general analysis would be welcome, we conclude that there is no incompatibility between the principles we have formulated and the yardstick motivation for competition. The new insight is that entry may be desirable even if the entrants enjoy no cost advantage over the incumbent and produce a close substitute on the competitive segment. The gains from yardstick competition are larger, the less regulators are informed about the incumbent's technology on the competitive segment, and the more similar the incumbent's and the competitors' technologies.[19]

3.4   Two Specific Concerns and Some Common Misperceptions about Ramsey Access Pricing

As we will see, the old practice and the new reforms all depart from the theoretical precepts just described, at the cost of substantial inefficiencies. Indeed, it is fair to say that the participants in the current regulatory debate are on the whole suspicious of Ramsey access pricing.[20] In our view, this mistrust is an amalgam of a legitimate concern that Ramsey pricing of access might be miscast within an otherwise incoherent regulatory framework, and of a misapprehension of its implications.

Two specific objections have been leveled at Ramsey prices: informational requirements and violation of the nondiscrimination rules.

3.4.1   Informational Requirements

Academic economists and policymakers both often argue that regulators do not have the information to set Ramsey prices. One leg of the argument, namely, the widespread shortage of relevant information, is correct. Regulatory agencies have a much smaller staff and less contact with markets than telecommunications operators.

But taken as a whole, this argument should look unconvincing to any observer of unregulated businesses. The latter indeed engage in sophisticated marketing strategies. They offer discounts to high-elasticity-of-demand customers, adjust their prices to competitive pressure, and

---

19. We should also note that in practice yardstick competition is likely to reveal more information about the incumbent's technology only if the competitors' market share is nonnegligible, so that the incumbent and its rival(s) operate in similar parts of the cost function.

20. This suspicion transpires in most regulatory documents. See, e.g. Oftel's consultative documents (December 1994, pp. 15–16; December 1995, p. 27), the WIK/EAC report commissioned by the European Union (1994, pp. 74–76), and the arguments leading to the adoption of forward-looking costs in the U.S. Telecommunications Act of 1996.

carefully coordinate the pricing of substitutes or complements. The *structure* of unregulated firms' prices (though not the level if the firms have substantial market power) thus reflects Ramsey-Boiteux precepts. This observation suggests that the most promising alley for implementing Ramsey prices in a regulatory context is to decentralize pricing decisions to the operator.

The idea of decentralizing pricing decisions may be foreign to those who favor heavy regulatory intervention. Yet, a key feature of the regulatory revolution of the 1980s was departure from the detailed setting of individual prices and flexibility to operators to adjust their price structure to demand and competitive pressure conditions. While the implications of this revolution for access prices have been overlooked (and will be the object of sections 4.7 and 4.8), we still find it surprising that regulators who routinely design price caps dismiss offhand Ramsey pricing as being informationally infeasible!

3.4.2   The Rhetoric of "Fair and Nondiscriminatory" Access Prices

We have observed that optimal access prices are usage based and thus discriminatory. Most experts oppose this implication of Ramsey access pricing and argue in favor of "fair and nondiscriminatory" access prices, a phrase that originated in the competition policy treatment of wholesale markets (e.g., the Robinson-Patman Act of 1936 in the United States) and made its way into almost all regulatory statutes governing the incumbents' wholesale transactions.

The ban on wholesale price discrimination applies to second- and third-degree price discrimination. Second-degree price discrimination consists in offering two different units at two different prices; for example, a two-part tariff involves a fixed fee as well as a variable price and thus implies a steep discount after the first unit of consumption. Menus of two-part tariffs, such as AT&T's retail optional calling plans[21] or the 80–90 percent discounts below retail currently offered by the U.S. long-distance carriers in wholesale transactions, also involve second-degree price discrimination. Third-degree price discrimination in contrast refers to the offering of different tariffs to different categories of users or, by stretching the definition of third-degree price discrimination a bit, for different usages (mobile, data, video, etc.). To be sure, exceptions have been made and have allowed operators to practice

---

21. See Mitchell and Vogelsang (1991) for a description.

some price discrimination at the wholesale level. In the United States, local exchange carriers have been given some flexibility to offer whole-sale discounts to respond to competitive access providers (CAPs), after it was perceived that uniform access pricing created some inefficient bypass entry. In the former U.K. regime set up in the early 1990s, BT's long-distance competitor, Mercury, paid higher charges when using BT's local network for international call origination than for domestic call origination (or termination) even though the access service is identical. An instance of third-degree price discrimination in many countries is the differential in access charges for fixed-link and mobile communications.

The ban on third-degree wholesale price discrimination applies both to discrimination between two nonaffiliated carriers in the adjacent, competitive segment, and, if the bottleneck owner is vertically integrated, between a nonaffiliated carrier and the bottleneck owner's division or subsidiary in the competitive segment. The interpretation of the latter nondiscrimination requirement is subject to debate. After all, the pricing of internal transactions is principally an accounting matter, which may have little connection with economic reality. Some experts have understood this form of nondiscrimination as saying that the access price charged to nonaffiliated buyers should be equal to marginal cost (that is, be cost based), since efficient transfer prices for transactions between two divisions of the same firm are equal to their marginal cost. Other experts have given it an "ECPR interpretation" by arguing that access prices that do not exceed the unit profit on the competitive segment (that is, the vertically integrated firm's opportunity cost, see section 3.2) allow a competitive subsidiary or a division of the bottleneck owner to break even when it is subject to accounting separation.

The origins of this deep-rooted fear of wholesale price discrimination can be found in competition policy. They are, therefore, worth a short digression into the economics of foreclosure.[22] Let us start with the paradigm of an inventor who holds a patent on an innovation and subcontracts the exploitation of the innovation to some licensees (one can alternatively think of a franchisor subcontracting to franchisees). The licensing contract is similar to an interconnection agreement: The licensees obtain access to the bottleneck (the innovation) at some access price (fixed fee or royalties). How can the inventor make money on

---

22. See Rey and Tirole (1996) for an extensive review of the foreclosure doctrine.

her innovation (which most of us would agree is a desirable outcome if society is to provide incentives for innovation)?

Let us start with the wrong way for the licensor to proceed. Suppose that she contacts prospective licensees separately and offers them independent contracts. It is clear that she cannot collect any money in this way, for the following reason: Suppose that she is expected to sign up n licensees. Once she has entered into n licensing contracts, nothing prevents her from contracting an $(n + 1)$st licensee, thus creating more competition for the existing ones. Anticipating this incentive to "flood the market," existing licensees would not be willing to pay much. Because the total licensing profit is bounded above by the downstream industry profit, stiff downstream competition hurts the licensor. In other words, downstream product market competition destroys the profit that could a priori be gleaned from the upstream monopoly position.[23] (Similarly, McDonald's would be unable to collect any money from franchisees if it could install new franchisees at the doorsteps of existing ones.)

To avoid this disastrous outcome, the licensor has at least three alternatives. First, she can sign an exclusionary contract with, say, one licensor, that stipulates that she will not be able to enter into further licensing agreements. That is, she can create a downstream monopoly contractually and demand the corresponding monopoly profit. Second, she can vertically integrate and undertake the exploitation of the patent herself; she will then have no incentive to engage in excessive licensing because such licensing amounts to expropriating herself. Third, she may ask for (or it may be imposed!) a legal ban on third-degree price discrimination (but not on second-degree price discrimination). In this legal environment, she can offer a fixed-fee/no-royalty licensing contract to all prospective licensees, with the fixed fee equal to the downstream monopoly profit.[24] It is clear that only one potential licensee will enter a licensing agreement, for duopolists in the downstream market would be unable to recoup the high fixed licensing fee.

---

23. This argument is drawn from Hart and Tirole (1990) to which we refer for modeling. The extent of profit dissipation depends on the nature of downstream competition and on the number of potential licensees (see Rey and Tirole, 1996). See also O'Brien and Shaffer (1992) and McAfee and Schwartz (1994) for key insights into the foreclosure doctrine.
24. Note the importance of the no-price-discrimination provision. Absent this provision, the licensor would still have incentives to bring in additional licensees by charging lower fees. Note also that the optimal royalty for the licensor would be positive if the licensor gained from licensing more than one licensee.

The economics of wholesale transactions in general are similar to those of licensing and franchising. An upstream bottleneck must find a way to "discipline" the downstream market if she wants to exploit her upstream monopoly power. Whether it is socially optimal to let an upstream bottleneck exploit this monopoly power is another matter. There seems to be intellectual consensus that the owner of an upstream bottleneck should be allowed to exploit *some* of this monopoly power in order to recoup the fixed investment: An inventor who would be prevented by competition policy from making money on licensing agreements and from integrating downward into development and production would not undertake R&D in the first place. Similarly, incumbent telecommunications operators would not build local loops if they expected not to be able to enjoy some markups when reselling or exploiting the local loops themselves. *How much* monopoly power should be enjoyed by owners of bottlenecks is a matter of intense debate in competition policy, and antitrust practice (probably rightly) differs substantially across applications. For example, a number of foreclosure practices are well tolerated in the context of licensing and frowned upon in other contexts.

What do those antitrust considerations have to do with the regulated environment of the telecommunications industry? Probably little as such, as they do not take into account the specificities of regulated industries. But there is no denying that such considerations resurface under some regulatory paradigms, and that new issues arise as well. We illustrate these two points in sequence. Let us return to the licensor's third way of reestablishing her market power. We saw that contracts with sharp discounts can enable the licensor to create a downstream monopoly while giving the appearance of nondiscrimination. Transpose this insight to the pricing of the local loop by incumbent local exchange carriers, and recall that ILECs have been allowed to offer substantial discounts to counter inefficient bypass by CAPs. This opportunity to practice nonlinear wholesale pricing raises the concern that an ILEC enters an agreement with a long-distance carrier, AT&T, say, specifying a very high fixed fee and a very low wholesale price. Such a "sweet deal" (a slight misnomer, since the deal would be available to anyone else as well) would not enable rival long-distance companies to compete effectively with AT&T, as they would not have access to the low wholesale price without paying a fixed fee so high that they would be unable to recover it in a competitive long-distance market!

Next, we return to the innovator's second way of restoring her monopoly power. We saw that she can integrate vertically, deny access to nonaffiliated potential licensees, and let her downstream affiliate charge monopoly prices on the applications of her patent. The equivalent situation in telecommunications is provided by a local loop owner serving an adjacent segment, say, long distance. The local loop company has little incentive to create its own competition and is therefore likely to foreclose its rivals on the competitive segment unless the latter are much more cost-efficient or else produce a sufficiently differentiated service.

Suppose now that the vertically integrated innovator is forced to distribute free or cheap licenses to independent licensees. The innovator then has a strong incentive not to cooperate with the licensees in order not to dissipate the downstream profit; for example, she will refuse to supply the missing specifications that makes the invention work or to provide expertise at the development stage. The same holds in telecommunications. As we will later argue, a bottleneck owner who is forced to sell access below or around marginal cost and is otherwise an unregulated competitor in the adjacent segment has an incentive to use nonprice methods to deny access to rivals. We will expand on this idea in section 4.8.

To sum up, one cannot directly apply foreclosure theory as developed for competition policy to regulated environments. Regulatory rules can change the private and social costs and benefits of foreclosure, and further analysis is required before all-encompassing statements such as those related to "fair and nondiscriminatory access" can be made.

4   Essential Facility and One-Way Access: Policy

4.1   General Issues for the Design of Access Policies

Access pricing rules are necessarily imperfect for several reasons, which we have regrouped into three categories. The first issue stems directly from the discussion in section 3.4: *Any* access pricing rule is an instrument of regulation of the bottleneck owner's rate of return on the bottleneck investment or for that matter of the owner's overall rate of return. As such, it governs the owner's incentives to build and maintain the bottleneck. There is then a trade-off between two considerations: "ex post efficiency," which goes in the direction of fostering competition through access beyond the level that would be spontaneously permitted by the bottleneck owner, and "ex ante efficiency," which suggests giving the bottleneck owner flexibility in exploiting the bottleneck.

The second snag in designing a good access policy comes from the difficulty in defining the notion of "service," and the third relates to the problems associated with the monitoring of compliance of the access policy once services have been defined. The last two difficulties echo those faced in the regulation of retail prices (see chapter 2), and so we will content ourselves with illustrating them with wholesale pricing examples.

4.1.1   Liberalization and Deregulatory Takings

A central issue in the creation of competition is whether it breaches the "regulatory contract" between the incumbent operator and the regulators and thus constitutes a taking of the incumbent's property. This issue has already taken center stage in the debates on the deregulation of the power and gas industries in the United States. For example, in the wake of the deregulation initiated by the Public Utility Regulatory Policies Act (PURPA) of 1978 and accelerated by the Energy Policy Act of 1992, which mandates wholesale wheeling, that is, access to a power utility's transmission grid, and eventually retail wheeling, vertically integrated utilities might be left with more than $200 billion of "stranded assets" in generation (the competitive segment). The utilities' earlier investments in nuclear power have proved very costly, and utilities had also been forced by regulators after PURPA to enter into costly supply agreements with "qualifying facilities" (cogenerators and small power producers). Electricity purchasers (large industrial users, distributors) were reluctant to pay the high embedded costs of utility generation, especially at the time when the price of gas had tumbled and new technological developments such as combined cycle gas turbines offered cheap alternative sources of energy.

The debate has centered on the contention that the utilities would have been able to generate a substantial profit "on the upside" if things had turned differently, given that the opening of competition leaves them with a substantial deficit "on the downside." Answering negatively amounts to admitting that the utilities' investment (here in generation) would not have been committed if utilities had been forewarned of incoming competition, or equivalently that, in the absence of proper compensation, liberalization constitutes a regulatory taking. Adopting this view, the California Public Utility Commission announced in 1995 that power utilities in its state will be entitled to full recovery of their stranded costs through an "electricity service surcharge" to be levied on transport (the equivalent of the access surcharge currently paid by long-distance carriers to local exchange carriers for access to the local loop bottleneck, and due to be eliminated in the wake of the Telecommunications Act). However, some other public utility commissions intend to leave a substantial part of the stranded assets burden on the incumbents' shoulders. And American jurisprudence has not yet brought clear guidance with respect to the treatment of stranded assets.[1]

---

1. See the well-known *Hope Natural Gas* (1944) and *Duquesne Light* (1989) cases.

Greg Sidak and Dan Spulber (1996) offer a fascinating account of the development of judicial and regulatory treatment of deregulatory takings. Incidentally, the trade-off between ex post increase in welfare due to entry and ex ante incentive to build has long divided courts and legislatures. For example, in 1837 the Supreme Court justices were divided about whether the building of a new bridge (first toll-collecting, and then toll-free) near the Charles River Bridge, which had been granted a charter in 1785 by the Massachusetts legislature, constituted a taking of property and called for compensation of the latter's owners (see Sidak and Spulber, 1996, pp. 42–46, for an account of *Charles River Bridge v. Warren Bridge*).

In a competitive environment various regulatory actions have the potential of constituting a taking: low access prices paid by entrants, of course, but also excessive collocation requirements, entry subsidies, rigidity of regulated prices before a competitive threat, uncompensated requirements to add transmission or switching capacity to accommodate new traffic, line-of-business restrictions, and so forth. Recently, the California Public Utility Commission's adoption of a bill-and-keep system (in which two interconnecting carriers do not pay access charges to each other) for interconnection between ILECs and CLECs was challenged by two incumbent local exchange carriers who claimed that the bill-and-keep rule was a taking on the basis that cross-networks call flows would be unbalanced. Sidak and Spulber (1996) argue that the California Public Utility Commission failed to recognize the existence of an obvious taking, despite a 1913 California Supreme Court decision hostile to a bill-and-keep rule (already in telecommunications) on exactly those grounds.

Of course, incumbents have strong incentives to claim that there is a taking whenever regulators and lawmakers contemplate a competitive move. Quite generally, competition-oriented policies must trade off the benefits of entry against the incumbents' incentives to build. No access pricing policy is likely to strike the right balance. The challenge is therefore to design rules that do not err too much with regard to this trade-off.

4.1.2   Definition of Services

As for retail services, the right to define the set of telecommunications wholesale services whose price is to be regulated is by no means obvious. Let us recall a few snags:

• *Changing services:* The configuration of the local loop (for example, of the feeder part), the switches' vertical features, and other elements of the local networks are changing rapidly with technological progress. Accordingly it is difficult for price regulators to keep up with the ever-changing range of services and elements to which competitors can have access.

• *Nonlinear tariffs:* As we noted in chapter 2, nonlinear tariffs amount to a multiplication of services. A linear price for a given service corresponds to a single service; a two-part tariff corresponds to two services: access to the service and variable consumption of the service; and menus of two-part or more-complex tariffs (such as those in optional calling plans) correspond to even more services. Discounted wholesale tariffs have made an appearance as a way of countering bypass; with the development of local competition, local exchange carriers will most likely want to enlarge their wholesale pricing options. These changes, of course, will raise the standard problem that current regulatory methods (backward- or forward-looking incremental cost, price cap) are designed for linear prices and are modified in a basically ad hoc way to reflect the nonlinearity of prices.

• *Bundling:* Relatedly, carriers may want to offer policies that bundle elements of the network or resale services.[2] Local loop resale is an example of bundling, but one can imagine that local exchange carriers will want to multiply menus of bundles in a competitive environment. Another dimension of bundling is intertemporal bundling. A three- or five-year access contract with volume requirements cannot easily be summarized by a single yearly price.

• *Level of deaveraging:* The number of access services and of access prices is an important aspect of access policies. The theory's precept is that there should be as many access services as possible: Maximal unbundling allows entrants to buy access only to what they need. This approach, however, ignores the transaction costs of defining and monitoring access charges. (Imagine, for example, the complexity of cost-based rules that would single out each technologically, chronologically, or geographically differentiated piece of a network as a separate element for which a cost must be assessed!) It also ignores the fact that the multiplication of imperfectly determined access charges increases the possibilities open to entrants in arbitraging by purchasing undervalued pieces and leaving others aside. However, access price averaging also creates scope for substantial arbitrage by entrants (if they can buy individual elements or services separately) by putting together in the same pricing formula services or elements that have different costs or values to the entrants. The level of unbundling and access charge aggregation does matter geographically, in view of varying topologies and customer densities. It also is a subject of an unresolved debate for time-of-day pricing of access. Telephone networks' marginal costs are very small off peak and quite high at peak. While economists rightly argue in favor of peak-load pricing of access (see Cave, 1993, and Mitchell et al., 1994), the implementation of peak-

---

2. In the same way long-distance carriers offer discounts to their business customers for bundling services such as long-distance calls, (toll-free) 800 services, credit card calls, and so forth.

load pricing still has to be carefully designed. Besides the standard issue of computing off-peak and peak marginal costs, the new and interesting issue in a competitive environment with access is that several operators are jointly responsible for the timing of the peak during the day. This fact may induce some gaming on their part, and in any case adds to the difficulty encountered when foreseeing the location of the peak.[3]

4.1.3 Information Requirements and Compliance Monitoring

A key feature of access pricing rules is their information requirement. To be realistic, access pricing rules must economize on the collection of information by the authorities that are in charge of enforcing them. All existing rules are information demanding. Cost-based rules require information about marginal costs of various elements and services in the bottleneck segment. They also require information about demand either if they make forecasts of capacity utilization (as is the case for forward-looking long-run incremental costs, see section 4.4) or if they attempt to adopt a time-of-day structure. ECPR requires information about marginal costs in the competitive segment. Price caps require information about cost and demand in order to set the weights in the caps properly.

Once the access pricing rule is in place, compliance with it must be ensured. Such compliance may be particularly problematic if the rule creates strong incentives for gaming by the incumbents. The only way to ensure compliance then, as we will argue, is to engage in heavy-handed regulation.

Information requirements and the complexity of compliance monitoring are key dimensions of access pricing rules. And one of our concerns with current regulatory reforms is that, beyond the liberalization and free-market rhetoric, one may be creating an environment that will lead to heavy-handed regulatory intervention.

4.2 Backward-Looking Cost-Based Pricing of Access

The traditional approach to computing interconnection charges consists in applying the methodology of cost-of-service regulation to the

---

3. The August 1996 FCC order does not require or forbid adoption of peak-load transport and termination pricing by states. It only requires peak-load prices to be based on a forward-looking (TELRIC) cost study or to comply with the FCC default prices.

operator's wholesale offerings. There are a variety of possible cost allocations. (See box 4.1 for a formal approach.)

A popular cost-of-service methodology is that of *additive or usage-proportional markups*. Suppose that several services utilize a common element. After the allocation of costs that are attributable to a particular service to the corresponding services, there remains a residual corresponding to the "fixed cost" or "common cost." This unallocated residual is then spread across services, and the additive markup on each price is the same for each service. In other words, a usage-proportional markup is tantamount to a *fixed (price-independent) excise tax*, whose magnitude is computed so as to cover the unallocated cost.

It is interesting to note that usage-proportional markups satisfy the ECPR. Recall from section 3.2 that ECPR requires the access price to be equal to the operator's opportunity cost on the competitive segment. The operator's price on the competitive segment is equal to total marginal cost, that is, the marginal cost of access plus the marginal cost of the segment itself, plus the markup. The access charge, which is equal to the marginal cost of access plus the markup, is thus equal to the difference between the price and the marginal cost on the competitive segment, that is, the opportunity cost.

Another popular approach to allocating the fixed cost is that of *uniform or price-proportional markups*.[4] The markup over the marginal cost of a service is proportional to this marginal cost. The uniform markup is thus akin to a *proportional (VAT type) tax*. Unlike additive markups, uniform markups do not satisfy ECPR. Because the total marginal cost of the competitive segment exceeds the marginal cost of the access facilities used by this segment, the price of the competitive segment is inflated more than that of the access segment, and so the access charge is set below the operator's opportunity cost. The burden of cost recovery then falls disproportionately on the competitive segments.

The benefit of fully distributed cost pricing is that it commits the regulator to allow the operator to recoup its investments and to break even. Thus, to a large extent, it solves the problem of regulatory takings. In particular, an operator who incurs a large fixed cost to install fiber optics in the local loop or to endow switches with new functions need

---

4. In a sense, the additive markups described here are also uniform. We reserve "uniform" for the case of price-proportional markups in order to conform with the terminology used (in the context of forward-looking costs) in the current debate in the United Kingdom and Europe.

Box 4.1
Additive and Uniform Markups

To illustrate the additive and uniform types of cost-of-service regulation in the presence of wholesale services, let us return to the example of a local-call monopoly with a long-distance-call duopoly (see box 3.1). The unallocated cost is k_0.

Additive or Usage-Proportional Markup

Let $Q = q_0 + q_1 + q_2$ denote the total number of calls using the local network. Under an additive markup, a markup equal to k_0/Q is tacked on the prices of all (wholesale or retail) services. And so the prices of local calls, long-distance calls offered by the operator, and access services are, respectively,

$$p_0 = 2c_0 + \frac{k_0}{Q}$$

$$p_1 = (2c_0 + c_1) + \frac{k_0}{Q}$$

$$a = 2c_0 + \frac{k_0}{Q}$$

Note that $a = p_1 - c_1$, so ECPR is satisfied. Let

$$B_0 = (p_0 - 2c_0)q_0$$
$$B_1 = (p_1 - 2c_0 - c_1)q_1$$
$$B_2 = (a - 2c_0)q_2$$

denote the net benefits in the operator's three lines of business (local, long distance, access). We check that the total benefit covers the fixed cost, so that the operator's budget is balanced:

$$B_0 + B_1 + B_2 = \frac{k_0}{Q}(q_0 + q_1 + q_2) = k_0$$

Uniform or Price-Proportional Markups

Under a proportional markup, prices are a given multiple of marginal costs:

$$p_0 = k(2c_0)$$
$$p_1 = k(2c_0 + c_1)$$
$$a = k(2c_0)$$

where the coefficient of proportionality $k > 1$ is chosen so as to allow the operator to recoup the fixed

$$(k - 1)[(2c_0)q_0 + (2c_0 + c_1)q_1 + (2c_0)q_2] = k_0$$

Note that

$$a = p_1 - c_1 - (k - 1)c_1 < p_1 - c_1$$

so the access charge is set below the ECPR level.

not be concerned that this investment will later be expropriated by the regulator's setting low access charges, for example.

Despite this advantage, as we discussed in chapter 2 in the context of retail pricing, fully distributed cost pricing has been as frequently decried by economists as it has been used in practice. It has well-known flaws. First, it is determined through a cumbersome process. For example, a rebalancing of access charges must be cost justified, a requirement which is likely to imply a delay of several months in the rebalancing. Second, fully distributed cost pricing is cost based and therefore does not encourage cost minimization. Third, it yields an improper price structure and is a vastly suboptimal way of financing the access deficit. Because it is cost-based, it "subsidizes" inelastic-demand segments to the detriment of elastic-demand ones. In the presence of competition, fully distributed cost pricing tends to create an inefficient amount of entry. For example, under uniform markups, an inefficient entrant producing the same service as the operator in the competitive segment finds it profitable to enter as long as its cost handicap relative to the operator is smaller than the markup on the operator's marginal cost on the competitive segment.[5] Furthermore, under all fully distributed cost methods, the markup on access invites inefficient bypass.

To alleviate the cost of the first and third drawbacks (delays in price revisions, inefficient entry in the competitive and bottleneck segments), the prices set by fully distributed cost methods have sometimes been interpreted as ceilings or caps, providing, in particular, flexibility to respond to competitive threats such as those by competitive access providers. By letting operators respond to competition, this downward flexibility has perhaps brought actual prices closer to Ramsey levels, but fully distributed cost methods still have only limited appeal.

4.3   Regulated and Deregulated Segments: The Problem of Cross-Subsidies

4.3.1   The Theoretical Argument

Incentives for cross-subsidies stem from a differential in the sharing of earnings across product lines. An operator gains from transferring costs from a segment in which it keeps a sizable fraction of its profits to another segment where consumers share a higher fraction of costs.

---

5. Using the notation of box 4.1, $p_1 - (a + c_2) > 0$ iff $(k - 1)c_1 \geq c_2 - c_1$.

Cross-subsidies are particularly attractive for the operator when some segment is fully deregulated while a substantial fraction of costs on another segment (for example, regulated through some cost of service methodology) is reimbursed. For example, if 80 percent of the operator's cost on one segment is reimbursed, a $1 cross-subsidy with a deregulated segment increases the operator's profit by 80 cents.

But the incentive for cross-subsidies also exists, albeit in a weaker form, when the regulated segment is subject to a price cap.[6] As is well known, the ratchet effect implies that high profitability today leads to a more stringent cap tomorrow, thus inducing profit sharing. Conversely, there sometimes exists an explicit or implicit regulatory insurance against low profitability, which adds a further mechanism for profit sharing.

4.3.2   Examples

There are two main categories of cross-subsidies: accounting cost allocation and managerial cost allocation. (The literature has focused on the first and neglected the second.)

4.3.2.1   Accounting Cost Allocation

Telecommunications technology gives rise to many joint and common costs. The allocation of these costs among product lines is by and large arbitrary and may be used to cross-subsidize some product lines. For example, an operator has an incentive to allocate expenses relative to maintenance personnel, product development, marketing, connection between the customer's home and the first switch, and so on to those services for which profit sharing is the greatest.

Cross-subsidies may also have an intertemporal dimension through the depreciation of investment expenditures. For example, a few years ago it was argued that U.S. local exchange carriers could install a fiber-optic network that was then useless in providing plain old telephone services but would later be a valuable asset when introducing new and innovative services such as interactive TV and video on demand. To the extent that the investment is (partly) depreciated before the new

---

6. Note that the Telecommunications Act calls for price-cap regulation of access and deregulation of competitive segments. Whether incentives for cross-subsidies will exist depends on whether the regulators stick to a (non-operator-contingent) engineering-based determination of access prices.

services are introduced, there may be a cross-subsidy from (current) regulated services to (future) unregulated ones.

4.3.2.2   *Managerial Cost Allocation*

In the presence of asymmetric profit sharing, the operator also has an incentive to allocate *real* resources strategically, thus generating social waste. The operator can allocate its best engineers and marketing agents to the competitive segment, and leave its less efficient or yet untrained personnel with its regulated segments.[7] The CEO and top executive team may devote most of their attention to competitive segments and neglect regulated ones, for which high costs are more lightly sanctioned. Investment choices that jointly affect the marginal costs on competitive and regulated segments may be distorted toward achievement of low cost on competitive segments and high cost on regulated ones.

It is thus clear that managerial decisions are not geared to the minimization of the production cost, but rather to the minimization of the cost as perceived by the operator. Coming back to the theory, it can be shown that, under some assumptions, a *uniform* power or intensity of the operator's incentive scheme is socially optimal even when detailed supervisory monitoring prevents accounting cost manipulation. That is, the sharing of profit between the operator and the consumers should be based solely on the operator's overall cost and thus make no use of disaggregated information about cost at the product line level (Laffont and Tirole, 1990a).

4.3.3   Can Cross-Subsidies Be Prevented?

It is by no means easy to prevent cross-subsidies once one has created incentives for them. One can require accounting separation and invest regulatory resources into checking that the actual cost allocation follows clearly defined accounting principles. This accounting supervision, although costly, bars the most flagrant accounting cross-subsidies. Accountants, however, cannot substitute their judgment for business judgment. They have neither the training nor the

---

7. Furthermore, if competitive environments provide more information about the quality of managers because they require more innovation on their part, the firm will overemphasize its fast-track policy of selecting its future top managers through the allocation of promising managers to competitive segments.

information necessary to evaluate investment and personnel allocation within the firm. It is thus difficult to measure and prevent cross-
subsidies.

The use of *benchmarking* has been advocated as a way to detect cross-
subsidies, in particular in the context of a telecommunications operator's purchase of equipment from a manufacturing affiliate. The basic
idea behind benchmarking is to compare the price paid by the regulated
operator to the unregulated affiliated equipment manufacturer with
external prices, in order to prevent the firm from engaging in cross-
subsidization by inflating the price of its equipment. There are two
distinct measures of external prices: prices charged by other manufacturers for similar equipment, and prices charged by the manufacturing
affiliate to external buyers for the equipment. While benchmarking is
useful, it is no panacea.

4.3.3.1   Comparison with the Price of Similar Equipment Sold by Nonaffiliated Manufacturers

There are two limits to benchmarking by comparison with the equipment of other manufacturers. First, equipment may be heterogenous
across manufacturers. They may differ in capacities, functions, stur-
diness, manufacturer's reputation, and the like. Second, pricing has
several dimensions, which may also differ among types of buyers: installation cost, financing, training, penalties for delays, prices of spare
parts, and so on.

4.3.3.2   Comparison with the Price of the Same Equipment Sold to External Buyers

There are three limits to comparing prices to those of equipment sold to
others. First, as we just noted, the equipment may not be well-defined
"equipment," since its features and pricing may be customized. Second,
the internal buyer must not collude with external buyers and induce
them to purchase at inflated official prices. Third, forcing such nondiscrimination between internal and external buyers affects the price paid
by external buyers, since the supplier may want to forgo transactions
with external buyers in order to be able to raise the price and engage
in cross-subsidization. Alternatively, the supplier may decide to keep
serving external buyers, but benchmarking still raises the price paid the
latter, as the link between the two prices creates a new and profitable
effect of a price increase through cross-subsidization.

4.4   Forward-Looking Cost-Based Pricing of Access

The dominant paradigm in current regulatory reforms is that of "forward-looking long-run incremental cost," which we will abbreviate LRIC. This paradigm was taken up in 1995 by Oftel in the United Kingdom and in 1996 in the Telecommunications Act and the FCC order in the United States; it is also advocated in the 1994 WIK/EAC report commissioned by the European Union. (The WIK/EAC report recommended long-run incremental costs with a proportional markup partly because of political economy considerations, reflecting the fact that the starting retail rate price structure in Europe followed something like an inverse Ramsey rule. Proportional markups were viewed by some of its authors as an intermediate step in the reform.Their recommendation implied no hostility to Ramsey access pricing.) The idea behind the use of LRIC is to set access prices on the basis of an efficient cost benchmark rather than on the operator's actual (embedded) costs. The main appeal of the LRIC approach is that it eliminates the "cost plus" feature of backward-looking cost-based access pricing; it thus provides much better incentives for static cost efficiency, although, as we will see, its impact on incentives for dynamic efficiency (investment, innovation) is quite mixed.[8] The practicalities of its implementation still have to be determined, but the general idea is to base the computation of the LRIC of an element of the network on the cost of the currently most efficient technology derived from an engineering model, on a forecast of the likely usage of the element, and on a rule for treating depreciation.[9]

This broad regulatory consensus[10] in favor of LRIC unfortunately is supported by little economic argument. As a matter of fact, an economic

8. Temin (1997) argues that the debate concerning the use of (high) historical costs or (low) forward-looking costs is an old one. He points out that, in the early 1960s, AT&T championed the use of the cost of a hypothetical new investment (that is, of a forward-looking long-run incremental cost) to justify the low Telpak rates while entrants supported historical, fully distributed cost measures; and that in the 1970s, AT&T argued in favor of fully distributed costs for its access charge for MCI's long-distance service in order to force MCI to pay part of the cost of the local network.
9. The current engineering models in the United Kingdom (called bottom-up models) use an annuity approach for depreciation that implies little depreciation in the early years of the asset's life and relatively more in later years. Annex D of Oftel's December 1995 consultative document "Pricing of Telecommunications Services from 1997" points out that this rule need not correspond to economic depreciation and calls for further investigation into the matter.
10. While there is a broad consensus about the concept, there are of course some differences in its contemplated applications. For instance, Oftel suggests individual caps on BT's access termination services but intends to give BT more flexibility at the originating

analysis reveals several concerns about the whole endeavor.[11] First, LRIC regulation gives regulators a key role in managing entry. On the one hand, the determination of long-run incremental costs is highly discretionary. On the other hand, long-run incremental costs, even if they can be obtained costlessly and impartially, preclude operators from making money in the access activity and give them strong incentives to favor their competitive affiliates by biasing access against their competitors. These perverse incentives call for heavy-handed supervision of incumbent operators. Both factors imply a high cost in terms of regulatory staff resources and also create scope for interest-group politics in which the different parties try to influence the regulators' exercise of regulatory discretion. This outcome is at odds with the official goal of making regulation more light-handed. Second, even if long-run incremental costs could be determined objectively and rivals' exclusion could be prevented costlessly, the associated access prices would still not be the efficient prices and thus would imply economic distortions. We detail these concerns, except the foreclosure one which is treated in section 4.5, in sequence.

4.4.1   Discretion in the Measurement of the LRIC

We first analyze the information requirements for proper computation of long-run incremental costs. We will conclude that, while some requirements are reasonable, others are strong and are therefore conducive to the exercise of discretion. In the examples developed here, we will consider situations in which LRIC may define the proper access charge, in order to abstract from conceptual caveats and to focus better on the problems involved in defining and measuring LRIC.

4.4.1.1   Knowledge of the Cost of Equipment
LRIC methods start from the lowest current cost of the equipment. A number of elements of telecommunications networks (say, a switch or a fiber-optic cable with standard specifications) have relatively well-defined market prices; in such cases, the computation of the cost of purchase of technologically up-to-date equipment should be straightforward. Two complications may arise, however. First, some elements

---

end (which is more subject to bypass) by defining a price cap on a basket of access origination services. The Telecommunications Act and the FCC order envision individual caps at both ends.
11. See also Sidak and Spulber (1996).

may be customized. For example, a software upgrade specific to the company's equipment may not have a well-defined market price. Furthermore, fictitious price quotations that can be solicited from suppliers by the regulator solely for regulatory purposes are unlikely to receive careful attention and to elicit truthful revelation by suppliers who do not face the prospect of selling to the operator.

Second, what constitutes efficient equipment in general depends on a forecast of the future usage of the elements. In turn, the forecast depends on local demographic considerations (population growth, evolution of the business/residential mix, etc.) as well as on the planned offerings (for example, quite different switches and transmission facilities are required for standard telephone services and for new, innovative services.)[12]

4.4.1.2   Forecast of the Element's Usage

As Hausman (1997) points out, the lumpiness of investments in telecommunications networks[13] implies that it is often efficient to install equipment and use it below capacity for some extended period of time; or, to put it differently, always installing long-term capacity that is instantly saturated may well be a bad policy.

This simple fact raises a practical issue: If one is to approximate the long-run incremental cost by some form of cost average, one must foresee its likely usage over the element's lifetime. This exercise would be simple if the element were always used at capacity.[14] But the forecast, which depends on endogenous variables (pricing, introduction of new services), is likely to be somewhat subjective in a world of below-capacity usage.

---

12. This difficulty exists even when one takes the operator's network configuration (location of switches and design of transmission facilities) as given. A more demanding cost standard would be obtained by optimizing with respect to the network's configuration as well, and thus not only with respect to the network's elements for a given configuration; see Gasmi et al (1997). Such a "greenfield" approach has been abandoned for the moment both in the United Kingdom (see Annex D of Oftel's December 1995 consultative document) and in the United States.

13. Lumpiness is quite realistic for some transmission elements. For example, the installation of fiber optic in the local loop will be a substantial one-shot investment. A software design is also a lumpy investment. The installation of switches also exhibits some lumpiness, although their capacity can later be expanded at a cost.

14. Assuming that an element's capacity does not change over time. For example, the capacity of twisted pairs of copper wires was unexpectedly increased by the advent of data compression techniques.

4.4.1.3   Forecast of the Rate of Technological Progress

As telecommunications experts have noted, technological progress reduces the price of switches and transmission over time. And so computing at each point of time an access price corresponding to the most efficient equipment to date would be confiscatory when equipment is long-lived.

To illustrate this issue, box 4.2 computes the rental prices of equipment supplied by a competitive manufacturing industry in which exogenous technological progress steadily reduces the production cost of the equipment. To obtain the simplest formula, it assumes that the production technology for equipment exhibits constant returns to scale and so there is no technological obstacle to perfect competition, that equipment is indeed installed and leased by a competitive industry, that there is no demand and cost uncertainty, and that demand does not fall over time. It is shown that the *competitive* access charge (rental price for equipment) satisfies the following relationship:[15]

Access charge at date t = LRIC

= Marginal cost of date-t production of the most efficient technology

   × (Interest rate + Rate of technological progress + Rate of physical
     depreciation of the equipment)

The right-hand side of this equality is the sum of the interest on the principal and the economic depreciation of the asset. For example, with a 10 percent interest rate and equipment costs falling at a rate of 10 percent per year, the yearly access charge for infinitely lived equipment should be equal to 20 percent of the current purchase price of this equipment.

Thus, proper determination of long-run incremental costs for setting current access charges requires some forecast of technological progress. To be fair, such forecasts are also often made in alternative regulatory modes. For example, price-cap regulation indexes the cap over the 3 or

---

15. This formula is also derived in Hausman (1997). As pointed out by Hausman, it is a well-known formula in the economics of lumpy investments. See, e.g., the paper by McDonald and Siegel (1986) and the very comprehensive book by Dixit and Pindyck (1994), as well as Crew and Kleindorfer (1992), Salinger (1997), and Sidak and Spulber (1997a). In his affidavit Hausman criticizes the FCC's TELRIC measure of LRIC for ignoring the existence of technological progress.

   Similar arguments can also be found in Sidak and Spulber (1996).

Box 4.2
Accounting for Technological Progress

Consider a constant-returns-to-scale, competitive-input-supply industry in which the instantaneous rate of technological progress $x \geq 0$ is exogenously determined and is constant over time. Ignoring operating costs and treating time as continuous, the production cost of one unit of equipment at date t is equal to

$$C_t = e^{-xt} C_0$$

where C_0 is the cost at the reference date, date 0. Let r denote the instantaneous rate of interest. The rental rate at date t—that is, the competitive price of access at date t—is called a_t. Let $\delta \geq 0$ denote the equipment's instantaneous rate of depreciation. That is, the expected productivity at date $t + \tau$ of a unit of equipment produced at date t is $e^{-\delta \tau}$ times its productivity at date t.

Suppose that in a competitive equilibrium new units of equipment are built at each instant (we will later need to check that this is indeed the case). Perfect competition in equipment manufacturing implies that at each instant the price of the equipment is equal to its production cost; besides, the price must be equal to the present discounted value of the stream of rental charges that can be collected by the owner of the equipment. And so, for all t,

$$C_t = \int_0^\infty e^{-r\tau} \left(e^{-\delta \tau} a_{t+\tau} \right) d\tau$$

The equilibrium access price is therefore

$$a_t = (r + x + \delta)\, C_t$$

since for this price pattern

$$\int_0^\infty e^{-r\tau} \left(e^{-\delta \tau} a_{t+\tau} \right) d\tau = \int_0^\infty e^{-(r+\delta)\tau} (r + x + \delta) C_t e^{-x\tau} d\tau$$
$$= C_t$$

In this constant-returns-to-scale environment, equilibrium prices are entirely cost determined. The demand side enters only in the determination of the stock Q_t of nondepreciated equipment at date t. Namely, if $Q_t = D_t(a_t)$ denotes the deterministic demand curve for the equipment at date t, one must have

$$Q_t = D_t[(r + x + \delta)C_t]$$

If the demand curve does not shift downward over time, the stock Q_t thus obtained remains constant or grows over time, and so, because the existing stock depreciates, there is indeed new production of equipment at each point of time, as we presumed.

4 years of its validity on a rate of expected technological progress (as well as inflation).

This toy model in a sense builds the most favorable case for the determination of long-run incremental costs, since it abstracts from a number of important complications. First, it assumes that the equipment is used at full capacity during its lifetime, and so regulators need not forecast its usage (this point was discussed earlier). Second, it is assumed that the demand for the equipment cannot fall over time and thus that the access charge computed previously cannot exceed what users are willing to pay for it. If this were not the case, the equipment's owners would be rationed (could not find users) at the access charge computed previously. Third, we have assumed that technological progress is exogenous. This is a good assumption in some cases; technological progress on microprocessors used in switches may be by and large driven by factors outside the telecommunications industry. However, the incentives for undertaking R&D on equipment that is largely specific to the telecommunications industry are determined by the prices at which this equipment will be sold to operators, and therefore depend on the regulatory determination of access charges. In such cases, the regulatory treatment of access affects the speed of technological progress.

Fourth, the rule derived earlier does not take into account the option value of discarding the asset if it becomes uneconomical to *exploit* (and not only to build) the asset after new generations of equipment supersede the old technologies. We illustrate the bias created when one ignores this option value by a simple modification of the previous competitive setup in which technological progress is random. We show in box 4.3 that the access pricing formula derived earlier (and applied by replacing the rate of technological progress by the expected rate of technological progress) remains valid as long as previous assets do not become economically stranded, but yields an upward bias in the access charge if there is a possibility of economic stranding. We say that an asset becomes *economically stranded* if it cannot compete with new generations even though its investment cost has already been incurred, that is, if its operating cost exceeds the competitive rental (access) charges on the new generation of equipment. For example, some sources of electricity have become uneconomical with the advent of combined cycle gas turbines and the fall in gas prices, even though the cost of building the plants for these sources has already been incurred. (Economic stranding is only one aspect of the issue of stranded assets in electricity and in other industries. Later, we will discuss the complementary and important notion of *regulatory stranding,* as emphasized, e.g., by Sidak and Spulber, 1996, 1997a, and 1997b, in their work on deregulatory takings.)

To sum up:

• Under economic stranding, using the expected rate of technological progress leads to an overestimation of the economic depreciation of the asset, and so we have

Access charge at date t

< Marginal cost of date-t production of the most efficient technology

   × (Interest rate + Expected rate of technological progress + Rate of
      physical depreciation of the investment)

• The necessary downward correction reflects the option value of discarding the asset after the arrival of new generations. It increases with the difference between the operating cost of the current generation and the sum of the operating cost and interest on investment of the new generation.

How relevant is the issue of economic stranding and thus the correction to be included in the computation of the long-run incremental cost? While operating costs in the electricity industry can be large, the ratio of operating over investment cost seems small for many elements of telecommunications networks. And thus perhaps the issue of economic stranding may not be substantial in the latter industry. It could arise, say, if the maintenance cost of serving customers in remote areas using wireline technology exceeded the cost of providing the same services through the new mobile technology. (However, if the maintenance cost is small, then the wireline installation is not economically stranded even though it has been superseded as a way to provide service to a remote area.) It is also possible that the asset will have to be discarded because of technological incompatibility with the rest of the network if the technology there has been enhanced.

4.4.1.4   Regulatory Takings

Let us return to the uncertain technological progress model of a competitive industry just discussed. When technological progress occurs, the equipment owner is forced to lower its access price to the LRIC (denoted a_L in box 4.3) of the new and more efficient technology, and thus

Box 4.3
Economic Stranding and Access Pricing

Let us return to the competitive-input-supply industry of box 4.2. We introduce a marginal cost of operation in order to allow for the possibility of economically stranded investment.

It will prove convenient to consider a random rate of technological progress. Instead of positing a continuous and deterministic rate, we consider two technologies, the current or old one and the future or new one, with the latter's date of arrival being random. The current technology has (per-unit) investment cost C_H and operating cost c_H per unit of time. The new technology will involve a (per-unit) investment cost C_L and operating cost c_L per unit of time. To simplify the analysis, we assume that the corresponding equipment does not depreciate physically ($\delta = 0$) and that the demand function for its services is invariant over time. As earlier, letting r denote the instantaneous rate of interest, we assume that

$$C_H + \frac{c_H}{r} > C_L + \frac{c_L}{r}$$

that is, the new technology involves a lower total cost (production plus present discounted value of operating cost) than the old one, and thus supersedes it when it arrives on the market. This fact, however, does not necessarily mean that the old technology is discarded once the new one arrives. Indeed if

$$c_H < c_L + rC_L$$

the old technology continues to be exploited even though it is no longer built. In contrast, if

$$c_H > c_L + rC_L$$

then the old technology is discarded. We will then say that it is *economically stranded*. The new technology's arrival date is given by a Poisson process with arrival rate y. The probability that it has not appeared by date t is thus e^{-yt}. The expected rate of technological progress is thus

$$x = y\frac{\left(C_H + \frac{c_H}{r}\right) - \left(C_L + \frac{c_L}{r}\right)}{\left(C_H + \frac{c_H}{r}\right)}$$

This formula illustrates that adjustment for the rate of technological progress must take into account not only the difference between the technologies in investment costs but also the difference in the present discounted value of operating costs (which were assumed away in box 4.2).

Let a denote the rental/access charge (or, equivalently, the long-run marginal cost) that prevails before the arrival of the new technology and a_L that which obtains thereafter (these are constant thanks to the stationarity of the model). From box 4.2, we know that

$$a_L = c_L + rC_L$$

(given that the asset does not depreciate and there is no further technological progress). Before the arrival of the new generation, the production cost of the

Box 4.3 (continued)

current technology is equal to the expected present discounted value of the profits derived from asset ownership. And so

$$C_H = \int_0^\infty y e^{-yt} \left[(a - c_H) \int_0^t e^{-r\tau} d\tau \right.$$

$$\left. + \max(a_L - c_H, 0) \int_t^\infty e^{-r\tau} d\tau \right] dt$$

That is, with probability $y e^{-yt} dt$, the new technology arrives between t and $t + dt$. In this case, the owner of one unit of the asset will have enjoyed profit per unit of time equal to $a - c_H$ until the arrival and gets either $a_L - c_H$ (if she rents it) or 0 (if she discards it) after the new technology arrives. Simple computations show that

$$a = c_H + rC_H + \frac{y}{r}(c_H + rC_H - c_L - rC_L) = (r + x)\left(C_H + \frac{c_H}{r}\right)$$

$$= \left(1 + \frac{x}{r}\right)(c_H + rC_H) \qquad \text{if } c_L + rC_L > c_H$$

and

$$a = c_H + (r + y)C_H$$

$$= \left(1 + \frac{x}{r}\right)(c_H + rC_H) - y\left[\frac{c_H - (c_L + rC_L)}{r}\right] \qquad \text{if } c_L + rC_L < c_H$$

We thus obtain a downward correction in the case of strandable assets.

Deterministic date of resolution of uncertainty: The Poisson arrival process depicts one polar case in which the date of resolution of uncertainty is completely random. The other polar case, in which uncertainty is resolved at a deterministic date T, is also straightforward. Let us assume that the date-0 technology remains the up-to-date technology until date T. At date T it is learned whether there is an innovation (which has probability y). In the absence of innovation the current technology remains the efficient one forever. In case of innovation, it is superseded by the more efficient one. It is easy to see that with a constant demand function, investment takes place only at two dates: date 0 (in the old technology) and date T (in the old technology in the absence of innovation, in the new one otherwise). Assuming the absence of economic stranding, it can be shown that the access charge a before date T satisfies

$$a = \left(1 + x\frac{e^{-rT}}{1 - e^{-rT}}\right)(c_H + rC_H)$$

where x is defined as before.

to price access below its own LRIC. (Box 4.3 assumes that the old technology is not economically stranded. The equipment owner incurs a similar loss in the case of stranding.) This capital loss results from the users' option of turning to the more efficient technology. To break even, competitive equipment owners must charge, before the innovation arrives, a markup over the naive LRIC, which is the level that ensures a zero instantaneous rate of return; this naive LRIC is equal to the asset's operating cost plus the interest charge on the investment cost plus the physical depreciation (that is, $c_H + rC_H$ in box 4.3, where we ignore physical depreciation for simplicity). In other words, the competitive equipment owners make *supranormal profit* [namely, $a - (c_H + rC_H)$] in order to compensate for the future capital loss.

This intertemporal cross-subsidization can be reinterpreted as a cross-subsidization among states of nature. (The deterministic-date-of-uncertainty resolution in box 4.3 may help the reader understand this point.) Suppose that an operator invests today in equipment that with some probability will still be the most efficient equipment tomorrow and with some probability will be superseded by a new "bypass" technology. For the operator to break even overall, a markup on access corresponding to the risk of technological progress must be charged as long as users do not have an alternative to the operator's equipment. This markup on access needed to compensate the owner for the one-sided option enjoyed by the user is similar to the premium received by an insurer when the insuree does not have an accident.

So far, so good. But suppose now that the regulator attempts to reduce even slightly the markup on access. Then no investment takes place until uncertainty is resolved, as the markup is no longer sufficient to offset the users' option value. The users' one-sided option combined with the regulator's pressure on access charges leads potential equipment owners to exercise their option to wait to invest in facilities.

4.4.2   Common Costs, Markups, and Deregulatory Takings

The standard rationale for adding a markup over and beyond the full marginal cost (which includes economic depreciation, as we have seen) is the existence of common costs—for example, those associated with the local loop. To illustrate this idea in an intertemporal context and to elucidate the link between markups and depreciation, let us first return to the example of random technological progress developed earlier, and let us introduce a fixed cost. This fixed cost might stem from the introduction of the initial (old) technology. For instance, the operator might sink an initial wireline investment to serve rural areas; this investment can be divided into a joint and common cost of reaching villages and hamlets and a per-line cost of connecting individual inhabitants. The new technology might be cellular telephony. (More generally, the fixed cost need not be related to the old technology and could just be some arbitrary fixed network cost. It can alternatively be interpreted as the cost of supply requirements imposed by the state, such as long-term national coal contracts or supplies from qualifying facilities in the electricity industry.) Let us assume for the moment that the operator's monopoly position on this segment is secured.

The theory of multiproduct pricing implies that efficient recovery of the fixed cost entails spreading of the burden on the old and new technologies in order to limit the distortion of consumption of the old vintage. In other words, at the social optimum,

Access charge for the old technology > LRIC of old technology

before the new technology accrues, and, when the new technology accrues,

Access charge for the old and new technology
> LRIC of new technology

where the long-run incremental cost of the old technology includes the economic depreciation as before. Concretely, social optimality requires that part of the depreciation of the initial fixed cost is allocated (delayed) to the new technology.[16]

We can now introduce the notion of "deregulatory taking".[17] Suppose that the operator is promised a *secure monopoly position* on this segment, with the depreciation computed in accord with the Ramsey principles stated earlier. The operator is then willing to accept the *slow depreciation* implied by Ramsey pricing, that is, to tolerate moderate charges for access to the old technology. Assume now that the new technology, when it accrues, can be offered equally efficiently by new

---

16. Conversely, if there were a fixed cost of installing the new technology, the depreciation of this fixed cost should partly be moved forward to the old technology implying yet another markup on that technology. But, underlying our discussion of liberalization following technological progress is an implicit assumption that the fixed cost of installing the new technology is low, and so we can ignore it for the purpose of the analysis.

17. The term was coined by Sidak and Spulber (1996).

entrants and that the regulator reneges on her promise and decides to open the market for competition. The incumbent can no longer include any depreciation in its access charge when the new technology arrives, since this access charge is brought down to the LRIC of the new technology by competitive pressure. The incumbent is then unable to recoup the initial investment.

Had it been notified of the prospective deregulatory move, the incumbent would have insisted in advance on a still higher markup on the old technology in order to make up for the missing markup on the new technology (or the incumbent would not have invested in the first place if the regulator had turned down this request). Concretely, the incumbent would have requested *faster depreciation* in order to offset the revenue shortage due to the liberalization (see box 4.4).

To sum up, we have identified two types of takings:

• *Regulatory takings* occur in a liberalized or monopoly environment in which the regulator does not allow the firm (a) to charge its full LRIC (including economic depreciation) or (b), if there is a fixed cost, to impute a reasonable markup over LRIC.

• *Deregulatory takings* stem from an incorrect expectation by the incumbent that its market will not be liberalized. It arises when some fixed cost (sunk investment, costly purchase obligations, etc.) must be recouped, and the incumbent depreciates it slowly with the expectation that depreciation can be carried forward into the future because of the absence of impending liberalization.

It is also worth reiterating the point that efficient recovery of the common cost requires usage-based pricing of access. Box 4.5 illustrates this point in the context of random demand. It shows that the markup on the access charge increases in states of high demand, at least as long

Box 4.4
Deregulatory Takings and Speed of Depreciation

In the random innovation model studied in box 4.3, the old technology involves a per-unit investment C_H and operating cost c_H. Let us further add a joint and common cost k_0 incurred at date 0. As earlier, the new technology's arrival process is a Poisson process with parameter y, and its per-unit investment cost is C_L and operating cost c_L. We assume that

$$c_H < c_L + rC_L < c_H + rC_H$$

Box 4.4 (continued)

(so there is no economic stranding when the new technology arrives). The demand curve $D(\cdot)$ for the use of this segment is stationary. Assuming away physical depreciation, it is easy to see that investment occurs only at two dates at most: The incumbent installs q_H units of the old technology at date 0 and $q_L = Q - q_H$ units of the new technology when it arrives, where Q is the updated stock.

Let a and a_L denote the access charges before and after innovation. So $q_H = D(a)$ and $Q = D(a_L)$. Let $S(\cdot)$ denote the net surplus from the usage of the segment. Then, the Ramsey optimum for a secured monopoly is given by

$$\max_{\{a,a_L\}} \left\{ \int_0^\infty y e^{-yt} \left[\int_0^t S(a) e^{-r\tau} d\tau + \int_t^\infty S(a_L) e^{-r\tau} d\tau \right] dt \right\}$$

or

$$\max_{\{a,a_L\}} \left\{ \left(\frac{r}{y+r} \right) \frac{S(a)}{r} + \left(\frac{y}{y+r} \right) \frac{S(a_L)}{r} \right\}$$

subject to

$$\left(\frac{r}{y+r} \right) \left[\frac{(a - LRIC_H) D(a)}{r} \right] + \left(\frac{y}{y+r} \right) \left[\frac{(a_L - LRIC_L) D(a_L)}{r} \right] \geq k_0$$

where

$$LRIC_H \equiv c_H + r C_H + \frac{y}{r} (c_H + r C_H - c_L - r C_L)$$

and

$$LRIC_L \equiv c_L + r C_L$$

are the long-run incremental costs of the two technologies. We here use the fact that the model is equivalent to a two-period model in which the relative weights of the two periods are $r/(y+r)$ and $y/(y+r)$, respectively. Letting $1 + \lambda$ denote the shadow price of the budget constraint, we obtain the standard Ramsey formulas:

$$\frac{a - LRIC_H}{a} = \frac{\lambda}{1+\lambda} \frac{1}{\eta_H}$$

and

$$\frac{a_L - LRIC_L}{a_L} = \frac{\lambda}{1+\lambda} \frac{1}{\eta_L}$$

where η_H and η_L are the elasticities of demand at prices a and a_L.

Now, suppose that the market is liberalized when the new technology arrives. Then the new access charge is cost based:

$$\hat{a}_L = LRIC_L$$

And so, to break even, the incumbent must charge a still higher access price before the innovation:

$$\hat{a} > a$$

Box 4.5
State-Contingent Markups

Consider the random demand extension of the Ramsey pricing formula. The investment cost k_0 is incurred before the uncertainty about demand is resolved. Let $V(q_1, q_2, \theta)$ denote the consumers' gross surplus in state of nature θ from consuming q_1 and q_2 units of the operator's and the competitors' services, respectively, on the competitive segment. The consumers' net surplus is then $S_0(p_0, \theta) + S(p_1, p_2, \theta)$ where $S(p_1, p_2, \theta) = \max_{\{q_1, q_2\}}\{V(q_1, q_2, \theta) - p_1 q_1 - p_2 q_2\}$, and $S_0(p_0, \theta)$ is the net surplus on local calls. The prior distribution of the demand parameter θ is given by $F(\theta)$, with density $f(\theta)$ on an interval $[\underline{\theta}, \bar{\theta}]$.

We impose the constraint that the incumbent breaks even in expectation. The Ramsey program can then be written

$$\max_{\{p_0(\cdot), p_1(\cdot), p_2(\cdot)\}} \int_{\underline{\theta}}^{\bar{\theta}} \{S_0[p_0(\theta), \theta] + S[p_1(\theta), p_2(\theta), \theta]\} f(\theta) d\theta$$

subject to expected profit being nonnegative:

$$\int_{\underline{\theta}}^{\bar{\theta}} \pi[p_0(\theta), p_1(\theta), p_2(\theta), \theta] f(\theta) d\theta \geq 0$$

Letting $(1 + \lambda)$ denote the (state-independent) multiplier of the budget constraint, the (state-contingent) optimal access price is given by the standard formula:

$$a(\theta) = 2c_0 + \frac{\lambda}{1 + \lambda} \frac{p_2(\theta)}{\hat{\eta}_2(\theta)}$$

If the final price $p_2(\theta)$ increases and the superelasticity $\hat{\eta}_2(\theta)$ does not increase with the demand parameter θ, then $a(\theta)$ increases with θ. In this sense, the access charge should increase in high-demand states.

as high demand does not reduce the (super) elasticity of demand for the competitors' offering.

4.5 Cost-Based Access Pricing and Exclusion

We will define *exclusion* as the incumbent's denying access to rivals through nonprice methods, with the goal of transferring the incumbent's untapped market power in the bottleneck segment to the competitive segment. Exclusion is an instrument, and not a goal, because it is not intended *per se* to hurt rivals, even though it actually does so.

4.5.1 The Theoretical Argument

Exclusion is tempting in the presence of asymmetric constraints on retail and wholesale prices. When facing a stringent ceiling on access charges and a looser constraint on final services, perhaps no constraint at all (as in the case of a deregulated competitive segment), an operator has a strong incentive to deprive its rivals in the final segments from access to the bottleneck through nonprice methods.

The reforms that are contemplated in the United States and the United Kingdom create such asymmetries among product lines because they intend to leave the incumbent with no marginal profit on the access segment through LRIC regulation of the access price.

To illustrate the theoretical argument, let us consider the simple case of an unregulated retail market, long distance, say, together with a price cap on the access charge to the local bottleneck. The access charge a must not exceed a cap $\bar{a}$ that lies below the monopoly price for access that the operator would charge if interconnection were not regulated:

$$a \leq \bar{a}$$

Suppose further, and to simplify the exposition, that the operator and its long-distance competitors produce perfect substitutes at equal and constant marginal cost $c_1 = c_2 = c$. (The reasoning extends straightforwardly to differentiated services and efficiency disparities.)

The cap on the access charge prevents the operator from exploiting its monopoly power on access to long distance. As a substitute the operator would then want to charge the monopoly price, p_1^m, say, on long distance. The long-distance price, however, is constrained by competition. That is, the operator must charge a long-distance price p_1 that is constrained by the total marginal cost of its competitors:

$$p_1 \leq \bar{a} + c$$

In other words, competitive pressure on the final market prevents the operator from translating its untapped monopoly power on access to the competitive segment. The operator, therefore, has an incentive to deny access to its competitors or to raise their costs, in order to loosen the competitive pressure on the final segment. This incentive is stronger, the lower the cap on the access charge.

Remark 1: Distinction between Exclusion and Predation   Unfortunately, the academic literature and the policy debate often blend the notions of exclusion and predation. The common features of these two behaviors are that they are profit maximizing and that they hurt rivals. The rationales for the two behaviors are quite different, however, and a regulatory environment may well generate incentives for one but not the other, as we will see.

The purpose of exclusion is not per se to hurt rivals. Rather, exclusion is meant to loosen the regulatory constraint. That is, hurting the competitor is an instrument, not a goal. Exclusion refers to a short- and long-run profit-maximizing strategy. In contrast, predation corresponds to a sacrifice of short-term profits in order to boost long-term gains by forcing rivals out of the market. Predation can be profitable only if it leads competitors to exit the market enduringly, for example, because their financial health does not allow them to incur necessary investments or to pay for operating expenses.

To sum up, exclusion increases the operator's profit while it is practiced. Predation lowers the operator's profit and therefore can be rational only if it creates sufficient losses for the rivals that they enduringly exit the market and if future monopoly gains offset current predation losses.

Remark 2: The Deregulation of Competitive Markets: A Sophism?   It is now almost universally accepted that a segment that is subject to strong competition should be deregulated. The two starting points for this belief are well taken: On the one hand, competition usually is a favorable substitute for regulation in competitive markets. On the other hand, past experiments with a mixture of regulation and competition, in particular in the telecommunications industry, have often been unsatisfactory. For example, regulators have generated some inefficient entry by fixing prices on competitive segments and by preventing operators from offering price discounts.

But when one of the competitors owns a bottleneck, it is less clear that flexible regulation, in which the operator enjoys downward flexibility in the competitive segments (and thus can respond to competitive moves) but no upward flexibility, is dominated by deregulation. The situation we have described shows that the operator would have much less incentive to exclude rivals if its final price itself were constrained, for he would not be able to exploit his monopoly power in the competitive segment once the rivals are excluded. We thus conclude that the deregulation of competitive segments is costly, since it substantially increases the monitoring requirements. It should be noted, though, that this deregulation, while complicating the regulation of access, reduces the regulatory burden in the relevant retail markets, especially when these markets experience frequent technological and pricing innovations.

4.5.2   Examples of Exclusionary Behavior

This theoretical argument has very practical implications for the telecommunications industry. Indeed it provides a unifying framework to analyze a number of concerns that have been expressed relative to the entry of the regional Bell operating companies (RBOCs) into the U.S. long-distance market.[18]

In particular, the long-distance incumbents and part of the Clinton administration have listed a number of exclusionary acts that the RBOCs, the owners of the local networks, may have employed or especially could use once they are allowed to enter the long-distance segment.

It is worth stressing that we do not take sides on whether these accusations are well founded. Besides, incentives to exclude are likely to depend on the extent of regulatory oversight as well as on the operators' desire to preserve goodwill (say, on the probability that the RBOCs attached to the possible revision of Modification of Final Judgment in case of "good behavior"). So, past experience may lead us to under- or overestimate the relevance of exclusionary behavior. Rather, we use the American debate to illustrate one of our key points: *Asymmetric regulations create perverse incentives and generate a suspicion against the integrated operator. They thereby call for heavy-handed regulatory monitoring.*

Even though all exclusionary practices described in the American debate are fundamentally related, it is useful to break them into three categories:

- *Refusals and delays in interconnection:*
  - Invocation by the operator of a high cost of providing supplemental capacity or of modernizing existing facilities to accommodate the demand for access by rivals.
  - Staggering of the upgrade of switches so as to delay the introduction of a new service by a competitor until the operator is technologically able to provide a similar service.
- *Raising rivals' costs:*
  - Tie-ins or refusal to unbundle, thereby forcing the rivals to purchase elements or functionalities that they do not need.

---

18. There are too many references for them to be listed here. The readers may in particular want to consult Bernheim and Willig (1994), which contains many of the long-distance companies' concerns and, on the RBOCs' side, the memorandum of Bell Atlantic, BellSouth, NYNEX, and Southwestern in support of their motion to vacate the MFJ.

• Requirement that the rivals purchase costly interface equipment.
• Technological choices (network configuration, standards, interface equipment) that favor the operator over its rivals.
• Requirements for rivals to disclose business plans or commercial information.
• *Lowering rivals' demand:*
  • Refusal or delays in providing number portability.
  • Imposing long access codes on the rivals' customers.
  • Insufficient maintenance of the network.

4.5.3   Exclusion or Efficient Behavior?

A natural response to this long list of possible exclusionary behaviors would be a per se prohibition of such practices. Such an attitude, however, is unwarranted, as most of these practices can be justified by efficiency considerations. For example, it may be that the new technologies demanded by rivals indeed require a costly upgrade of the network, and that rivals attempt to build a market niche that is profitable only if the operator bears part of the upgrade costs. Number portability may be costly to install in the short run. The disclosure of the rivals' business plans may allow a better dimensioning of the operators' network capacity. And so forth.

Thus the regulator can assess the grounding of accusations of exclusionary behaviors only through a detailed analysis of the operator's technological and commercial environment, and to some extent by substituting her judgment for the operator's business judgment. A *rule of reason* approach, which, as we have seen, is conceptually far superior to a per se stance, requires sufficient regulatory staffing, knowledge of the technology, and independence vis-à-vis the lobbies.

There are, therefore, two possible options. Either one uses asymmetric regulation and thus creates incentives for exclusion, and one sets up heavy-handed regulation that controls exclusionary practices. In our view this stance (1) involves substantial regulatory cost for the government and the firms, (2) is limited by the need to substitute for business judgment, and possibly (3) is subject to strong lobbying pressures.

Or, one eliminates the perverse incentives set up by the regulatory framework in the first place and reorients regulatory resources toward the monitoring of more circumscribed behavior, such as predation. This possibility will bring us to a discussion in section 4.7 of the notion of a global price cap, which aims at reestablishing the symmetry between product lines and thus provides incentives for a better allocation of resources.

4.6   ECPR and Its Applications

Recall from section 3.2.5 that the efficient component pricing rule, or Baumol-Willig rule, allows the incumbent to charge access prices equal to her opportunity cost on the competitive segment.

4.6.1   The Theoretical Debate

ECPR has been criticized repeatedly by economists in the policy litera-ture.[19] And several regulatory agencies and laws have recently argued against its use for telecommunications. In its December 1994 consulta-tive document "A Framework for Effective Competition,"[20] the British Office of Telecommunications (Oftel) states, "The ECPR approach has some useful properties in limiting inefficient entry and would allow an incumbent to recover common costs." It nevertheless argues against the use of ECPR on the following grounds: (a) The entrant's full cost on the competitive market is likely to exceed the incumbent's incremental cost on that market. (b) The incumbent's retail tariff guides the access price, and thus entrants must adjust their retail prices when the incumbent does. (c) ECPR may force the entrants to contribute to the incumbent's cost inefficiency.

A different critique is leveled at ECPR by U.S. regulators. Consistent with the Telecommunications Act of 1996, the FCC states that ECPR is an improper method to set prices for interconnection and network ele-ments because the method is not cost based and because ECPR provides no mechanism for forcing retail prices to competitive levels.

While the U.S. and U.K. regulators converge to broadly consistent policies (cost-based access pricing using, if possible, forward-looking long-run incremental costs), their objections to ECPR are markedly dif-ferent and result partly from the different regulatory environments in the two countries. In the United States, the incumbent local ex-

---

19. See, e.g., Economides and White (1995), Ergas and Ralph (1994), Ralph (1994), and Tye and Lapuerta (1996), as well as the influential WIK/EAC report written for the European Commission (see WIK/EAC, 1994).

20. See pages 14–15. See also the director general's July 1995 statement "Effective Com-petition: Framework for Action" and the December 1995 consultative document "Pricing of Telecommunications from 1997."

change carriers' (ILECs') long-distance prices will be unregulated once these carriers are allowed to enter the long-distance market. Like New Zealanders, who no longer have a telecommunications regulator, American authorities note that ECPR is only a partial rule and cannot by itself fully regulate incumbents. And indeed, as William Baumol and Robert Willig themselves have repeatedly emphasized, ECPR has been designed for regulatory environments that differ from those encountered in the United States and New Zealand.

Returning to Oftel's concerns, argument a refers to the existence of fixed entry cost or, more generally, to increasing returns to scale for the entrant. Such costs imply that at equal marginal costs and with perfect substitutes, entry is inefficient, unless entry is not desired per se but rather is motivated by its use as a yardstick to evaluate the incumbent's cost performance. We refer to section 3.3 for a discussion of entry with fixed entry costs. Argument b raises the issue of the speed with which the incumbent's retail prices are adjusted. An alternative interpretation of ECPR is that the incumbent sets access prices for entrants and is then free to adjust retail prices subject to the floors defined by ECPR.[21] Argument c points out that ECPR is a partial rule not only with respect to the determination of bottleneck costs, but also with respect to the provision of incentives to minimize cost on the bottleneck segment. The point of view of ECPR proponents, however, is that incentives to minimize costs on the bottleneck segment should be provided by instruments other than the access charge.

Last, ECPR may be (and has been criticized for being) informationally demanding. The operator's marginal cost on the competitive segment may not be measured precisely. And to the extent that its computation is based on accounting data (which is likely to be the case), the operator has an incentive to bias its investment choices so as to reduce its marginal costs on the competitive segments and thus to comply more easily with ECPR. For the same reason, it also has an incentive to exert a greater effort to reduce its costs in the competitive segments.

4.6.2   An Application

The design in the early 1990s of BT's access charges by Bryan Carsberg (director general of the Office of Telecommunications until 1992) draws its inspiration from ECPR. Box 4.6 sketches its main features.

---

21. That is, ECPR is used in its weak inequality version: $a \leq p_1 - c_1$, or $p_1 \geq a + c_1$.

Box 4.6
The Oftel Rule

The British Office of Telecommunications' (Oftel's) interconnection policy for British Telecom (BT) in force from the early 1990s through 1997 drew its inspiration from ECPR. (The following schematizes the policy in order to highlight its main features better. See Cave [1993], or the director general's statement "Policy on Separation and Interconnection" [1992] for more details.) Start from the access deficit (AD) to be covered by markups. In our context, it is equal to the fixed cost of the local network:

$$AD = k_0$$

The Oftel rule is a usage-based rule. The competitors pay a "tax" or "markup" or "access deficit contribution" (ADC) on a call proportional to the profitability of that call for British Telecom. In our basic model, there is a single good (long-distance calls) produced by competitors. The access charge is then

$$a = 2c_0 + ADC = 2c_0 + \frac{AD}{q_1} \frac{B_1}{B_0 + B_1 + B_2}$$

where the benefits are defined by $B_0 = (p_0 - 2c_0)q_0$, $B_1 = (p_1 - 2c_0 - c_1)q_1$, and $B_2 = (a - 2c_0)q_2$.[22]

Several remarks are in order here:

• All benefits, in particular B_2, depend on the access price. The access price is then the outcome of a fixed-point process. In practice, the access deficit contribution can only be based on historical data or on forecasts.

• The preceding formula can easily be generalized to the existence of multiple competitive segments. It then yields differentiated access prices. Oftel defines two main access prices for Mercury, in respect to national and international calls (Oftel's director general can subdivide categories into subcategories in order to define more appropriate access deficit contributions if needed). Let $B_3 = (p_3 - c_0 - c_3)q_3$ denote BT's profit on international calls, where c_3 is its nonlocal marginal cost[23] and q_3 its international output. (An international call uses only one BT local loop, the one corresponding to origination, whereas domestic calls use two.) The benefits from Mercury's access charges a_1 and a_3 for domestic and international calls are now

$$B_2 = (a_1 - 2c_0)q_2 \quad \text{and} \quad B_4 = (a_3 - c_0)q_4$$

where q_4 is Mercury's international output. The access prices charged to Mercury on the two competitive segments—domestic long distance and international—are, respectively,

---

22. There are actually minor differences in detail that we ignore, since we are aiming at a schematic account of the policy. In practice, both c_0 and the access deficit are calculated on a fully allocated cost basis.

23. For notational simplicity, we assume that BT and Mercury do not pay access charges for termination to foreign operators, and that BT receives no foreign calls. While these assumptions are blatantly incorrect, the notational modifications needed to reflect reality are straightforward.

Box 4.6 (continued)

$$a_1 = 2c_0 + \frac{AD}{q_1} \frac{B_1}{B_0 + B_1 + B_2 + B_3 + B_4}$$

and

$$a_3 = c_0 + \frac{AD}{q_3} \frac{B_3}{B_0 + B_1 + B_2 + B_3 + B_4}$$

The linkage with BT's profitability in practice implies that the access price per end (origination or termination) is higher for an international call than for a domestic call.[24]

• The preceding formulas do not define British Telecom's consumer prices p_0, p_1, and p_3. These are regulated by a price cap.[25]The basket of goods subject to this price cap includes the final goods, but not the access good, whose price is determined separately by the formulas. Such a price cap is a "partial price cap."

• The Oftel rule takes a very simple form *when the telephone operator's budget is balanced.* Suppose that

$$B_0 + B_1 + B_2 + B_3 + B_4 = AD$$

Then

$$a_1 = p_1 - c_1$$

and

$$a_3 = p_3 - c_3$$

Under budget balance, access prices are exactly equal to the telephone operator's "opportunity costs." In other words, the telephone operator's external price for access (a_i, $i = 1$ or 3) is equal to a notional internal transfer price ($p_i - c_i$, $i = 1$ or 3) computed by assuming that BT's competitive divisions charge their marginal cost (including the internal transfer price) on the competitive markets. Under budget balance, the Oftel rule boils down to the *efficient component pricing rule.*

• Application of the Oftel rule (like that of some other rules) requires proper separation between the bottleneck and the competitive segments. For example, a transfer of accounting costs or a real resource reallocation between the bottleneck segment and a competitive segment in the form of a decrease in B_0[26] and an equal increase in B_1, say, raises the access charge without imposing a cost on British Telecom. This result is due to the fact that the price cap is a partial one, so that an increase in the access charge has no direct impact on the operator's price flexibility. (We will come back to this theme from a different perspective in the next section.)

---

24. There is also a local-call ADC rate, which by the same logic is smaller than the ADC rates for international and national calls. In practice, most of these ADCs have been waived by the director general (except for Mercury's international calls) in order to promote competition (see section 3.3).

25. Subject to some further constraints (e.g., the RPI + 2 constraint on rentals that slows down rate rebalancing).

26. Keeping the measure of the access deficit constant.

4.7   Global Price Cap

The most promising avenue for basing of the rate structure on demand considerations and reducing the scope for the capture is to delegate pricing to the telephone operator through a price cap. Some will counter that the firm itself may have imperfect knowledge of the demand curve. But imperfect knowledge of the demand curve has never prevented unregulated firms from practicing subtle forms of price discrimination, charging low prices for products with elastic demands and high prices for products with low elasticities, adjusting prices to reflect the intensity of competition, and correcting prices upward when selling substitutes and downward when selling complements.

In theory, the Ramsey pricing structure can be obtained by imposing a *global price cap*[27] on the incumbent, with the following features:

1. The intermediate good (access) is treated as a final good and is included in the computation of the price cap (this is the definition of a global price cap).

2. Weights used in the computation of the price cap are exogenously determined and are proportional to the forecasted quantities of the associated goods.

That is, a price cap induces a firm to select the proper Ramsey structure as long as all goods (including, here, access goods) are included in the definition of the cap and the weights are *exogenously* fixed at the level of output that will be realized (see box 4.7).

The intuition for this result is straightforward: An unregulated firm with market power does not maximize social welfare because it does not internalize the increase in consumer net surplus brought about by a price reduction. A $1 decrease in the price of a service increases consumer net surplus by an amount equal to the consumption of that service. Let us now look at profit maximization by a regulated operator subject to a price cap covering all its services. The global price cap forces the firm to internalize the increase in consumer net surplus in proportion to the weights in the cap (the coefficient of proportionality is the shadow cost of the price cap constraint). Therefore, if the weights in the global price cap are equal to realized consumption quantities and

---

27. Global price caps were proposed in Laffont and Tirole (1996). They were also briefly discussed in Laffont and Tirole (1994). We refer to Baumol, Ordover, and Willig (1997), Grout (1996), and Schwartz (1996) for careful discussions of the concept.

the level of the cap is chosen appropriately, the operator perfectly internalizes net consumer surplus when maximizing profit.[28]

This result holds for any demand structure and, in particular, allows for the possibility of substitutability between access goods and final goods. That is, a global price cap in principle allows a proper usage-based pricing structure apparently without a need for the regulator to know the demand functions. As we will see, however, the exogeneity of weights qualifies this encouraging result, as weights based on realizations of output create some difficulties.

The global price cap assumption is at odds with standard practice. Actually, the very debate about access pricing rules reflects the general view that intermediate and final goods should be treated asymmetrically. A global price cap implicitly denies the difference between access services and other services.

Remark 1. Price Cap and Profit Sharing It is important to point out that we give the phrase "price cap" a more general meaning than contemporary regulatory usage. A price cap is logically consistent with profit-sharing rules, although its usage has been restricted to situations in which the regulated firm is (theoretically) residual claimant of profit. That is, once a price cap has been set, any profit-sharing mechanism can be superimposed without affecting the implementation of the structure of Ramsey prices.[29]

Remark 2: Cross-Subsidies A global price cap makes the operator residual claimant of profit until the next regulatory review. Any cross-subsidy can only reduce profit during that period. But we should also ask whether the intertemporal profit sharing associated with the ratchet

---

28. Formally, let $\pi(\mathbf{p})$ and $S^n(\mathbf{p})$ denote the firm's profit and the consumers' net surplus for price vector $\mathbf{p}$. A social-welfare-maximizing firm subject to a budget constraint would maximize $\pi(\mathbf{p}) + S^n(\mathbf{p})$ subject to $\pi(\mathbf{p}) \geq 0$. That is, it would maximize $\pi(\mathbf{p}) + \alpha S^n(\mathbf{p})$ for some $\alpha \in (0, 1]$. When increasing price p_k by one unit, a profit-maximizing firm ignores the impact $(-q_k)$ on the net consumer surplus, where q_k is the demand for good k. However, a profit-maximizing firm subject to price cap $\Sigma_k w_k p_k = \mathbf{w} \cdot \mathbf{p} \leq \bar{p}$ maximizes $\pi(\mathbf{p}) + \beta(\bar{p} - \mathbf{w} \cdot \mathbf{p})$ and therefore chooses the proper relative prices if the weights are exogenous and proportional to the realized outputs.
29. Suppose for simplicity that the regulated firm has private information about a cost parameter β. Then, under certain conditions (see Laffont and Tirole, 1993, chap. 3), optimal regulation can be decomposed into two rules: a price cap rule, $\sum_{k=1}^{n} w_k(\beta)p_k \leq \bar{p}(\beta)$, where the weights $w_k(\beta)$ are proportional to the forecasted output $\bar{q}_k(\beta)$, and a profit-sharing rule, in which a firm keeps $t = a(\beta) + b(\beta)\pi$ of its realized profit π, where $0 < b(\beta) < 1$.

Box 4.7
Partial and Global Price Caps

In our basic setup, in which the incumbent sells local calls, long-distance calls, and access services, a *global price cap* takes the following form:

$$w_0 p_0 + w_1 p_1 + w_2 a \leq \bar{p}$$

where w_0, w_1, and w_2 are the weights in the cap. Suppose that one adopts instead a *partial price cap*:

$$w_0 p_0 + w_1 p_1 \leq \bar{p}$$

together with ECPR, namely, $a = p_1 - c_1$ (which is an approximation of the Oftel rule reviewed in box 4.6). The incumbent then maximizes profit

$$(p_0 - 2c_0)q_0 + (a - 2c_0)q_2 + (p_1 - 2c_0 - c_1)q_1 - k_0 =$$
$$(p_0 - 2c_0)q_0 + (p_1 - 2c_0 - c_1)(q_1 + q_2) - k_0$$

subject to the partial price cap. Suppose further that the weights w_0 and w_1 are chosen proportional to anticipated (Ramsey) outputs $\bar{q}_0$ and $\bar{q}_1$, say,[30]

$$\bar{q}_0 p_0 + \bar{q}_1 p_1 \leq \bar{p}$$

Then, assuming correct expectations ($q_0 = \bar{q}_0$ and $q_1 = \bar{q}_1$), the incumbent biases its rate structure relative to the Ramsey optimum. Long-distance prices and the access charge are too high while local calls are too cheap. *By not including the access charge in the price cap, a partial price cap de facto subsidizes noncompetitive segments to the detriment of competitive ones.*

In contrast, a *global* price cap is able to achieve the Ramsey price structure. To achieve the Ramsey structure, weights must be proportional to actual quantities, say,

$$\bar{q}_0 p_0 + \bar{q}_1 p_1 + \bar{q}_2 a \leq \bar{p}$$

Suppose that ECPR ($a = p_1 - c_1$) is appended to the global price cap (the rationale for doing so as well as its cost will be discussed later). The global price cap then becomes a partial price cap, with weights that differ from the standard ones:

$$\bar{q}_0 p_o + (\bar{q}_1 + \bar{q}_2)p_1 \leq \bar{p}'$$

The comparison between formulas for this modified global price cap and the partial price cap illustrates clearly the limits of a partial price cap and the merits of a global one. Under ECPR, an increase in the final price p_1 also raises the access price. From the point of view of profit, the price increase thus affects *total demand on the competitive segment.* However, in the partial price cap constraint, the price increase is reflected only through its impact on the incumbent's demand on the competitive market. The pricing incentives, therefore, are biased in favor of high prices in the competitive segments under a partial price cap. In contrast, *a global price cap eliminates the discrimination between the incumbent and the competitors' outputs in the price constraint* and restores proper pricing incentives.

---

30. In contrast, British Telecom's price cap's weights were proportional to each product's revenue share.

Box 4.7 (continued)

Weight Setting

To implement Ramsey prices through a price cap, weights must be set proportional to the forecasted outputs. A precise forecast may demand information not available to regulators. In practice, weights are often based on recent outputs or revenues (for example, British Telecom's weights were the previous year's revenue shares for the various products). That is, if one does not have good forecasts of actual quantities, one must grope through a *tâtonnement* process. To limit the pricing distortions induced by endogenous weights and to accelerate convergence toward Ramsey prices, regulators must under a partial price cap come up with a reasonable forecast of the total demand on the competitive segment and of the market share of the incumbent. It is interesting to note in this respect that the exogenous-weights global price cap cum ECPR requires for the competitive segment only *a forecast of total demand* on that segment. While this task is arduous, it is still easier than the one that is needed to define a partial price cap and that consists in predicting (demand-, technology-, and regulatory-policy-contingent) production for the incumbent.[31]

---

31. The careful reader may object that the estimate of the competitors' market share resurfaces in the computation of the cap $\bar{p}' = \bar{p} + c_1\bar{q}_2$. In practice, though, the price cap is set iteratively and reacts to past profit performance. So, $\bar{p}$ and $\bar{p}'$ are the outcomes of a *tâtonnement* process. We leave it to future research to determine which of the *tâtonnement* on weights and that on the level of the cap is most affected by the ignorance of $\bar{q}_2$ (this will clearly depend on the level of c_1).

effect (see section 4.3.1) can recreate incentives for cross-subsidies. To the extent that the revision of the global price cap at the regulatory review is based on the operator's overall profitability (not on individual segments), the operator cannot gain by reducing its current profit through cross-subsidies (otherwise, it could also gain by "burning money").

4.8   Global Price Cap and Incentives to Exclude

Recall that a major drawback of LRIC regulation is that it does not allow the operator to make a margin on its bottleneck segment. The operator then has strong incentives to deny access to its rivals through nonprice methods, which in turn call for close monitoring by regulatory agencies. Incentives for exclusion are much attenuated if treatment of access services as a normal business segment is allowed and the operator can make money on them.

Under a global price cap (GPC), the operator manages its product lines "symmetrically," as it has no built-in incentive to favor one over another. In particular, excluding buyers of interconnection services amounts to mutilating a potentially quite profitable activity. A global price cap provides the operator with the flexibility to choose which product lines, retail or wholesale, are profitable. The theoretical analysis confirms that behavior that excludes rivals, raises their costs, or limits their demand tends to reduce the operator's profit. This reduction is particularly clear in the case where rivals have no market power and the exclusionary practice consists in raising the rivals' cost. The exclusionary practice then is tantamount to the operator's raising its own cost of providing the retail service through the competitive rivals. In contrast, we saw that even in this simple case the operator has a strong incentive to exclude under fragmented regulation.[32] Therefore, one should not hastily transpose concerns that are legitimate under fragmented regulatory schemes to global price cap regulation.

Global price caps thus enable regulation to be more light-handed, for global price caps reduce perverse incentives and therefore diminish the need for regulatory oversight of the operator's decisions. A global price cap scheme, therefore, is more compatible with deference to the operator's business judgment than existing schemes. A global price cap, however, still involves discretion with respect to the weights in the cap and to their revision process.

Global Price Cap and Predation   Global price caps raise the possibility of predation. To the extent that predation is often mingled with exclusion, a more common practice, this fear may be exaggerated, for we have observed that a global price cap tends to eliminate, rather than create, incentives for exclusion.

A price squeeze, however, is easy to carry out under a global price cap: The operator can increase the access charge and reduce its final price while keeping the price cap constraint satisfied. It thereby hurts its rivals on the retail market considerably. One can then conceive of

---

32. Box 4.8 shows that a price *floor* on access charges may need to be added to the global price cap to avoid exclusionary behaviors aiming at diverting the rivals' demand. (The price floor then serves to prevent the operator from charging a very low price on access to relax the price cap constraint and then to deny interconnection.) The price floor may possibly be set by the operator's rivals, who have the incentive to avoid exclusion.

Box 4.8
Global Price Caps and Incentives to Exclude

Recall our basic framework: The operator sells retail service 1 (long distance) at price p_1 and has marginal cost c_1. A competitive fringe sells retail service 2 (long distance) at price $p_2 = a + c_2$, where a is the access charge and c_2 marginal cost. Let $q_1 \equiv D_1(p_1, p_2)$ and $q_2 \equiv D_2(p_1, p_2)$ denote the demands for the two services. The operator also owns the local loop and sells access. Its marginal cost at each end is c_0. For convenience let us ignore local calls. A global price cap (GPC) has the following form:

$$w_1 p_1 + w_2 a \leq \bar{p}$$

where w_1 and w_2 are the weights on the retail and access services. In an idealized GPC, these weights are equal to Ramsey-realized quantities, $\bar{q}_1$ and $\bar{q}_2$, of the two services. The competitive-fringe assumption implies $p_2 = a + c_2$. Thus, in the absence of exclusionary behavior, the operator solves

$$\max_{\{p_1, p_2\}} (p_1 - 2c_0 - c_1)D_1(p_1, p_2) + (a - 2c_0)D_2(p_1, p_2)$$

$$= (p_1 - 2c_0 - c_1)D_1(p_1, p_2) + (p_2 - 2c_0 - c_2)D_2(p_1, p_2) \tag{1}$$

subject to

$$w_1 p_1 + w_2 p_2 \leq p + w_2 c_2 = p'$$

Let

$$m_1 \equiv p_1 - 2c_0 - c_1$$

and

$$m_2 \equiv a - 2c_0 .$$

denote the margins on the operator's two product lines. The first-order conditions (when $w_i = q_i$) are

$$m_1 \frac{\partial D_1}{\partial p_1} + m_2 \frac{\partial D_2}{\partial p_1} = (\mu - 1)q_1 \tag{2}$$

$$m_1 \frac{\partial D_1}{\partial p_2} + m_2 \frac{\partial D_2}{\partial p_2} = (\mu - 1)q_2 \tag{3}$$

One can show that

• The multiplier μ of the GPC constraint is lower than 1. ($\mu = 0$ is the unconstrained monopoly solution. $\mu = 1$ corresponds to $m_1 = m_2 = 0$, that is, to a zero gross profit and therefore to a negative profit once fixed costs are taken into account.)

• Privately optimal prices have a Ramsey structure. They are equal to Ramsey prices if the operator's profit (net of fixed costs) is equal to zero.

Let us now introduce exclusionary behavior indexed by a parameter f (f stands for "foreclosure" and is equal to zero in the absence of foreclosure).

1. Let us first assume that exclusion consists in *raising rivals' costs* (refusal to unbundle, requirement of point-of-termination bays, bias in the network's design, and so forth). The competitors' marginal cost becomes $c_2 + f$, where $f \geq 0$. Program (1) then becomes

$$\max_{\{p_1, p_2, f\}} (p_1 - 2c_0 - c_1)D_1(p_1, p_2) + (p_2 - 2c_0 - c_2 - f)D_2(p_1, p_2)$$

Box 4.8 (continued)

subject to

$$w_1 p_1 + w_2(p_2 - f) \le \bar{p} + w_2 c_2 = \bar{p}'$$

Let us assume that the optimal amount of foreclosure for the operator is f^*. Equations (2) and (3) still hold except that now

$$m_2 \equiv p_2 - 2c_0 - c_2 - f^*$$

Using the envelope theorem, the derivative of the operator's profit π with respect to f at $f = 0$ is thus

$$\frac{\partial \pi}{\partial f}_{\,|\,f=0} = (\mu - 1)q_2 < 0$$

Hence, if regulatory supervision leaves scope only for small amounts of foreclosure, then $f^* = 0$. Intuitively, the exclusionary practice amounts for the operator to raising its cost of producing indirectly (through the competitors) service 2.

Let us note that $f^* = 0$ is not optimal when access is subject to a separate strict price cap. Suppose for example that LRIC is applied, and so $a = 2c_0$. Then

$$\pi = (p_1 - 2c_0 - c_1)D_1(p_1, 2c_0 + c_2 + f)$$

and thus, if $p_1 > 2c_0 + c_1$ and the retail services are substitutes, the firm's profit grows strictly with f. More generally, the incentive to foreclose increases when the access charge decreases (and the operator's retail price increases). Relaxing the constraint on the access charge and tightening the constraint on the final price goes in the direction of a GPC and reduces the incentive to exclude.

Let us now return to the global price cap and relax the assumption that regulatory supervision leaves scope only for small amounts of foreclosure. The result stated earlier—the operator has no incentive to foreclose—no longer holds as it stands, especially if services 1 and 2 are fairly good substitutes: From some level of f on, the operator no longer mutilates its access business by raising f because there is no longer a demand for service 2 and therefore no demand for access; but an increase in f keeps relaxing the price cap constraint. Large amounts of foreclosure may then become optimal while small amounts are not!

Here is what we would recommend in such a situation: *Let entrants set an access charge floor!* However incongruous this policy might look, it obeys a clear logic. Entrants have an incentive to prevent their exclusion from the market. They can prevent foreclosure by making sure that the access segment is profitable enough for the operator. Suppose they set an access charge floor equal to the Ramsey level $a = a^R$ (the one that prevails in the absence of foreclosure). Then, from the price cap constraint, p_1 is bounded above by its Ramsey level. Quite importantly, the operator can no longer reduce a and increase f so as to keep $a + f$ (and therefore demands) constant while relaxing the price cap constraint. It can be shown that the operator chooses not to foreclose ($f = 0$) despite the absence of regulatory supervision in the matter. (Suppose first that the operator chooses $a = a^R$. Then π is clearly decreasing in f, and so $f = 0$. Then $p_1 < p_1^R$ and $p_2 < p_2^R + f$, where superscript R refers, as earlier, to the Ramsey levels. The

Box 4.8 (continued)

operator would then gain by "rebalancing" the pricing structure by choosing $f = 0$ for the given levels of p_1 and a.)

2. The other broad category of exclusionary behavior consists in *reducing the demand for the competitors' services* (refusal or delays in interconnection, lack of number portability, and so forth). It can be formalized as follows: Demand functions are $q_1 = D_1(p_1, p_2, f)$ and $q_2 = D_2(p_1, p_2, f)$, with $\frac{\partial D_1}{\partial f} > 0 > \frac{\partial D_2}{\partial f}$. One must further assume that exclusionary behavior (in the sense of an increase in f) is wasteful. Intuitively, foreclosure is socially detrimental if an increase in f lowers D_2 much more than it raises D_1. Note that, for the Ramsey prices obtained through the GPC and for $f = 0$, foreclosure reduces the operator's profit:

$$\frac{\partial \pi}{\partial f} = m_1 \frac{\partial D_1}{\partial f} + m_2 \frac{\partial D_2}{\partial f} < 0$$

if $|\frac{\partial D_1}{\partial f}| \ll |\frac{\partial D_2}{\partial f}|$. (One can find a lower bound for m_2/m_1 if services are substitutes.)

Once again, it is important to note that at *Ramsey prices*, interconnection is a profitable activity for the operator. In contrast, a tighter constraint on the access price creates incentives for foreclosure. In particular, if $a = 2c_0$, that is, if $m_2 = 0$, then necessarily

$$\frac{\partial \pi}{\partial f} = m_1 \frac{\partial D_1}{\partial f} > 0$$

We nevertheless have built an example in which

a. Foreclosure implies an almost perfect switch of clientele from service 2 to service 1, and thus has hardly any effect on total demand.

b. The operator has an incentive to exclude under a GPC. The intuition for this example is that (1) at Ramsey prices the operator loses little money in this switch of clientele, and (2) the operator can reduce its access price a toward marginal cost $2c_0$ (taking marginal cost as a floor, any price cap faces serious trouble if prices can be below marginal cost, as low prices and rationing create substantial opportunities for profiteering), ration access, raise p_1, and increase its profit.

We have not fully investigated the likelihood of this scenario. Two remarks, however, are in order:

1. Even in this pessimistic scenario, the GPC generates the same prices and incentive to exclude as a regulation based on incremental cost pricing of access ($a \simeq 2c_0$). Also, because of the revision of weights, the long-term profitability of the strategy remains to be examined.

2. There is a simple way for entrants to avoid foreclosure: They can insist on an *access price floor!* (The following argument resembles that underlying the efficiency wage theory.) A high access price makes interconnection a profitable activity and protects the entrants against exclusion. For example, in the

Box 4.8 (continued)

symmetric case, entrants could require (under a GPC) that the access price exceed the ECPR level (which, we recall, is optimal in the symmetric case):

$$a \geq p_1 - c_1$$

For any price satisfying this condition, the optimal choice for the operator is $f = 0$, even when foreclosure does not reduce overall demand. (Hence the entrants will not insist on $a > p_1 - c_1$!)

use of this strategy for predatory purposes. That is, the operator might reduce its profit until the next price review, but eliminate rivals who otherwise would have been used by the regulator as benchmarks in the future. The profitability of such predatory behavior unfortunately has not yet been analyzed; one can only presume that the threat of predation is more relevant when competitors do not have a long purse and when their assets cannot easily be purchased and managed by another company in case of bankruptcy.

As is the case in antitrust, rules against predation in the context of a regulated firm subject to a global price cap are imperfect and require further analysis. *In our current state of knowledge,* we feel that the efficient component pricing rule (ECPR) designed by Baumol and Willig is a reasonable rule against predation (see Baumol, Ordover, and Willig, 1997, and Laffont and Tirole, 1996, for further discussions of predation). This rule defines a ceiling on an access charge equal to the difference between the price and the marginal cost of the operator on the corresponding retail segment using the access facility. It therefore prevents the incumbent from operating such a price squeeze on an entrant. To be sure, we have seen in chapter 3 that in the absence of symmetry access prices above ECPR levels are sometimes vindicated; in such cases, using ECPR as a predation test unduly constrains the incumbent. We feel that *ECPR as a predation test is a good rule of thumb,* even though we acknowledge that some refined analysis may sometimes be required.

5   Multiple Bottlenecks and Two-Way Access

with Patrick Rey

5.1   Background

Although one-way access has been the central issue and will remain a key one for the opening of a number of segments to competition, the design of two-way access policies is quickly gaining prominence in the public debate. Until local competition is developed, two-way access in telecommunications will have been mainly confined to two types of interconnection:

• *International calls:* Telecommunications carriers have traditionally enjoyed a monopoly position in their respective countries and cooperated in the determination of termination access charges. For example, France Telecom pays a "settlement charge," or termination charge, to Deutsche Telekom when a French subscriber calls someone in Germany. These settlement charges are determined in private negotiations between the carriers. Interestingly, they are set above the marginal cost of terminating calls, especially in agreements with operators in less developed countries. As we will note, such high termination charges may be quite inefficient even from the point of view of profit maximization. The high level of termination charges in a number of countries has to be explained mainly by the fact that traffic is unbalanced (and not only by the high termination costs in these countries); because of income, price, and other effects, developed countries call less developed countries much more than they are called, and so the latter can draw revenue from high termination charges.[1]

---

1. In August 1997 the FCC announced benchmarks for pricing settlement rates (of 15, 19, and 23 cents per minute for high-, middle- and low-income countries), with the intent of reducing drastically the price of international calls to and from the United States. The average price of international calls for U.S. customers is 88 cents per minute, versus 13 cents per minute for domestic long-distance calls, which have only slightly lower costs.

It is to be noted, though, that international agreements among monopoly operators do not always generate large access charges. Indeed, termination charges for postal services within the European Union are set below cost, a policy which encourages inefficient rerouting of mail. (The domestic mail of country A may be routed to country B to be sent back to country A and benefit from the low international termination charges.)

• *Fixed-mobile interconnection:* The offering of mobile services by companies other than the incumbent fixed-link operator has given rise to a second set of two-way termination access charges. Charges for termination on a mobile network are often set quite high.

The experience with international settlements and with fixed-mobile interconnection may not shed much light on what will prevail for local competition. Fixed-link incumbents were monopolies and so did not compete for market share. France Telecom and Deutsche Telekom were just agreeing to put together two complementary inputs, their national networks, to offer an additional service, international calls. And, to some extent, mobile services have been more a complement than a substitute for fixed-link services, although this situation is changing rapidly with the price cuts for mobile services. In contrast, interconnection between local providers will involve substantial competition for market share between interconnecting networks.

While cooperation among competitors in setting access charges is relatively new in the telecommunications industry, it is commonplace in some other industries. Consider the joint ventures Visa and MasterCard in the credit card industry. These associations are each owned by thousands of member banks, which compete for customers on one side of the market and for merchants on the other side. The merchant's bank, the "acquirer," and the customer's bank, the "issuer," must be bound by an interconnection agreement if the transaction between the customer and the merchant is to use a Visa card or a MasterCard. This interconnection agreement involves an access charge, the "interchange fee," set at the association level;[2] see figure 5.1. There are many other examples of (potential or actual) cooperation between competitors: ATM

Unfortunately, the study of international settlements lies outside the scope of this book. See in particular Malueg and Schwartz (1998) for an interesting account of the many ways an international settlement may be gamed.

2. In contrast, for proprietary cards such as American Express, the issuer and the acquirer are the same company, and so the interchange fee is internal.

Figure 5.1
Credit card association

(automatic teller machine) networks, railroad trackage rights or combined transportation (railroad-trucks), airline interlining, and so on. One should be careful, though, before importing lessons drawn from one industry into another, since networks can differ substantially.

The telecommunications industry and regulators are currently defining principles for interconnection. Should it be a purely private matter, with operators agreeing on a wholesale transaction with a possible recourse to private arbitration in case of conflict, or should the regulator get involved? Should market forces be trusted to bring about efficient entry into the local market as well as competition-preserving agreements between established local operators?

New Zealand has embraced the laissez-faire view and refused to regulate access charges. In contrast, the FCC in its August 1996 order interpreting the U.S. Telecommunications Act of 1996 has recommended a fairly prescriptive approach. It proposed to set cost-based, nondiscriminatory access charges at the originating and terminating ends at forward-looking long-run incremental costs ($a = c_0$ at each end in our terminology).[3] Access charges are also meant to be reciprocal between carriers, unless there is a rebuttal of symmetry (symmetry may be violated if traffic is unbalanced or if access costs are very unequal). The FCC also suggests that states be allowed to impose a "bill-and-keep" regime (carriers do not pay any access charges to each other, that is, $a = 0$) if there is no rebuttal of symmetry. Such bill-and-keep arrangements had surfaced in the United States, for example, before the passage of the Telecommunications Act of 1996.[4]

---

3. In 1997, though, the FCC offered to adopt a less prescriptive approach by applying a price cap to LEC access charges. Similarly, Oftel in the United Kingdom has argued for substantial regulatory involvement, especially in the matter of termination charges (see chapter 1).
4. Sidak and Spulber (1996) note that the debate about the bill-and-keep rule is not new. In 1913, in *Pacific Telephone & Telegraph Co. v. Eshleman* (166 Cal. 640, 137 P.1119, 1913), the

This chapter, which borrows heavily from our joint work with Patrick Rey (Laffont, Rey, and Tirole, 1998a, 1998b), builds an economic theory of two-way access. One key assumption is an extension of the "sender pays" principle:

Calling company pays termination charge: The call receiver's network charges an amount a per minute to the caller's network for termination. The call receiver pays nothing.

This assumption reflects the widespread practice of relieving call receivers from any charge. Indeed, the entire policy debate is built on this premise. This practice is usually motivated by the telephone users' reluctance to have to pay anything for what they consider nuisance calls. It should be noted, though, that the call receiver is not accountable for charges that are imposed by his/her company onto other companies and their customers. The practice, therefore, may have some unappealing incentives implications. We should thus take a broader view, and consider the possibility of making the call receivers internalize the externalities they impose on calling parties; see section 5.7 for a very preliminary discussion of this view.

Another key assumption of our analysis is

Unregulated retail markets: Telecommunications carriers are free to set the prices they wish to final consumers.

This retail-deregulation assumption also deserves some comments. Again, it corresponds to a view commonly held among regulators

---

California Supreme Court found the bill-and-keep rule to be a taking. More recently: In two 1995 decisions, regulators in California and Washington summarily rejected the argument that a "bill and keep" system of reciprocal compensation between interconnected local telephone companies amounted to a taking of the incumbent's property because the volume of calls in its direction grossly outnumbered those originating on its sytem and terminating on the entrant's. (Sidak and Spulber, 1996, p. 10)

Before the start of either form of competition, the CPUC (California Public Utilities Commission) adopted for one year, beginning January 1, 1996, "interim" rules concerning the compensation to be paid by carrier A for having carrier B terminate A's calls on B's local exchange network. Rather than order carriers to price terminating access on the basis of some measure of cost (however defined), the CPUC adopted the "bill and keep" system advocated by the CLCs (new competitive local carriers), which the commission described as follows:

"'Bill and keep' is a method by which each LEC and CLC terminates local traffic for all other LECs and CLCs with which it interconnects, bearing its own capital and operating costs for these functions. Under this approach, individual LECs or CLCs theoretically bear a proportional share of the overall costs associated with reciprocal traffic exchange." (ibid., p. 119)

and industry experts, who envision head-to-head competition between telecommunications networks. This assumption of retail deregulation is usually built on two different premises. The first is that, once the local bottleneck has been eliminated, unfettered competition in all retail segments will ensue and there will therefore be no need for regulation of retail prices. The second and quite distinct premise is that telephone offerings change very fast, making retail regulation very awkward to implement in practice whether or not it is desirable in theory.

The second comment concerning retail deregulation is that some contemplated policies do in effect constrain retail pricing. In particular, the efficient component pricing rule (ECPR, see section 4.6) links retail and wholesale prices, and so any regulation of wholesale prices restricts flexibility in the setting of retail prices.[5]

Chapter 5 is organized as follows. First, section 5.2 notes that noncooperative access price setting is in general very damaging for both consumers and the industry. We then consider cooperation among competitors and ask: Will cooperative agreements in the wholesale market foster collusion in the retail market? Section 5.3 reviews a standard competition policy concern about wholesale market agreements. Section 5.4 shows that the competition policy concern has some validity, but section 5.5 points out that the telecommunications industry does not fit the standard paradigm. Indeed, it identifies four reasons why wholesale agreements may fail to facilitate retail collusion: (a) sidestepping termination charges through the buildup of market share, (b) volume discounts, (c) termination-based price discrimination, and (d) reception subsidies. Section 5.6 provides a first analysis of the impact of interconnection agreements on facilities-based and unbundled entry as envisioned by the Telecommunications Act of 1996. Section 5.7 concludes with brief discussions of two omitted topics. First, one can abandon the assumption that the calling company pays the termination charge and investigate the possibility that the call receiver be made accountable for any excess payment imposed on termination by his/her company. Second, a different (and more costly) type of competition may involve multiple active lines to the home (e.g., telephone and cable).

---

5. We will not study the impact of ECPR in a two-way access context. See Laffont, Rey, and Tirole (1998a) for an extensive analysis of the meaning and implications of ECPR in this context.

5.2   Ineffectiveness of Noncooperative Access Price Setting

To illustrate the need for wholesale agreements, consider first the case in which there is no competition for market share. Suppose that there are 100 networks, each with one captive consumer. The 100 consumers call each other. Each of the 100 networks noncooperatively sets an access price (a_i for network i) for terminating calls. Each network's perceived per-minute cost of conveying a call for its customer is its technological marginal cost up to the interface with the call receiver's network plus the termination charge. Assuming that the price of calls is independent of the terminating network, this termination charge is the *average* of the 99 termination charges chosen by the other networks. This assumption implies that an individual network's termination charge has a very small impact on the average termination charge paid by any other network, and therefore on the retail prices charged by the other networks. Each network then has an incentive to charge very high termination charges, since these hardly affect the number of calls it will receive; this policy results in high perceived marginal costs and in high final prices.

Although the inefficiency of noncooperative wholesale price setting is most striking with a large number of networks, it exists with only two networks. Consider the issue of settlement rates for international calls between two countries, each serviced by a monopoly operator, so that there is no competition for market share.[6] A noncooperative setting of access charges would necessarily result in the well-known double marginalization, each country adding its monopoly market to its perceived marginal cost. The originating country charges the monopoly price for the domestic demand for international calls, given its perceived marginal cost, which includes a monopoly markup on termination.[7] Box 5.1 reminds the reader of the standard double marginalization argument.

---

6. In the case of international calls, when countries are serviced by a single operator, retail price discrimination based on country destination is equivalent to retail price discrimination based on the network on which the call terminates, and so the relevant paradigm is that of a two-country world.

7. This point has been noted by a number of authors including Carter and Wright (1994), Economides and Woroch (1995), and Armstrong (1998). See Hakim and Lu (1993) and Malueg and Schwartz (1998) on arbitrage (say, through call-back), Yun, Choi, and Ahn (1997) on asymmetric development and domestic competition, and O'Brien (1991) on discrimination of settlement rates between competitors. Also see Einhorn (1997) for an extensive review of the literature on international settlements.

Box 5.1
The Chain-of-Monopolies or Pancaking Problem

Suppose, in a two-country world, that the demand curve for international calls in country A is $q = D(p) = p^{-\eta}$, where η is the elasticity of demand. Country A and country B are serviced by two monopoly operators, which maximize their profits. Country B first sets its access charge a, and then country A sets its retail price p for international calls (and symmetrically for international calls in country B, but we will not need to consider these for the argument). Keeping the notation of chapters 3 and 4, let c_0 denote the marginal cost of termination and $c = 2c_0 + c_1$ denote the total cost of a call (c_0 is also the origination cost, and c_1 is a trunk cost, say). So the marginal cost of an international call for country A is $c_0 + c_1 + a = c + a - c_0$.

For a given termination charge a set by operator B, operator A sets $p^*(a)$ so as to maximize

$$[p - (c + a - c_0)]p^{-\eta}$$

yielding, from the first-order condition, the inverse elasticity rule

$$\frac{p^*(a) - (c + a - c_0)}{p^*(a)} = \frac{1}{\eta} \tag{1}$$

Now consider operator B. The demand curve for termination of international calls, expressed as a function of the access charge a, is given by

$$\hat{D}(a) = [p^*(a)]^{-\eta} = \left(\frac{c + a - c_0}{1 - \frac{1}{\eta}}\right)^{-\eta}$$

Defining $\hat{p} \equiv c + a - c_0$, the maximization of

$$(a - c_0)\hat{D}(a) = (\hat{p} - c)\frac{\hat{p}^{-\eta}}{\left(1 - \frac{1}{\eta}\right)^{-\eta}}$$

yields

$$\hat{p} = \frac{c}{1 - \frac{1}{\eta}}$$

and so the equilibrium retail price for international calls is

$$p^* = \frac{\hat{p}}{1 - \frac{1}{\eta}} = \frac{c}{\left(1 - \frac{1}{\eta}\right)^2} \tag{2}$$

The profits are $c^{1-\eta}/(\eta - 1)[1 - (1/\eta)]^{-2\eta}$ at the terminating end (country B here) and $\eta/(\eta - 1)$ times this at the originating end (country A here). The fact that profits at the originating end exceed those at the terminating end is related to the familiar result that, in a symmetric price competition situation, the Stackelberg follower makes more profit than the Stackelberg leader (while, in contrast, the Stackelberg leader is more profitable under quantity competition). Here, the terminating network moves first by choosing a, and the originating network, the Stackelberg follower, reacts by choosing p^*. [The reader may, for example, check this result on a diagram for the case in which a finite price

Box 5.1 (continued)

equilibrium exists when the two networks select their absolute margins simultaneously, namely, when $\eta > 2$. The absolute margins for the terminating and
originating networks are $m_T \equiv a - c_0$ and $m_O \equiv p^* - (c + m_T)$, respectively. Using equation (1), the (upward-sloping) reaction curves are $m_i = (c + m_j)/(\eta - 1)$
for $i \in \{O, T\}$ and $j \neq i$.]

Were the two companies to get together, they could obtain the lower vertically integrated monopoly price

$$p^m = \frac{c}{1 - \frac{1}{\eta}}$$

for instance, by using two-part tariffs in which each operator sells terminating
access at marginal cost c_0, plus possibly a fixed fee. In particular, if the countries
are symmetric, they can agree on setting a reciprocal access charge equal to
marginal cost

$$a = c_0$$

and obtain the monopoly profit. Both operators, as well as the consumers,
would gain from the elimination of the second marginalization.

Remark   Equation (2) generalizes to a chain of n monopolies. For example, one
may have in mind n countries or states operating each a railroad network, a gas
pipeline, or an electric grid. If a transaction between two points must use the
infrastructure (tracks, pipelines, high-voltage lines) of the n countries or states,
then noncooperative access price setting yields final price p^* such that

$$\frac{p^*}{c} = \left(\frac{p^m}{c}\right)^n \tag{3}$$

where c is the total marginal cost and p^m is the monopoly price that would
prevail if prices were coordinated so as to maximize total profit.

It is worth recording here the *common fallacy that small players do not
have market power and should therefore face no constraint on their termination
charges*. This fallacy results from a misunderstanding of the definition
of a market. A network operator may have a small market share in
terms of subscribers; yet it is still a monopolist on the calls received
by its subscribers. Indeed, under the assumption that retail prices do
not discriminate according to where the calls terminate, *the network has
more market power, the smaller its market share*: whereas a big operator
must account for the impact of its wholesale price on its call inflow
through the sensitivity of its rivals' final prices to its wholesale price,
a small network faces a very inelastic demand for termination and thus
can impose higher markups above the marginal cost of terminating
calls.

This argument assumes that market shares are exogenous. As we will see, there is in such situations an incentive for networks to build market share in order to evade the high termination "taxes" and offer better deals to their customers. The chain-of-monopolies problem persists, however, when there is competition for market share.[8] Thus there is a general concern that noncooperative access price setting results in inefficiently high price equilibria.

5.3 Do Wholesale Agreements Promote Retail Collusion? The Patent Pool Analogy

Let us consider a highly stylized situation in order to illustrate the possibility that wholesale agreements can serve as a collusive device.[9] Two firms, $i = 1, 2$, compete in a retail market. To take an extreme case, suppose that they produce the same final output at marginal cost c. Each owns a patent, and the two patents refer to two distinct but equivalent technologies that enable production of the final output at cost c. We will further assume that competition in the final market is vigorous, namely that Bertrand competition prevails. (This assumption maximizes the gains from collusion.)

Under Bertrand competition, each firm charges its marginal cost,

$$p = c,$$

and so the duopolists make no profit. For future reference, we let p^m denote the monopoly price, that is, the price that would be charged by the firms if they were allowed to fix the retail price.

Suppose now that the duopolists create a joint subsidiary or joint venture, the "patent pool venture." The two patents are transferred to the venture, which then charges the firms a royalty (access charge, transfer price) a per unit of output, that is, per unit of usage of the

---

8. See Laffont, Rey, and Tirole (1998a).

9. The specific concern about patent pool agreements analyzed here is only one of the many concerns voiced by antitrust authorities. Others include the possibility that patent pooling allows the owners of substitute patents to collude in the market for licensing to third parties, the possibility that the patent pool agreement specifies ancillary restraints (such as geographic market division among the owners or retail price fixing), and the possibility that a covenant in which the owners agree to pool future patents reduces R&D competition and dulls the incentives to innovate. For more on this topic, see Andewelt (1984).

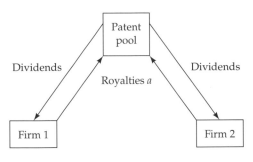

Figure 5.2
The standard competition policy concern

patents.[10] If the usage price a exceeds the marginal cost, 0, of making the ideas contained in the patent available for use by the firms, the patent pool venture makes a profit that is redistributed equally between its two owners in the form of dividends; see figure 5.2.

Each firm's *perceived* marginal cost of production is then the technological marginal cost c, plus the unit charge for having access to the patent, a, minus the dividend, $a/2$, received per unit of final output as an owner in the patent pool venture, or

$$c + \frac{a}{2}$$

Because Bertrand competition yields a price equal to perceived marginal cost, if

$$p^m = c + \frac{a}{2} \qquad \text{or} \qquad a = 2(p^m - c)$$

then the monopoly price prevails at the retail level. The downstream divisions of the duopolists make no profit because of Bertrand competition, but their joint upstream division receives the monopoly profit that is then redistributed to the firms.[11]

---

10. To do so, the two firms also agree on mechanisms for the disclosure and monitoring of their respective outputs.

11. Note that the same reasoning applies to n downstream competitors, with

$$a = \left(\frac{n-1}{n}\right)(p^m - c)$$

With a large number of firms, the access charge is approximately equal to the monopoly markup $p^m - c$.

5.4   Application to Two-Way Access Pricing in Telecommunications

On the basis of the standard antitrust concern about wholesale agreements between competitors, it is tempting to conclude that the determination of mutual access charges by the industry should allow carriers to enforce collusion even if they compete fiercely on the retail market. While there is a grain of truth in this analogy, it is also misleading. But let us begin with the grain of truth.[12]

Laffont, Rey, and Tirole (1998a, LRT in this chapter) builds the following symmetric framework for the study of two-way access. Two networks already in place, $i = 1, 2$, compete for consumers. Consumers solve a two-step problem. First, they must decide which network to join. Second, they must choose their variable telephone consumption (the number of calling minutes).

An "on-net" call is a call that terminates on the same network. That is, the caller and the receiver belong to the same network. In contrast, an "off-net" call occurs when the two parties belong to different networks.

Two simplifying assumptions are made:

• *Reciprocal access pricing:* Each network charges a per-minute access charge a for terminating its rival's off-net calls. The access charge or termination charge is thus the same for both networks. For the determination of the retail market equilibrium, it is irrelevant whether the access charge has been picked by a regulator or whether it stems from a private negotiation between the two operators. But we will, of course, investigate the levels of the access charge most preferred by the regulator and by the industry, respectively.

• *Balanced calling pattern:* We assume that the fraction of calls originating on a network that terminates on the other network is proportional to the latter network's market share.

It is easy to find examples in which the balanced-calling-pattern assumption is violated. Internet service providers, customer service centers, pizza parlors, pager subscribers, or cab companies almost exclusively receive calls, whereas phone-marketing agencies originate calls. If one network enlists the former type of customers and the other network the latter, then a very unbalanced calling pattern ensues. We

---

12. In independent work, Armstrong (1998) has obtained results that are similar to those described in this section.

will discuss the incentives to enlist customers with specific calling patterns in section 5.5.

Box 5.2 describes the LRT model. The key points of the analysis are discussed in the following subsections.

5.4.1   Endogenous Marginal Costs

Under the balanced-calling-pattern assumption, the fraction of calls originating on a network and terminating off net is equal to the rival network's market share of subscribers. If terminating access is priced at marginal cost, then the cost for a network of a call originated by one of its subscribers is independent of whether the call terminates on or off net. In contrast, if the termination charge exceeds (lies below) the marginal cost of terminating calls, then the average marginal cost of a call for a network grows (decreases) with its rival's market share. Hence, high termination charges create a strong incentive for networks to increase their market share in order to reduce their average marginal cost of producing calls; we come back to this *endogenous-marginal-cost effect* in section 5.5.1. Note for the record that this effect is negligible if the access charge is close to marginal cost.

Also, for given (positive) market shares, a network's perceived average marginal cost increases with the access charge. Thus, ignoring market share effects, a higher access charge induces networks to raise their retail price. This *raise-each-other's-cost effect* underlies the validity of the "grain of truth."

In this respect, it is worth recording the *bill-and-keep fallacy*. It is sometimes argued that if networks' inflows and outflows are balanced, so that the net payment between them is equal to zero, one might as well forget about access charges and not record any wholesale transactions. This "bill-and-keep" arrangement amounts to setting an access charge equal to zero. It is correct that a change in the access charge need not affect the (absence of) net payment between the operators, but the access charge affects each network's perceived marginal cost and therefore retail prices. It is, therefore, *not* neutral even if traffic is balanced.

5.4.2   Network Competition

LRT provides sufficient conditions for an equilibrium to exist (and be unique). The (symmetric) equilibrium price is then increasing with the

Text continues on p. 195.

Box 5.2
The Access Charge as a Factor Facilitating Collusion

(The duopoly framework developed in this box will also be used in boxes 5.3 through 5.6.)

Cost Structure

Let us assume (until section 5.6) that the two networks have full coverage and thus can connect any consumer at fixed cost f per customer. This fixed cost stands, for instance, for the cost of connecting the customer's home to the curb and for billing and servicing the customer.

As in chapters 3 and 4, we assume that a carrier incurs marginal cost c_0 both at the originating and terminating ends of a call. And we let c_1 denote the marginal cost in between (switching, trunk lines, . . .). The total marginal cost of a call is therefore

$$c = 2c_0 + c_1$$

Each network carries its customers' off-net calls on its network up to the terminating end where the call is handed over to its rival; and so the calling network incurs marginal cost $c_0 + c_1$ plus the access charge a. Thus, the *perceived* marginal cost for an off-net call is

$$c_0 + c_1 + a = c + a - c_0$$

Note that a network's average marginal cost of a call is endogenous. Letting α_j denote network j's market share, the balanced-calling-pattern assumption implies that a fraction α_j of calls originating on network i are off-net calls. Hence network i's marginal cost of calls is

$$c + \alpha_j(a - c_0)$$

Demand

For the moment, we assume that firms charge *linear retail prices* to their customers. Let p_i denote carrier i's retail price.

Networks are differentiated according to a symmetric Hotelling model. A customer who elects carrier i then has demand $q_i = D(p_i)$. In this simple model, consumers' variable demand is unrelated (except through the impact of prices) to their preference between networks. Let η denote the elasticity of this variable consumption with respect to price.

The networks' prices, of course, do not solely determine their customers' consumption. They also condition the allocation of consumers between the two networks. By symmetry, the networks share the market if they charge equal prices (so their market shares α_1 and α_2 satisfy $\alpha_1 = \alpha_2 = 1/2$). Let σ denote the sensitivity of firm i's market share to a unit increase in net consumer surplus. That is, remembering that a unit price decrease brings about an increase in net consumer surplus equal to his/her consumption q_i, then

$$\frac{\partial \alpha_i}{\partial p_i} = -\sigma q_i$$

Box 5.2 (continued)

The substitution parameter σ is equal to zero in the case of international calls provided by domestic monopolies. It tends to infinity (provided the market is shared) when the networks become close substitutes.

Illustration   In the symmetric Hotelling model that we have discussed, consumers differ along a characteristic indexed by x on the segment $[0, 1]$. The distribution of consumers' preferences on this segment is uniform. The networks are located at the two extremities of the segment ($x_1 = 0$, $x_2 = 1$). Letting v_0 denote the fixed gross surplus enjoyed by consumers from being connected and $u(q)$ their variable gross surplus from consuming q units of calls, then a consumer located at x and selecting network i obtains total gross surplus

$$v_0 + u(q) - t|x - x_i|$$

where t is Hotelling's differentiation parameter or "transportation cost" of not consuming a brand corresponding exactly to the consumer's tastes.
   Letting

$$v(p) \equiv \max_q \{u(q) - pq\}$$

with $v'(p) = -q(p)$, that is, (minus) the demand function, then the market shares are given by

$$\alpha_i = \frac{1}{2} + \sigma[v(p_i) - v(p_j)]$$

where $\sigma \equiv 1/2t$. (For some technical results, LRT uses a constant-elasticity demand function.)

Access Surplus or Deficit

The balanced calling pattern assumption implies that a fraction α_j of network i's call volume $\alpha_i q_i$ terminates on rival network j, and conversely. Because termination yields a per-minute profit (or loss) $a - c_0$, network i's access surplus (or deficit) is

$$A_i \equiv \alpha_i \alpha_j (q_j - q_i)(a - c_0)$$

Of course

$$A_1 + A_2 = 0$$

Note that the access deficits are equal to zero if either access is priced at marginal cost ($a = c_0$) or if call volumes per customer are the same for the two networks. This relation would obtain even if we introduced some asymmetry in network preferences so that $\alpha_i \neq \alpha_j$ (under symmetric demand functions, $q_i = q_j$ necessarily implies that $\alpha_i = \alpha_j = 1/2$). A third configuration without access deficit results when one carrier corners the market, that is, when one of the market shares is equal to zero; there are then no off-net calls (in contrast, the fraction $\alpha_1 \alpha_2$ of calls that terminate off net is maximized at equal market shares).

Box 5.2 (continued)

Ramsey and Monopoly Benchmarks

For future reference, let us compute the retail prices that maximize social welfare subject to the industry breaking even (the Ramsey price), and maximize the firms' profit, respectively. By symmetry, the Ramsey and monopoly allocations involve equal prices and market shares for the two firms.

Because we ignored joint and common costs (across consumers) the Ramsey price p^R is such that carriers break even on each consumer:

$$(p^R - c)q(p^R) \equiv f \tag{1}$$

In contrast, the monopoly price does not depend on the fixed cost of connecting a consumer (provided a monopoly provider is viable) and is given by the inverse elasticity rule:

$$\frac{p^M - c}{p^M} = \frac{1}{\eta} \tag{2}$$

Retail Price Competition

Fixing an arbitrary reciprocal access charge, a, we look at the outcome of (unregulated) retail price setting by the duopolists. Remembering that the average cost per call for network i is $c + \alpha_j(a - c_0)$, network i's profit is thus

$$\pi_i = \alpha_i \left\{ [p_i - c - \alpha_j(a - c_0)]q(p_i) - f \right\} + \alpha_i\alpha_j(a - c_0)q(p_j)$$

or

$$\pi_i = \alpha_i(p_i, p_j)\pi(p_i) + A_i(p_i, p_j)$$

where

$$\pi(p_i) \equiv (p_i - c)q(p_i) - f$$

is the retail profit on individual consumers, and

$$A_i(p_i, p_j) \equiv \alpha_i(p_i, p_j)[1 - \alpha_i(p_i, p_j)](a - c_0)[q(p_j) - q(p_i)]$$

is the access revenue (if positive, deficit if negative).

Straightforward computations show that the first-order condition for a symmetric equilibrium at price p^* is

$$\frac{p^* - \left(c + \frac{a - c_0}{2}\right)}{p^*} = \frac{1}{\eta}\left[1 - 2\sigma\pi(p^*)\right] \tag{3}$$

(LRT provide sufficient conditions for existence and uniqueness of equilibrium. We will later come back to the issue of existence.)

Interpretation   Equation (3) is a variation on Lerner's inverse elasticity rule. On the left-hand side of this equation lies the Lerner index. Firms share the market in a symmetric equilibrium, and so half of the calls are off net. The marginal cost perceived by each operator is thus $c + [(a - c_0)/2]$. To understand

Box 5.2 (continued)

the right-hand side, first assume that, as in the case of international calls with monopoly national carriers, the firms do not compete for market share, and so $\sigma = 0$. Then, the right-hand side is the inverse elasticity as in the standard monopoly formula. In general, though, firms do compete for market share, and so each firm faces an elasticity not only for its variable demand but also for its subscribership. The two combine into a modified and larger elasticity $\eta/[1 - 2\sigma\pi(p^*)]$.

How demand elasticity is modified to incorporate the market share effect depends on the substitutability parameter σ and on the net profit per consumer $\pi(p^*)$ that is forgone when losing a customer to the rival. [At equal prices, there is no access deficit or surplus, and so the per-firm profit is $\pi(p^*)$.]

Implications   Let us begin with the "grain of truth": Equation (3) defines an *increasing function* $p^*(a)$. So by raising a, the firms raise the equilibrium price provided the equilibrium exists. Indeed, it can be shown that the equilibrium exists (and is unique) if a is close to c_0. Then an increase in the reciprocal access charge does promote retail collusion by raising the competitors' perceived costs.

Second, we can ask what access charges, a^R and a^M, would be selected by a benevolent regulator and by the industry, respectively [subject to the caveat that the equilibrium characterized by equation (3) indeed exists]. The Ramsey access charge a^R must result in $\pi(p^R) = 0$, and so from equation (3)

$$a^R < c_0 \tag{4}$$

In contrast, the monopoly or collusive access charge must yield $p^* = p^M$; or, using equations (2) and (3),

$$a^M > c_0 \tag{5}$$

Joint and Common Costs

Let us now add a sunk network cost, say, of laying wires in trenches along the curb. Each network has incurred sunk cost $C/2$ per household, say, of building its network. To this fixed cost must be added the per-customer fixed cost of connecting the household's home to the curb and of servicing the household. The per-customer fixed cost, unlike the network fixed cost, is avoidable in the sense that the network does not incur the corresponding cost if it does not gain the consumer's business. The modified Ramsey benchmark (recalling that each network serves half of the consumers and thus that the joint cost per subscriber to be recovered is C) becomes

$$(p^R - c)q(p^R) - f = C$$

or

$$\pi(p^R) = C \tag{1'}$$

Box 5.2 (continued)

The sunk cost is otherwise irrelevant, in that it affects only the firms' profits but not their incentives. The analysis and results (3) and (5) are unchanged. However, combining (1′) and (3) shows that the comparison of the Ramsey access charge and marginal cost is now ambiguous:

$$a^R \lessgtr c_0 \tag{4'}$$

access charge, as a result of the raise-each-other's-cost effect. In this sense, the access charge is an instrument of tacit collusion.

Consequently, *the networks benefit from setting the access charge above the marginal cost of access.* By so doing, they mutually raise their rival's cost and generate higher profits without colluding in the retail market.

What about the socially optimal access charge? In a first step, let us assume that the networks' only fixed cost is an (avoidable) per-customer cost of, say, connecting the customer's home to the curb and billing and servicing the customer. That is, we ignore at this stage any joint and common cost incurred by a network when serving a group of consumers (e.g., the cost of bringing the network to the curb in their neighborhood). Thus, although there are increasing returns to scale at the consumer level (the marginal cost of a call is lower than the average cost, owing to the existence of a per-customer fixed cost), the technology exhibits constant returns to scale across consumers.

In the absence of a joint and common cost, the socially optimal termination charge lies below the marginal cost of terminating access. The intuition for this result is straightforward. From chapter 3, we know that the efficient access charge in a regulated environment without returns to scale is equal to the marginal cost of giving access. Here we do have constant returns to scale, but retail prices are deregulated and thus are only constrained by competition. The networks, provided they are differentiated, enjoy some market power and so are able to set prices above their (perceived) marginal cost. Offseting such markups requires, as in the standard monopoly problem, subsidizing the output. This purpose can be accomplished here by subsidizing one of the inputs, namely, terminating access (which is used in fixed proportions for given market shares). Unlike the textbook monopoly case, though, the subsidy is not paid by taxpayers, but rather by the other firm in the form of a termination charge below marginal cost. So, the two networks subsidize each other in the socially efficient solution, while they tax each other under the wholesale agreement that would prevail, were the networks free to negotiate their mutual access conditions.

In the presence of a joint and common cost, however, two opposite effects lead to an ambiguous comparison between the socially efficient access charge and the marginal cost of access. On the one hand, the subsidy (or market power correction) argument stated earlier is still valid, calling for below-cost access pricing. On the other hand, the presence of joint costs to be recouped requires, as shown in chapter 3, a markup on access. So, above-cost mutual access charges may well be desirable in the presence of nonnegligible joint costs.

Dessein (1998) investigates the relative incentive for networks to enroll low and heavy users.[13] This incentive depends on whether heavy users call more or less than they are called. Let us assume for conciseness that they call more than they are called. A price reduction now has two effects on the undercutting network's access deficit. First, all its customers call more, generating an outflow as discussed previously. Second, and a new effect, the price cut changes the *composition* of the network's customers. Heavy users are more price sensitive than low users because they gain more from a price reduction. So a price cut increases the fraction of heavy users in the network's clientele. If heavy users call more than they are called, then the impact of a retail price cut on the access deficit is strengthened. In this case, an access markup has a bigger collusive effect under consumer heterogeneity.[14]

5.5   Four Reasons Why High Access Charges May Not Facilitate Collusion

This section provides a number of caveats to the view developed in the previous section that networks can raise each other's costs and facilitate retail collusion through high access charges. For this purpose, it relaxes in sequence several assumptions underlying this view: weak endogenous-marginal-cost effect, absence of second- and third-degree price discrimination, and pricing of calls to the caller only.

---

13. In his model, consumers have constant elasticity demand functions ($q = kp^{-\eta}$, where k is smaller for low than for heavy users). Networks are otherwise differentiated (for heavy and low users alike) as in box 5.2.

14. However, price competition is tougher than under consumer homogeneity (at least if the access charge is close to the marginal cost of access), since heavy users are both more price sensitive and more profitable customers.

   See Dessein (1998) for other extensions of the model, including the case of "narcissistic calling patterns" that arise when customers tend to call customers of the same type more than other customers.

5.5.1   Evasion of the Access Tax through the Buildup of Market Share

In order to obtain the monopoly price at the retail level, the networks must agree on an access charge above marginal cost. How much above that cost depends on the substitutability between the networks. Were they not to compete for market share, as in the case of international telecommunications with monopoly national carriers, it would be optimal for the domestic monopolies to set the settlement charge at marginal cost. The companies' perceived marginal costs would then be equal to the true marginal costs, and each would charge the monopoly price in its reserved territory. In general, though, competition for market share erodes markups, and so the enforcement of collusion requires raising the access charge in order to bring the retail price back to its monopoly level. Tougher retail competition, therefore, calls for higher deviations from marginal cost pricing of access.

The question then is, Does a high markup above the marginal cost of access indeed generate high retail prices? To see that this is not a foregone conclusion, let us return to the two effects unveiled in the previous section. First, for given market shares, a higher access charge raises marginal costs and thus retail prices. This is the raise-each-other's-cost effect we have focused on. Second, for a given access charge set above marginal cost, a network's perceived marginal cost per call decreases with its market share; this is the endogenous-marginal-cost effect.

A network's perceived marginal cost of a call depends on the product of the access charge *markup* (difference between the access charge and the marginal cost of access) and of the rival's market share. Thus, as long as the access charge departs little from marginal cost, a reduction in the rival's market share does not much affect the network's perceived marginal cost. And indeed, LRT shows that *for small departures from marginal cost pricing of access,* an equilibrium in retail prices exists and is unique, and *the retail price is indeed an increasing function of the access charge.* The endogenous-marginal-cost effect is small and is dominated by the raising-each-other's-cost effect.

When retail price competition is intense, however, the networks want to impose substantial markups on access in order to make up for the lack of markup at the retail level. But as the access charge grows, the endogenous-marginal-cost effect becomes more important, and a market share buildup starts reducing the networks' perceived marginal cost substantially. This cost reduction creates the temptation to charge low retail prices in order to avoid paying the "access tax."

Indeed, as the access charge grows above marginal cost, there comes a point at which the networks are no longer willing to charge a high retail price and instead want to undercut. Where this point lies depends on network substitutability. If networks are very substitutable, then small price cuts reduce perceived marginal costs substantially.

As an illustration, suppose that the networks succeed in generating the retail monopoly price through a high access charge. In a symmetric equilibrium, the networks share the market and furthermore do not make *net* access charge payments to each other because the flows in and out of a network are balanced. If networks are very substitutable, then a network can corner the market, that is, double its market share, through only a modest price cut. At the lower price, the undercutting network makes a little bit less than the monopoly profit on each customer, but has twice as many customers; and it still does not incur an access deficit, since the rival network has no subscribers and therefore there are no off-net calls. Ironically, *it is precisely when very high access charges are required in order to sustain collusion that only small price cuts are needed for networks to reduce their fraction of off-net calls substantially.* And indeed LRT shows that no retail equilibrium exists with high substitutability and high enough access charges.

Last, let us compare the network interconnection problem with the patent pool paradigm of section 5.3. The key difference between the two situations is that in the patent pool paradigm the firms cannot evade the wholesale tax. In particular, if a firm stops sharing and corners the retail market, this firm must pay (at least) twice as much to the patent pool venture and thus to its rival for the use of the patents. In contrast, a telecommunications carrier's net access payment does not increase when it stops sharing the market and corners it. Put differently, the firms' perceived marginal production cost is exogenous in the case of payments to a patent pool joint venture, and endogenous in the case of two-way access to local networks.

5.5.2   Nonlinear Pricing

Under linear retail pricing, a high access charge may facilitate collusion because a network cannot sell more telecommunications services to its subscribers without incurring an access deficit. This reluctance to boost per-customer volume is what gives rise to high retail prices. Under linear pricing, a network is torn beween the desire to expand market share in order to benefit from the fat premium from enlistment of customers and the concern about generating an access deficit, since both are associated with a price cut.

Suppose now that networks offer two-part retail tariffs: a monthly subscriber charge (cum perhaps a connection charge) and a per-minute calling rate or usage price. We previously assumed that the monthly subscriber charge is set equal to zero, or, more generally, that it is exogenously set. Let us, in contrast, assume that the networks' monthly subscriber charges, and not only the per-minute calling rates, are unconstrained. *Networks now have two instruments each, and can separate the building of market share from the generation of call volume.* While an increasing call volume is still associated with a decrease in the usage price, a network can use the subscriber charge to build market share without inflating its outflow.

Indeed, the higher the per-customer profit generated by high access charges, the tougher the competition for market share. Thus networks compete fiercely on the fixed-fee dimension and offer low, perhaps negative, subscriber charges. (An example of a "negative" subscriber charge is the giveaway by mobile operators of telephone handsets or sharp subsidies to their purchase.) A case in point is the U.K. market in which high termination charges lead to high connection subsidies for mobile subscribers (Armstrong, 1997b).

Following the analysis in LRT, box 5.3 considers a simple example of competition in two-part tariffs. The consumers' variable demand is known by the operators; actually it is the same for all consumers. A standard result on two-part tariffs is that with known consumer demand, firms optimally set the usage price at marginal cost and then extract consumer surplus through a fixed fee.

The application of this result to our context requires two remarks. First, the extraction of consumer surplus in oligopoly is limited by the extent of competition. Under tough competition (high substitutability), little surplus can be extracted from the consumer. Second, *the usage price is set equal to the relevant marginal cost, namely, the network's perceived marginal cost.* An access markup implies that the perceived marginal cost lies above the true marginal cost. That is, under an access markup the networks reduce volume, just as under linear pricing. The raise-each-other's-cost effect still prevails; however, it does not enable firms to collude because they wage a fierce war along the fixed-fee dimension.

In the example studied in box 5.3, the access charge is no longer an instrument of collusion. Indeed, the firms' equilibrium profit is entirely

Box 5.3
Building Market Share without Raising One's Access Deficit

Let us return to the framework of box 5.2 and assume that the networks charge two-part tariffs

$$T_i(q) = F_i + p_i q,$$

where F_i is the monthly subscriber charge and p_i the usage price. Defining, as earlier,

$$v(p_i) \equiv \max_{q}\{u(q) - p_i q\}$$

and letting

$$w_i(q) \equiv v(p_i) - F_i$$

the market shares are now given by

$$\alpha_i = 1/2 + \sigma\left(w_i - w_j\right)$$

Because networks know the consumers' variable surplus function $u(q)$, their optimal two-part tariffs involve usage prices equal to their perceived marginal cost, or

$$p_i = c + \alpha_j(a - c_0)$$

Networks then make no profit on calls and derive their profit solely from the markup on the monthly charge, namely, the difference between the monthly charge F_i and the per-consumer fixed cost f. Intuitively, two-part tariffs make network competition resemble Hotelling's model of duopoly competition for consumers with unit demands, where the unit demand here refers to the consumers' 0–1 decision on subscribing to a network.

Simple computations, indeed, show that the equilibrium profit is equal to the Hotelling profit, or here

$$\pi_i = \frac{1}{4\sigma}$$

In particular, it is independent of the access charge (provided that the access charge does not depart too much from marginal cost; see LRT for details).

While the networks are not affected by the level of the access charge, social welfare is maximized when

$$a = c_0$$

The networks then set the usage price p_i at the true marginal cost c of calls and recoup the per-customer fixed cost (with a differentiation-contingent markup) through their monthly charges F_i.

Interestingly, Dessein (1998) shows that the access charge still has no impact on the equilibrium profit when there are high and low users and the networks use two-part or fully nonlinear tariffs (that is, second-degree price discrimination).

determined by the extent of their differentiation and is independent of the access charge. While this result is extreme, it illustrates well the general logic of the erosion through nonlinear pricing of the fat profits generated by access charge markups.

5.5.3   Termination-Based Price Discrimination

We have assumed that networks do not discriminate on the basis of whether the call terminates on their network or on the rival network. Yet, in the presence of an access markup (or for that matter, discount), a network's marginal cost depends on whether the call is on or off net. With an access markup, say, off-net calls are privately more costly to produce than on-net calls, and so, on purely cost-based grounds, networks would like to charge more for off-net calls. Note incidentally, that there is no technological obstacle to such price discrimination. In some instances there are no institutional constraints either,[15] and it is indeed used. For example, in many countries, calls terminating on mobile networks are more expensive that those terminating on fixed networks. In the United Kingdom, cable companies (which offer local service) partly engage in termination-based price discrimination in that they offer free calls to subscribers belonging to their networks. In contrast, the incumbent BT does not engage in such termination-based price discrimination. This section, based on Laffont, Rey, and Tirole (1998b), explores the implications of allowing networks to discriminate in this manner.

An interesting feature of this new form of competition is that termination-based price discrimination reintroduces network externalities among consumers. Interconnection together with uniform (non-termination-based) pricing implies that consumers, when choosing a network, do not take into account the choice of network by the people they will want to call.[16] In contrast, if on-net calls are cheaper than off-net calls, consumers are better off if the people they want to call select the same network. More generally, it is easy to see that an access markup (access charge above marginal cost) or an access discount (access charge below marginal cost) generates, respectively, positive or negative net-

---

15. Even in the presence of legal prohibitions against termination-based price discrimination, operators may attempt to find (imperfect) substitute forms of discrimination. For example, if entry is targeted at financial centers and company premises in large cities, then regional tariff differentiation may accomplish some of the goals of termination-based price discrimination. The two policies, however, do not quite have the same implications.
16. As long as consumers do not care about being called.

work externalities among consumers. Such externalities can be labeled *tariff-mediated network externalities.*

Interestingly, the presence of tariff-mediated network externalities does not create difficulties for the analysis; see box 5.4. We here ignore technicalities and just state the main insights.

First, *high access charges do not facilitate collusion as well as under uniform pricing.* The reason is basically the same as for nonlinear pricing. Suppose that the networks set two prices, one for on-net calls and the other for off-net calls; so, we consider a particular form of third-degree price discrimination but retain the linear pricing assumption. (The analysis is not much altered when combining the two forms of price discrimination; see Laffont, Rey, and Tirole, 1998b.) Whereas networks cannot build market share without incurring an access deficit under uniform pricing, they can do so with termination-based price discrimination. The access deficit depends on the volume of off-net calls, and therefore on the off-net price, but not on the on-net price; so a network can build market share by reducing its on-net price without increasing its access deficit. The reason why collusion may fail, as with nonlinear pricing, is that the network can compete along a dimension (on-net price here, monthly subscriber charge under nonlinear pricing) that does not inflate the access tax bill.

The second interesting insight relates to the welfare implications of allowing termination-based price discrimination. At first sight, one might believe that such discrimination is socially wasteful because it is neither cost nor demand based. Or, to be more precise, it is generated by a divergence between the privately perceived and the social costs of calls. The networks have no demand-based incentive to price discriminate according to termination, because a consumer's willingness to call another consumer is independent of the identity of the latter consumer's network. We conclude that termination-based price discrimination introduces a distortion in the consumers' marginal rates of substitution between on- and off-net calls.

We should, however, remember that the industry is in a second-best situation, and so adding a distortion to a set of existing distortions may turn out to increase social welfare. This is actually the case here in some circumstances. First, price discrimination intensifies competition, as we already noted. Second, when the networks are poor substitutes, price discrimination tends to alleviate the second marginalization generated by an access markup. Overall, *the welfare implications of termination-based price discrimination are ambiguous.*

Box 5.4
Termination-Based Price Discrimination

We return to the framework of section 5.4 and this time modify it by assuming that network i, $i = 1, 2$, charges two different prices, p_i for on-net calls and $\hat{p}_i$ for off-net calls. Again, we take the termination charge a as exogenous at the price-setting stage; this termination charge has been set earlier by a regulator or in a wholesale agreement between the two networks. Figure 5.3 summarizes the cost and price structures.

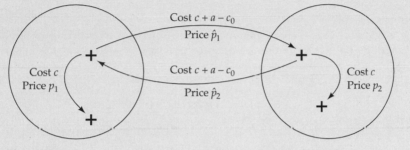

Figure 5.3

For tractability, we will assume that consumer demand has a constant elasticity η:

$$u(q) = \frac{q^{1-1/\eta}}{1 - \frac{1}{\eta}} \quad \text{or} \quad q = p^{-\eta}$$

Tariff-Mediated Network Externalities

Let us begin with an analysis of demand for given prices charged by the two networks. As earlier, letting

$$v(p) \equiv \max_q \{u(q) - pq\}$$

and introducing

$$w_i \equiv \alpha_i v(p_i) + \alpha_j v(\hat{p}_i) \tag{1}$$

(which reflects the assumption that a fraction α_i of the calls issued by a subscriber of network i are on net, and a fraction α_j off net), network i's market share is now

$$\alpha_i = 1/2 + \sigma(w_i - w_j) \tag{2}$$

Note that market shares depend on the difference of the net surpluses offered by the two networks. But this difference itself depends on market shares due to price discrimination. Market shares are thus obtained through "fixed-point reasoning." Letting

$$M_i = 1/2 + \sigma\left[v(\hat{p}_i) - v(p_j)\right]$$

denote the fictitious market share that network i would attract if all consumers

Box 5.4 (continued)

(incorrectly) expected all other consumers to join network j, simple computations yield

$$\alpha_i = \frac{M_i}{M_i + M_j} \tag{3}$$

Laffont, Rey, and Tirole (1998b) show that the demand equilibrium (that is, the allocation of consumers between networks for given prices) is unique except when M_1 and M_2 are both negative. In the latter case, however, there exists a unique stable equilibrium,[17] and this equilibrium is selected in the rest of the analysis.

Next, we turn to the determination of the price structure and level. A simple "proportionality rule" holds for the price structure. Specifically, the ratio of the off-net price over the on-net price is equal to one plus the relative access markup ("relative" meaning that the access markup is divided by the total cost of a call):

$$\frac{\hat{p}_i}{p_i} = 1 + \frac{a - c_0}{c} \tag{4}$$

That is, the network's optimal price structure is uniform ($p_i = \hat{p}_i$) under marginal cost pricing of access ($a = c_0$). There are positive network externalities ($p_i < \hat{p}_i$) under an access markup, and negative network externalities ($p_i > \hat{p}_i$) under an access discount.

Price Structure

Equation (4) has a simple interpretation. Its right-hand side is the relative perceived cost $(c + a - c_0)/c$ of off- to on-net calls. That prices are proportional to costs results from the constant elasticity of demand: View the choice of a network's price *structure* as a (dual) Ramsey program of maximizing profit subject to providing the network's subscribers with a given surplus. The standard Ramsey conclusion (see chapter 2) is that the Lerner indices of the different services are proportional to the inverse elasticities of demand. But here the elasticities of demand for on- and off-net calls are identical, and so are the Lerner indices, hence the proportionality rule.

Price Level

We refer to Laffont, Rey, and Tirole (1998b) for a fuller study of price competition. Let us simply mention that, for a given access charge $a > c_0$, price discrimination raises the off-net price and lowers the on-net price, as one would expect. For small markups, the average price is lower than under uniform pricing, which is a sufficient condition for consumers' welfare to increase, owing to the convexity of their net surplus function.

---

17. "Stable" refers to a fictitious time *tâtonnement* process in which the consumers at stage $n + 1$ select their networks on the basis of the stage n market shares.

5.5.4   Reception Subsidies

Last, let us observe that networks may still compete away high access charges even if they charge linear prices and if they cannot discriminate on the basis of call termination. We have until now assumed that the call receiver neither paid nor received anything for receiving calls. In the presence of access charge premiums or discounts, though, networks may want to let the call receiver internalize the net benefit or cost to the network of terminating the call. In particular, when the access charge exceeds the marginal cost of terminating the call, the network may want to give the call receiver money for receiving the call.

Although the point can be made generally, it is most simply illustrated in the case of a very unbalanced calling pattern. Suppose that there are two types of consumers: those who only call, and those who are called and never call. Suppose further that the networks are undifferentiated. Then, in an equilibrium, both networks charge a linear price equal to the marginal cost of calls plus the access premium for calls, and pay a subsidy equal to the access premium for call reception. That is, both networks tag the full access premium onto the price of calls and subsidize call reception to the level of the access charge premium. See box 5.5 for more detail. The basic point, thus, is that *the access charge premium is competed away by the networks, which fight fiercely to enroll customers on the receiving end.*

Remark 1: Relationship to the Credit Card Industry   In section 5.1 we mentioned the analogy with the treatment of access between members of a credit card association (Visa, MasterCard). This particular illustration is indeed highly reminiscent of the credit card industry for two reasons. First, we assumed an extremely unbalanced calling pattern (some consumers are always called, some always call) that is similar to the credit card situation, where clients are on the debit side and merchants on the receiving side. Second, and more important, pricing on both sides is rather unconstrained.[18] We refer to Rochet and Tirole (1999) and Schmalensee (1998) for analyses of access charges in the credit card industry.

Remark 2: Relationship to Two-Part Tariffs   Reception subsidies create yet another dimension of competition along which the profits from high

---

18. True enough, issuers do not charge for the use of the card; but they compete along several dimensions to enroll clients: interest rates (APRs), credit limits, service, gifts, and frequent user programs, and so forth.

Box 5.5
Reception Subsidies

Returning to our framework, let us suppose that there is no per-customer fixed cost ($f = 0$), that type 1 consumers call type 2 consumers, and that the access charge a exceeds the marginal cost of access c_0. As usual, we let c denote the total marginal cost of a call. With undifferentiated networks, let us suppose that the networks, $i = 1, 2$, offer unit prices

$$p_i = c + (a - c_0)$$

for calls, and unit subsidies

$$s_i = a - c_0$$

for call reception. In this equilibrium, the networks just break even. First, note that a network cannot benefit by changing a single price: The perceived termination cost is $a - c_0$ regardless of where the call terminates, and so the cost of issuing a call is indeed $c + a - c_0$. Conversely, each network obtains a benefit on call termination equal to $a - c_0$ whether or not it has originated the call. Thus the subsidy on call reception also amounts to marginal cost pricing.

Might a network want simultaneously to subsidize call reception less and reduce its price on calls? If it did so, it would lose all type 2 consumers to its rival, and so its total per-unit cost of issuing calls would be $c + a - c_0$; however, it cannot charge more than $c + a - c_0$ per call if it wants to attract type 1 customers. More generally, the reader will check that a network cannot make a profit by moving both prices from their equilibrium levels. Last, one can prove that the equilibrium is unique. [First, fixing prices for calls, Bertrand competition for call receivers yields $s_1 = s_2 = a - c_0$. Then Bertrand competition for callers yields $p_1 = p_2 = c + (a - c_0)$.]

access charges may be competed away. Indeed, if the "demand" for call reception is perfectly inelastic and if all consumers receive the same volume of calls, the per-unit subsidy is equivalent to a fixed subsidy, and so we are back to the point made earlier that a high access charge promotes low or even negative monthly subscriber charges or connection charges. In general, though, consumers differ in the volume of calls they receive. (It is interesting to note that in environments with high access charges, operators have offered nice deals to call receivers [mail order companies, etc.]. Competitive access providers have eagerly signed up Internet service providers to pick up termination charges. And some local exchange companies have vertically integrated into call-in phone services so as to boost their call termination volume.) Furthermore, the demand for call reception is not inelastic; the call receiver has an impact on the length of the call or may choose to have an unlisted number and to give his/her number to a limited set of people. For these two reasons, call reception subsidies are not redundant even in the presence of monthly subscriber charge subsidies.

Remark 3: Ratcheting   If the access charge is determined by a regulator, the introduction by a network of reception subsidies may have only a short-run effect, for it signals to the regulator (or to the political principal or public opinion, if the regulator already knows it) that the access charge is well above the marginal cost of terminating calls. This result is likely to lead to a reduction in the access charge. This political concern may induce networks to refrain from arbitraging the access markup through reception subsidies.

5.6   Unbundling- and Facilities-Based Entry

Our analysis so far has focused on competition in a mature industry, in which network owners have built large-scale facilities that allow them to serve all potential customers. This "full coverage" situation is unlikely to prevail in the short run. Entrants will provide local service themselves only in limited areas, that is, have *partial coverage*, or else will not build facilities at all, but rather content themselves with renting the incumbent's facilities to offer their own local service, that is, to have *zero coverage*. We have seen that regulators in the United Kingdom do not want to encourage the second form of entry, but hope to promote entry by local service providers with partial coverage such as cable companies; in contrast, U.S. regulators aim at also encouraging entry by carriers who own no local facilities and rent the local facilities from the incumbent. Let us analyze the two types of entry in sequence.

5.6.1   Unbundling-Based Entry

Let us consider the common situation in which an incumbent covers the entire territory and incurs a per-customer cost of connecting and servicing the customer. This cost is incurred by the incumbent regardless of the identity of the operator selected by the customer.

An entrant can lease the local loop from the incumbent in order to provide the same service to the customer as the latter. The entrant may install facilities (switches, trunk lines) between local loops (in this sense, the entry may be "unbundling based," where "resale" refers to the special case in which the entrant provides no facilities at all), but the entrant has zero coverage at the local loop level. Leasing the local loop, however, allows the entrant to have de facto full coverage.

One must now consider two access charges; see box 5.6. First, the entrant leases from the incumbent the connections to the customers that it enrolls. Let us call this per-customer charge the *local loop rental charge*. Second, the entrant must pay the incumbent a per-minute *termination charge* whenever its customers call the incumbent's subscribers; unlike the local loop rental charge, the termination charge goes both ways in that the incumbent also pays a termination charge when its customers call the entrant's subscribers.

In the linear pricing situation studied in section 5.4, the termination charge is still an instrument of tacit collusion; that is, an increase in the termination charge, as long as the latter does not depart too much from marginal cost, raises the firms' marginal costs and their retail prices. More interestingly, *an increase in the local loop rental charge also softens competition. The reason is that the local loop rental charge is a cost for the entrant and a revenue for the incumbent.* A high local loop rental charge makes it very costly for the entrant to enroll subscribers and thus makes it an inoffensive competitor. Interestingly enough, a high local loop rental charge also makes the incumbent a soft competitor, since the incumbent does not lose much money from abandoning subscribers to the entrant. The monopoly outcome prevails for very high local loop rental charges.

The regulator, in contrast, would like to promote competition, while not expropriating the incumbent. From our previous analysis, competition can be promoted either through a low local loop rental charge or through a low termination charge. The two instruments, however, are not equivalent: *It is more efficient to encourage competition through a low termination charge than through a low local loop rental charge. The former, unlike the latter, preserves a level playing field by not expropriating the incumbent.*

In the absence of joint and common cost of building the incumbent's full coverage network, the implementation of the social optimum requires the following policy: the termination charge (as in section 5.4) is set below the marginal cost of terminating calls. In contrast, the local loop rental charge must equal the per-customer cost of connecting the customer (minus the cost of billing the customer if this service is provided by the entrant).

In general, though, the incumbent must recover the *joint and common cost* of building the local network (besides the local loop), and so *a markup must be added onto the local loop rental charge so as to allow cost recovery, and solely on this charge. This markup is equal to the per-line joint*

Box 5.6
Optimal Local Loop Rental Charges

Let us return to the formal framework of box 5.2. The incumbent, firm 1, incurs cost f of connecting individual customers. (For notational simplicity, we ignore the cost of billing and servicing the consumer, or, equivalently, we assume that these are provided by the incumbent and thus included in f.) And let C denote the per-line joint and common cost of building the local network. The fixed cost per customer to be recouped by the incumbent is therefore $f + C$.

The Ramsey price, p^R, is given by the industry's budget-balance condition:

$$(p^R - c)q(p^R) = f + C$$

Letting $\mathcal{A}$ denote the local loop rental charge paid by the entrant, the incumbent's profit is

$$\hat{\pi}_1 = \alpha_1(p_1 - c)q(p_1) + A_1 - (f + C) + \alpha_2 \mathcal{A}$$

where

$$A_1 = -A_2 = \alpha_1\alpha_2(a - c_0)\left[q(p_2) - q(p_1)\right]$$

as earlier denotes firm 1's access revenue.

The profit of the entrant, firm 2, is

$$\hat{\pi}_2 = \alpha_2(p_2 - c)q(p_2) + A_2 - \alpha_2 \mathcal{A}$$

Note that, given that the incumbent incurs cost $(f + C)$ per line regardless of subscribers' network choice, the networks' perceived fixed costs of enrolling a subscriber are the same and are equal to $\mathcal{A}$. In this sense, the level playing field is always established *at the margin*.

Setting $\mathcal{A} = f + C$, the *full* fixed cost, yields

$$\hat{\pi}_i = \alpha_i\left[(p_i - c)q(p_i) - f - C\right] + A_i$$

for $i = 1, 2$.

The symmetry of the profit functions implies that this particular choice of $\mathcal{A}$ establishes a level playing field not only at the margin, but *also on average*. Note further that the analysis of box 5.2 applies with per-customer fixed cost $f + C$ rather than f. A termination discount $(a < c_0)$ still serves to curb market power.

and common cost of building the network, that is, the overall joint and common cost of building the network divided by the total number of lines (whether the lines connect the incumbent's or the entrant's subscribers).

The intuition for this simple result goes as follows: The incumbent pays for all local facilities, be they the local network or individual connections to this local network. By setting the local loop rental charge equal to the *full* fixed cost per customer (marginal cost of connecting a consumer plus the per-line common cost), the regulator guarantees that the incumbent and the entrant face the *same* fixed cost per customer they enroll (not only at the margin, but also on average). This policy defines a level playing field that is a prerequisite for an efficient allocation of resources. The existence of market power is then as usual tackled through a discount on the termination charge.

5.6.2   Facilities-Based Entry

Suppose now that the entrants cannot lease from the incumbent and must install their own facilities. Before starting to enroll customers, the entrants must build local networks. Typically they choose partial coverage; that is, they stand ready to serve only a fraction of the population. Competitive access providers target central business districts; cable companies upgrade their networks in cities to offer telephony; and mobile operators may cover only a fraction of the country's territory. An obvious reason for this partial coverage strategy is that entrants pick areas in which network duplication is not too costly and where demand is high. As we will see, this may not be the only motivation.

Partial coverage by the entrants raises the question of whether the incumbent can and is allowed to charge different retail prices to its customers depending on whether they can alternatively be served by the entrants. Clearly the incumbent would like to charge higher prices to captive customers who do not reside in the area covered by the entrants than to customers who enjoy a network choice. For conciseness, we focus on the situation in which, for regulatory reasons, say, the incumbent cannot price discriminate and must offer *uniform* conditions all over its territory. As in section 5.6.1, we assume a single entrant for the sake of the argument. We only sketch the main lessons of the analysis and refer to Laffont, Rey, and Tirole (1998a, 1998b) for further details.

5.6.2.1   No Termination-Based Price Discrimination
Let us first assume that the networks are not allowed to price discriminate on the basis of where the call terminates. We assume that the access charge is reciprocal, and we examine strategic pricing by the networks, the choice of coverage by the entrant, and the possibility of a cooperative determination of the reciprocal access charge.

Strategic Pricing   It is easy to see that *an entrant with partial coverage undercuts the incumbent.* The reason is that the entirety of the entrant's market is competitive, while part of the incumbent's market is captive. As we observed, the incumbent would like to charge a high price to the captive customers and a low price to the customers residing in the entrant's territory. When constrained to charge a uniform price, the incumbent charges something "in between" and so sets a price above that of the entrant, whose entire market is competitive. By the same reasoning, *the incumbent's price is higher, the smaller the entrant's coverage is* (at least for access charges close to the marginal cost of access). The fraction of the incumbent's market that is captive decreases with the entrant's coverage, and so a territorial expansion by the entrant triggers more aggressive price behavior from the incumbent. A corollary to this analysis is that the entrant generates a larger outflow than the incumbent (because it prices more aggressively to its customers) and thus (voluntarily) incurs an access deficit (unless it targets net-inflow customers, of course).

Extent of Entry and Access Charge Negotiation The choice of coverage by the entrant and the private negotiation of a reciprocal access charge cannot be separated. (For simplicity, we will assume that the access charge by law must be reciprocal.)

A key determinant of industry behavior and performance is the institutional environment in which the private negotiation takes place, and, more precisely, the *default rule* in case of disagreement. One possibility is that networks are not interconnected in case of disagreement. An alternative default rule is that the regulator intervenes if the parties fail to agree and sets the access charge at some arbitrary level (e.g., marginal cost).

The entrant's coverage strategy is highly dependent on the default rule. In the latter default rule—*mandated interconnection* at some price—the entrant is not at a disadvantage relative to the incumbent, regardless of the level of coverage. The entrant then has an incentive to limit the size of its coverage, since we have seen that reduced coverage softens the incumbent's pricing. *The entrant, therefore, has an incentive to keep a low profile* as far as coverage is concerned. As for the access charge negotiations, the asymmetry between the operators implies that they have different preferences about the level of termination charge. The entrant prices more aggressively and thus tends to generate more off-net calls.[19] *The entrant's preferred access charge, therefore, is lower than*

---

19. Assuming that the access charge does not exceed the marginal cost of access by a large amount. For high access markups, there is another and potentially countervailing effect: The entrant's perceived marginal cost per call $[c + a_1(a - c_0)$, letting firm 1 be the incumbent] is then substantially larger than the incumbent's $[c + a_2(a - c_0)]$. The analysis for large markups, however, is complicated by the fact that a pure-strategy equilibrium may not exist, for the same reason as in section 5.5.1.

the incumbent's.[20] And the entrant has a stronger bargaining position, the lower the default access charge is. Whether the entrant will advocate a "bill-and-keep" arrangement (the absence of access charge) depends on the relative importance of its net outflow and the raise-each-other's-cost effect.

Assume, in contrast, that the default rule is the *absence of interconnection.* Clearly, the entrant is then at a strong strategic disadvantage if its network has a small coverage (unless customers form small clubs, covered by the entrant, of clients calling each other, as in the case of private networks). Unless the entrant has wide coverage, its offering has very limited appeal in the absence of interconnection because its customers cannot reach a number of people they want to call. The incumbent can charge high prices, perhaps even the monopoly price, and yet lose no customer to the entrant. *The entrant now has an incentive to overinvest in coverage in order to force the incumbent to negotiate interconnection.* In contrast, we saw that when the default rule is mandated interconnection, the entrant underinvests in coverage so as to soften price competition. Paradoxically, the incumbent may be better off under the mandated interconnection default rule, even though (or rather because) the latter puts the entrant in a stronger bargaining position.

5.6.2.2   *Termination-Based Price Discrimination*
Assume now that networks can discriminate on the basis of whether their customers' calls terminate on or off net. A mandated interconnection default rule with a high access charge then amounts to the absence of interconnection. For a high access charge, each network charges a high price for off-net calls, and so customers almost exclusively call on net. Thus, an incumbent facing small-scale entry can enjoy its monopoly profit and has little incentive to negotiate alternative interconnection agreements. In contrast with the case where termination-based price discrimination is banned, the incumbent remains in a secured position as long as the default rule specifies a high access charge and the entrant does not build a large coverage network.

In practice, though, incumbents are rarely allowed to engage in termination-based price discrimination, and so the concerns just noted are unlikely to apply.

---

20. This conclusion relies on competition in linear prices. As Wouter Dessein pointed out to us, under nonlinear pricing, the incumbent may charge a high fixed fee (to extract the captive market's surplus)) and a low usage price (to reflect its low average marginal cost).

5.7   Alternative Policies

Two-way-access policies have historically received little attention in the policy debate, except perhaps for international telecommunications. They are bound, as we have seen, to become more and more prominent over time. The policy debate and the theoretical analysis have by and large focused on particular approaches, namely, those of regulated or privately negotiated determination of reciprocal access charges. While these are reasonable paradigms, others are worth investigating as well. Without any pretense at exhaustive and careful analysis, we record two alternative possibilities.

5.7.1   Making the Receiver Accountable

A striking feature of interconnection frameworks in which the calling network pays the termination charge is that if termination charges are not set reciprocal, call receivers do not internalize an externality—the termination charge paid by other networks—generated by one of their decisions—their choice of network.

Let us entertain the possibility that networks freely set their own termination charges and have call receivers pay the termination charge set by their elected networks (this termination charge being the same for all calls, whether they originate on or off net). Networks would then be unable to "tax" other networks through a high termination charge.[21]

A possible objection—and a standard one for motivating the absence of retail charge on the receiving side—is that call receivers do not like to pay for being called; this is particularly the case for nuisance calls. But there are ways of accommodating this concern. Suppose for example that *the call receiver is charged the difference between the termination charge set by his network and a benchmark termination charge (the calling network would then pay the benchmark termination charge)*. This benchmark termination charge could be derived from a cost model, or else (and perhaps more in line with the idea of using market-determined access charges) be an average of termination charges set by other comparable networks. In this case, the call receiver would pay nothing for receiving calls if this network adopts the benchmark termination charge. Yet, the

---

21. Doyle and Smith (1998) argue that the price of calls to mobiles in the United Kingdom would be lower if receivers were to pay for the access charge set by their mobile operator.

call receiver would still be fully sensitized to changes in his network's termination charge.[22]

What would be gained and lost relative to the institution of a jointly set reciprocal access charge? The potential benefit is that a network can more easily reflect its termination cost specificity and transmit the corresponding signal to customers. So, for instance, a mobile network with sparse (excess) capacity can translate its marginal cost of termination into a high (low) termination charge. Similarly, a wire-based network would not set the same termination charge as a wireless network. But does this policy bring any benefit? Let us entertain two possible hypotheses concerning the elasticity of demand for termination—that is, the sensitivity of receiving minutes to a per-minute termination charge imputed to the subscriber.

Suppose first that the subscriber has no control over the volume of calls he receives: His demand for termination is *inelastic*. The termination charge then has no impact on call termination, and a unit increase in the termination charge is equivalent to an increase in the fixed fee (monthly subscriber charge) equal to the volume of calls received. Note, though, that this impact on the "generalized monthly subscriber charge" is not uniform across consumers. While the payment of a termination charge by the customer has no effect on the volume of calls received, it allows the phone company to have a better measurement of phone usage and thus of the customer's willingness to pay for receiving calls. This knowledge may enable the phone company to engage more effectively in price discrimination (although this discrimination may be complex when the fraction of calls that are nuisance calls—and thus do not raise the willingness to pay for being connected—varies across customers). With an inelastic demand for termination we would thus expect a type of competition resembling that described in section 5.5.2, with a couple of twists, though: For example, customers who mainly receive calls would tend to migrate away from high-termination-cost networks, and this migration would create a socially beneficial reallocation of consumers.

Second, let us assume that the demand for termination is somewhat *elastic*. In practice, consumers may give their phone number to a restricted set of acquaintances and require that their number be unlisted,

---

22. Another, and complementary, method to deal with the nuisance-call problem might be to make the customer accountable (at the margin) from the second minute on, but not for call setup and for the first minute.

and they may abbreviate the calls they receive. Making customers accountable, then, may have costs and benefits. The benefit is that consumers are induced to receive fewer calls and to abbreviate calls when their network's termination cost is high. A potential cost of making customers accountable is that networks would not fully internalize the externality on callers. A network's high termination charge induces its subscribers to abbreviate calls. The externality on callers belonging to the same network is internalized by the network, but not that on callers subscribing to the rival network. We should be careful not to draw conclusions, however, since we have not conducted an analysis of industry behavior in this framework analogous to that developed for reciprocal access charges.

5.7.2   Multiple Terminating Lines

The possibility that not only local networks but the very connection to the customer's home may be duplicated raises new possibilities as well as questions about the likely industry behavior and performance. This point has been known for a while with regard to call origination: For example, a large user can be connected by, and actively subscribe to, two operators, and use real-time least-cost routing to decide which network to use at each instant. But it is evident that similar possibilities arise at the termination level. Suppose that a customer's home is connected both by a telephone company and by a cable company that has upgraded its line to carry telephony. Whether the customer subscribes to one or both networks for originating calls, there is now a potential choice of operators for terminating calls. Networks originating calls, or the receivers themselves if they are charged for call termination, can select the least-cost termination. Again, it would be worth investigating the implications of such competition for termination for industry behavior and performance.

6

Universal Service

6.1 The Need for a New Paradigm

For years, network industries have implemented broad subsidy programs. Telecommunications companies (but also electricity, postal, and railroad companies) have refrained from charging high prices to high-cost areas such as remote, rural areas and from closing services in these areas. Business users of telecommunications have in most countries subsidized residential users; and in some countries low-income consumers have been provided support financed by charges on specific services.

This system of subsidies typically operated through "distortions" in the relative prices of the incumbent monopoly.[1] The monopoly was compensated for its losses on subsidized services (or more generally, from a Ramsey perspective, for insufficient cost recovery on those services) by unusually high markups on specific, unsubsidized offerings. That is, cross-subsidies were internal to the firm and were part of the regulatory contract between the firm and the regulator.

This mechanism of cross-subsidies is coming to an end in developed countries. On the one hand, price caps encourage the firm to rebalance its tariffs in a businesslike manner (see chapters 2 and 3). The firm is no longer willing to serve high-cost areas at low prices or to subsidize low-income customers. To be more precise, providing the firm with such an incentive under price cap regulation requires either a substantial manipulation of the weights in the price cap so as to, for instance,

---

1. What is meant by "distortions" is sometimes unclear in the literature. By distortions we mean that prices differed substantially from Ramsey prices computed for a social welfare function equal to the sum of the consumers' net surpluses. Or, put more technically, the ratio of the Lerner indices differed from those of an unregulated monopoly. (Recall that the Ramsey-Boiteux formulas can be written $L_k = \theta L_k^m$ for all k where m stands for monopoly and $0 < \theta < 1$.)

heavily penalize price increases for targeted customers, or a uniform pricing requirement. And, indeed, such adjustments to the price cap paradigm were made systematically when price caps were introduced in the 1980s. Incumbent operators were often required to keep charging uniform prices throughout their territory, and the speed of tariff rebalancing was severely constrained—for instance, through the imposition of constraints on the rate of increase in monthly subscriber charges.

While the introduction of price caps led to some changes in the way cross-subsidies were implemented, a more decisive blow to the existing cross-subsidy mechanism comes from the liberalization movement. Because operators must make substantial profits on subsidizing segments in order to pay for subsidized ones, entrants have a strong incentive to enter the former (and neglect the latter). This point raises two concerns. First, even inefficient entrants may be enticed by the incumbent's price umbrella in the high-price segments. Second, the "tax base" from which some services are subsidized is eroded, undermining the entire system of cross-subsidies.

Universal service is a knotty and explosive problem. It has been (or will be)[2] a central issue in the political debate surrounding regulatory reform in all network industries and in most countries. On the consumer side, the interest groups receiving those subsidies (e.g., residential customers and rural inhabitants) have, of course, lobbied heavily for their preservation; powerful interest groups on the other side, such as large business users in telecommunications and electricity, have pushed for deregulation as a means to remove the subsidies and enjoy lower prices. On the producer side, incumbent operators have often used universal service as an argument against liberalization; it has thus been observed that "cross-subsidies are the enemy of competition, *because* competition is the enemy of cross-subsidies."[3] Conversely, entrants sometimes attempt to incapacitate the incumbent operator by forcing the entire burden of universal service on the latter, or to create arbitrage possibilities by imposing constraints such as uniform pricing on the incumbent only. Overall, universal service considerations add a fair dose of politics to the deregulatory process.

This chapter discusses various proposals that are meant to preserve universal service in a "competitively neutral" way. But, first, we must define universal service more precisely and investigate its rationale.

---

2. Unless regulators conclude (as Oftel did in the United Kingdom) that the benefits of providing universal service match its costs.
3. Larry White, quoted by Farrell (1996).

6.2   The Foundations of Universal Service

Our discussion will focus on the (primarily Anglo-Saxon) concept of *universal service*, which consists in "ensuring quality telecommunications services at affordable rates to consumers, including low-income consumers, in all regions of the nation, including rural, insular, and high-cost areas."[4] Let us ignore for the moment the tricky issue of choosing "targeted services" and defining a level of "quality" for these services. Let us simply note the two common rationales for universal service:

• *Redistribution* toward needy customers. The definition of need, of course, is subject to question, but it generally includes low-income residents, handicapped customers, the elderly, and rural customers with limited geographical mobility, who arguably might need to be protected against the sharp increases in rates that would be associated with full rate rebalancing.[5]

• *Regional planning* attempting to encourage a more harmonious distribution of residents away from large congested metropolitan areas. This rationale is based on the existence of externalities: noninternalized congestion externalities in large cities; social benefits from maintaining a rural habitat (this perception is often dear to the French, for example).

Two important remarks are in order at this stage. First, these objectives *per se* do not vindicate universal service. It is not a priori clear that the needy and the high-cost-area customers are best helped through distortions in the price systems of network industries. We will shortly investigate the possible foundations for universal service obligations (USOs). Second, some countries (most notably France) have embraced a broader concept of "public service" that incorporates other objectives,

---

4. See, e.g., Federal Communications Commission, "In the Matter of Federal-State Joint Board on Universal Service," CC Docket no. 96–45, Nov. 8, 1996.

5. The case for protecting medium- and high-income customers in rural areas, of course, cannot stem from purely redistributive concerns. Rather, if a case is to be made (independently of the regional planning argument to be stated later), it ought to do with a possible implicit promise by governments that citizens deciding to live in high-cost areas would not be penalized by high utility prices. If such an implicit promise was made (an assertion which is open to question), then the scrapping of the corresponding subsidies implies an expropriation of those who have made the (relational, professional, psychological,or physical) investment of living in high-cost areas. So, if the existence of an implicit promise is established, compensation is called for, although it need not necessarily take the form of a subsidy on utilities' services.

such as (a) the need to secure supplies of a vital input and to contribute to the provision of national defense, (b) the need to defend unrepresented future generations by undertaking long-term investments that would be neglected in an unregulated private industry, and (c) the objective of linking citizens so as to strengthen the nation.[6] The first two arguments are rarely invoked in the context of telecommunications. The third argument deserves some inquiry into why citizens care about being linked beyond the standard economic benefit of being able to call each other. However, we will not discuss them further.

6.2.1   A Negative Result on Taxation by Regulation

As we discussed before, the imposition of universal service obligations on operators is *not* a foregone conclusion of the adhesion to redistributive and regional planning objectives. There may be better (less distorting) ways to help the targeted consumers. And, indeed, a well-known result due to Atkinson and Stiglitz (1976) may cast some doubt on the entire universal service enterprise.

The Atkinson-Stiglitz theorem indicates simply that the best way to redistribute income may be the direct way, through the taxation of income, and that (indirect) manipulation of the relative prices of goods and services may be an inefficient policy. The Atkinson-Stiglitz result rests on the following assumptions (see box 6.1 for more details):

1. Consumers differ in their ability to earn money (e.g., their hourly wage), and these abilities are unobserved by tax authorities.

2. Their incomes are perfectly verifiable by tax authorities.

3. There is no constraint on the design of the income tax schedule.

4. The consumers' preferences are separable between their labor input (say, the number of hours they work) on the one side and a basket of consumption goods or services on the other side. That is, their relative preference for two goods is independent of the amount of their labor input. (Technically, their marginal rate of substitution between the two consumption goods is independent of labor input.)

5. There are no consumption externalities.

---

6. In Europe, Article 90–1 of the Treaty of European Union (1957) allows member states to assign economic missions of general interest to their operators, as long as these do not conflict with rules governing competition. Article 90–2, however, implies that competition should not conflict with the pursuit of such missions.

The distribution of abilities gives rise to a distribution of income that society may find too unequal. Income may then be redistributed from the rich to the poor through adoption of a progressive income tax, albeit at the cost of reduced work incentives for the most able.[7] *The thrust of the Atkinson-Stiglitz result is that, under the five assumptions listed, the income tax is all that is needed for redistributive purposes.* This result on the undesirability of indirect taxation has several implications. The consumption of goods and services should be taxed at a uniform rate, zero, say.[8] Relatedly, and more to the point for our analysis, regulated firms should not distort their relative prices. Indeed, they may as well sell all services at their marginal cost. (Of course, such a policy would require a concomitant lump-sum subsidy from the overall budget of the state.)

The logic behind the Atkinson-Stiglitz result is simple: While the government may want to redistribute from the rich to the poor, it should not substitute for consumers and decide what they want to consume. Subsidizing some goods and taxing others amounts to forcing consumption choices on consumers. If all consumers, rich and poor, have the same relative preferences for the goods, then there is absolutely no rationale for distorting the system of relative prices.

The Atkinson-Stiglitz result applies to the redistributive motivation. But the same line of argument is relevant for the *regional planning* dimension of universal service. Suppose one wants to encourage people to live in rural (high-cost) areas. It is not clear a priori why one would want to induce them to consume specific phone services or telecommunications services more generally rather than other goods and services. It may be preferable to boost their income, say, through location-based income-tax breaks, rather than deciding for them what they should consume.

6.2.2   Arguments in Favor of Indirect Taxation

Though unrealistic, the Atkinson-Stiglitz benchmark model is important on two grounds. First, it shows that universal service is not to be

---

7. The reader will here recognize the structure of Mirrlees' famous 1971 analysis of the income tax problem, which is based on the five assumptions listed. Assumption 4 is satisfied trivially in Mirrlees' analysis, since he assumes a single, composite consumption good.

8. This argument assumes that there are no foreign tourists consuming domestic goods and services. Departures from the zero and uniform tax rules can in practice be motivated by foreign consumption of domestic goods.

Box 6.1

The Case against Taxation by Regulation

Let us sketch the Atkinson-Stiglitz argument. There are $(n+1)$ goods: n consumption goods and labor. Consumers have utility

$$U = U(q_1, \ldots, q_n, \ell)$$

where $(q_k)_{k=1,\ldots,n}$ denote the consumptions of the n goods and ℓ the labor supply. Consumers differ in their ability to earn money, described by their hourly wage w. There is a density $g(w)$ of consumers on the interval $[\underline{w}, \bar{w}]$. The tax authority observes neither w nor ℓ, but observes perfectly the consumer's income $I = w\ell$. The tax authority selects a disposable income function $D(I)$ or, equivalently, an income tax schedule $I - D(I)$.

A consumer with "ability" w facing this income tax schedule and consumer prices $p = (p_1, \ldots, p_n)$ chooses labor supply and consumption so as to solve

$$(I) \quad \max_{\{q_1,\ldots,q_n\ell\}} U(q_1, \ldots, q_n, \ell) \tag{1}$$

subject to

$$\sum_k p_k q_k \leq D(w\ell) \tag{2}$$

yielding the first-order conditions

$$U_k = \lambda p_k \qquad k = 1, \ldots, n \tag{3}$$
$$U_\ell = -\lambda w D'(w\ell) \tag{4}$$

where λ is the multiplier of program (I).

Under complete information about w the tax authority would maximize a social welfare function

$$\int_{\underline{w}}^{\bar{w}} \phi(U) g(w) dw \tag{5}$$

under the budget constraint

$$\int_{\underline{w}}^{\bar{w}} \left[(p_k - c_k) q_k + w\ell - D(w\ell) \right] g(w) dw \geq K \tag{6}$$

where K is a fixed cost of producing the goods and c_k is the marginal cost of producing good k (which, for simplicity, is assumed constant).

We can choose to normalize the price system so that $p_1 = c_1$. Then the maximization of function (5) under constraint (6) immediately gives the classical result (e.g., Debreu, 1959) that it is optimal to price goods at marginal cost and to cover the fixed cost and perform the redistributive function through lump-sum transfers.

Under incomplete information we must add an incentive constraint. Let $U(w)$ denote the maximal value of program (I) as a function of w. By the envelope theorem

$$\dot{U}(w) = \lambda \ell D'(w\ell) = -\frac{\ell}{w} U_\ell \tag{7}$$

6.2 The Foundations of Universal Service

Box 6.1 (continued)

As in Mirrlees (1971), condition (7) is the first-order incentive constraint (we neglect technical considerations here). It describes the rate at which the consumer's rent under asymmetric information, $U(w)$, must evolve to induce truthful revelation of the w's.

The problem of the tax authority is now to maximize function (5) under the budget constraints (2) and (6) and the information constraint (7).

The state variable of this control problem is U. Using formula (2) we can eliminate q_1

$$c_1 q_1 = D(w\ell) - \sum_{k>1} p_k q_k \tag{8}$$

so that we have only n control variables $q_2, \ldots, q_n, \ell$.

Consumption efficiency requires prices to be equal to marginal costs. But, under incomplete information one might want to tolerate departures from marginal cost pricing in order to extract rents better and thus perform the redistributive function. However, it is inefficient to distort consumption signals if the control variables $q_2, \ldots, q_n$ (affected by relative prices if we decentralize them) do not affect the informational rents, that is, do not affect the right-hand side of equation (7), that is, U_ℓ.

The condition for the validity of the Atkinson-Stiglitz result is therefore

$$\frac{dU_\ell}{dq_k} = 0 \qquad k = 2, \ldots, n$$

or

$$U_{\ell k} + U_{\ell 1} \frac{dq_1}{dq_k} = 0 \qquad k = 2, \ldots, n$$

or, from equation (8)

$$U_{\ell k} - U_{\ell 1} \frac{p_k}{c_1} = 0 \qquad k = 2, \ldots, n.$$

Condition (3) then implies

$$U_{\ell k} - U_{\ell 1} \frac{U_k}{U_1} = 0 \qquad k = 2, \ldots, n$$

which is equivalent to

$$\frac{d}{d\ell}\left(\frac{U_k}{U_1}\right) = 0 \qquad k = 2, \ldots, n \tag{9}$$

From Leontief's 1947 theorem, equation (9) amounts to the existence of an aggregator function $\wedge(q_1, \ldots, q_n)$ such that

$$U(q_1, \ldots, q_n, \ell) = \tilde{U}[\wedge(q_1, \ldots, q_n), \ell]$$

that is, weak separability of labor and good consumptions.

taken for granted. Second, it suggests factors that may possibly justify some amount of taxation by regulation. At least one of assumptions 2 through 5 underlying the Atkinson-Stiglitz result must be relaxed in order to build arguments for such taxation.

This exercise may appear quite academic. Yet, the many abuses committed under a universal service cover have led many to be deeply skeptical about the very idea of having USOs. Why "should subscribers in a [New Jersey] urban, low-income, largely African-American city be subsidizing telephone subscribers among the rural gentry in the horse country of New Jersey through a statewide scheme, or prosperous ranchers in the freedom-loving expanses of Montana through an interstate scheme?"[9] Why should schools of wealthy cities with average incomes exceeding $100,000 a year receive substantial Internet subsidies?[10]

Of course, it is to be understood that behind the official redistributive and regional planning discourse lie interest-group politics. A case in point was a recent attempt by the staff of the Federal Communications Commission to design policies to help the homeless and the seasonal workers, who certainly count among the least prosperous Americans. Relatively low subsidies seemingly could have helped them to have access to voice mail services or community phone banks, thus enabling them to keep contact with others (family, potential employers, etc.).[11] Congress never seriously considered employing the FCC staff's proposal, as one might expect from the fact that the homeless and the seasonal workers do not vote.

The importance of political economy considerations suggests, as usual, two possible reactions. The first is to investigate the underpinnings of political abuse and look for institutions that reduce the role of regulatory capture.[12] The second is to clarify the rationale for and the implementation of universal service so as to reduce the scope for regulatory discretion and capture. These two approaches are comple-

---

9. Farrell (1996, p. 215).
10. Hausman (1998).
11. See FCC Docket no. 96–45, "In the Matter of Federal-State Joint Board on Universal Service," section VIII. Although our prior view is that this policy would have been a fairly inexpensive way of helping people who actually need help, we have not studied the matter and so do not want to assess the cogency of this policy.
12. See Laffont and Tirole (1993, chaps. 11–16). To the best of our knowledge, little attention has been paid to a formal treatment of regulatory capture in the context of universal subsidies.

mentary. The second approach eliminates unnecessary discretion and identifies unavoidable discretion; the first then studies the institutional reactions to the existence of discretion. In the following discussion, we will pursue solely the second, purely normative approach, and ask, What is it that USOs are trying to achieve, and are USOs part of an optimal array of policies to achieve these goals?

6.2.2.1   Imperfect Observability of the Source of Inequality

Let us relax assumption 2 and assume either that there is tax evasion or else that the possibility of tax evasion constrains the progressivity of income tax schedules and therefore income redistribution. If we simultaneously relax assumption 4 according to which consumers have identical preferences over consumption goods, then one sees that it may be worth taxing goods that are primarily consumed by the rich and subsidizing the goods for which the poor have a relative preference. For example, if musical education is correlated with income and further enhances the pleasure derived from listening to operas, operas should be taxed more heavily than other goods. (In practice, though, opera is heavily subsidized, providing an illustration of regressive taxation. Similarly, it would be quite difficult to justify the substantial subsidies enjoyed by Internet users on such grounds!)

Box 6.2 analyzes the offering of toll limitation services on precisely such grounds. There has been much discussion lately of subsidizing toll-limitation and toll-blocking services for low-income consumers. Toll blocking prevents the placement of long-distance calls for which the subscribers would be charged. Toll-limitation services limit the toll charges subscribers can incur during a billing period. The Federal Communications Commission, for instance, observed that disconnection for nonpayment of toll charges is a significant barrier to universal service (the main reason subscribers lose their telephone services is excessive toll bills), and proposed offering subsidized toll blocking and toll limitation as an option for low-income consumers. Comments on the Notice of Proposed Rule Making were mixed and included some questions as to why such services should be part of USOs.

Box 6.2 develops a model through which an analysis of this question can start. It assumes that there are two categories of low-income consumers that are undifferentiated to the tax authorities' eye: true indigents who may end up being unable to pay their bill, and less destitute

Box 6.2
Toll Limitation as an Instrument of Redistribution

As explained in text, suppose that there are two categories of consumers: the mildly needy and the indigent. The only difference between the two categories is that the mildly needy have some source of unobserved income (moonlighting, family support). The state would like to help the latter more that the former, but does not have the required information to redistribute income directly.

Consumers all have the same preferences for telecommunications. A consumer's demand is ex ante uncertain. It may be "low" (for instance, receiving calls and placing urgent calls only) with probability α, or "high," with probability $1 - \alpha$. The low consumption always yields gross surplus v_1 while the high consumption, when there is a demand for it, yields gross surplus v_2.

The total costs for the operator of the low and high levels of service for a given consumer are c_1 and c_2, respectively. We assume that the flexibility may be socially valuable, that is,

$$v_2 - c_2 > v_1 - c_1 \tag{1}$$

We will also assume that the operator incurs no fixed cost, and so marginal cost and Ramsey pricing coincide.

A key feature of this model is that there is a delay between telephone consumption and the corresponding payment. A consumer is disconnected in case of nonpayment at the end of the period. Her value of not being disconnected is taken, in reduced form, to be V. We will assume that V is sufficiently large so that a consumer who has money to pay the bill indeed pays the bill.

As mentioned before, indigent consumers may not be able to pay their bill. We will assume that while they always have enough to pay c_1, they, with probability y, are unable to pay c_2. Given the assumption made on V and assuming that indigent consumers do not know whether they will be able to pay later on when they choose their telephone consumption, this assumption implies that at marginal cost pricing indigent consumers do not value the flexibility of choice while mildly needy ones, who know they will be able to pay, value this flexibility. The timing is summarized in figure 6.1.

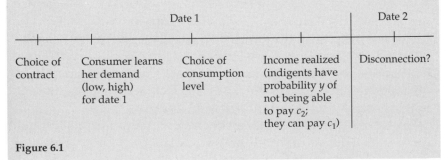

Figure 6.1

Box 6.2 (continued)

Marginal Cost/Ramsey Pricing

Suppose the low and high services are sold at c_1 and c_2, respectively. As we observed, if

$$v_2 - (1-y)c_2 - yV < v_1 - c_1 \tag{2}$$

then the indigent consumer limits her consumption even if she has high demand, while condition (1) implies that the mildly needy person does not. The date-1 surpluses, therefore, are

$$v_1 - c_1$$

for the indigent, and

$$\alpha(v_1 - c_1) + (1-\alpha)(v_2 - c_2)$$

for the mildly needy. Note that the mildly needy consumers are given a *free* option to purchase the extra units. We now observe that a redistributive scheme consists in having them pay for the option and in redistributing the proceeds to the true indigents.

Toll Limitation

Suppose now that the operator no longer offers a flexible contract (low consumption at price c_1, high consumption at price c_2), but rather a *menu* of contracts. The toll-limitation contract, as its name indicates, limits consumption to the low level at the subscription price p_1. The regular service is a "two-part tariff" offering the low consumption at price $\hat{p}_1 > p_1$ together with the option of electing the high consumption at incremental price equal to incremental cost $c_2 - c_1$.

The indigent is made better off as long as

$$p_1 < c_1$$

Cross-subsidies are feasible if $\hat{p}_1$ can be chosen sufficiently above c_1 to ensure budget balance while not providing mildly needy consumers with an incentive to choose toll limitation:

$$v_1 - p_1 \leq v_1 - \hat{p}_1 + (1-\alpha)[(v_2 - v_1) - (c_2 - c_1)] \tag{3}$$

While the exact amount of feasible redistribution depends on the relative proportions of the two categories, it is always feasible to find a balanced-budget menu satisfying formula (3) and

$$p_1 < c_1 < \hat{p}_1$$

(p_1 should be "close" enough to c_1).

The basic insight is that the indigents have a lower marginal disutility of toll limitation and therefore can be offered low prices without being mimicked by other consumers.

Box 6.2 (continued)

Remark   In this version of the model, there exist alternative and equivalent ways of achieving the same redistribution. In the same spirit, the mildly needy consumers could be offered an option to buy the extra units together with a penalty if the option is not exercised. The point worth noting, though, is that if $v_2 - v_1$ is random, then it is in general efficient to offer the extra units at incremental cost $c_2 - c_1$ (this is a version of the "perfect two-part tariff").

poor people who have some unobserved source of income (moonlighting, family support, etc.) and thus can pay their bills. In this situation, offering subsidized toll limitation is a way of discriminating in favor of the neediest. The indigent do not value the flexibility of choice provided by regular servicing as much as less needy consumers, because the former are frightened of not being able to pay their bill and of being disconnected. Toll limitation is a screening device that allows offering of a lower quality service at an affordable price.

Remark 1   In practice, it is not possible to offer menus that screen all types of consumers. For example, Oftel has computed that the offer of a new "lifeline" service package designed for the indigents might be selected by about 10 percent of the current low-user scheme (see chapter 3 for a description of this scheme).

Remark 2   In a similar vein, and with regard to the regional planning motivation, one may argue that a customer's address is imperfectly observed—say, because the inhabitant of a metropolitan area may give a fictitious or secondary residence address in the countryside—and so direct redistributions from the low-cost to high-cost areas through the income tax system may not be feasible. In contrast, the ratio of marginal willingnesses to pay for telecommunications, postal, or electricity services in the countryside and in cities is higher for those who actually live in the countryside. That is, the consumption of telephone, electricity, or postal services is likely to be a better indicator than the declared address of where the individual actually lives, and so may be a better base for subsidies. And so, subsidies through utility pricing may substitute for a priori more efficient but infeasible redistributions through the income tax system.

We have emphasized the imperfect observability of income. Other limitations on income tax redistribution stem from the existence of constraints on tax schemes. Such constraints can only be rationalized through political economy considerations, which, for brevity, we will not analyze.[13]

Budget Balance Constraints   Fearing runaway budget deficits, various countries have adopted mechanical rules (budget balance amendments in the United States, Maastricht convergence criteria in the European Union) that make it harder to provide subsidies through the overall budget. There is, therefore, an incentive to shift subsidies to the industry level so that they not be recorded in the overall budget, and to use other industry services to finance these subsidies.

Compartmentalization and Utility Budget Balance   An important assumption of the Atkinson-Stiglitz model is that the state faces a single budget constraint. Under this and the other underlying assumptions, marginal cost pricing—or, more generally, the "Frisch-Allais rule" of a uniform tax rate—is the optimal utility pricing rule. In practice, though, utilities are subject to separate budget balancing and generally do not receive subsidies from the state. This constraint is precisely what motivated Ramsey-Boiteux pricing in the first place. There are several hypotheses for why one may subject regulated industries to budget constraints, such as the need for regulatory accountability, or the desire to strengthen the budget constraint credibly so as to force the regulated firm to limit costs.[14]

6.2.2.2   Consumption Externalities

Subsidies, as is the case of free inoculations against contagious diseases, are sometimes motivated by the existence of (uninternalized) externalities. This argument in favor of subsidies is sometimes applied to network industries. For instance, consumers benefit from being able to call or send faxes to other consumers, and this benefit may not be fully internalized by the latter when choosing whether to subscribe to a telephone network or purchase a fax machine. This argument suggests subsidizing the initial connection charge as well as the monthly subscription charge of telephone subscribers. Note, however, that a

---

13. Note, though, that if political economy considerations constrain tax schemes, they may also constrain the design of universal service.
14. See Laffont and Tirole (1993, chap. 15 and pp. 681–682, respectively) for formal analyses of these two rationales for budget constraints. See also section 2.2.1.

profit-maximizing firm (whether subject to a price cap or not) would take this consideration into account when choosing its price structure. A larger network increases the value of telephone services to consumers and thus enables the company to charge higher prices for variable consumption.

Another form of club effect arises in high-cost areas. For example, bringing a telephone wire or electricity to a remote hamlet is quite expensive and can be justified only if a substantial fraction of the hamlet purchases the associated service. In any case, no inhabitant would want to connect first if he has to pay the total incremental cost of connecting the hamlet. There are, then, two standard solutions: Either the operator subsidizes the first subscriber substantially and sets prices above the within-hamlet marginal connection cost to the subsequent users. Or, as is sometimes done, the operator charges the full cost to the first subscriber, who then acquires property rights in the line and thus can charge subsequent users for within-hamlet connections.[15]

Network or club externalities are no longer at the forefront of the universal service debate (except perhaps for new services such as Internet), partly because networks are largely developed in the OECD countries and partly because it is recognized that network externalities are to a large extent internalized by operators.

6.2.2.3   *Other Factors*
Several other violations of the Atkinson-Stiglitz paradigm have been pointed out in other contexts, most notably education. They play a much more minor role in the telecommunications industry, but we briefly record them for completeness, using the case of subsidies to education. Many feel that a relatively distortion-free method of redistributing utility is to subsidize education. Again, the case for such subsidies is not a foregone conclusion in view of the Atkinson-Stiglitz result. Why should one force the poor to consume education, and not redistribute income to them and let them decide what to do with it? Four arguments have been made to explain why such a deviation from the Atkinson-Stiglitz result might be warranted: consumption exter-

---

15. Each solution has drawbacks. On the one hand, the operator may have less information than the first subscriber about the demand of the other potential subscribers (or the future development of the hamlet); so, in the first paradigm, the operator may end up subsidizing lines that benefit only a small number of consumers. On the other hand, the second paradigm may expose the first subscriber to liquidity problems and to income risk (which may be nonnegligible in a low-income area), and may create inefficient and possibly unpleasant bargaining among the inhabitants of the hamlet.

nalities (education increases the productivity of coworkers), imperfect information among the poor about the rate of return on education (although there might be ways of informing the poor about this rate of return), credit rationing (even after some amount of income redistribution, the poor may still find it difficult to borrow to pay the cost of education), and within-family principal-agent problems (the state may deem that some parents, who control the within-family allocation of income, would not internalize their children's welfare sufficiently and would therefore underinvest in their education). Let us note, finally, that some educational subsidies may possibly be provided by the telecommunications industry. The current U.S. reform project aims at subsidizing 20 to 90 percent of the cost of Internet access and communications of schools and libraries, up to a ceiling of $2.25 billion per year.

6.3   The U.S. Telecommunications Act of 1996 and Universal Service Obligations

In the United States the Federal Communications Commission is designing rules to deal with the practicalities of the universal service reform set in motion by the Telecommunications Act of 1996. Let us briefly review existing programs as well as the currently favored reform.[16]

6.3.1   Existing Programs

Simplifying a bit, universal service in the United States can be divided into two programs corresponding to the two motivations for universal service obligations: income redistribution and regional planning.

Support for low-income consumers is composed of a Lifeline Assistance program ("lifeline") and a Lifeline Connection Assistance program ("link up"). Both benefit (means-tested) qualifying consumers and are financed through taxes on long-distance services. In most states lifeline reduces the monthly subscriber charge of qualifying consumers by $7.[17] The link-up program defrays $30 from the connection cost for low-income consumers (or more precisely pays for half of the connection price, with a ceiling at $30).

---

16. For more detail, see, e.g., FCC document CC Docket no. 96–45, "In the Matter of Federal-State Joint Board on Universal Service" (Nov. 8, 1996).

17. Technically, the federal subscriber line charge (SLC), equal to $3.50, is fully or partly waived, and states must match the reduction.

Support for rural, insular, and high-cost areas is currently provided through three mechanisms. To understand the mechanism behind the Universal Service Fund (or high-cost assistance fund), one should recall that the jurisdictional separations rules (arbitrarily) assign 25 percent of each local exchange company's (LEC's) loop cost to the interstate jurisdiction. That is, such allocated costs must be recovered from interstate services. This fraction is raised in the case of LECs that have above-average loop costs (namely, those whose accounting/embedded loop costs exceed the national average by 15 percent). The increase amounts to a subsidy by long-distance services. The subsidies may be substantial and create a disincentive for the LEC to reduce its loop costs. (The FCC notes that some local companies receive a dollar from the interstate jurisdiction for each dollar of loop costs above 150 percent of the national average loop cost.)

There are two other support mechanisms for high-cost areas. The "Dial Equipment Minutes Weighting" mechanism provides subsidies to LECs with fewer than 50,000 access lines (which may not be able to take advantage of returns to scale in switching) by similarly allocating a higher fraction of switching costs than normal to the interstate jurisdiction. Last, the soon defunct "LTS program" supports some carriers with higher-than-average subscriber line costs.

These support mechanisms for high-cost areas raise two main concerns. First, they are based on embedded costs and therefore provide poor incentives for cost reduction . Second, they go to the incumbent local exchange carrier (ILEC). The advent of competition in the local segment calls for new, competitively neutral mechanisms that do not favor the ILECs to the detriment of the entrants (competitive local exchange carriers, or CLECs).

6.3.2   Reform Projects

For expository purposes, we decompose the design of a universal service policy into four steps: definition of supported services, choice of quality levels, pricing, and choice of a tax base to finance the subsidies. Because an optimal policy must balance the costs and benefits of universal service subsidies, it is clear that these decisions should be taken simultaneously, rather than sequentially.

Defining Universal Service   The first step in designing a universal service policy is the definition of services to be included in the subsidized basket. It may be useful to return to a discussion of the Atkinson-Stiglitz result. The very choice of a basket of subsidized services is not per se an obvious matter. It implies that the supported group (low-income consumers, residents of high-cost areas) not only are induced to favor telecommunications services over nontelecommunications goods and services, but also that they are encouraged to consume a subset of such services rather than other telecommunications services. In the case of low-income consumers the argument probably is that they have a relative preference for the very services that are included in the support basket. Let us note also that according to this logic, the supported services need not be the same for low-income consumers and for high-cost areas (unless the support for high-cost areas really has a redistributive function rather than a regional planning one). For example, one can imagine reasons to subsidize Internet and long-distance services for businesses in high-cost areas, whereas one would not subsidize these services for low-income consumers.

In any case, the FCC has listed a set of services that will benefit from universal service support: voice grade access to the public switched network, Touch-Tone (which is important for access to voice mail, information services, etc.), single-party services, operator, directory and emergency services, and access to long distance (the ability to connect to a long-distance company). This list, of course, is not exhaustive. We have discussed the (aborted) project for the homeless and seasonal workers, and we have analyzed support for toll-blocking and toll-limitation services. There is also some discussion concerning the provision of toll-free Internet access and other subsidies for health care providers serving rural areas.

Quality   After defining the set of supportable services, the regulators must impose some minimum level of quality. For example, offering operator assistance is meaningless if the operator rarely answers. More generally, it may be tempting for an operator to provide the supported services and skimp on quality. Delineating the areas covered by "local service" is also a complex issue.

The setting of minimum quality levels is further complicated when different technologies compete for the provision of supportable services. For example, it becomes more and more apparent that a cost-effective way of serving remote areas not yet connected by wire telephony is to go wireless. But wireless services do not have the same quality characteristics as wire-based services. They allow mobility, but they often have lower quality, lower completion rate, and so forth. Uninformed regulatory choices on the respective quality standards for wire-based and wireless services might well bias the outcome of the competition.

Another issue is whether quality should be the same everywhere. For example, local providers currently fear that if they provide high-speed Internet access to their urban consumers, they will also be forced to provide the same service at a similar price to their high-cost rural consumers. This fear may inhibit the diffusion of new technology.

Pricing   The next step after the definition of supportable services and minimum quality is to pick maximum prices. To some extent this choice is a political decision. But there are also some technical problems at this stage. Even basic services exhibit substantial price discrimination—for example, through time-of-day pricing or various forms of nonlinear pricing (menus of offerings differing in the fixed subscriber fee, the per-minute charge, the number of free local calls, and so forth). While there is nothing wrong with such price discrimination, it raises the administrative question of which price is the relevant price.

Financing   The last step consists in selecting a tax base to finance the supported services. Presumably, and in conformity with Ramsey principles (see chapters 2 and 3), taxes must be chosen so as to distort least the consumptions of other telecommunications services. Exercises such as the one performed by Hausman (1998) are useful in this respect. Hausman computes the social deadweight loss associated with the possible financing of a specific subsidy, that to schools and libraries, by long-distance services. Recall the project of subsidizing 20 to 90 percent of the cost of consumption of some telecommunications services by schools and libraries, up to a ceiling of $2.25 billion a year. Assuming that all increases in access go directly into an increase in the price of long distance, Hausman estimates a deadweight loss equal to $1.93 billion a year. That is, each dollar raised through an extra markup on long-distance services costs $1.86 = (2.25 + 1.93)/(2.25) to consumers in terms of welfare.

This shadow cost of funds of .86 must be compared to various estimates of the shadow cost of public funds, that is, the deadweight loss associated with one dollar of general tax revenue.[18] These estimates lie

_____

18. Universal service obligations could alternatively be financed through general taxation rather than from markups on telecommunications services. For example, in the United Kingdom, subsidies to the winners of auctions for universal-service railroad franchises come from the general revenue.

between .25 and .40, well below the shadow cost of funds obtained in this specific matter. Hausman attributes this high shadow cost to three factors: a nonnegligible elasticity of demand for long-distance services (.7), the existence of other taxes on long-distance services,[19] and a very high markup by the long-distance companies above their perceived marginal cost (technological marginal cost plus taxes on long-distance services).[20] Hausman further argues that a replacement of the tax on long-distance services by one on the monthly subscriber charge would have a much lower social cost.[21]

6.3.2.1   Use of Proxy Models for the Definition of Universal Subsidy Vouchers

The leading contender for universal service reform at this stage is the use of proxy models. Recall that proxy models aim at estimating the forward-looking cost of various elements of the network from engineering data.

---

19. The FCC is actually planning to lower taxes on long-distance services. See "In the Matter of Access Charge Reform: First Report and Order," May 16, 1997. Currently, as we have seen, the long-distance companies pay per-minute access charges (CCL or common carrier line charge) to local exchange carriers that include a fraction of local loop and other non–traffic sensitive costs. The plan is to phase out these taxes and to recover the corresponding revenue loss through flat-rated charges. Officially, the flat-rated charges will still be recouped from long-distance companies. The latter will pay a presubscribed interexchange carrier charge (PICC) per subscriber that they enroll. (A consumer who does not subscribe to a long-distance company will pay the PICC anyway. The LEC may collect the PICC directly from the end user who has not presubscribed an interchange carrier.) To the extent that the long-distance companies pass this monthly charge along to their customers, the PICC de facto amounts to an increase in the monthly subscriber charge (a direct increase in this monthly subscriber charge seems politically difficult, a fact which may justify this disguised approach). The FCC is thus in the process of substantially rebalancing rates in favor of long-distance and other highly taxed services and to the detriment of subsidies on monthly fees.

20. The big long-distance companies have installed high-capacity fiber networks. Therefore, they have incurred substantial sunk costs and have very low marginal costs. Without some amount of tacit collusion, most would face deep financial problems. The existence of a large markup in the long-distance market certainly inflates the welfare cost. It makes it hard, however, to compute the impact of a change in the access tax on the price of long distance. (This impact would be one-for-one if the long-distance market were competitive, but it may differ substantially from one-for-one in a more collusive environment.)

21. As we discussed earlier, the impact of an increase in the monthly subscriber charge is somewhat hard to compute, since the elasticity of demand (currently quite small) is likely to increase at higher monthly charges and since the demand for the second line and for secondary residences is higher than that for the first line in primary homes. Also, states may be reluctant to raise the monthly subscriber charge. Hausman's qualitative conclusion that the deadweight loss can be reduced seems robust, though.

Suppose that one has estimated the marginal cost of offering the bundle of supported services in a given area (we will later come back to the choice of area size); and that one has made the political choice of offering the bundle to all consumers at some maximum price p^*. A high-cost area is an area where $c > p^*$. The regulator then can define a level of subsidy per line, s, to which any carrier offering the universal service bundle would be entitled:

Subsidy = Forward-looking cost − National benchmark price

or

$$s = c - p^*$$

This method has two main benefits. First, to the extent that the cost is not an embedded cost the current cost-plus nature of universal service subsidies is eliminated; local exchange carriers in high-cost areas then have strong incentives to reduce their costs. Second, the subsidy is competitively neutral. Any carrier who wants to serve the area (and meets some requirements; see section 6.3.3.3) can benefit from the subsidy. The subsidy is similar to a voucher, which the consumer can allocate to the carrier of her choice.

6.3.3   Some Difficulties

This paradigm for universal service raises some issues, some of which are specific to the use of proxy models, while some others apply to any form of universal service funding.

6.3.3.1   General Issues Affecting Proxy Models

Forward-looking long-run incremental costs can be computed either by looking at an optimized network that would be built now, or, alternatively, by taking as a given the existing network, which inherits historical choices of wire center locations, equipment, and technology. In either case, the technological choices are supposed here to reflect the least-cost provision of the supported services, although of course carriers are free to make alternative choices, for example, to be able to offer advanced services as well.[22] As we have observed, there are a num-

---

22. Nothing, of course, guarantees that this technological choice will be socially optimal. Suppose, for instance, that the basic technology costs c per line and allows the company to offer only the supported services. Let $s = c - p^*$ denote the per-line subsidy, where p^* denotes the target price for the basic, supported service. An improved network (e.g.

ber of discretionary items involved in the process of computing such forward-looking costs: area size, distribution of households within the area, soil conditions, choice of the fiber-copper crossover line (how the feeder line is deployed) and size of switches, distance of households from roadways, forecast of usage (in particular fill factor of the feeder cables), treatment of joint costs, physical depreciation, and economic depreciation. At this stage, proxy models still yield widely divergent estimates.[23]

6.3.3.2   Distinction between Technological and Opportunity Costs

Companies will offer not only the basic supported services, but also complementary and more advanced services (call forwarding, call waiting, video, and so forth). Indeed a major justification for creating competitively neutral support mechanisms is that consumers will face a fair choice of suppliers of complementary services. These complementary services will bring extra revenue, which must be subtracted from the technological cost of supplying the supported services in order to compute the more relevant opportunity cost of supplying the supported services. The extra revenue, however, is likely to vary substantially with the served area. For example, the set of high-cost areas includes very rich and very poor areas; and it includes areas well and poorly served by satellite television (a competitor for video services).

Another (and probably more minor) source of divergence between opportunity and technological cost is the brand name and advertising

---

ISDN on an analog technology) involves per-line cost $c' > c$, but allows the firm to offer a complementary, advanced service on top of the basic service. Suppose that the firm makes an average per-line profit π and generates an average consumer net surplus S from this avanced service. The firm will opt for the advanced technology if and only if $p^* + s - c = 0 \leq p^* + \pi + s - c'$, or $c' - c \leq \pi$.

If $\pi \leq c' - c < \pi + S$, the firm selects the basic technology even though the advanced one is socially optimal. This point is unrelated to the existence of universal subsidy and is nothing but the standard point that firms have an incentive to underinvest in a new product or an upgrade if they do not internalize the associated increase in consumer surplus. (More generally, with multiple products the firm may introduce a socially overoptimal number of products; see, e.g., Tirole, 1988. Here we have a choice between two products, but the profit on one of them is constrained by regulation to be equal to zero.)

23. For example, as of the fall of 1997, the Hatfield Model (sponsored by long-distance companies AT&T and MCI) yielded a monthly per-line local loop cost equal to $18.58. The Benchmark Costing Model (BCM1 was sponsored by MCI, NYNEX, Sprint/United Management, and U.S. West; BCM2 was sponsored by Sprint and U.S. West) put that number at $41.12. The Cost Proxy Model (CPM, sponsored by PacTel, an LEC) gave a number of $29.14.

spillovers of the provision of universal service. The U.K. regulator (Oftel) has thus argued that the incumbent operator (BT) benefits from its national coverage and from the provision of public phone booths in terms of name recognition.

These two sources of divergence between opportunity cost and technological cost (offering of complementary services, brand name) focus on the demand side. On the *cost* side, returns to scope may imply that the cost of supplying an area depends on whether the company also serves adjacent areas. The extent of these returns to scope depends heavily on the size of the area. There are probably small returns to scope of serving both Toulouse and Bordeaux rather than each city individually. However, there are certainly large returns to scope from serving everyone in a neighborhood or from serving adjacent neighborhoods. Returns to scope are of course part of the question of how forward-looking costs are computed; we here just take note of the fact that for small area sizes a proper computation requires knowing whether the company serves adjacent areas.

6.3.3.3   *Definition of Geographical Area*

The current proposals emphasize the use of relatively small areas. "Census block groups," or CBGs (used by the BCM model), encompass about 400 households. Alternatively, one can use geographical areas such as 3,000-foot-by-3,000-foot grids, combined with census data to determine the location of households (as the CPM model does). Or else, one can focus the analysis on wire centers.

What are the *trade-offs* involved in the choice of an area size? There are three potential drawbacks to choosing a small area size. First, a small area size implies returns to scope across areas and therefore makes the notion of the cost of an area ambiguous, as we already noted. Second, a fine grid generates a large number of areas (350,000 CBGs in the United States!). This fact increases the transaction costs of defining area-specific subsidies.

At least theoretically, there is a third potential drawback: Small areas may increase the amount of private information held by incumbent LECs. Even very carefully designed proxy models will always miss some unobserved/unmeasured specific features of the terrain, distribution of consumers, and so forth. It *may* prove that, owing to the law of large numbers, regulators and entrants face lower asymmetries of information when the area size is large than when it is small (in the same way that uninformed investors are much better protected against informed ones when trading the stock index than when trading an individual stock). We are not aware of any reflection on this argument; nor can we offer an informed guess on its empirical validity.

The key benefit of small area size is the reduced opportunity for cream skimming. Two remarks are in order before we explain the argument. The first is that it is widely recognized that there will always be heterogeneity within a given size area:

A clearly defined obligation to serve is necessary because customers in each CBG are heterogeneous with respect both to cost and to other factors, such as the level of services they demand, that would affect their attractiveness to the carriers. If the regulator had perfect knowledge, and could call out exactly the correct amount of support for each customer—the precise amount that would just elicit supply from a carrier—then no obligation to serve would be necessary, since every customer would be served voluntarily. Unfortunately, no commission has that perfect knowledge, and in any event it would not be practical to administer a plan on a customer-specific basis. Therefore, any real-world Universal Service Plan must offer an average amount of support within each area. The only way to ensure that every customer is served at an average support level—when customers are heterogeneous—is to link the average support payment to an obligation to serve any customer who requests service.[24]

Accordingly, section 214(e)(1) of the Telecommunications Act of 1996 states that a common carrier designated as an eligible telecommunications carrier must advertise the availability of supported services and their charges using media of general distribution throughout the service area. Most observers agree that all carriers eligible to receive universal service subsidies should be willing to serve and advertise to all consumers in the area. In the following, we will sometimes follow common usage by calling those carriers who accept a commitment to advertise and supply supported services to all consumers in an area COLRs (carriers of last resort).

The second remark is that the presumption of reduced heterogeneity for small areas is related to the argument that average costs may be more precisely estimated for larger areas.

Box 6.3 develops a simple model of cream skimming in an area with heterogeneous consumers, namely, consumers with different costs of serving. To give local competition its best chance, it assumes away economies of scope in the delivery of local services. That is, the

---

24. Comments of GTE submitted to the California Public Utilities Commission, Auctions Proposals for Universal Service, 1997.

Box 6.3
The Universal Service Obligation and Cream Skimming

Consider an area with heterogeneous consumers. In this area, a carrier must incur per-customer cost c_H of serving a "high-cost consumer" and cost c_L of serving a "low-cost consumer." High- and low-cost consumers are in proportions α and $1 - \alpha$, respectively. Let us assume for the sake of the argument that the regulator's estimate of the average cost $c = \alpha c_H + (1 - \alpha)c_L$ is unbiased (that is, the regulator knows the fraction of high-cost customers) although the regulator cannot tell low- from high-cost consumers. So the per-line subsidy s will be uniform. We will assume, in contrast, that firms can tell the two types of consumers apart.

In a high-cost area, c exceeds the price benchmark p^* selected for the universal service bundle. Let us further assume that

$$c_L < p^* < c_H$$

so that some customers do not require a subsidy to be served at the benchmark price. We now argue that a subsidy that would pay each COLR (carrier accepting the universal service contract offered by the regulator, thereby agreeing to serve any consumer in the area at maximal price p^*) the difference between the area's average per-line cost and the benchmark price,

$$s_0 = c - p^*$$

is subject to cream skimming and is not sustainable. A COLR accepting this subsidy faces two types of cream skimming, by non-COLRs and by other COLRs, if any.

Cream Skimming by Non-COLRs

Let us first assume that there is a single COLR, facing entry by non-COLRs. Non-COLRs have no incentive to target the high-cost consumers because these can purchase at price p^* from the COLR, and cost $c_H > p^*$ to serve. In contrast, non-COLRs can make offers at price c_L to low-cost consumers. The COLR will find it profitable to keep these customers (by charging $c_L - \varepsilon$, for small enough ε), because the net cost of serving these customers is the technological cost c_L minus the per-line subsidy s.

The COLR indeed agrees to be a COLR if it does not lose money overall, or

$$\alpha(p^* + s - c_H) + (1 - \alpha)(c_L + s - c_L) \geq 0$$

or

$$s \geq s_1 = \alpha(c_H - p^*) > s_0 = \alpha(c_H - p^*) + (1 - \alpha)(c_L - p^*)$$

The required subsidy s_1 exceeds the level s_0 that is obtained from the average per-line cost estimate. The competitive pressure by non-COLRs on low-cost consumers creates a partial revenue loss on these consumers that must be offset by an increase in the subsidy. Or, equivalently, entry prevents any low-cost consumers from cross-subsidizing high-cost ones, thus contributing to universal service.

Box 6.3 (continued)

Note also that cream skimming is potential rather than actual: Non-COLRs in this example create a competitive threat, but do not bite into the COLR's market share. The COLR remains the sole supplier in this market, and the total subsidy per line is equal to s_1.

Note also that neither the prices faced by the two types of consumers nor the required total subsidy changes if the COLR is prevented from responding to the competitive threat by non-COLRs, say, through the prohibition of price discrimination in the area. The COLR then charges p^* but serves only the high-cost consumers. The low-cost consumers turn to the non-COLRs and purchase the service at price c_L, as earlier. The *nominal* per-line subsidy to the COLR must be raised from $s_1 = \alpha(c_H - p^*)$ to

$$s_2 = c_H - p^*$$

but the *average* per-line subsidy remains the same, as

$$\alpha s_2 = s_1$$

The only difference between the two situations is the COLR's market share. Entry is actual, and not only potential, when price discrimination by the COLR is prohibited.

Cream Skimming by Other COLRs

Assume now that there is more than one COLR. Let us suppose further that COLRs either can price discriminate or that they sell complementary services consumed by all consumers, on which they can make targeted, below-cost offers. That is, the COLRs can charge different prices to high- and low-cost consumers. Therefore, they offer a price equal to their net cost $c_L - s$ to low-cost consumers (and so non-COLRs cannot compete and do not even play the role of potential competitors). Because COLRs make no profit on the low-cost consumers, they must receive subsidy $s_2 = c_H - p^*$ in order to be willing to be COLRs.

The comparison with the case of a single COLR facing non-COLRs is the following. The total subsidy is now $s_2 > s_1$. The high-cost consumers still pay p^*. But the price paid by low-cost consumers has decreased by the amount of the subsidy (s_2). That is, the low-cost consumers receive the universal service subsidy over and above an already low price. The losers are the consumers of services that contribute to the financing of the universal service program. To the extent that the low-cost consumers' demand for connection is inelastic in the relevant range (as we have assumed here), and that the demand for services that are taxed to finance universal service is elastic, welfare has been reduced by allowing multiple COLRs.

marginal cost of connecting a consumer is independent of the number of other consumers connected by the firm; this marginal cost, however, varies across consumers. The model shows that *the average per-line cost in an area is not a proper basis for defining universal service subsidies in a competitive environment.* In a nutshell, entry erodes the tax base; consumers who are relatively cheap to serve receive low prices. Thus carriers that provide universal service (accept the COLR status) can no longer count on low-cost consumers to complement the universal service subsidy to compensate their losses on high-cost consumers.

The size of the increase in the total universal service subsidy depends on the number of COLRs. If there is a single COLR, the competitive pressure faced by this COLR for low-cost consumers comes solely from non-COLRs that do not receive the subsidy.[25] In contrast, with multiple COLRs, the latter compete even more fiercely for low-cost consumers, since their cost of serving low-cost (as well as high-cost) consumers is reduced by the amount of the subsidy. In the latter, and in contrast with the former competitive paradigm, the low-cost consumers not only do not contribute to the financing of the universal service provision, but also receive the subsidy themselves. Thus, *the increase in the total universal service subsidy to be borne by consumers of other services* (such as long-distance) *is higher in the case of multiple COLRs.*

The model thus makes the points that consumer heterogeneity and competition raise the cost of providing universal service and also condition the amount of the required subsidy. Its implication in terms of choice of area size is the following: To the extent that the regulator cannot easily identify low-cost consumers (as is assumed in the model), selecting a smaller area size does not a priori reduce the required level of subsidies. However, if the regulator can identify two areas, one with high-cost consumers and the other with low-cost consumers, lumping them together in a single area with a uniform universal service subsidy may raise the required amount of subsidy.

Remark   We have assumed that consumers select a single company. In practice, though, consumers may want to subscribe to both wireless and wire-based services. Whether wireless services are non-COLR (say, because they do not want to cover the entire high-cost area) or COLR, then cream skimming by wireless services is less a concern than is de-

---

25. It may be argued that, for the United States, cream skimming by non-COLRs may not be a very big problem, given the very low price picked by regulators for residential service. (This situation corresponds to the case $p^* \leq c_L$ in box 6.3.)

picted here. The possibility of multiple subscriptions, however, raises new issues. In particular, assuming such a rule can be enforced in practice (which is not obvious), should a multiple-subscription customer be entitled to only one COLR subsidy? The answer to this question may well depend on the precise rationale for universal service support. Support to the needy may not justify multiple subsidies for customers subscribing to both wireless and wire-based services; in contrast, multiple subsidies may be justified if the rationale is to contribute to regional development.

6.4   Universal Service Auctions

The major obstacle to good regulation lies in the asymmetric information between the regulator and the regulated firms. Here, even with proxy models, we must expect that a sizable asymmetry of information will remain in the evaluation of the cost of universal service. This motivates the possible use of auctions as a market-based (as opposed to prescriptive) method of determining universal service subsidies.

6.4.1   Current Proposals

The use of proxy models to compute universal service support is a prescriptive approach. That is, the subsidy is set by the regulator rather than by market forces. In view of the difficulties involved in estimating the true cost of universal service, it is worth considering alternative support mechanisms in which this cost is elicited from the market participants through an auction mechanism. A small set of companies (notably GTE) and their experts have embraced the concept of universal service auctions. And the California Public Utility Commission, in its 1996 order adopting the universal service plan has argued, "An auction mechanism appears to be the most efficient mechanism for reviewing the subsidy amounts in the future." The FCC at the date of this writing is more circumspect and tends to view the auction mechanism more as an interesting alternative to be studied for possible future use than as a mechanism whose details are settled well enough to qualify for immediate implementation.

There is nothing unusual about the use of auctions to select companies to provide some service to a local or national authority. For example, in the United Kingdom, universal service auctions are used to select franchisees to operate railroad services, including a basket of basic services associated with minimum quality requirements in specific geographical areas. Auctions are also widely used in state procurement contracts and in the "concession" system, in which a contractor is selected to provide highway, local transportation, water, or sewerage services at prespecified prices.

The current proposals perhaps depart from standard franchising by the state in that they promise to allow *competition in the market as well as competition for the market*. That is, several franchisees (COLRs in the specific case) may be selected and may compete ex post in the market, while most auctions allow only ex ante competition for an ex post monopoly position. To be certain, split awards are commonplace in defense procurement,[26] but the motive for selecting multiple contractors there is not ex post competition for consumers. A number of other auctions (such as spectrum auctions for PCS services) split the awards in order to create ex post competition; however, they usually do not involve output-proportional subsidies of the kind considered for local telecommunications service auctions.

6.4.1.1   The GTE Proposal

Let us briefly describe one of the proposals. The GTE proposal[27] considers the auction of universal service support in a small area, a CBG, say. In this auction, bidders announce the minimum per-line subsidy that they are willing to take in order to accept COLR status. The auction is a single-round, sealed-bid auction. Its key features are that the market structure is endogenous and that the subsidy is uniform across winning bidders. Winning bidders are determined as follows:

If at least two valid bids have been submitted in the auction for a given CBG, the number of winning bidders will be determined by the relative levels of their bids. In general,the closer together the bids are, the greater the number of bids that will be accepted.

When bids are far apart, fewer bids will be accepted. The proposed decision rule is as follows:

1. If at least one bid does not exceed the lowest bid by more that 15 percent of the sum of the lowest bid and the basic service price, then all bids within that range will be accepted.

---

26. See Anton and Yao (1987, 1989, 1992), Auriol and Laffont (1992), McGuire and Riordan (1995), and Stole (1994) for formal models of split-award auctions and dual sourcing.
27. See GTE (1997). The proposal described here was elaborated in particular by Paul Milgrom (1996, 1997), building on earlier work by David Salant and Richard Steinberg. See also Kelly and Steinberg (1997).

2. If no competing bid is within the range described in (1), but one is within 25 percent, then the two lowest bids will be accepted.

3. If no bid is within the range described in (2), then only the lowest bid is accepted.[28]

The main feature of this selection rule is that the second, third, . . . lowest bidders are selected if they are not too inefficient compared to the lowest bidder. This suggests a trade-off between the benefits of in-the-market competition (which may increase, presumably at a decreasing rate, with the number of selected firms) and the cost inefficiency associated with not allocating the market to the most efficient bidder (an inefficiency that is present even when there are no returns to scale over the area under consideration). Leaving aside for the moment the question of the nature of the benefits of ex post competition, the premise of this rule is that the latter inefficiency can be tolerated only if the cost differential between the lowest bid and the other winners is low. Unfortunately, little theoretical research has been devoted to the study of the foundations of this interesting proposal. Box 6.4 reviews one of the rare models of endogenous market structure, namely that of Dana and Spier (1994).[29]

Let us briefly describe *some* practical aspects of the GTE proposal. First, as in the case of subsidies built from proxy models, the *area size* would be small, namely, census block groups (20,000 in California).The supporters of the proposal argue that a small area size reduces the scope for cream skimming (see section 6.3 for a formal analysis of cream skimming) and that it facilitates entry by allowing entrants to start with small territories.

On the cost side, we have seen that the smaller the area size, the higher the cost synergies across areas. In the case of auctions, this relationship implies that, when bidding for area A, a carrrier would like to know whether it will also serve adjacent areas B and C, in view of the substantial returns to scope. The second cost of a small area size is that it creates a large number of auctions. This result increases transaction costs; and it is also likely to facilitate tacit collusion because the competition between the telephone companies is often repeated.[30]

---

28. Comments of GTE submitted to the California Public Utilities Commission, Auction Proposals for Universal Service (1997, pp. 23–24).

29. See also Milgrom (1996) and Auriol and Laffont (1992).

30. See, e.g., Tirole (1988, chap. 6) for a review of the tacit collusion argument and of factors facilitating collusion.

Text continues on p. 250.

Box 6.4
Auctions with Endogenous Market Structure

Dana and Spier (1994) have developed a model in which the market structure is endogenously determined as a function of the firms' announcements of their bids. Here we describe a special case of their more general analysis.

Suppose there are two potential suppliers, $i = 1, 2$, with cost functions

$$C_i(q_i) = \begin{cases} \theta_i + c_i q_i & \text{for } q_i > 0 \\ 0 & \text{for } q_i = 0 \end{cases}$$

where θ_i is firm i's fixed cost and q_i is the firm's output. We assume that firm i's fixed cost θ_i (or equivalently, its opportunity cost of not being able to devote its attention to another market) is private information to the firm. From the point of view of the auction designer and the firm's rival, θ_i is distributed according to cumulative distribution function $F_i(\theta_i)$ with density $f_i(\theta_i)$ on some interval $[\underline{\theta}, \bar{\theta}]$. (For the standard technical reasons, we make the assumption that the hazard rate f_i/F_i is decreasing.) There is asymmetric information only on the fixed cost.

The firm's profits (gross of any payment made in the auction) and the consumer net surplus are defined in reduced form and depend on the selected market structure. All are equal to zero if no firm is selected. If firm i receives a monopoly position, its profit is a function $\pi_i^m(\theta_i)$ with $\pi_i^{m'} = -1$; the consumer net surplus is S_i^m (presumably, it is independent of the firm's fixed cost as long as the firm stays in operation). Similarly, if both firms are selected, their duopoly profits are $\pi_i^d(\theta_i)$ with $\pi_i^{d'} = -1$, and the consumer net surplus is S^d. Competition destroys profits:

$$\pi_i^d(\theta_i) \le \pi_i^m(\theta_i)$$

and

$$\pi_1^d(\theta_1) + \pi_2^d(\theta_2) \le \max\left\{\pi_1^m(\theta_1), \pi_2^m(\theta_2)\right\}$$

and raises consumer welfare:

$$S^d \ge \max\left\{S_1^m, S_2^m\right\}$$

Social welfare, W, is equal to the sum of the firms' profits net of payments b_i, namely, $\pi_i - b_i$ for firm i, plus the consumer net surplus, plus the (positive or negative) proceeds $(\Sigma_i b_i)$ from the mechanism times one plus the shadow cost of funds $(1 + \lambda)$, so

$$W = [\Sigma_i(\pi_i - b_i)] + S + (1 + \lambda)(\Sigma_i b_i) \tag{1}$$

The shadow cost of funds stands for the deadweight loss associated with the levying of funds in the industry.

Let us start with the benchmark of *symmetric information*, in which the regulator knows all cost parameters. Because $\lambda > 0$, it is optimal to have each firm pay (or receive) the amount of its profit: $b_i = \pi_i$. The regulator then chooses among three market structures:

• Nonprovision, yielding social welfare normalized at zero.

Box 6.4 (continued)

- Monopoly to firm i, yielding

$$W^i = S^m_i + (1 + \lambda)\pi^m_i(\theta_i)$$

- Duopoly, yielding

$$W^d = S^d + (1 + \lambda)\left[\pi^d_1(\theta_1) + \pi^d_2(\theta_2)\right]$$

Because the fixed costs are just subtracted from a basic profit, the solution to $\max\{0, W^1, W^2, W^d\}$ can be depicted for symmetric costs, i.e., $c_1 = c_2$ as in figure 6.2 (where D means that both firms are selected, M_i that only firm i is selected, and ϕ that no firm is selected).

When the regulator has *incomplete information* about the firms' fixed costs, the firms' profits must be replaced by the "virtual profits" (for an exposition, see, e.g., chap. 7 of Fudenberg and Tirole, 1991):

$$\pi^m_i(\theta_i) - \left(\frac{\lambda}{1+\lambda}\right)\left(\frac{F_i(\theta_i)}{f_i(\theta_i)}\right) \qquad \text{if firm } i \text{ only is selected}$$

and

$$\pi^d_i(\theta_i) - \left(\frac{\lambda}{1+\lambda}\right)\left(\frac{F_i(\theta_i)}{f_i(\theta_i)}\right) \qquad \text{under duopoly}$$

(and still 0 if no firm is selected). The computation of the virtual profits amounts to subtracting an "information cost" as perceived by the regulator from the actual profits. To understand the nature of this information cost, note that under

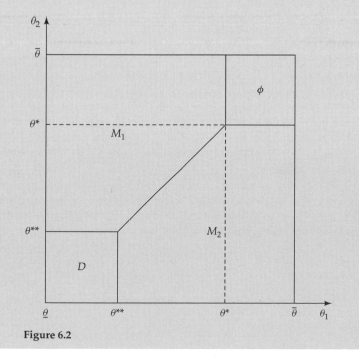

Figure 6.2

Box 6.4 (continued)

asymmetric information, and provided that firm i is selected, firm i's profit decreases one-for-one with its fixed cost. Selecting firm i under regime $r \in \{m, d\}$ yields extra profit, valued at the cost of funds, equal to $(1 + \lambda)\pi_i^r(\theta_i)$. The probability that firm i has parameter θ_i in $[\theta_i - d\theta_i, \theta_i]$ is $f_i(\theta_i)d\theta_i$. Selecting the firm when its cost is in this interval raises the rent of types in $[\underline{\theta}, \theta_i]$, which have probability $F_i(\theta_i)$, by $\pi_i^{r\prime}(\theta_i) \cdot d\theta_i = -d\theta_i$. This, together with the fact that rents have unit social cost λ (see equation [1]), yields the virtual profits.

The choice of market structure is now determined by

$$\max\{0, \hat{W}^1, \hat{W}^2, \hat{W}^d\}$$

where

$$\hat{W}^i = S_i^m + (1 + \lambda)\left[\pi_i^m(\theta_i) - \frac{\lambda}{1 + \lambda}\frac{F_i(\theta_i)}{f_i(\theta_i)}\right] < W^i$$

and

$$\hat{W}^d = S^d + (1 + \lambda)\left[\Sigma_i[\pi_i^d(\theta_i)] - \frac{\lambda}{1 + \lambda}\Sigma_i\left(\frac{F_i(\theta_i)}{f_i(\theta_i)}\right)\right] < W^d$$

Because virtual production costs are equal to technological costs plus information costs, the region of nonproduction (ϕ) expands. More interestingly, the region in which both firms are selected (D) shrinks. To induce firms to report their types truthfully, the regulator makes a low report less advantageous by decreasing the probability that the firm is selected. In this model where the regulator does not control quantities, there is no other instrument to decrease the information rents. It is for this reason that the region where both firms are selected shrinks and the region of no production expands. Competition *for* the market, that is, for a monopoly franchise, becomes more attractive relative to competition *in* the market when the regulator is poorly informed about the firms' costs.

Let us now turn to implementation. For simplicity, we consider only the symmetric case. The optimal mechanism can be implemented by the following two simultaneous auctions:

Each bidder i selects a bid to be a monopolist, b_i^m, and a bid to be a duopolist, b_i^d.

• *First auction:* The auction to be a monopolist is a first-price auction with reservation price $\pi^m(\theta^*)$.
• *Second auction:* The auction to be a duopolist is an all-pay auction with reservation price $\pi^d(\theta^{**})$. That is, if both firms bid at least $\pi^d(\theta^{**})$ in the second auction, a duopoly is created and each firm pays $\pi^d(\theta^{**})$. Otherwise, the only relevant auction is the first-price auction to be a monopolist.

Furthermore, if, in the first auction, both bid strictly more $\pi^m(\theta^{**}) - \int_{\theta^{**}}^{\theta^*}[1 - F(u)]du \Big/ [1 - F(\theta^{**})]$ a duopoly is created. (This outcome will not occur on the equilibrium path.)

Box 6.4 (continued)

For this auction, the following strategies are equilibrium strategies:

$$b^m(\theta_i) = 0 \qquad\qquad\qquad\qquad\qquad\qquad \text{if } \theta_i > \theta^*$$

$$= \pi^m(\theta_i) - \int_{\theta_i}^{\theta^*} [1 - F(u)]du \Big/ [1 - F(\theta_i)] \qquad \text{if } \theta^* \geq \theta_i > \theta^{**}$$

$$= \pi^m(\theta^{**}) - \int_{\theta^{**}}^{\theta^*} [1 - F(u)]du \Big/ [1 - F(\theta^{**})] \qquad \text{if } \theta_i \leq \theta^{**}$$

$$b^d(\theta_i) = 0 \qquad \text{if } \theta_i > \theta^{**}$$

$$= \pi^d(\theta^{**}) \qquad \text{if } \theta_i < \theta^{**}$$

The proof is straightforward.

Remarks Note that *the decision to create a duopoly is linked here to the absolute values of the bids and not to the comparison between bids.* (To obtain rules such as the ones discussed later that grant duopoly when bids are close enough, we would need private information about cost with larger positive externalities when types are closer, or about demand with complementarity of products which are greater when types are closer, or about nonconstant marginal costs; see following discussion.)

The optimal auction can be implemented in dominant strategies. It is obvious that the bid in the auction for a duopoly is a dominant strategy. As usual the first-price auction to be monopolist is equivalent to a dominant-strategy Vickrey auction; see also the material on combinatorial auctions in box 6.8. (The possibility of dominant-strategy implementation occurs because valuations are independent and the assumptions of Mookherjee and Reichelstein [1992] are satisfied. See Dasgupta and Maskin [1998] for the case of common values.)

Auriol and Laffont (1992) consider a regulation problem with cost functions

$$C_i(q_i) = \theta_i q_i + 1/2(q_i)^2 \qquad \text{for } q_i > 0$$
$$= 0 \qquad\qquad\qquad \text{for } q_i = 0$$

where θ_i is the unknown marginal cost with cumulative distribution $F(\cdot)$ in $[\underline{\theta}, \bar{\theta}]$. Here, production levels are observable and regulated.

Duopoly is now optimal if the difference in marginal costs is not too large, that is, if

$$\left| \theta^1 - \theta^2 \right| \leq q^m \left[\min(\theta^1, \theta^2) \right]$$

where $q^m(\theta)$ is the optimal production for parameter θ in the monopoly regime.

Again asymmetric information decreases $q^m(\cdot)$ and contracts the duopoly region, as depicted in figure 6.3.

Box 6.4 (continued)

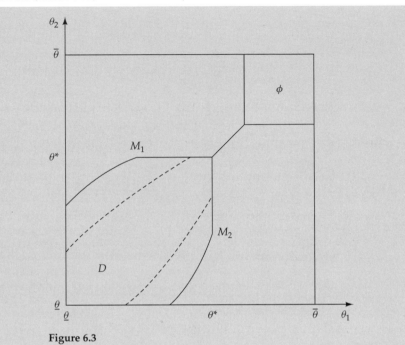

Figure 6.3

A second practicality is the nomination process. GTE proposes that at regular intervals firms be able to nominate any area for bidding.[31] The auction for this area would then be a single-round, sealed-bid auction.

---

31. GTE proposes that firms interested in prompting an auction in a given CBG should nominate that area for bidding. "Every six months there would be a preannounced two-week interval during which the CPUC [California Public Utilities Commission] would accept nominations from qualified carriers. Each qualified carrier would provide the CPUC with the list of CBGs for which it wished to submit bids, and for which it was interested in assuming the COLR obligation.

If an auction had been previously held in a given CBG, and if, as a result of that auction, at least one new firm had been selected to be a COLR there, then no new nominations would be accepted for that CBG for a period of three years.

Immediately after the close of the two-week nomination window, the CPUC would make public the list of the nominated CBGs, and the nominating firms for each CBG."

Comments of GTE submitted to the California Public Utilities Commission: Auction Proposals for Universal Service (1997, pp. 19–20).

6.4.2   The Benefits of In-Market Competition

The policy discussions on auctions for universal service often take the benefits of in-market competition for granted. The environments in which these auctions will possibly be implemented, however, are not traditional environments, since they are substantially regulated. One should, therefore, not rely on the economist's gut feeling that competition is a priori good for the consumer, and one should rather investigate the nature of the benefits in this specific environment. It is useful in this respect to distinguish between two types of services: supported services, and nonsupported or complementary services.

At first sight, one may wonder about the nature of the benefits to be expected from in-market competition for *supported services*. After all, the premise of universal service policies is that the regulator imposes a price ceiling (chosen in a prescriptive manner in the case of proxy models, or through a market mechanism as is the case here), as well as a minimum quality level that prevents carriers from escaping the price constraint by lowering quality. Thus, if any benefit is to be expected from in-market competition for supported services, either the bidders must "overestimate" the required subsidy to the point that the price constraint is not binding ex post, or the regulator must be unable to define or monitor some aspects of quality, and so competition may keep universal service providers on their toes.

Concerning the first possibility, one may have in mind the existence of random technological progress between two successive auctions; such progress is likely if the time interval between auctions is long, in particular if firms cannot easily nominate areas for bidding. Box 6.5, however, shows that this downward flexibility is a mixed blessing of in-market competition, as it increases the subsidy that must be granted to the area: Under competition *for* the market solely—that is, under a monopoly franchise—the winner of the auction faces a lottery in which the area will ex post be profitable in case of technological progress and unprofitable otherwise. The required subsidy is then equal to the difference between the expected cost and the target price. In the presence of in-market competition, the upside does not exist because the market price adjusts downward with technological progress; and so *the required subsidy is higher in the presence of in-market competition.* (We will make a very similar point when we discuss competition for complementary services.)

Box 6.5
In-Market Competition and Price Adjustment

Suppose that the current technology corresponds to a per-line cost c in the area subject to competitive bidding. This cost exceeds the target price p^* for universal service. With probability α, a technological innovation will drive the per-line cost to $c' < p^*$ (and with probability $1 - \alpha$, the per-line cost will remain $c > p^*$). To simplify computations, we assume that technological progress, if any, accrues just after the auction and thus applies to the whole time interval until the next auction. Also for simplicity, we assume that the carriers do not offer complementary services (see box 6.7 for an analysis of complementary services). Last, we assume that technologies are available to all firms and that there are at least two firms.

Under a *monopoly franchise* (competition for the market), the price to consumers does not adjust to technological progress and thus remains equal to p^*. The subsidy that emerges from the auction, therefore, is equal to the difference between the expected cost and the target price, or

$$s^m = [\alpha c' + (1 - \alpha)c] - p^*$$

Under *in-market competition* (competition for and in the market, in which at least two bidders are selected), the price adjusts from p^* to $c' - s$ in the case of technological progress. Because the selected firms make no profit in the case of technological progress, they must break even in the absence of technological progress, and so the required subsidy is

$$s = c - p^* > s^m$$

That is, competition in the market raises the level of subsidy and therefore of distortions in the consumption of services that contribute to the financing of the universal service obligation.

The second possible benefit of in-market competition for supported services is that their quality level is higher under competition. As we discussed, it may be that the regulator is able to impose some quality standards but cannot monitor the level of quality in some other dimensions. In order to create incentives for competing COLRs to provide quality beyond the level specified in the universal service obligations, however, the subsidy must exceed the level that would obtain under monopoly franchising. Furthermore, *competition for the market when in-market competition is allowed need not result in levels of subsidies that are sufficiently high to create competition in those nonspecified dimensions of quality;* see box 6.6.

We now turn to the second category of potential benefits derived from in-market competition, those related to *nonsupported services.* Here, we must distinguish between two cases. A polar case is that of reliable access policies. That is, the resale and unbundling policies

Box 6.6
In-Market Competition and Quality of Supported Services

Suppose that the regulator is able to specify some level of quality in the provision of universal service. The per-line cost of supplying this basic level of quality is c. However, it would be socially desirable to provide better service. Let $v(\xi)$ denote the per-line consumer surplus generated by extra quality ξ ($\xi = 0$ for the basic, specified quality) and $\psi(\xi)$ denote the per-line cost of providing extra quality ξ. Assume that $v(\cdot)$ and $\psi(\cdot)$ are continuously increasing and that $v(\xi) - \psi(\xi)$ is quasi-concave with an optimum at $\xi^* > 0$. As usual we use p^* to denote the target price, and we assume that all firms have the same technology. The question is, Is the socially optimal level ξ^* the outcome of a universal service auction?

Under a *monopoly franchise*, the bidders all bid

$$s^m = c - p^*$$

and the winner ex post chooses $\xi^m = 0$. The quality is at the minimum level specified by the regulator because the winning firm cannot benefit from quality improvements by raising its price beyond p^*.

Let us now turn to *in-market competition*. Suppose, for example, that two firms (the two lowest bidders) out of $n > 2$ firms are selected. It is easy to see that the same outcome prevails as under monopoly franchising. Ex ante competition for the market drives the subsidy down to s^m. The level of subsidy is too low to provide incentives to supply extra quality and gain market share ex post, since the equilibrium subsidy already guarantees that the providers just break even for the minimum quality level.

The socially optimal level ξ^* could be obtained by prescribing subsidy

$$s = c + \psi(\xi^*) - p^* > s^m$$

and letting competition operate rather than letting an auction set the subsidy level. The firms then charge p^* and select quality level ξ^*, since, up to $\xi = \xi^*$, firms find it cheaper to compete for customers in quality than in price. They make no profit in equilibrium. This prescriptive mode of setting the subsidy, however, requires more information for the regulator than an auction.

described in chapter 2 create a level playing field for complementary services that penalizes neither the bottleneck owners nor the suppliers of stand-alone complementary services. In this case, in-market competition does not bring any benefit relative to nonsupported services because the provision of the latter is disconnected from the production of the supported services. Therefore, the assertion that in-market competition for basic services generates benefits in the provision of nonsupported services amounts to recognition of the limitations of access policies, at least for a subset of nonsupported services that will end up being provided jointly with the supported ones.

We therefore turn to the other polar case in which access policies are inoperative (at least for a subset of complementary services) and the complementary services can be provided only by a carrier also supplying the basic services. Box 6.7 analyzes the impact of in-market competition under these circumstances.

The first key insight of this analysis is that *in-market competition is a mixed blessing,* for a reason that was analyzed earlier: *Competition* lowers profits on the complementary segment, and therefore *raises the equilibrium subsidy that is demanded by the bidders.* In a sense there is no free lunch. In-market competition is desirable if the deadweight loss associated with the absence of competition in the complementary segment exceeds the increase (associated with the increase in the subsidy) in the deadweight loss on other telecommunications segments financing the universal service plan.

The other main insights relate to the questions whether *simple auctions with endogenous market structures* deliver the efficient market structure and whether, if they do, the optimal subsidy emerges. With respect to the first question, it is clear that, for the usual reason, the optimality of the emerging market structure cannot be guaranteed. While the optimality of monopoly franchising versus in-market competition hinges on a comparison of deadweight losses, the outcome of an auction depends only on profits and therefore cannot reflect consumer surplus considerations.

As to the second question, we study auctions in which bids are accepted if they lie within a specified range of the lowest bid, and we make three main points. First, *ascending auctions* (that is, auctions in which the subsidy starts at a low level and is raised, and bidders choose when to announce their intent to acquire COLR status) *give rise to collusion* (in the sense of equilibrium coordination on a high-subsidy equilibrium), a point already made by Milgrom (1996). Second, *descending auctions do yield the monopoly franchising outcome* (with the efficient level of subsidy) *provided the range for bid acceptance above the lowest bid is small enough.* Third, *descending auctions yield in-market competition if the bid acceptance range is large enough, but then give rise to inefficiently high subsidies.*

We are unaware of formal analyses of universal service auctions with endogenous market structure.[32] We have tried to provide a framework

32. The Dana-Spier model reviewed earlier does not formalize the benefits of in-market competition.

Text continues on p. 260.

Box 6.7
In-Market Competition and Complementary Services

Consider the by-now familiar framework in which the basic service costs c per line. This cost exceeds the target price p^* defined by universal service objectives. In the absence of complementary services, therefore, the required subsidy would be

$$s = c - p^*$$

Auctions with Predetermined Market Structure

Assume now that the providers of the basic service (and only they) can offer a complementary service at marginal cost $\hat{c}$ per line. So, the total cost of the bundle of basic and complementary services is $c + \hat{c}$. As earlier, all firms have the same technology.

While the demand for the basic service is inelastic (in the relevant range of prices $p \le p^*$), the demand for complementary services is elastic. At (incremental) price $\hat{p}$ for the complementary service, a fraction $x(\hat{p}) \in (0, 1)$ of consumers subscribing to the basic service also purchase the complementary service. The function $x(\cdot)$ is decreasing. Let

$$\hat{\pi}^m \equiv \max_{\hat{p}}\{(\hat{p} - \hat{c})x(\hat{p})\}$$

denote the monopoly profit on the complementary segment and $\hat{p}^m$ denote the associated monopoly price. Universal service taxes are levied on telecommunications services other than these two services. As in the case of basic services, we analyze successively the cases of bidding for a monopoly franchise and of in-market competition.

• *Monopoly franchise:* The winner of the universal service auction charges p^* for the basic service and the monopoly price $\hat{p}^m$ for the complementary service. The opportunity cost of the winner of the universal service auction is $c - \hat{\pi}^m$ per line. And so ex ante competition for the market yields subsidy

$$s^m = c - \hat{\pi}^m - p^*$$

• *In-market competition:* Suppose that at least two firms are selected to supply the basic services, and that their competition on the complementary segment brings the price down to the marginal cost, $\hat{p} = \hat{c}$. The COLRs then make no money on the complementary segment and demand

$$s^d = c - p^*$$

subsidy for supplying the basic service.

Comparing the two arrangements, we see that *in-market competition lowers the price of the complementary service* ($\hat{c} < \hat{p}^m$) *but raises the required subsidy* ($s^d > s^m$). Whether in-market competition is desirable depends on the relative distortions imposed by the markup $\hat{p}^m - \hat{c}$ on the complementary service and by the increase $s - s^m$ in the universal service taxes levied on other telecommunications services. In particular, if the demand for the complementary segment is

Box 6.7 (continued)

relatively inelastic, in-market competition shifts the financing of universal service from a distortion-free markup to distorting levies on other telecommunications services, and therefore reduces social welfare. More generally, either monopoly franchising or in-market competition may be optimal.

Remark   The feasible set also includes a continuum of "intermediate arrangements" in which there is in-market competition but the complementary segment is taxed at rate $\tau \in [0, \hat{p}^m - \hat{c}]$ per line, in a lump sum fashion. The tax is then used as a contribution to the universal service fund, reducing the total subsidy to be covered by other telecommunications services. The case $\tau = 0$ corresponds to our paradigm of in-market competition, while $\tau = \hat{p}^m - \hat{c}$ is equivalent to monopoly franchising. Under all arrangements, the firms make no profit. The only difference is the relative amounts contributed by the complementary segment and other telecommunications services to the universal service fund. For expositional simplicity, we will not consider taxes on the complementary segment in the following discussion of auctions.

Universal Service Auctions with Endogenous Market Structure

The first part of the box has assumed that the regulator knows in advance whether in-market competition is desirable or not and has looked at auctions with exogenous market structures.

Let us now investigate whether standard auctions with endogenous market structure yield the socially desirable outcome, which, recall, is either a monopoly franchise or in-market competition. For this purpose, let us assume there are two firms, $i = 1, 2$. These two firms produce bids b_1 and b_2 corresponding to demands for per-line subsidies (the way these bids are produced depends on the type of auction; see the following subsections). We consider a selection rule in the spirit of the GTE proposal. Let b^{min} and b^{max} denote the lower and the higher bids, respectively. Both firms obtain COLR status if their bids are not too far apart. That is, if for some fixed $x > 0$, if $b^{max} \leq (1 + x)b^{min}$, both firms are selected and in-market competition ensues. If $b^{max} > (1 + x)b^{min}$, only the lower bidder is selected and a monopoly franchise is created. The subsidy in either case is the highest accepted bid (as in the GTE proposal).

Under in-market competition firms make no profit. And given subsidy s and target price p^* for the basic service, the prices for the basic and complementary services are

$$p = \min(c - s, p^*)$$

and

$$\hat{p} = \hat{c}$$

We will assume that, despite the fact that they make no profit, the duopolists prefer a higher subsidy; and that a firm making zero profit prefers to be in the market rather than out of the market. Such "lexicographic preferences" can be justified by taking the limit of competition with differentiation between the two firms when the differentiation vanishes to produce perfect substitution.

Box 6.7 (continued)

Ascending Auction and Collusion

In an ascending auction, the subsidy is initially set equal to zero and moves up, continuously, say. Each firm must decide when to enter, that is, when to announce that it is ready to take on COLR status at the current subsidy level (and a fortiori at higher subsidy levels). The level of subsidy at which a firm enters is called its bid. Under the general rule enunciated earlier, if the first firm (the leader) to announce its intent to serve the market does so at level b^{min}, then there is in-market competition if and only if the other firm follows suit before or when the slide reaches level $(1 + x)b^{min}$. The subsidy in this case is the latter level; from our previous assumption, it is clear that the equilibrium subsidy when the leader bids b^{min} is then $(1 + x)b^{min}$, because the follower has no incentive to step in before that level. If the follower does not step in at $(1 + x)b^{min}$, the leader receives a monopoly franchise with subsidy b^{min}.

$$\uparrow \\ \dashv c - p^* \\ \dashv 0$$

In this ascending auction, firms can coordinate and obtain an arbitrarily high subsidy. It suffices that the firms wait until the corresponding level of subsidy (or, more precisely, this level divided by $1 + x$) is reached. A firm faces no risk when waiting for higher subsidies. If the other firm happened to step in prematurely at some b^{min}, then the firm could always follow suit at $(1 + x)b^{min}$ and still be in the market. *The possibility of in-market competition destroys the incentive for preemption in ascending auctions.*

Thus, even in the absence of bid rigging or collusion enforced by the repeated nature of universal service auctions of many areas, a different form of "collusion," namely, coordination on a favorable equilibrium within the auction, is likely to arise. This obviously calls for the imposition of a subsidy ceiling, perhaps determined from proxy models. Such a ceiling is presumably difficult to set because the very motivation for the introduction of auctions is that the proxy models deliver an unreliable estimate of the required subsidy. Although it would be interesting to study the "preemption games" induced by the existence of such reservation subsidies, we will for conciseness not analyze the outcome of the ascending auction with a subsidy ceiling, and we turn, rather, to descending auctions.

Descending Auction

In the descending auction, the initial subsidy is initially set very high, so that both bidders are willing to accept COLR status initially. The subsidy is

Box 6.7 (continued)

decreased continuously, say, toward zero. The first to call it quits, at some level of subsidy b^{max}, will be called the leader ("call it quits" of course does not mean that the firm will not receive COLR status; its bid may still be within x percent of the follower's bid). The other firm, the "follower," then chooses a subsidy level b^{min} at which to quit. Given the auction rules, only two strategies are available to the follower. One is that it allows in-market competition by quitting in the interval $[b^{max}/(1+x), b^{max})$; the exact choice of b^{min} in this interval is irrelevant because the equilibrium subsidy to which the two firms are entitled is then b^{max}. The other is that the follower "undercuts," quits slightly below $b^{max}/(1+x)$, and obtains a monopoly franchise. The universal service subsidy for the franchisee is then $b^{max}/(1+x)$. Quitting later would not benefit the follower because this tactic would just reduce the subsidy.

The outcome of the auction depends on the profitability of the market for the complementary service. For a given x, we will say that the complementary market exhibits low profitability if

$$(1+x)s^m > s^d = c - p^*, \quad \text{or } \hat{\pi}^m < \frac{x}{1+x}(c - p^*)$$

or that the complementary market exhibits high profitability if

$$(1+x)s^m < s^d = c - p^*, \quad \text{or } \hat{\pi}^m > \frac{x}{1+x}(c - p^*)$$

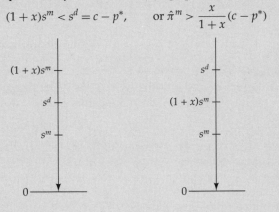

Case 1:
Low-profitability
complementary market

Case 2:
High-profitability
complementary market

In the following analysis, it is useful to remember that s^m and s^d are the levels of subsidy that allow the firms to break even under monopoly and duopoly, respectively. Note also that a firm never has an incentive to quit before the subsidy has reached $(1+x)s^m$: If it did, the other firm could undercut and make a strictly positive profit as a monopoly franchise, while it makes zero profit as a duopolist (even a high subsidy is competed away by in-market competition). Last, the equilibrium in both cases will exhibit zero profit, and so any inefficiency in the outcome does not stem from rents left to the firms.

Box 6.7 (continued)

Low-Profitability Complementary Market
We claim that the outcome is then a *duopoly with subsidy level* $(1 + x)s^m$. On the
one hand, a firm that quits at this level is guaranteed the corresponding outcome, since the other firm then prefers the zero-profit duopoly outcome to a
negative-profit monopoly position, which can only be obtained by undercutting below s^m. On the other hand, if the firm continues, one of four outcomes
may result: (a) the other firm quits at $(1 + x)s^m$, yielding the same outcome any-
how; (b) the final allocation is a duopoly at a lower level of subsidy; (c) the firm
becomes a negative-profit monopoly; and (d) the firm ends up being eliminated
from the market by its rival. From our lexicographic preference assumptions,
outcomes b through d are dominated by outcome a, which is equivalent to the
one obtained by the firm when quitting at $(1 + x)s^m$.

This duopoly outcome is *inefficient*, even if the optimum is in-market competition. The market prices for the basic and complementary services, respectively, are

$$p = c - (1 + x)s^m < p^*$$

and

$$\dot{p} = \ddot{c}$$

That is, the subsidy is too high, or, equivalently, the price of the basic service
too low. A high "tolerance level" x leads to excessive subsidies.

High-Profitability Complementary Market
In the high-profitability case, the unique outcome in symmetric strategies is a
monopoly franchise with subsidy s^m. The game is technically difficult to analyze
and is best approached by using limits of discrete decrements in the subsidy
(for an exposition of the techniques involved here, we refer to Fudenberg and
Tirole, 1985, and Simon, 1988). Let us simply describe the outcome and provide an intuition. In the equilibrium with symmetric strategies, each quits first
with probability 1/2 at (about) $(1 + x)s^m$, and the other then undercuts to (close
to) s^m. With probability 1, a monopoly franchise emerges. To see that there
cannot be another outcome in symmetric strategies, note first that for subsidy
$t > (1 + x)s^m$, it cannot be the case that firms call it quits with probability $y(t)dt$
in the interval $[t, t - dt]$ (recall that the auction is a descending one). If a firm
stops, the other firm undercuts, while, if it continues, it becomes a profitable
monopoly with probability $y(t)dt$ and can always quit and obtain zero profit (it
is then undercut) if it does not. So, there is no bid above $(1 + x)s^m$, and therefore
no possible monopoly profit. So, with probability 1, no firm makes a positive
profit. Next, the equilibrium probability of ending with in-market competition
must be equal to zero, since in-market competition yields strictly negative profit
below s and so the firms would make strictly negative profit overall. Similarly,
the equilibrium probability that a monopoly at subsidy strictly below s^m (and

Box 6.7 (continued)

therefore with strictly negative profit) occurs must also be equal to zero. Hence the only possible equilibrium is the one already described.

We thus conclude that the equilibrium outcome (with symmetric strategies) delivers a monopoly with subsidy s^m. The equilibrium outcome is then socially optimal only if a monopoly franchise is efficient.

within which analysis of such auctions can begin. The first insights thus gleaned do not build as strong a case for the introduction of competition as we had expected. First, and a fact mostly ignored in the literature, in-market competition raises the level of the subsidy and is therefore a mixed blessing. Second, the use of simple auctions may deliver the wrong market structure or the wrong subsidy level even in simple environments. Of course, further work is warranted before we draw definitive conclusions.

6.4.3   Some Further Difficulties

Let us discuss three further issues affecting the design of universal service auctions.

6.4.3.1   Historical Asymmetries

Much of the discussion on universal service auctions proceeds as if all competitors were building their network from scratch. This may be a fine assumption for newly settled areas or when substantial network upgradings are contemplated. In practice, however, many high-cost areas are already partly covered by a wire-based incumbent operator able to provide the supported services with its existing technology. While the incumbent operator's network may have been very costly to build, once in place it has a low (short-term) marginal cost. And so facilities-based entrants (e.g., offering wireless services) may find it hard to compete with the incumbent. In our view, more attention should be devoted to this aspect of universal service provision.

6.4.3.2   Provision of Universal Service by Non-Facilities-Based Entrants

Experts view unbundling and resale as possible mechanisms of entry into the provision of universal service. That is, the entrants would not build their own facilities (local loop, switches), but rather rent them from the incumbent operator. Non-facilities-based entrants will qualify for universal service support. This view raises two issues. The first is practical and may be temporary. The use of forward-looking long-run incremental cost for renting unbundled network elements is being challenged (successfully) in court by the incumbent local exchange carriers. A non-facilities-based entrant bidding in a universal service auction, therefore, faces uncertainty about the price at which it will be able to rent the incumbent's network. The second issue is more conceptual. Recall that auctions are motivated by the unreliability of cost estimates. Auctions with entrants renting the incumbent's network may suffer the same criticisms as the direct use of a proxy model to compute a universal service subsidy.

Last, and to the extent that there can be real competition between the incumbent and the entrants, auctions may be more drastic than prescriptive subsidies in that the incumbent may be shut out of the market. The transfer of the incumbent's capital to winning entrants (either through rentals or through an acquisition) may give rise to the usual concerns about the impact of "second sourcing" on the incumbent's incentives to invest in the quality of its network (Williamson, 1976; Laffont and Tirole, 1988a).

6.4.3.3   *Absence of Combinatorial Auctions*

The concept of "minimum subsidy demanded by a bidder to accept COLR status" is not well defined for two reasons. First, a firm's profitability usually decreases with the number of competitors in the market. Second, there may be cost synergies across areas, and so a firm's willingness to serve a market at a given subsidy depends on whether this firm also serves adjacent areas. Indeed such synergies motivated the use of simultaneous ascending auctions for spectrum licenses in the United States.[33]

In theory, it suffices to organize "combinatorial auctions," auctions with allocations based on the bidders' announcement of their demands for the various configurations. For example, bidder 1 could announce which per-line subsidies it would want to receive in areas A and B if it wins areas A and B and loses area C, and faces competition from bidder 1 in area A and 2 and 3 in area B. As one can imagine, such auctions quickly become extremely complex to organize. There is actually in the current state of our knowledge a discrepancy between the conceptual

---

33. For descriptions of these auctions, see, e.g., Chakravorty et al. (1995), Cramton (1995), McAfee and McMillan (1996), and McMillan (1994).

simplicity of combinatorial auctions (see box 6.8) and the complexity of their implementation. Economists struggle to translate their theories into workable mechanisms. At this stage, only rough adjustments to standard auctions, such as the simultaneity of auctions (to account for synergies across auctions) and the possibility of withdrawing a winning bid (in particular to permit reactions to the number of winners), have been designed. More research in the area is, of course, warranted.

Box 6.8
Vickrey Combinatorial Auctions

In 1961, Vickrey demonstrated a few remarkable properties of second-price auctions, auctions in which the winner is the lowest bidder (in a procurement situation as is the case here) and is paid the second-lowest bid. First, for each firm, announcing its true cost is a "dominant strategy"; that is, regardless of the behavior of other bidders, a bidder cannot do better by announcing something differing from its cost. Second, and under a series of assumptions (in particular, private values and uncorrelated cost parameters, symmetric distributions for the cost parameters), the second-price auction yields the same expected cost for the buyer as the first-price auction (in which the winner also is the lowest bidder but pays its bid), and both minimize the expected cost among all conceivable auctions.

Let us show that the logic of the Vickrey result is quite general in that second-price auctions can be adapted to allow for multidimensional valuations of the bidders. Suppose that there are n bidders, $i = 1, \ldots, n$, and m possible allocations, $k = 1, \ldots, m$. An "allocation" provides a full description of the outcome of the auction or of a set of auctions. For example it specifies which bidders will serve area A, which will serve area B, and so on, and the per-line subsidy paid by each selected bidder in each area. The allocation, however, does not include the transfers made to (or received from) the bidders.

Let $v_i(k)$ denote bidder i's gross surplus (or gross profit) for allocation k, and p_i denote bidder i's payment to the auction designer [depending on the interpretation, $v_i(k)$ and p_i may be positive or negative]. Bidder i's net surplus or net profit when allocation k prevails is

$$v_i(k) - p_i$$

The auction designer in general does not know the gross profits. The auction designer designs a "combinatorial auction" in which each bidder i announces the whole vector of valuations, that is, $\{b_i(k)\}_{k=1,\ldots,m}$.

A Vickrey combinatorial auction works as follows:

• First, the selected allocation k^* is the one that maximizes the total announced gross surplus,

Box 6.8 (continued)

$$\max_{k} \left\{ \sum_{i} b_i(k) \right\} \tag{1}$$

Let

$$B^* \equiv \sum_{i} b_i(k^*) = \max_{k} \left\{ \sum_{i} b_i(k) \right\}$$

and

$$B^*_{-i} = \max_{k} \left\{ \sum_{j \neq i} b_j(k) \right\}$$

• Second, bidder i pays p_i^* so that its net surplus computed from its announcement of the gross surplus function and from the optimal choice of allocation is equal to the increase in total gross surplus brought about by the inclusion of its bid function:

$$b_i(k^*) - p_i^* = B^* - B^*_{-i}$$

or

$$p_i^* = \left[\max_{k} \left\{ \sum_{j \neq i} b_j(k) \right\} \right] - \left[\sum_{j \neq i} b_j(k^*) \right] \tag{2}$$

Equation (2) defines an *externality payment*: The presence of i in the auction leads to a choice of allocation k^* that may differ from the optimal choice for the set of other bidders only.

The key insight is that for this auction bidders have a dominant strategy, to announce their true profit function:

$$b_i(\cdot) = v_i(\cdot)$$

Indeed for arbitrary bids $\{b_j(\cdot)_{j \neq i}\}$ by other bidders, suppose that by distorting its announcement $[b_i(\cdot) \neq v_i(\cdot)]$, bidder i succeeds in shifting the optimal allocation from k^*, which would prevail if it announced the truth, to k. Bidder i's net surplus when announcing the true $v_i(\cdot)$ is

$$\max_{k} \left\{ v_i(k) + \sum_{j \neq i} b_i(k) \right\} - B^*_{-i} = v_i(k^*) + \sum_{j \neq i} b_i(k^*) - B^*_{-i}$$

By inducing k, bidder i obtains

$$v_i(k) + \sum_{j \neq i} b_i(k) - B^*_{-i}$$

(note that B^*_{-i} has not changed, because only bidder i's announcement is altered). By definition,

$$v_i(k^*) + \sum_{j \neq i} b_i(k^*) \geq v_i(k) + \sum_{j \neq i} b_i(k) \qquad \text{for all } k$$

Box 6.8 (continued)

and so telling the truth is optimal regardless of the other bidders' announcements.

The Vickrey auction is *efficient* in that it allocates scarce resources in a way that maximizes total surplus. It need not maximize revenue, however. For example, in a context of cost synergies in which some bidders are interested in bundles while others care about some specific items (a model designed by Krishna and Rosenthal, 1996), Branco (1995, 1996) shows that optimal auctions need not be efficient and studies their implementation. (The study of auctions with cost synergies is still in its infancy. Other interesting early contributions are due to Harstad and Rothkopf [1995] and Rothkopf, Pekec, and Harstad [1995].)

7   Concluding Remarks

7.1 Internet and Internet Telephony

We would be remiss not to discuss the Internet in a book devoted to competition in telecommunications. The Internet offers a wide variety of new services, as well as new ways to provide old services like telephony. Internet telephony, as its name indicates, refers to telephony over the Internet; unlike a traditional phone call, for which a circuit is opened and dedicated to a single conversation for the whole length of the call, messages sent over the Internet are decomposed into tiny data packets, which may or may not take the same route, and which are reassembled at termination. Internet telephony uses the transmission control protocol/Internet protocol (TCP/IP), which more generally supports transmission of packets over the Internet regardless of their application (voice, audio, video, . . .).

Internet telephony currently has a low market share, and arguably this market share is inflated by favorable regulatory treatment.[1] The low market share in part results from the low quality of calls; Internet telephony, like other premium services such as videoconferencing and unlike e-mail, requires very low delays of transmission over the Internet. Such low delays are not yet guaranteed, and one of the key challenges for the development of Internet telephony is precisely the definition of protocols and interconnection agreements involving prioritization of premium services that will enable networks to promise

---

1. It may be argued that the playing field is currently tilted in favor of Internet telephony. In the United States, telephone calls that are made over the Internet, either from computer to computer or when a consumer dials from his or her phone via a local call to an Internet service provider, do not pay access fees. This fact creates difficulty in generating funds for the universal service fund (see chapter 6). At some point, it is likely that Internet service providers will have to pay access fees.

their customers an adequate quality of service. Most experts predict a rapid growth of Internet telephony in the next few years. This section briefly discusses the future of the Internet more generally, as well as two key challenges currently facing its development: broadband access to the home and interconnection. These challenges raise issues of one- and two-way access, respectively. Their full analysis lies outside the scope of this book, and we will content ourselves with a description of the main issues.

7.1.1   Broadband Access

Currently, most consumers can connect to the Internet from their home or small business premises through dial-up access at very low speeds.[2] Broadband access to the home would provide speeds of transmission, say, one hundred times faster than current speeds, as well as an "always-on" capability.

Several technologies are envisioned to break this "bandwidth-to-the-home bottleneck":

• *DSL technologies:* By installing new-generation modems at the customer's premises and at the location of the first switch, the owner of the copper line or else an entrant having "unbundled access" to the copper line can substantially improve its performance. ("Unbundled" refers to the fact that the entrant purchases only access to the naked copper line and not other services such as switching.) Several operators are currently performing commercial experiments with these technologies. We will come back shortly to the issue of local loop unbundling (LLU).

• *Cable:* Cable transmission facilities, which historically have been used to transmit content to the home, usually have only one-way capability (cannot offer interactivity). But once cable modems are set in place, they are able to provide two-way, higher bandwidth capability.

• *Fiber to customer premises:* Bringing fiber to the home would be an ideal system of delivery to a fixed location, with data delivery rates much

---

2. The data transmission rate through the copper line at the time the Telecommunications Act of 1996 was debated in the United States was 9,600 bits per second (now a couple of tens of thousands per second). In contrast, transmission speeds in the backbone can reach tens or even hundreds of megabits per second. (DS-3 lines transmit information at 45 Mbps, most recent networks operate at 155 to 622 Mbps.) The new DSL technologies should provide local access at speeds from a few hundred thousand bits up to, say, 10 or 20 megabits per second.

larger than those for DSL technologies. Alas, the cost of putting fiber to the home is very high, and this solution is unlikely to be adopted in the short run. (Of course, businesses with large usage already have fiber to their premises.)

• *Power line:* There is currently some experimentation to modify power distribution networks in order to provide customers with high-speed access to the Internet through electricity wires. Like fiber to the home, this is not a realistic possibility in the short run.

• *Radio spectrum and satellites:* A number of wireless solutions are currently being considered. For example, some consortia are considering using a satellite constellation to provide "local access."[3]

Let us return to the issue of local loop unbundling. *Simplifying a lot,* there are three forms of access to bandwidth that can be offered to an entrant:

1. *Rental of naked copper line:* The entrant rents the copper line from the home to the first switch from the incumbent operator and collocates with the operator so as to be able to install its modems. The bandwidth then belongs to the entrant, who can make the commercial use of it that he wishes (offer his own services or rent bandwidth to providers of final services). Presumably, the incumbent and the entrant then compete in packages or bundles, in the same sense in which two cable services providers (e g , wireline and wireless) compete in bundles for the customer. The customer will choose her supplier, who then will install the modems and will provide a range of services using the bandwidth (produced in house or outsourced).

2. *Exclusive bitstream access:* The incumbent installs the modems on behalf of the entrants (as well as for himself). The entrants then do not rent only access to the copper pair, but rent the entire bandwidth. There is

---

3. See, e.g., the Teledesic and SkyBridge projects. The Teledesic project (Microsoft, Motorola, Boeing, Matra, etc., planned for the year 2003) wants to deploy 288 satellites at low orbit (less than 500 miles) to offer very-high-speed access. The SkyBridge project (Loral Space & Communications, Toshiba, Mitsubishi, Aerospatiale, etc.) plans to use 80 satellites orbiting at an altitude of 913 miles, and to deliver per-user traffic capacity in the megabits (higher in the downstream direction than in the return link).

Satellite constellations for traditional mobile telephony have existed since 1998, when Iridium services were introduced. The Iridium consortium (Motorola, Lockheed-Martin, Telecom Italia, . . .) uses 66 satellites orbiting at an altitude of 482 miles. The 48 satellites of Globalstar (Loral, Daimler-Benz, France Telecom, . . .), its rival, will be operational in 2000.

no competition in building facilities, but there is competition in bundles of services. Thus the key difference with the first option is that the investment in extra facilities (in particular, the modems) is here always borne by the incumbent, whereas it is borne by the entrant (provided the consumer chooses the entrant) in the first option.

3. *Nonexclusive bitstream access:* As under exclusive bitstream access, the incumbent keeps a monopoly on the building of new facilities, but instead of renting the entire bandwidth to a single entrant, he sells pieces of this bandwidth to different entrants at some access price per unit of bandwidth. This solution allows an entrant who does not wish to offer a full range of services to contract directly with the customer.

The choice of regulatory framework will be crucial for the development of broadband access to the home. Key issues[4] include the choice of technology (xDSL technologies are still improving) and their compatibility with the services that entrants and incumbents desire to offer; the optimal sharing of the investment risk between incumbent, entrant, and customer (in view of rapid technological progress in these and alternative technologies and of an important uncertainty about demand for the new services, economic depreciation ought to be large); the design of regulatory commitments against takings of the new facilities; the definition of proper access charges (cost oriented versus demand-and-cost oriented, measurement of cost, nondiscrimination rules, relationship between local loop rental and consumer's monthly subscriber charge, etc.); and relationship to universal service. These issues are highly reminiscent of the themes of chapters 3, 4, and 6. For conciseness, we will not further discuss the matter, which would deserve a full treatment of its own.

7.1.2   Interconnection in the Commercial Internet

Probably the largest stakes in telecommunications today lie in the Internet. Yet, little is known about the future industrial organization of the Internet. Indeed, the biggest part of the initial network, the NSFNET, was privatized only in 1995, and thus the commercial era is just begin-

---

4. Some of these issues are not specific to traditional local loop unbundling. Whether cable companies should unbundle their broadband networks to ISPs is being debated. Some fear that such unbundling may slow investment in broadband. AT&T and TCI (a cable company) announced that their merger would be called off if the FCC were to require unbundling (the FCC approved the merger in March 1999).

ning. Until recently the Internet community was largely one of engineers working cooperatively to take the Internet off the ground. Nowadays, financial stakes are huge, and the Internet is turning into a fascinating commercial battleground.

Again, we content ourselves with a brief description of the issues, starting with a description of the players.[5] End users include residential users and businesses, who have access to the Internet either through dial-up (over the phone line using modems) or through dedicated access. On the other side lie web sites, which provide a wide variety of free or fee-based content as well as offerings of services (e-commerce, . . .). In between can be found a host of intermediaries. Some intermediaries provide users with guidance as to whether to connect, what to buy, and so forth: search engines, portals, infomediaries, . . . Other intermediaries provide transmission services: internet service providers (ISPs), internet backbone providers (IBPs). We will focus on the latter, keeping in mind that the dividing line between the various players is not always clear-cut: For example, America Online (AOL), an ISP offering Internet access to residential users, also offers content as well as search capabilities (for example, through its acquisition of Netscape, which produces a browser with search-engine capability).

Internet backbone providers direct traffic over large regions of the world using long-haul fiber-optic cables. IBPs connect to each other at multiple points under the so-called "peering agreements" (see following paragraphs). IBPs pick up the traffic generated by ISPs (as well as that of their own customers) and carry it over long distances. They also have the most sophisticated routing of all Internet players.

The Internet is a network of interconnected networks. Indeed, one of the main appeals of the Internet is its current almost ubiquitous connectivity: From almost any point (URL address) in the network can be sent messages to almost any other point. One may wonder how a network of 7,000 ISPs and 4 to 50 IBPs (depending on the exact definition of IBPs[6]) can offer such ubiquitous connectivity. The basic structure is

---

5. For more details, as well as an analysis of some strategic considerations, see Crémer, Rey, and Tirole (1999).

6. The four big IBPs are MCI, Sprint, WorldCom, and GTE. Following an investigation by the U.S. Department of Justice and Directorate General 4 of the European Commission concerning the WorldCom-MCI merger, MCI Internet assets were divested to allow the merger to go through. (Together, MCI and WorldCom's market share was estimated to lie between 40% and 70% depending on the methodology.)

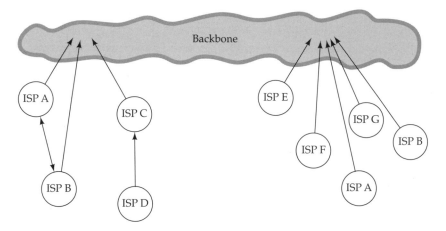

Figure 7.1

hierarchical. As illustrated in figure 7.1, IBPs sit on top of the hierarchy, customers lie at the bottom, and ISPs and regional networks stand in between.

IBPs "peer" with each other. In so doing, they accept for routing all traffic that is destined to their own customers, the customers of their customers, and so on. Peering used to occur at public peering points, NAPs (network access points), or MAEs (metropolitan access exchanges). The slow expansion of the capacity at these points (Internet traffic grows at a rate of up to 1000% a year) has led IBPs to turn to private peering, that is, to exchanging traffic pairwise at a number of bilateral interfaces. The importance of public peering points, where an arbitrary number of networks exchange traffic, is waning. IBPs impose a number of conditions to accept each other as peers: number of points of interface,[7] national high-speed network, and so on. Currently, peering arrangements are of the bill-and-keep type; that is, each peer terminates without charge the traffic originating with other peers. This feature is probably a leftover of the transition process. One may wonder

---

7. One motivation for this condition is to make sure that an IBP will not suffer asymmetrically from "hot potato routing." Suppose that a customer of IBP 1 in San Francisco sends a message to a customer of IBP 2 in Boston. IBP 1 will get rid of the message as quickly as possible and will therefore transmit it to IBP 2 near San Francisco. Because of this shortest-exit strategy, the message will therefore be carried mostly by the receiver's network. Conversely, the return message (say, a web page download) will be handed over to IBP 1 near Boston.

whether IBPs will keep running their two-way interconnection arrangements through bill-and-keep.

IBPs do not make money from their peering relationships. To cover the huge investments they have made in infrastructure, they charge their customers, who in turn charge their own customers. Charges often are related to the capacity of the link between the network and its customer, but can also depend on usage. Thus the Internet can be seen as a pyramid, in which monies are collected at the bottom.

To be certain, the organization of the Internet is not purely hierarchical. For example, it may make sense for two ISPs in the same city, such as ISPs A and B in figure 7.1, to exchange traffic directly (engage in "secondary peering") rather than let their mutual traffic move up and then down the hierarchy. Such sideways interconnections do not upset the hierarchical nature of the Internet.

The design of interconnection arrangements is crucial for the future of the Internet. In the short term, it conditions the prices charged to dial-up and dedicated access users and to web sites, and thereby the use and organization of the network. In the "long run" (a few months in the Internet world, owing to the growth of traffic and technological progress), it determines the networks' incentives to build up their capacity and to cooperate.

The framework for two-way interconnection for traditional voice telephony reviewed in chapter 5 provides a number of insights that will be useful for our understanding of Internet interconnection. However, as it stands, it is inappropriate, in that it does not reflect the specificities of the Internet. These specificities not only are technical (packet switching versus dedicated circuit), but they also have important economic dimensions. For example, unlike voice telephony, the party who requests the message may receive rather than send this message, as is the case when a user downloads a web page. Such specificities require a careful consideration of the interaction between the wholesale market (interconnection arrangements) and the retail markets (pricing to end users and web sites and commercial interaction between these).

A second important issue related to interconnection is the development of premium services. Premium services on the Internet (IP telephony, video on demand, videoconferencing, etc.) require low delays in packet transmission and therefore a higher quality of service throughout the network than is currently observed. Several scenarios may be envisioned. First, some large Internet operators may develop proprietary standards and offer such services on a limited basis (between their customers), hoping that the lack of ubiquity will be mitigated by tipping, or at least that the proprietary offering will create a comparative advantage. Second, networks may agree on standards and two-way access charges for the premium services to attempt to achieve ubiquity. The incentives for cooperation and the design of two-way access charges for premium services are important topics for research.

7.2   Regulatory Institutions

The received paradigm for telecommunications regulation is being called into question. The traditional oversight of telecommunications operators by national regulatory agencies (NRAs) no longer seems appropriate. Examples of timely questions about the structure and the scope of regulatory institutions include these: Should telecommunications regulators be specializing in that industry, or should we opt for multisector regulators as in Australia? How much regulation should be conducted at the federal level and how much at the national or state level? Should we give up regulation and, as in New Zealand, rely on competition policy?

The economics literature does not provide a systematic analysis of these important questions, which lie beyond the scope of this book. We content ourselves with a mention of the general issues and with a discussion of some of the trade-offs involved. We start by listing some factors that have led to the current concern about the adequacy of existing structures. We then discuss potential institutional reforms of the regulatory structure, and we conclude with a discussion of the possible substitution of competition policy for regulation.

7.2.1   Unsettling Factors: Innovation, Convergence, Proliferation of Operators, and Globalization

The traditional paradigm for utility regulation rests on the regulation of a well-defined set of services offered by a well-identified operator (or small group of operators) in a well-circumscribed geographical area. Recent evolution in telecommunications has shattered each of these foundations:

• *Innovation:* While plain old telephone services (the POTS) such as local, long-distance, and international calls remain important sources of revenue for the operators, new services (the PANS) keep gaining prominence. Furthermore, marketing innovations change the pricing structure of POTS. As was discussed in chapters 2–4, neither price-cap regulation nor older regulatory approaches are at ease with either rapid technological progress or complex nonlinear pricing and discriminatory tariffs.

• *Convergence:* It is commonplace to note that the telecommunications, broadcasting, and computer industries are coming together. Fundamentally, audio, video, voice, and Internet data are digital bits, ones and zeros. Internet service providers are starting to offer broadcasting and IP telephony. Broadcasters are entering Internet provision and offer telecommunications services. Telecommunications operators offer Internet access and services and want to enter the video-on-demand and cable markets.

Convergence means that new players from formerly distinct industries have entered telecommunications: electronic publishers, broadcasters, Internet service providers, content creators, software companies, hardware companies, . . . The new players are either unregulated (as in the case of information technology) or else regulated by different regulatory bodies (as for broadcasting). This fact raises issues of licensing, standards, level playing field with traditional operators, and coherency of the overall regulatory approach.[8]

• *Proliferation of operators:* Similar issues are raised by the entry into telecommunications of utilities and franchisees overseen by other regulatory bodies. Recently, water companies, cable operators, railroads, power companies, and highway franchisees have provided infrastructures to telecommunications entrants or have become operators themselves. The multiplicity of regulators raises issues of regulatory competition, cross-subsidization, and commitment.

• *Globalization:* It becomes more and more obvious that the "right" geographical boundary for telecommunications regulation is unlikely to coincide with political boundaries. While some markets, such as international fixed and mobile telephony and global corporate services, have long been understood to be international in nature, the trend is accelerating; for example, Internet services truly represent worldwide markets. Yet, much power still resides at the "local" level (member

---

8. For further questions raised by convergence, see, e.g., the European Commission's "Green Paper on the Convergence of the Telecommunications, Media, and Information Technology Sectors, and the Implications for Regulation" (Dec. 1, 1997).

states in the European Union due to the subsidiarity principle; states in the United States, although the FCC has substantial control rights). A fortiori, there is no worldwide regulatory body. The imperfect overlap between the operators' geographical coverage and their regulators' geographical jurisdiction raises issues of regulatory externalities as well as competency and regulatory arbitrage (or forum shopping in which operators seek the most lenient treatment).

7.2.2   The Structure of Regulatory Institutions: Theoretical Considerations

We content ourselves here with a mention of a few theoretical contributions to serve as a guide for the interested reader. We do not go into the arguments in any detail; nor do we assess their relevance for the forthcoming telecommunications environment.

7.2.2.1   One versus Several Regulators

Were regulators well-informed and benevolent, their number would not matter much. Regulators would always coordinate to achieve what's best for society. In practice, though, regulators, like other economic agents, are self-interested. They, like anybody, must be provided with incentives to become (economic and technological) experts, to think hard about specific regulatory issues, and to shun putting their career concerns or the stakes of their favored interest groups or causes first.

The presence of multiple regulators raises a concern about the coordination of their decisions. Several recent theoretical approaches, though, have stressed some benefits obtained by splitting the regulatory tasks among several regulators. The first motivation is benchmarking. Regulatory policies in different states in the United States or different member states in the European Union are often compared. From a theoretical perspective, provided that the information acquired by the regulators in their activities is correlated or that the performances on the tasks they oversee are correlated, having several regulators enables a form of yardstick competition among the regulators.[9] This benchmarking is effective if regulators do not collude. Second, having specific industry regulators enhances their technological expertise, although it may fa-

---

9. See Neven, Nuttall, and Seabright (1993).

cilitate their colluding with the industry.[10] Third, splitting regulatory tasks may inhibit capture by the industry.[11] Fourth, the provision of incentives within government agencies is often facilitated by focused missions[12] and by the creation of advocates.[13]

Last, we should note that, all along, we have assumed away subsidies from outside the telecommunications industry. While realistic, this is not an obvious assumption. Theoretical finance[14] has always stressed the benefits from a broad "tax base" that permits spreading the distortionary burden of tax finance. In this book, we have assumed, for example, that the fixed costs associated with local loop provision must be financed through markups on various telecommunications services, but not on non-telecommunications-related goods and services; that is, we have artificially constrained the number of commodities that can be "taxed" by the telecommunications industry. While this approach seems reasonable, it can be vindicated only by a theory of political institution design relating incentive considerations and the separation of powers; see section 2.2.4 for some relevant arguments in this respect.

7.2.2.2   Federal versus State Regulation

The centralization of regulation at the federal level would appear to be the leading contender for institutional design because it eliminates competition between and externalities across regulatory bodies. As for the broader issue of the optimal number of regulators, though, things are more complicated. The arguments cited in the previous subsection apply with appropriate reinterpretations. For example, decentralization may give control rights to more accountable bodies.[15] Or, adapting to decentralization an argument made by Shapiro and Willig (1991) in favor of privatization, decentralizing information-collecting rights

---

10. See Faure, Grimaud, Laffont, and Martimort (1998).
11. See Laffont and Martimort (1999).
12. See Dewatripont, Jewitt, and Tirole (1999).
13. See Dewatripont and Tirole (1999).
14. See, e.g., Atkinson and Stiglitz (1980).
15. Adam Smith (1776) was in favor of decentralization for political economy reasons:
"Public works of a local nature should be maintained by local revenue" because "the abuses which sometimes creep into the local and provincial revenue, how enormous so ever they may appear, are in reality, however, almost always very trifling, in comparison with those which commonly take place in the administration and expenditure of the revenue of a great empire" (p. 689).
   See also Seabright (1996). Caillaud et al. (1996) and Laffont and Zantman (1998) argue that local political life produces a pool of information that is most efficiently used under decentralization.

may create an information barrier and prevent nonbenevolent federal politicians from unduly interfering with business; relatedly, decentralization is sometimes justified by the lack of commitment at the federal level.[16]

7.2.3   Competition Policy versus Regulation

In view of the difficulties involved in regulating the new telecommunications environment the old-fashioned way, one may rationally consider substituting competition policy for regulation.[17] Indeed, there are some signals in the Anglo-Saxon world that point in this direction. The Merger and Monopoly Commission in the United Kingdom and the Department of Justice and the courts in the United States have intervened in the telecommunications industry in order to promote competition. And the New Zealand telecommunications regulatory agency has been abrogated altogether, leaving the regulatory task to competition policy. Another signal of the growing influence of competition policy is provided by recent Internet cases, which involve a worldwide market without any regulator.[18]

Let us say right away that there are many forms of regulation as well as various approaches to antitrust enforcement, making it difficult to provide a clean comparison of "antitrust" and "regulation." Furthermore, there are alternative techniques of (what we will label generically) "industry oversight." For example, compulsory arbitration in which the parties must defer to a designated arbitrator if they fail to come to an agreement is sometimes proposed as a way of regulating interconnection.

While they differ in several respects, the premises of antitrust and regulation are roughly the same. Industry oversight aims at promoting economic efficiency. Regulatory agencies, although not competition officials, are often further instructed to perform redistributive functions across consumers and across geographical areas, although there is some

---

16. Klibanoff and Poitevin (1997).
17. See IDEI (1997) for more detailed reflection on the trade-offs between competition policy and regulation. That section was written jointly with Patrick Rey.
18. Besides, in the United States, the 1996 Telecom Act specifies that the Internet will remain unregulated. A recent Internet case is the 1998 merger between MCI and WorldCom, in which the Department of Justice and the European Commission (in coordination) requested the divestiture of about half of the merged entity's Internet assets (the MCI Internet assets were divested).

debate as to whether such redistribution should be performed through the regulation of the telecommunications industry rather than by other means (see chapter 6). In contrast, competition policy is a priori not meant to perform redistributive functions, which are left to other government agencies; therefore, cross-subsidies are often more transparent under a competition policy regime.

Another point of convergence between antitrust and regulation is that they strike the same rocks: lack of information about costs, demands, and competitive pressure; capture by interest groups; limited commitment ability.

A third point of convergence is that both use an advocacy process. The enlistment of advocates helps reduce the informational handicap faced by the industry overseer.

Let us now come to a couple of lines of departure between competition policy and regulation:

• *Procedures and control rights:* By and large, regulatory agencies have wider control rights than competition agencies and courts. Competition policy assesses the lawfulness of *conduct*. In contrast, regulatory agencies engage in detailed regulation of wholesale and retail prices, profit sharing, and investments, and impose lines-of-business restrictions.

Furthermore, courts are subject to stronger consistency requirements than regulatory agencies. They must refer to the decisions of other courts and apply criteria that are uniform across industries.

To be certain, regulatory discretion is limited by procedural requirements, by statutory limits on the ability to commit in the long term, by safeguards against regulatory takings, by legal constraints on the mode of regulation (e.g., price cap, rate of return, nondiscriminatory, and cost-based regulation of access), and by the parties' possible resort to courts among other things. But, as a first approximation, it is fair to say that regulatory agencies have more extensive powers than antitrust enforcers.

• *Timing of oversight:* By and large, competition policy operates ex post (after the fact), with the exception of merger control (in this sense, a merger task force bears strong resemblance to a regulatory agency). Conversely, regulators operate ex ante by defining the prices of utilities or the rules for the industry, with the exception of the ex post disallowance-of-investments process. The judicial process is a lengthy one, while the regulatory process can (must) be more expedient.

The difference in timing (ex post versus ex ante) has a couple of implications. First, the players in the telecommunications industry perhaps face more uncertainty under competition policy (this effect may be offset by the larger discretion enjoyed by regulatory agencies, as discussed earlier), since, under regulation, the uncertainty is partly resolved before operators take their private decisions. Second, antitrust enforcement benefits from the late accrual of information. That is, what constitutes acceptable conduct may become clearer after the fact.

Perhaps the implication of all this is that the decision rights endowed upon regulatory agencies and antitrust enforcers have a different nature. Regulators define ex ante a set of feasible moves for operators. Antitrust enforcers, in contrast, check ex post that anticompetitive moves in the feasible set were not selected.

• *Information intensiveness and continued relationship:* Regulators often have expertise superior to that of their antitrust counterparts, although the use of specialized courts and antitrust officials tends to reduce the informational wedge between the two. This wedge has three origins: Regulatory oversight is industry specific; antitrust enforcement is not. Regulators have long-term relationships with regulated firms; antitrust enforcers (Judge Greene notwithstanding) do not. Last, regulators have larger professional staffs as well as continued procedures of data collection.

The relative shortage of data available to antitrust enforcers implies that they are usually more at ease with cases based on *qualitative* evidence (price discrimination, price fixing, vertical restraints, . . .) than those based on *quantitative* evidence (predation, tacit collusion, access pricing, . . .). In contrast, regulators are more at ease with quantitative evidence, which they often use to set very detailed regulations, as in the case of cost-based pricing rules.

There are costs of being too well-informed, though. Too much information about profitability, for example, coupled with limited commitment power, aggravates the ratchet effect (which, recall, ex post penalizes operators who have proved efficient or have invested). Furthermore, to the extent that expertise is partly associated with the existence of a long-term relationship between the regulator and the industry, expertise may also be correlated with a higher risk of capture by the industry.

• *Political independence:* Although many regulatory agencies are in principle independent of the political power, they probably are less so than

courts. In effect, politicians exert some influence on the so-called independent agencies through the appropriation process and through
nominations. The costs and benefits of agency independence transcend
the telecommunications industry (for example, they have been much
discussed in the context of central bank independence) and are well
known. The cost of independence is a certain lack of accountability. Its
benefits are that regulators are less concerned about the electoral impact of their decisions and therefore less biased in favor of domestic
firms or powerful interest groups, and, to the extent that they include
fewer political appointees, their staff may be more professional.

Our view is that in the context of network industries, independence
(of regulatory agencies or courts) is a virtue. Regulatory decisions in the
telecommunications industry are usually very technical for an outsider,
and their economic impact is unlikely to be understood by the public.
For such industries, the political accountability mechanism is unlikely
to operate well.[19]

7.2.3.1   *Toward the Demise of Regulation?*

We have stressed a number of shortcomings of the regulatory framework in the new telecommunications environment. Our brief overview
of the comparison between antitrust and regulation is insufficient to
conclude that antitrust should substitute for regulation, even though
we feel that competition policy should be given a more prominent role
in the overall process.

Consider a key issue treated in this book: interconnection policy.
Reaching good decisions in the matter requires (1) a sophisticated
understanding of the economics of network interconnection, (2) technological expertise, and (3) some or a lot of cost and demand information (depending on the approach). Unsurprisingly, traditional
antitrust enforcement has been ill at ease with the few access-pricing
cases it confronted, despite a well-established practice of dealing with
essential-facility cases.

Besides, antitrust enforcement and regulation need not be incompat-
ible, even though their coexistence may jeopardize the coherency of
the oversight institution. Several cases can be made for their complementarity: reduction in the scope for capture, creation of more focused

---

19. Similarly, juries are unlikely to build enough expertise to understand the economic
and technological issues involved in a telecommunications case.

missions through the separation of tasks, and reduction in the incentives for "cover-ups" through a separation of ex ante (regulation) and ex post (antitrust) decisions between two unrelated players (regulatory agency and antitrust enforcers).

In fine, what matters most is not the labels one gives to industry overseers, but rather their attributes: expertise, information, independence from politics and industry, commitment ability, and overall organization of the oversight process. We leave a more detailed investigation of the industry oversight process for future research.

Glossary

Access charge (interconnect charge in United Kingdom)   Wholesale price to be paid to a network by an interconnecting network for access to a segment of the former network.

Access deficit (U.K.)   Loss incurred (usually by the incumbent operator) in providing local service.

ADSL (more generally *x*DSL)   Asymmetric digital subscriber loop, technique allowing higher-speed access through the existing local loop by installing equipment on the premises and before the first switch. That is, *x*DSL technologies exploit the copper-pair cable for high-speed data transmission. ADSL runs at 1.5 Mbps and HDSL (H for high-speed) at 6 Mbps. An important distinction must also be made between asymmetrical devices such as ADSL, which allow different rates for incoming and outgoing information, and symmetrical ones, for which the rate is the same in both directions. DSL modems transform digital information into analog format, allowing the signal to be transmitted over the traditional pair of copper wires that link the customer's premises to, say, the first switch.

Analog signaling   Transmission by electromagnetic waves (analogous to sound waves). Still used mainly over the local loop.

ATM (asynchronous transfer mode)   A new switching and transmission technique to transmit data and video services at high speed on a broadband ISDN network.

Basket of services   Collection of services, which are usually subject to a price cap.

Bill-and-keep   Rule under which two local exchange networks do not charge each other for terminating off-net calls.

Bottleneck (or *essential facility*)   Unique input to the production process that cannot be cheaply duplicated.

CAP   Competitive access provider.

Central office   See *end office.*

Centrex   Business switching service using the public switched telephone network's central offices.

CLEC   Competitive local exchange carrier.

Coaxial cable   Cable with a copper wire surrounded by an insulating material, encased in a conductor and a protective plastic covering. The coaxial cable can span longer distances at higher speeds than the twisted pair of copper wires.

COLR   Carrier of last resort, company that is licensed by the regulator to fulfill universal service obligations. In exchange for the benefits for the carrier associated with the universal service policy (subsidies, protection from competition, etc., depending on the policy), the carrier accepts a number of obligations such as offering a number of basic services at a given price to all consumers and advertising this offering.

Common carrier   Companies in the United States that offer communication services to the public, and whose tariffs are approved by the Federal Communications Commission.

Digital power line (DPL)   New technique offering the prospect of high-speed access to the Internet through the local (low-voltage) electricity network. Would make power companies a competitor in local access for telecommunications companies.

Digital signaling   Transmits 0–1 bits. More efficient and cheaper to maintain than an analog system. Long-distance calls have been converted to digital in most countries.

DSL   See *ADSL.*

Efficient component pricing rule (ECPR)   Rule for determining access prices by an integrated carrier, under which the access charge is equal to the loss in profit incurred on the competitive segment by the provider of access when it provides access to a rival.

800 number   Toll-free number. The call receiver is charged, usually for a dedicated access line.

Embedded costs   Historical accounting costs, as opposed to a theoretical cost that would be obtained from a proxy model or a benchmark cost obtained by looking at other companies' cost of supplying a similar service or element of a network.

End office (also called *local central office* or *central office*)   First switch, usually located a few kilometers from the subscriber.

Equal access   Absence of bias in the connection to the local network between alternative providers of long-distance, international, or any other service requiring access to the local network for the provision of the service. For instance, users of MCI and Sprint in the United States and of Mercury in the United Kingdom needed to dial a longer access code than those of the incumbents, AT&T and BT, respectively, in the early days of long-distance competition.

Essential facility   See *bottleneck*.

Facilities-based operator   Operator that builds its own facilities (as opposed to renting them from another operator).

FCC   Federal Communications Commission (U.S. regulator of the telecommunications industry).

Features   Services added to the basic telephone services, such as call forwarding or call waiting.

Fiber optics   Very high capacity transmission medium using light to carry signals. Optical fibers are made of ultrathin glass.

Fixed cost   Cost that does not vary with the scale of production.

Forward-looking cost   Theoretical minimized cost of producing a service or installing an element of a network at a given date. Usually obtained through an engineering model. Could also be obtained through benchmarking as long as other operators themselves minimize cost. Not a backward-looking (historical, embedded) cost.

Fully distributed costs (FDC)   Regulatory rule allocating total revenue requirements among the firm's several services. The allocation is done on the basis of arbitrary accounting rules. See Kahn (1971, vol. 1, p. 150) for more detail.

Global price cap (GPC)   Price cap applied to a large basket of services including both retail and wholesale services.

ILEC   Incumbent local exchange carrier.

Incremental cost   Cost that arises as a result of the provision of an "increment." This notion generalizes that of marginal cost to noninfinitesimal increments. For example, for a single product firm with cost function $C(q)$, starting from quantity q_1, the incremental cost of $(q_2 - q_1)$ units is $C(q_2) - C(q_1)$, or in per-unit terms $[C(q_2) - C(q_1)]/(q_2 - q_1)$; the marginal cost is $C'(q_1)$.

Interexchange carrier (IXC)   U.S. long-distance company (handles inter-LATA traffic).

Interconnect charges   U.K. terminology for *access charges* (which is U.S. terminology).

Internet protocol (IP)   Protocol for the Internet, used for routing and transporting text, image, video, and sound.

ISDN   Integrated services digital network, a network providing end-to-end digital connectivity, allowing a wider range of services. ISDN's main goal is to integrate voice and nonvoice services. It was initially developed in a narrowband version. B-ISDN (Broadband ISDN or integrated broadband network) runs over optical fibers and operates at high speeds.

ISP   Internet service provider. In the United States, ISPs are classified as "enhanced service providers" and their rates are unregulated. ISPs purchase local phone lines and are considered business users; this "end user" status allows them not to pay various "taxes" imposed on long-distance companies, which are considered "carriers."

Joint and common costs   Costs incurred to allow the production of multiple services, to which incremental costs of producing individual services may need to be added. (In the literature, the notion of joint cost often implies that the services are necessarily produced in fixed proportions, whereas common costs allow the services not to be produced in fixed proportions.)

LATA   Local access and transport area (U.S.), roughly as big as the area covered by one area code.

LEC   Local exchange carrier.

Local area network (LAN)   Privately owned network within a building or campus.

Local loop   Connection between the subscriber's premises and the end office.

LRIC   Long-run incremental cost.

Market power   The ability for a firm to charge a price above marginal cost. Market power is not inconsistent with the absence of profit or free entry into the market, because the profit generated by the markup may be offset by the fixed cost of producing and marketing the good or service.

Markup   Difference between the price and the marginal cost of a service.

Mbps   Million bits per second (measure of speed of transfer of digital information).

Microwave transmission   Transmission in straight line of above-100-MHz waves between a transmitting and a receiving antenna. MCI originally entered the U.S. long-distance market using microwave transmission. (Its network is now a fiber-optic network.)

Modified Final Judgment (MFJ)   Settlement of the U.S. antitrust suit against AT&T to divest itself of its local exchange operations, creating seven regional Bell operating companies (RBOCs).

Narrowband   Refers to lines operating at low speed.

Natural monopoly   Activity that is most cost-effectively carried out by a single company rather than by several.

Network externality   Arises when users of a service benefit when more people use the service.

NTS   Non–traffic sensitive. The cost of a piece of equipment is non–traffic sensitive if it does not vary with the usage at current usage levels.

Number portability   Possibility for subscribers to keep the same phone number when they change the network to which they are connected.

Off-net calls   Calls originating and terminating on different networks.

Oftel   Office of Telecommunications. U.K. regulator of the telecommunications industry.

On-net calls   Calls originating and terminating on the same network.

Origination access charge   Access charge paid for the use of the network at the origination of a call.

PBX   Private Branch Exchange. Private telephone system or switch that allows callers to obtain an outside line by dialing an access code.

Located at the periphery and not belonging to the public switched network.

PCS   Personal communications services.

Price cap   Form of regulation that sets a ceiling on the average price that can be charged by the regulated firm, but allows some or full flexibility in the price structure.

Proxy model   Engineering model used to determine the cost of supplying various elements of a network using the currently available technology.

PSTN   Public switched telephone network.

Rate rebalancing   Change in a regulated firm's price structure toward business-oriented rates.

Rate-of-return regulation (or *cost-of-service regulation*)   Form of regulation under which rates are set so as to generate just enough revenue to cover the firm's operating cost plus a fair rate of return on its capital.

RBOC   Regional Bell operating company.

Resellers   Purchasers of switched (mainly long-distance and international) services, who then offer services at retail. For example, there are hundreds of long-distance resellers of long-distance services in the United States. They have often found a market niche (e.g., small businesses) neglected by the larger carriers, from whom they lease lines.

Retail services   Services sold to the final consumers.

Router (also referred to as *gateway*)   Special-purpose computer processing the Internet protocol information to deliver a message.

Stand-alone cost   The stand-alone cost of a service (or set of services) is the cost of producing solely this service (or set of services).

Stranded asset   Can be roughly defined as an asset whose cost cannot be recovered because of the advent of competition. Joskow (1996) defines the utility's costs that are potentially stranded by the expansion of competitive opportunities as the difference between (1) the revenues that utilities would receive in the future to compensate them for the costs of these historical investments and contractual obligations pursuant to regulatory institutions prevailing when the commitments were made, and (2) the revenues that they will receive in the future when services are sold in a competitive market. *Business Week* (April 28, 1997,

p. 117) estimates that the decline in value of high-cost assets from increased competition is $200 billion for electric utilities and $30 billion for local phone companies. Joskow (1996) argues forcefully that there is no way to calculate the magnitude of stranded costs with certainty "upfront" because future market prices as well as future operating costs are unknown.

TELRIC Total element long-run incremental cost, namely, the incremental cost of supplying a specific element of a network. It is defined as a forward-looking cost.

Termination access charge (*transport and termination charge* in United States) Access charge paid for the use of the network at the termination of a call.

Twisted pair of copper wires Oldest transmission medium consisting of two insulated copper wires. Almost all premises are still connected by a twisted pair. They can be used for either analog or digital transmission.

Telecommunications Act of 1996 (United States) Law aiming at promoting local competition in the United States and defining the conditions of entry by the RBOCs into long distance.

TSLRIC Total service long-run incremental cost, namely, the incremental cost of supplying the entire service. It is defined as a forward-looking cost.

Value-added services Examples: 800 services (toll-free numbers), videotext, e-mail.

Video on demand Program sent by content supplier upon request by an individual customer. (In contrast, the traditional "one-way" broadcast model involves sending the same program to all subscribers to a cable service or consumers owning a TV set.)

Wholesale services Services sold to other firms rather than to the final consumer.

Wireless communications Communications that do not use a wire—not quite the same as mobile communications. (A portable computer allows mobility but can be plugged into a telephone jack; conversely, wireless fixed telephony does not offer mobility.)

References

Andewelt, R. (1984). "Analysis of Patent Pools under the Antitrust Laws." *Antitrust Law Journal*, 53:611–639.

Anton, J., and D. Yao. (1987). "Second Sourcing and the Experience Curve: Price Competition in Defense Procurement." *Rand Journal of Economics*, 18:57–76.

——. (1989). "Split Awards, Procurement and Innovation." *Rand Journal of Economics*, 20:538–552.

——. (1992). "Coordination in Split Award Auctions." *Quarterly Journal of Economics*, 107:681–707.

Armstrong, M. (1997a). "Local Competition in UK Telecommunications." Regulation Initiative Discussion Paper Series no. 016, London Business School.

——. (1997b). "Mobile Telephony in the UK." Regulation Initiative Discussion Paper Series no. 015, London Business School.

——. (1997c). "Competition in Telecommunications." *Oxford Review of Economic Policy*, 13:64–82.

——. (1998). "Network Interconnection." *Economic Journal*, 108:545–564.

Armstrong, M., S. Cowan, and J. Vickers. (1994). *Regulatory Reform: Economic Analysis and British Experience*. Cambridge, MA: MIT Press.

Armstrong, M., C. Doyle, and J. Vickers. (1996). "The Access Pricing Problem: A Synthesis." *Journal of Industrial Economics*, 44(2): 131–150.

Armstrong, M., and J. Vickers. (1991). "Welfare Effects of Price Discrimination by a Regulated Monopolist." *Rand Journal of Economics*, 22:571–580.

——. (1996). "Multiproduct Price Regulation under Asymmetric Information." Mimeo, Oxford University.

Atkinson, A. B., and J. Stiglitz. (1976). "The Design of Tax Structure: Direct and Indirect Taxation." *Journal of Public Economics*, 6:55–75.

——. (1980). *Lectures on Public Economics*. New York: McGraw-Hill.

Auriol, E., and J.-J. Laffont. (1992). "Regulation by Duopoly." *Journal of Economics and Management Strategy*, 1:507–533.

Baumol, W. J., J. Ordover, and R. Willig. (1997). "Parity Pricing and Its Critics: A Neces-sary Condition for Efficiency in the Provision of Bottleneck Services to Competition." *Yale Journal on Regulation,* 14:145–163.

Baumol, W. J., J. Panzar, and R. Willig. (1982). *Contestable Markets and the Theory of Industry Structure.* New York: Harcourt Brace Jovanovich.

Baumol, W. J., and G. Sidak. (1994a). *Toward Competition in Local Telephony.* Cambridge, MA: MIT Press.

———. (1994b). "The Pricing of Inputs Sold to Competitors." *Yale Journal on Regulation,* 11:171–202.

Baumol, W. J., and R. Willig. (1987). "How Arbitrary is 'Arbitrary'? Or Toward the De-served Demise of Full Cost Allocation." *Public Utilities Fortnightly,* 120.

Bernheim, D., and R. Willig. (1994). "An Analysis of the MFJ Line of Business Restric-tions." Affidavit submitted relative to the petition of Bell Atlantic Corp., Bell South Corp., NYNEX, and Southwestern Bell Corp. to vacate the Modified Final Judgment.

Boiteux, M. (1956). "Sur la Gestion des Monopoles Publics Astreints à l'Equilibre Bud-gétaire." *Econometrica,* 24:22–40. Published in English as "On the Management of Public Monopolies Subject to Budgetary Constraints." *Journal of Economic Theory,* 3:219–240, 1971.

Bradley, I., and C. Price. (1988). "The Economic Regulation of Private Industries by Price Constraints." *Journal of Industrial Economics,* 37:99–106.

———. (1991). "Average Revenue Regulation and Regional Price Structure." *Regional Science and Urban Economics,* 21:89–108.

Branco, F. (1995). "Multi-Object Auctions: On the Use of Combinatorial Bids." Mimeo, Universidade Catolica Portuguesa.

———. (1996). "Multi-Object Auctions with Synergies." Mimeo, Universidade Catolica Portuguesa.

Brock, G. (1986). "The Regulatory Change in Telecommunications: The Dissolution of AT&T." Chapter 7 in *Regulatory Reform: What Actually Happened,* ed. by L. Weiss and M. Klass. Boston: Little, Brown.

Caillaud, B., B. Jullien, and P. Picard. (1996). "National vs. European Incentive Policies: Bargaining, Information and Coordination." *European Economic Review,* 40:91–111.

California PUC. (1994). "In the Matter of Alternative Regulatory Frameworks for Local Exchange Carriers." Decision 94–09–065, Public Utilities Commission of the State of Cal-ifornia.

Carter, M., and J. Wright. (1994). "Symbiotic Production: The Case of Telecommunications Pricing." *Review of Industrial Organization,* 9:365–378.

Cave, M. (1993). "Interconnection Issues in UK Telecommunications." Paper presented at the conference Access Pricing in Regulated Industries, London, November 12, 1993.

CEPR (Center for Economic Policy Research). (1998). *Europe's Network Industries: Conflict-ing Priorities.* London.

Chakravorti, B., W. Sharkey, Y. Spiegel, and S. Wilkie. (1995). "Auctioning the Airwaves: The Contest for Broadband PCS Spectrum." *Journal of Economics and Management Strategy*, 4(2): 345–373.

Chang, M. C. (1996). "Ramsey Pricing in a Hierarchical Structure with an Application to Network-Access Pricing." *Journal of Economics*, 64:281–314.

Coase, R. (1945). "Price and Output Policy of State Enterprise: A Comment." *Economic Journal*, 55:112–113.

Congressional Quarterly. (1995). *Special Report. The Fine Print: A Side-by-Side Comparison of the House and Senate Telecommunications Bills*. Washington, DC, September 23.

Cramton, P. (1995). "Money out of Thin Air: The Nationwide Narrowband PCS Auction." *Journal of Economics and Management Strategy*, 4(2): 267–343.

Crémer, J., P. Rey, and J. Tirole. (1999). "Interconnection in the Commercial Internet." Mimeo, IDEI, Toulouse.

Crew, M., and P. Kleindorfer. (1992). "Economic Depreciation and the Regulated Firm under Competition and Technological Change." *Journal of Regulatory Economics*, 4:51–61.

Curien, N., B. Jullien, and P. Rey. (1998). "Pricing Regulation under Bypass Competition." *Rand Journal of Economics*, 29:259–279.

Dana, J., and K. Spier. (1994). "Designing a Private Industry: Government Auctions with Endogenous Market Structure." *Journal of Public Economics*, 53:127–147.

Dasgupta, P., and E. Maskin. (1998). "Efficient Auctions." Harvard, HIER DP 1857.

Deaton, A. (1977). "Equity, Efficiency and the Structure of Indirect Taxation." *Journal of Public Economics*, 8:299–312.

Debreu, G. (1959). *The Theory of Value*. New York: Wiley.

Dessein, W. (1998). "Network Competition: Effects of Customer Heterogeneity, Unbalanced Calling Patterns, and Targeted Entry." Mimeo, ECARE, Université Libre de Bruxelles.

Dewatripont, M., and J. Tirole. (1999). " Advocates." *Journal of Political Economy*, 107:1–39.

Dewatripont, M., I. Jewitt, and J. Tirole. (1999). "The Economics of Career Concerns, Part II: Application to Missions and Accountability of Government Agencies." *Review of Economic Studies*, 66:199–217.

Dixit, A., and R. Pindyck. (1994). *Investment under Uncertainty*. Princeton, NJ: Princeton University Press.

Doyle, C., and J. Smith. (1998). "Market Structure in Mobile Telecoms: Qualified Indirect Access and the Receiver Pays Principle." *Information Economics and Policy*, 10:471–488.

Economides, N., and L. White. (1995). "Access and Interconnection Pricing: How Efficient Is the 'Efficient Component Pricing Rule'?" *The Antitrust Bulletin*, Fall, 557–579.

Economides, N., and G. Woroch. (1995). "Strategic Commitments in the Principle of Reciprocity in Interconnection Pricing." Mimeo.

Einhorn, M. (1997). "International Accounting and Settlements: A Review of Literature." U.S. Department of Justice, Antitrust Division.

Ergas, H., and E. Ralph. (1994). "The Baumol-Willig Rule: The Answer to the Pricing of Interconnection?" Mimeo, Trade Practices Commission, Canberra.

European Commission. (1998). "Notice on the Application of the Competition Rules to Access Agreements in the Telecommunications Sector." March.

Farrell, J. (1996). "Creating Local Competition." *Federal Communications Law Journal*, 49:201–215.

Faure Grimaud, A., J. J. Laffont, and D. Martimort. (1998). "A Theory of Supervision with Endogenous Transaction Costs." Mimeo, IDEI.

Feinstein, J., and F. Wolak. (1991). "Econometric Implications of Incentive Compatible Regulation." In G. H. Rhodes (ed.) *Advances in Econometrics*, 9:159–204. Greenwich, CT: JAI Press.

Feldstein, M. (1971). "The Pricing of Public Intermediate Goods." *Journal of Public Economics*, 1:45–72.

Freixas, X., R. Guesnerie, and J. Tirole. (1985). "Planning under Incomplete Information and the Ratchet Effect." *Review of Economic Studies*, 52:173–192.

Fudenberg, D., and J. Tirole. (1985). "Preemption and Rent Equalization in the Adoption of New Technology." *Review of Economic Studies*, 52:383–402.

———. (1991). *Game Theory*. Cambridge, MA: MIT Press.

Gagnepain, P. (1996). "Effet des structures contractuelles sur les coûts: l'exemple du transport urbain." Mimeo, GREMAQ, Toulouse.

Gasmi, F., M. Ivaldi, and J.-J. Laffont. (1994). "Rent Extraction and Incentives for Efficiency in Recent Regulatory Proposals." *Journal of Regulatory Economics*, 6:151–176.

Gasmi, F., J.-J. Laffont, and W. Sharkey. (1997). "Empirical Evaluation of Regulatory Regimes in Local Telecommunications Markets." *Journal of Regulatory Economics*, 12:5–25.

Gomez-Lobo, A. (1997). *Three Essays in Applied Regulation*. Ph.D. thesis, London School of Economics, London.

Green, R., and M. Rodriguez-Pardina. (1997). "Resetting Price Controls for Privatized Utilities: A Manual for Regulators." Economic Development Institute, World Bank.

Grout, P. (1996). "Structure of the Price Cap: Arguments for Global Price Cap and Answers to Oftel's Questions." Mimeo, University of Southampton.

GTE. (1997). "Comments of GTE Submitted to the California Public Utilities Commission: Auction Proposals for Universal Service." Mimeo, June 20.

Hakim, S., and D. Lu. (1993). "Monopolistic Settlement Agreements in International Telecommunications." *Information Economics and Policy*, 5:147–157.

Harstad, R., and M. H. Rothkopf. (1995). "Combinatorial Auctions with Synergies." Mimeo.

Hart, O., and J. Tirole. (1990). "Vertical Integration and Market Foreclosure." *Brookings Papers on Economic Acitvity, Microeconomics*, 205–285.

Hatfield Associates. (1994). "The Enduring Local Bottleneck." Mimeo.

Hausman, J. (1995). "Proliferation of Networks in Telecommunications." *Networks, Infrastructure, and the New Task for Regulation.* University of Michigan Press.

———. (1997). "Valuing the Effect of Regulation on New Services in Telecommunications." *Brookings Papers on Economic Activity: Microeconomics,* 1–38.

———. (1998). "Taxation by Telecommunications Regulation." In J. Poterba (ed.), *Tax Policy and the Economy,* 12, pp. 29–48. NBER and MIT Press.

Hausman, J., and T. Tardiff. (1995). "Efficient Local Exchange Competition." *Antitrust Bulletin,* Fall, 529–556.

Henry, C. (1997). *Concurrence et Services Publics dans l'Union Européenne.* Paris: Presses Universitaires de France.

Holmström, B., and P. Milgrom. (1991). "Multi-Task Principal-Agent Analyses: Incentive Contracts, Asset Ownership, and Job Design." *Journal of Law, Economics and Organization,* vol. 7, special issue: 24-52.

Huber, P. (1987). *The Geodesic Network 1987 Report on Competition in the Telephone Industry,* prepared for the U.S. Department of Justice. Washington, DC: Government Printing Office.

IDEI. (1997). "Network Industries and Public Service." Report for the European Commission.

Joskow, P. (1996). "Does Stranded Cost Recovery Distort Competition?" *Electricity Journal,* 9:31–45.

Kahn, A. (1971). *The Economics of Regulation: Principles and Institutions,* vols. 1 and 2. New York: Wiley. Reprinted 1988, Cambridge, MA: MIT Press.

Katz, M. (1997). "Ongoing Reform of U.S. Telecommunications Policy." *European Economic Review Papers and Proceedings,* 41:681–690.

Kelly, F., and R. Steinberg. (1997). "A Combinatorial Auction with Multiple Winners for COLR." Mimeo, University of Cambridge.

Klein, B., R. Crawford, and A. Alchian. (1978). "Vertical Integration, Appropriable Rents and the Competitive Contracting Process." *Journal of Law and Economics,* 21:297–326.

Klibanoff, P., and M. Poitevin. (1997). "A Theory of (De)centralization." Mimeo.

Krishna, V., and R. W. Rosenthal. (1996). "Simultaneous Auctions with Synergies." *Games and Economic Behavior,* 17(1): 1–31.

Laffont, J.-J. (1997). "Game Theory and Empirical Economics: The Case of Auction Data." *European Economic Review,* 41:1–35.

Laffont, J.-J., and D. Martimort. (1998). "Collusion and Delegation." *Rand Journal of Economics,* 29(2): 280–305.

———. (in press). "Separation of Regulators against Collusive Behavior." *Rand Journal of Economics.*

Laffont J.-J., and M. Meleu. (1997). "Reciprocal Supervision, Collusion and Organizational Design." *Scandinavian Journal of Economics,* 99:519–540.

Laffont, J.-J., P. Rey, and J. Tirole. (1998a). "Network Competition: I. Overview and Nondiscriminatory Pricing." *Rand Journal of Economics*, 29:1–37.

———. (1998b). "Network Competition: II. Price Discrimination." *Rand Journal of Economics*, 29:38–56.

Laffont, J.-J., and J. Tirole. (1986). "Using Cost Observation to Regulate Firms." *Journal of Political Economy*, 94:614–641.

———. (1987a). "Auctioning Incentive Contracts." *Journal of Political Economy*, 95:921–937.

———. (1987b). "Comparative Statics of the Optimal Dynamic Incentives Contract." *European Economic Review*, 31:901–926.

———. (1988a). "Repeated Auctions of Incentive Contracts, Investment and Bidding Parity." *Rand Journal of Economics*, 19:516–537.

———. (1988b). "The Dynamics of Incentive Contracts." *Econometrica*, 56:1153–1175.

———. (1990a). "The Regulation of Multiproduct Firms: I and II." *Journal of Public Economics*, 43:1–66.

———. (1990b). "The Politics of Decision-Making: Regulatory Institutions." *Journal of Law, Economics and Organization*, 6:1–32.

———. (1990c). "Bypass and Creamskimming." *American Economic Review*, 80:1042–1061.

———. (1991a). "Provision of Quality and Power of Incentive Schemes in Regulated Industries." In *Equilibrium Theory and Applications: Proceedings of the Sixth International Symposium in Economic Theory and Econometrics*, ed. W. Barnett, B. Cornet, C. d'Aspremont, J. Gabszevicz, and A. Mas Colell, pp. 161–196. Cambridge University Press.

———. (1991b). "The Politics of Government Decision-Making: A Theory of Regulatory Capture." *Quarterly Journal of Economics*, 106:1089–1127.

———. (1992). "Cost Padding, Auditing and Collusion." *Annales d'Economie et de Statistique*, 25/26:205–226.

———. (1993). *A Theory of Incentives in Regulation and Procurement*. Cambridge, MA: MIT Press.

———. (1994). "Access Pricing and Competition." *European Economic Review*, 38:1673–1710.

———. (1996). "Creating Competition through Interconnection: Theory and Practice." *Journal of Regulatory Economics*, 10(3): 227–256.

Laffont, J.-J., and W. Zantman. (1998). "Information Acquisition, Political Game and the Delegation of Authority." Mimeo.

Law, P. (1995). "Tighter Average Revenue Regulation Can Reduce Consumer Welfare." *Journal of Industrial Economics*, 43:399–404.

Leontief, W. (1947). "Introduction to a Theory of the Internal Structure of Functional Relationships," *Econometrica*, 15:361–373.

Malueg, D., and M. Schwartz. (1998). "Where Have All the Minutes Gone? Asymmetric Telecom Liberalization, Carrier Alliances, and Gaming of International Settlements." WP 98–08, Georgetown University, Washington, DC.

Marcus, M., and T. Spavins. (1993). "The Impact of Technical Change on the Structure of the Local Exchange and the Pricing of Exchange Access: An Interim Assessment." Paper presented at the October, 1993 Telecommunications Policy Research Conference.

Marcus, S. (in press). *How to Design Wide Area Internetworks*. Addison-Wesley Longman.

Martimort, D. (1997). "The Life Cycle of Regulatory Agencies: Dynamic Capture and Transaction Costs." INRA, Toulouse.

Masmoudi, H., and F. Prothais. (1994). "Access Charges: An Example of Application of the Fully Efficient Rule to Mobile Access to the Fixed Network." Mimeo, Ecole Polytechnique and France Télécom.

McAfee, P., and J. McMillan. (1987). "Auctions and Bidding." *Journal of Economic Literature*, 35:699–738.

———. (1996). "Analyzing the Airwaves Auction." *Journal of Economic Perspectives*, 10:159–175.

McAfee, P., and M. Schwartz. (1994). "Opportunism in Multilateral Vertical Contracting: Nondiscrimination, Exclusivity, and Uniformity." *American Economic Review*, 84:210–230.

McDonald, R., and D. Siegel. (1986). "The Value of Waiting to Invest." *Quarterly Journal of Economics*, 101:707–728.

McGuire, T., and M. Riordan. (1995). "Incomplete Information and Optimal Market Structure: Public Purchases form Private Providers." *Journal of Public Economics*, 56(1):125–141.

McMillan, J. (1994). "Selling Spectrum Rights." *Journal of Economic Perspectives*, 8:145–162.

Milgrom, P. (1996). "Procuring Universal Service: Putting Auction Theory to Work." Lecture at the Royal Swedish Academy of Sciences, Dec. 9.

———. (1997). "An Auction Proposal for Universal Service." Transparencies, March 19.

Miravete, E. (1997). "Estimating Demand for Local Telephone Service with Asymmetric Information and Optional Calling Plans." Mimeo, Insead, Paris.

Mirrlees, J. (1971). "An Exploration in the Theory of Optimum Income Taxation." *Review of Economic Studies*, 38:175–208.

Mitchell, B., W. Neu, K. H. Neumann, and I. Vogelsang. (1994). "The Regulation of Pricing of Interconnection Services." Paper presented at the conference Networks and Competition, Toulouse, Oct. 20–22.

Mitchell, B., and I. Vogelsang. (1991). *Telecommunications Pricing: Theory and Practice*. Cambridge University Press.

Mookherjee, D., and S. Reichelstein. (1992). "Dominant Strategy Implementation of Bayesian Incentive Compatible Allocation Rules." *Journal of Economic Theory*, 56:378–399.

Neven, D., R. Nuttall, and P. Seabright. (1993). *Merger in Daylight*. London: CEPR.

O'Brien, D. P. (1991). "Regulating by Manipulating Bargaining Power: Price Discrimination Policy in International Telecommunications." Unpublished paper, Charles River Associates, Inc.

O'Brien, D. P., and G. Shaffer. (1992). "Vertical Control with Bilateral Contracts." *Rand Journal of Economics* 23(3): 299–308.

Oftel. (1994). "A Framework for Effective Competition." Consultative document, December.

Public Utilities Commission of the State of California. (1994). Decision 94–09–065, In the Matter of Alternative Regulatory Frameworks for Local Exchange Carriers. [This decision is partly based on I–87–11–033, filed in November 1987.]

Ralph, E. (1994). "A New Mechanism for Establishing Interconnect Fees." Mimeo, Duke University, Durham, NC.

Ramsey, F. (1927). "A Contribution to the Theory of Taxation." *Economic Journal*, 47.

Rey, P., and J. Tirole. (1996). "A Primer on Foreclosure." Mimeo, IDEI, Toulouse. Forthcoming, *Handbook of Industrial Organization*, ed. M. Armstrong and R. H. Porter.

———. (1998). "Divergence of Objectives and the Governance of Joint Ventures." Mimeo, IDEI.

Riordan, M., and D. Sappington. (1987). "Second Sourcing." *Rand Journal of Economics*, 20:41–58.

Rochet, J. C., and L. Stole. (1997). "Competitive Nonlinear Pricing." Mimeo, IDEI, Toulouse and University of Chicago.

Rochet, J. C., and J. Tirole. (1999). "Cooperation among Competitors: The Economics of Credit Card Associations." Mimeo, IDEI, Toulouse.

Rothkopf, M. H., A. Pekec, and R. M. Harstad. (1995). "Computationally Manageable Combinatorial Auctions." Mimeo.

Salinger, M. (1997). "Regulating Prices to Equal Forward-Looking Costs: Cost-Based Prices or Price-Based Costs?" Mimeo, MIT Sloan School and Boston University.

Sappington, D., and D. Weisman. (1996). *Designing Incentive Regulation for the Telecommunications Industry*. Cambridge, MA: MIT Press, and Washington, DC: AEI Press.

Scherer, M. (1964). *The Weapons Acquisition Process: Economic Incentives*, Cambridge, MA: Harvard Business School Press.

Schmalensee, R. (1989). "Good Regulatory Regimes." *Rand Journal of Economics*, 20:417–436.

———. (1998). "Payment Systems and Interchange Fees." Mimeo, MIT.

Schwartz, M. (1996). "Telecommunications Reform in the United States: Promises and Pitfalls." In *Telecommunications and Energy in Systemic Transformation*, ed. P. Welfens and G. Yarrow. Heidelberg: Springer Verlag.

Seabright, P. (1996). "Accountability and Decentralization in Government: An Incomplete Contracts Model." *European Economic Review*, 40:61–90.

Shapiro, C., and R. Willig. (1991). "Economic Rationales for the Scope of Privatization." In E. N. Suleiman and J. Waterbury (eds.), *The Political Economy of Public Sector Reform and Privatization*, pp. 55–87.

Sidak, G., and D. Spulber. (1996). "Deregulatory Takings and Breach of the Regulatory Contract." *New York University Law Review*, 4:851–999.

———. (1997a). "Givings, Takings and the Fallacy of Forward-Looking Costs." *New York University Law Review*, 5:1068–1164.

———. (1997b). *Deregulatory Takings and the Regulatory Contract*. Cambridge: Cambridge University Press.

Simon, L. (1988). "Simple Timing Games." Mimeo, University of California, Berkeley.

Smith, A. (1776). *An Inquiry into the Nature and Causes of the Wealth of Nations*. New York: Modern Library, 1937.

Spavins, T. (1990). "An Introduction to the Economics of Price Cap Regulation." Mimeo, FCC.

Spence, M. (1975). "Monopoly, Quality and Regulation." *Bell Journal of Economics*, 6:417–429.

Stole, L. (1994). "Information Expropriation and Moral Hazard in Optimal Second-Source Auctions." *Journal of Public Economics*, 54(3): 463–484.

———. (1995). "Nonlinear Pricing and Oligopoly." *Journal of Economics, Management and Strategy*, 4:529–562.

Tanenbaum, A. (1996). *Computer Networks*, 3rd ed. Prentice Hall.

Temin, P. (1987). *The Fall of the Bell System*. Cambridge: Cambridge University Press.

———. (1997). "Entry Prices in Telecommunications Then and Now." Mimeo, MIT.

Thomas, A. (1995). "Regulating Pollution under Asymmetric Information: The Case of Industrial Wastewater Treatment." Mimeo, INRA, Toulouse.

Tirole, J. (1988). *The Theory of Industrial Organization*. Cambridge, MA: MIT Press.

Tye, W., and C. Lapuerta. (1996). "The Economics of Pricing Network Interconnection: Theory and Application to the Market for Telecommunications in New Zealand." *Yale Journal on Regulation*, 13:419–500.

Vickers, J. (1997). "Regulation, Competition, and the Structure of Prices." *Oxford Review of Economic Policy*, 13:15, 26.

Vickers, J., and G. Yarrow. (1988). *Privatization: An Economic Analysis*. Cambridge, MA: MIT Press.

Vickrey, W. (1961). "Counterspeculation, Auctions, and Competitive Sealed Tenders," *Journal of Finance*, 16:1–17.

Vogelgesang, I., and J. Finsinger. (1979). "Regulatory Adjustment Process for Optimal Pricing by Multiproduct Monopoly Firms," *Bell Journal of Economics*, 10:157–171.

Waterson, M. (1992). "A Comparative Analysis of Methods for Regulating Public Utilities." *Metroeconomica*, 43:205–222.

WIK-EAC. (1994). *Network Interconnection in the Domain of ONP*. Final Report for DG XIII of the European Commission, November.

Wildman, S. (1997). "Interconnection Pricing, Stranded Costs, and the Optimal Regulatory Contract." *Industrial and Corporate Change, Telecommunications Policy Issue*, 6:741–755.

Wiley, Rein, & Fielding. (1996). "Summary of the FCC's Report and Order (FCC 96–325). Regarding Implementation of the Local Competition Provisions in the Telecommunications Act of 1996." August 9.

Williamson, O. (1975). *Markets and Hierarchies: Analysis of Antitrust Implications*. New York: Free Press.

———. (1976). "Franchise Bidding for Natural Monopoly—in General and with Respect to CATV." *Bell Journal of Economics*, 7:73–107. Elaborated version: O. Williamson, *The Economic Institutions of Capitalism*. New York: Free Press.

Willig, R. D. (1978). "Pareto-Superior Nonlinear Outlay Schedules." *Bell Journal of Economics*, 9:56–69.

———. (1979). "The Theory of Network Access Pricing." In H. M. Trebing (ed.), *Issues in Public Utility Regulation*. Michigan State University Public Utilities Papers.

Wilson, R. (1993). *Nonlinear Pricing*. Oxford: Oxford University Press.

Wolak, F. (1994). "An Econometric Analysis of the Private Information Regulator Utility Interaction." *Annales d'Economie et de Statistique*, 34:13–69.

Wunsch, P. (1994). "Estimating Menus of Linear Contracts for Mass Transit Firms." Mimeo, CORE, Belgium.

Yang, C. (1991). "The Pricing of Public Intermediate Goods Revisited." *Journal of Public Economics*, 45:135–141.

Yun, K. L., H. W. Choi, and B. H. Ahn. (1997). "The Accounting Revenue Division in International Telecommunications: Conflicts and Inefficiencies." *Information Economics and Policy*, 9:71–92.

Index